Sonia Purnell is a biographer and jou........ the *Guardian*, *Daily Telegraph* and *Sı*...... Lady: *The Life and Wars of Clementine* .... year in the *Daily Telegraph*, *Independent* and *Lenny Letter*, and was shortlisted for the Plutarch Award for Best Biography. Her first book, *Just Boris: A tale of Blond Ambition*, was longlisted for the Orwell Prize.

'Purnell's account of Hall's hectic, amphetamine-fuelled exploits never falters. It recalls Caroline Moorehead's wonderful book, *Village of Secrets*, but has an added touch of Ben Macintyre's brio ... A rousing tale of derring-do' Richard Davenport-Hines, *The Times*, Book of the Week

'Soon to be a film starring Daisy Ridley, Purnell's life of the SOE agent Virginia Hall is a cracking story about an extraordinarily brave woman' *Telegraph* Best Holiday Beach Reads

'The extraordinary facts of [Hall's] life are brought onto the page here with a well-judged balance of empathy and fine detail. This book is as riveting as any thriller, and as hard to put down' Mick Herron, *New York Times*

'Riveting ... one of the most breath-taking stories yet told of female courage behind enemy lines ... An intimate and moving portrayal' Sarah Helm, author of *If This Is A Woman* and *A Life in Secrets*

'Brimming with moving tales of courage in the face of tyranny, this is a worthy tribute to an incredible figure' Deirdre O'Brien, *Sunday Mirror*

Also by Sonia Purnell

Just Boris: A Tale of Blond Ambition
First Lady: The Life and Wars of Clementine Churchill

A WOMAN OF NO IMPORTANCE

The Untold Story of WWII's Most
Dangerous Spy, Virginia Hall

SONIA PURNELL

virago

VIRAGO

First published in Great Britain in 2019 by Virago Press
This paperback edition published in 2020 by Virago Press

3 5 7 9 10 8 6 4

A CIP catalogue record for this book
is available from the British Library.

ISBN 978-0-349-01016-8

Typeset in Dante by M Rules
Printed and bound in Great Britain by
Clays Ltd, Elcograf S.p.A.

Papers used by Virago are from well-managed forests
and other responsible sources.

Virago Press
An imprint of
Little, Brown Book Group
Carmelite House
50 Victoria Embankment
London EC4Y 0DZ

An Hachette UK Company
www.hachette.co.uk

www.virago.co.uk

For Sue
1951 to 2017
Courage comes in many forms

'The ideal subject of totalitarian rule is not the convinced Nazi or the convinced Communist, but people for whom the distinction between fact and fiction (i.e., the reality of experience) and the distinction between true and false (i.e., the standards of thought) no longer exist.'

HANNAH ARENDT,
The Origins of Totalitarianism

'It is from numberless diverse acts of courage and belief that human history is shaped. Each time a man stands up for an ideal, or acts to improve the lot of others, or strikes out against injustice, he sends forth a tiny ripple of hope, and crossing each other from a million different centers of energy and daring, those ripples build a current that can sweep down the mightiest walls ... '

ROBERT F. KENNEDY,
speech at the University of Cape Town, 6 June 1966

'The Resistance was a way of life ... We see ourselves there utterly free ... an unknown and unknowable version of ourselves, the kind of people no one can ever find again, who existed only in relation to unique and terrible conditions ... to ghosts, or to the dead. [Yet] I would call that moment of my life: "Happiness"'.

JEAN CASSOU,
Toulouse Resistance leader and poet,
La Mémoire courte

CONTENTS

Prologue   1

1. The Dream   7
2. Cometh the Hour   29
3. My Tart Friends   60
4. Goodbye to Dindy   90
5. Twelve Minutes, Twelve Men   125
6. Honeycomb of Spies   142
7. Cruel Mountain   172
8. Agent Most Wanted   190
9. Scores to Settle   222
10. Madonna of the Mountains   254
11. From the Skies Above   289
12. The CIA Years   325

Epilogue   351

Agent Names   355
Selected Bibliography   357
Notes   363
Acknowledgements   379
Index   383

Prologue

France was falling. Burned-out cars, once strapped high with treasured possessions, were nosed crazily into ditches. Their beloved cargoes of dolls, clocks and mirrors lay smashed around them and along mile upon mile of unfriendly road. Their owners, young and old, sprawled in the hot dust, were groaning or already silent. Yet the hordes just kept streaming past them, a never-ending line of hunger and exhaustion too fearful to stop for days on end.

Ten million women, children and old men were on the move, all fleeing Hitler's tanks pouring across the border from the east and the north. Entire cities had uprooted themselves in a futile bid to escape the blitzkrieg that threatened to engulf them. The fevered talk was of German soldiers stripped to the waist in jubilation at the ease of their conquest. The air was thick with screams and smoke and the stench of the dead. The babies had no milk, and the aged fell where they stood. The horses drawing overladen farm carts sagged and snarled in their sweat-drenched agony. The French heatwave of May 1940 was witness to this, the largest refugee exodus of all time.

Day after day a solitary vehicle weaved its way through the crowd, a striking young woman at the wheel. Private Virginia Hall often ran low on fuel and medicines but still pressed on in her French Army ambulance towards the advancing enemy. She persevered even when the Stukas came screaming down to drop fifty-kilo bombs onto the convoys all around her, torching the cars and cratering the roads. Even when fighter planes swept over the treetops to machine-gun the ditches where women and children were trying to take cover from the carnage. Even though French soldiers were deserting their units, abandoning their weapons and running away, some in their tanks. Even when her left hip was shot through with pain from continually pressing down on the clutch with her prosthetic foot.

Now, at the age of thirty-four, her mission marked a turning point after years of cruel rejection. For her own sake as much as for the casualties she was picking up from the battlefields and ferrying to hospital, she could not fail again. There were many reasons why she was willingly risking her life far from home in aid of a foreign country when millions of others were giving up. Perhaps foremost among them was that it had been so long since she had felt so thrillingly alive. Disgusted at the cowardice of the deserters she could not understand why they would not continue the fight. But then she had so little to lose. The French still remembered sacrificing a third of their young menfolk to the Great War and a nation of widows and orphans was in no mood for more bloodshed. Virginia, though, intended to go on to the end, wherever the battle took her. She was prepared to take whatever risks, face down any dangers. Total war against the Third Reich might perversely offer her one last hope of personal peace.

Yet even this was as nothing to what was to come in a life that drew out into a Homeric tale of adventure, action and seemingly unfathomable courage. Virginia Hall's service in the summer of 1940 was merely an apprenticeship for what soon became a near suicide mission against the tyranny of the Nazis and their puppets in France. She pioneered a daredevil role of espionage, sabotage and subversion in an era when women barely featured in the prism of heroism; when their part in combat was confined to the supportive and palliative. When disabled women – or men – were confined to staying at home and leading often narrow, unsatisfying lives. The fact that a young woman who had lost her leg broke through the tightest of constrictions and overcame prejudice and even hostility to help the Allies win the Second World War is astonishing. The fact that a female guerrilla leader of her stature remains so little known is incredible.

Yet that is perhaps how Virginia would have wanted it. She operated in the shadows, where she was happiest. Even to her closest allies in France, she seemed to have no home or family or regiment, merely a burning desire to defeat the Nazis. They knew neither her real name or her nationality, nor how she had arrived in their midst. Constantly changing in looks and demeanour, surfacing without notice across whole swathes of France only to disappear again as suddenly – she remained an enigma throughout the war and in some ways after it too. Even now, tracing her story has involved three solid years of detective work, taking me from the National Archives in London via the Resistance files in Lyon and the parachute drop zones in the Haute-Loire to the judicial dossiers of Paris and even the white marble corridors of the CIA headquarters at Langley. My search led me through nine levels of security clearance and into the heart of today's world of espionage; I have discussed the pressures of operating in enemy territory with former members of Britain's special forces. I have tracked down files that have gone missing and discovered that others remain lost or unaccounted for. I have spent days drawing organigrams matching dozens of codenames with her scores of missions, months hunting down remaining extracts of those strange 'disappeared' papers, years digging out hundreds of forgotten documents and memoirs. Of course, the best guerrilla leaders do not intend to keep future historians happy by keeping perfect records of their overnight missions, and those that do exist are often patchy or contradictory. Where possible, I have stuck to the version of events as told by the people closest to them. At times, however, it has been as if Virginia and I have been playing our own game of cat and mouse; as if from the grave she remains, as she used to put it, 'unwilling to talk' about what she did.

Nor have governments made it easy to fill in the gaps. Scores of relevant documents are still classified for another generation – although I managed to have a number released to me with the invaluable aid of two former intelligence officers. Still more went up in flames in a devastating fire at the French National Archives in the 1970s, leaving an unfillable hole in the official accounts. Whole batches of papers at the National Archives and Records Administration (NARA) in Washington, DC have apparently been mislaid or possibly mis-filed; a handy list of them apparently forgotten in a move between two buildings. Only 15 per cent of the original papers from Special Operations Executive – the British secret service that Virginia worked for from 1941 to 1944 – survive. Yet for all these challenges and twists and turns down dark and hidden alleys, Virginia's story has never once disappointed: in fact, it has repeatedly turned out to be more extraordinary, its characters more vivid, its significance far greater than I could have imagined. She helped to change espionage and the views of women in warfare for ever – and the course of the fighting in France.

Virginia's enemies were more cunning and deadly, her conduct more gallant and daring than in many a Hollywood blockbuster. And yet the swashbuckling tale is true and Virginia a real-life hero who simply kept going even when all seemed lost. The pitiless universe of deception and intrigue that she inhabited might have inspired Ian Fleming to create James Bond, yet she came closer to being the ultimate spy. Every bit as ruthless and wily as the fictional 007, she also understood the need to blend in and keep her distance from friend and foe alike. Where Bond was known by name to every baddie, she slipped past her enemies, unseen. Where Bond drove a flashy Aston Martin, she travelled by train or tram or, despite her disability, on foot. Where Fleming's character seemed to rise effortlessly to the top, Virginia had to battle for every inch of recognition. Her struggle made her the great figure she became, one who survived, even thrived, in a clandestine life that broke many apparently far more suited to the job. No wonder today's MI6 chief has revealed that he searches specifically for recruits who do not shout loud and show off but who have had to 'fight to get on in life'.[1]

Virginia was a human being with the flaws, fears and insecurities of the rest of us – perhaps even more – but they helped her understand her enemies. Only once did her instincts let her down – with catastrophic consequences. For the most part, though, she conquered her demons and won the trust, admiration and ultimately gratitude of thousands in the process. Until the moment she retired in the 1960s from her post-war career in the CIA, she was a woman ahead of her times who has much to say to us now.

Controversy still rages about women fighting alongside men on the front line, but nearly eight decades ago Virginia was commanding men deep into enemy territory. She experienced six years of war in Europe in a way that very few other Americans did. She gambled again and again with her own life, not out of a fervent nationalism but for the love and respect for the freedoms of another land. She blew up bridges and tunnels and tricked, traded and, like Commander Bond, she had a licence to kill. What she pursued was a very modern form of warfare based on propaganda, deceit and the formation of an enemy within to topple a regime – techniques now increasingly familiar to us all. But her goals were noble: she wanted to protect rather than destroy, to restore liberty rather than remove it. She neither pursued fame nor glory, nor was she really granted it.

This is not a military account of the battle for France, nor an analysis of the shifting shapes of espionage or the evolving role of special forces, although they of course provide a rich and dramatic background to Virginia's tale. This book is rather an attempt to reveal how one woman really did help turn the tide of history. How adversity and rejection and suffering can sometimes turn into resolve and ultimately triumph, even against the backdrop of a brutal and horrifying conflict that casts its long shadows over the way we live today. How women can step out of the construct of conventional femininity to defy all the stereotypes, if only they are given the chance. And how the desperate urgencies of war can open up opportunities that normal life keeps closed.

Of course Virginia did not work alone. The supporting cast of doctors, prostitutes, farmers' wives, teachers, booksellers and policemen have been forgotten, but often paid dearly for their valour. Just as what they did for the cause was inspired in part by lofty romance and ideals, so also were they aware that failure or capture meant a lonely and grisly death. Some of the Third Reich's most venal and terrifying figures were obsessed by Virginia and her networks and strove tirelessly to eliminate her and the whole movement she helped to create. But when the hour of France's liberation came in 1944, the secret armies she equipped, trained and sometimes directed defied expectations and helped bring about complete and final victory for the Allies. Even that, though, was not enough for her.

Chapter One

The Dream

Mrs Barbara Hall thought she had it all worked out. She had raised her youngest child and only daughter, Virginia, born on 6 April 1906, in the expectation of an advantageous marriage. As an ambitious young secretary in the previous century, Barbara had triumphed by marrying her boss Edwin Lee Hall (known as Ned), a wealthy Baltimore banker and cinema owner, and never wanted to look back. Such a steep social elevation had, even according to her own family, made her 'snooty'. After all, Ned's father, John W. Hall, may have run away to sea at the age of nine on one of the family's sailing ships, but he had gone on to marry an heiress and become president of the First National Bank. John's brother, Virginia's great-uncle Robert, had been the grandest grandee of the exclusive Maryland Jockey Club. Barbara saw how the senior Halls led a fancy life – the hallway of their opulent Baltimore townhouse was reputedly wide enough to turn round a coach and horses – and wanted the same. But Ned had, to Barbara's frustration, failed to maintain the family fortune, let alone enlarge it, and now the Halls' domestic arrangements were more modest. Ned and Barbara's family house at Boxhorn Farm in Maryland was genteel but did not have central heating and pumped its water in from a stream. Their apartment in central Baltimore, although elegant, was only rented. It was Virginia's duty to haul the family back up to the Halls' former social heights by marrying money.

In her old life, Barbara had watched Virginia being chased by well-to-do young suitors with maternal satisfaction. Such was her appeal that Virginia was known to her friends at her posh private school, Roland Park Country, as Donna Juanita. Tall and rangy with sparkly nut-brown eyes and a melting smile (when she chose to use it), she was unusually spirited and presented an irresistible challenge for those young men who dreamed of taming her. Virginia held such displays of male ardour in contempt, however, and would assert her independence by wearing tomboy trousers and checked shirts whenever she could. 'I must have liberty,' she proclaimed in her school leavers' book in 1924, 'withal as large a charter as I please.' Little she said or did accorded to her mother's great plan.

Virginia took pleasure in defying convention. She hunted with a rifle, skinned rabbits, rode horses bareback and once wore a bracelet of live snakes to school. Just like her sea-going grandfather, it was clear that the fearless young Dindy, as her family called her, yearned for adventure even if it meant enduring discomfort. The fact that Roland Park Country pursued a Dickensian insistence on keeping its windows open, even in below-freezing weather – meaning the girls took their lessons in coats, gloves and hats – seems not to have bothered her at all.

Dindy described herself as 'cantankerous and capricious'[1] – a view shared by her classmates who nevertheless also recognised her gifts for organising and initiative. They viewed her as their natural leader and voted her in as their class president, editor-in-chief, captain of sports and even 'Class Prophet'. Her elder brother John studied chemistry at the University of Iowa and then dutifully went to work with his father as had been envisaged since birth. By contrast Virginia liked to explore pastures new, encouraging her classmates to expect from her nothing less than the unexpected. Considered by her peers at school the most 'original' among them – an accolade she evidently enjoyed – she admitted that she strove to live 'up to her reputation at all times'.[2] If Ned was indulgent of this unconventional outlook, then Barbara had quite different views. Mrs Hall was intent on her daughter forsaking her interest in adventure for the greater prize of a rich husband and a fashionable household. At the age of nineteen Virginia dutifully became engaged and appeared destined for the narrow life of many other society women reaching adulthood in the 1920s.

However eligible her fiancé might have been in her mother's eyes, Virginia still bridled at his entitlement and cheating. Yes, young 'ladies' such as Virginia had long been expected to defer to their menfolk, but now rebellion was in the air, with the advent in Baltimore as elsewhere of the independence-loving flappers. They were a new breed of young women who broke the Prohibition on drinking and scandalised their elders by cutting their hair short, smoking and dancing to jazz. They rejected the one-sided restrictions of traditional marriage and were taking a more active role in politics, not least because in 1920 (after a century of protests) American women had been granted the vote. Virginia now looked around her: home life was stifling but the world outside seemed to offer enticing new freedoms. And so – to her fiancé's evident indignation – she ditched him. (It turned out to be the right call as he later reputedly went through three unhappy and adulterous marriages.)

Virginia may have shared her mother's sense of vaulting

ambition, but she began to direct it towards a career and explor-
ing the world rather than bagging a feckless husband, however
well-heeled. Barbara had seemingly had little choice in her youth
but to work as a secretary – few other options were open to a
single woman of modest fortune in the late nineteenth century.
She was now mystified by her daughter's desire for a job instead
of a lifetime of married leisure, but Virginia's regular family
trips to Europe as a child and the influence of her crisply dressed
German nanny had inspired a hunger for independent travel. She
had excelled at languages at school and dreamed of using them
to meet what she termed 'interesting' people by becoming an
ambassador, apparently undeterred by the fact that such exalted
positions had hitherto always been reserved for men. Dindy was
set on proving herself an equal in a masculine world. To that
end it was her doting father, to whom she was unusually close,
who allowed her to spend the next seven years studying at five
prestigious universities.

    She had begun in 1924 in Cambridge, Massachusetts, at
Radcliffe (now part of Harvard) but the bluestocking atmosphere bored her and in 1925 she moved to the more metropolitan
Barnard College in Manhattan where she enjoyed the theatres on
Broadway. She was still conscious, however, that after dispatching one suitor she was expected to conform and quickly catch
another suitable husband. She failed to find one. Nor did Virginia
impress her tutors, who noted her down as 'an average student'
who failed to participate in campus life or turn up to physical
education classes. French and maths were her favourite subjects
(she loathed Latin and theology) but although she left in 'good
standing' her grades were mainly Cs and she did not graduate.
She knew she required a college education but was now anxious
to begin her life in the real world. Barnard was perhaps still too
much like home for her to thrive.

Paris seemed to offer wider horizons and she persuaded her parents that she would do better if only she could go abroad. Like many well-to-do East Coast Americans before and after her, Virginia viewed the French capital as the elegant gateway to liberation. Hundreds of young Americans boarded Cunard liners for Europe every week sending back word on how fashionable women in Paris – the so-called *garçonnes* – were positively expected to be independent, athletic and androgynous in appearance and to work and love as they pleased. So in 1926 the twenty-year-old Virginia moved to the other side of the Atlantic from her mother's wearying disappointment to enrol at the École Libre des Sciences Politiques on the Rive Gauche at the height of the so-called Années Folles. In place of Prohibition and racial segregation, she found a thrillingly diverse art, literary and music scene that drew in such writers as F. Scott Fitzgerald, Gertrude Stein and Ernest Hemingway and the legendary black dancer Josephine Baker (famous for her charleston performances at the Folies Bergère and later for her service in the Resistance). In the cafés of Saint-Germain and the jazz clubs of Montmartre, Virginia met actresses, racing drivers, intellectuals and budding politicians. The adventurous young woman from Baltimore smoked, drank and danced with them all, far more enthralled by what she learned from her new friends in France than from her teachers. Here, she felt free at last to be herself.

This freewheeling lifestyle continued when she moved in autumn 1927 to the Konsular Akademie university in Vienna to study languages, economics and the press. In contrast to her time in New York she coasted in her classes, achieving the required grades with the minimum of effort and finding plenty of time to revel in the city's frantic round of parties. Tall, slender and now elegantly attired in the latest European fashions, Virginia attracted plenty of male attention, especially from a dashing

Polish army officer called Emil who escorted her on romantic walks along the banks of the Danube. He adored her as a free spirit and in so doing won her heart in a way that no one had before, but Ned (seemingly egged on by Barbara) took exception to his uncertain origins and the idea of his daughter settling in Europe for good and forbade her from seeing him again. Although distraught, the normally wilful Virginia obeyed her beloved Ned (as she also called him) and broke off the unofficial engagement. She kept a photo of Emil for some time afterwards but her independence ran only so far. She never saw her lover again, and was later to discover that he had probably perished in spring 1940, one of thousands of Polish officers executed in cold blood by Russia's secret police during the Second World War and buried in mass graves in the forest at Katyn.

Once she got over her heartbreak, Virginia left Europe a very different woman to the one who had set sail in 1926. She carried with her not only a degree at last, but a burning belief in female emancipation. Those three carefree years instilled in her a deep and abiding love of France and the freedoms its people had offered her. That passion was to withstand all the barbarity that was to come and drove her to put her life on the line to defend what she would call her second country. She had also honed her collection of five foreign languages – most usefully French and German but also Spanish, Italian and Russian – although she was never able to shake off her American drawl. She had, however, become unusually well-versed in European culture, geography and most of all politics. When she was in Vienna she saw fascist groups on the rampage during outbreaks of bloody political unrest. On trips over the border she witnessed Adolf Hitler's National Socialist Party rising fast in popularity on the back of his pledge to put Germany first, with his Nuremberg rallies becoming massive displays of Nazi paramilitary power. In nearby Italy, the dictator

Benito Mussolini had already declared war on democracy itself back in 1925 and had been building up a police state ever since. She was thus witness to the dark clouds of nationalism gathering on the horizon. Peace in Europe and Virginia's intoxicating *belle vie de Paris* were already under threat.

Dindy returned home to Maryland and Boxhorn Farm in July 1929, shortly before the family fortune was wiped out in the Wall Street Crash and the Depression that followed. John lost his job in the now-beleaguered family construction and finance business and the general gloom appears to have affected Virginia's graduate studies in French and economics at George Washington University in Washington, DC. Her attendance was erratic but her grades sufficient to apply to the State Department to become a professional diplomat, still her fervent dream. With the confidence of youth – plus her languages and extensive academic study – she expected to succeed in the requisite entrance exam. The fact that only six out of fifteen hundred Foreign Service officers were women should have been due warning. The rejection was quick and brutal.

The high echelons of the State Department seemed unwilling to welcome women into their ranks, she told her friend Elbridge Durbrow, but refusing to countenance defeat she planned to 'enter by the back door'.[3] In the meantime, she would try to support her father as he lurched from one business calamity to another, agonised by the plight of the thousands now out of work and facing the prospect of personal ruin. On 22 January 1931, as he emerged from his office in downtown Baltimore, Ned collapsed on the pavement from a massive cardiac arrest and died a few hours later. His loss at just fifty-nine was a cruel blow to his family, and perhaps Virginia most of all. He had doted on his daring young Dindy, indulging her fondness for traditionally male pursuits such as hunting, even buying his daughter her own gun. Now he had gone, and so had much of the money. John and his wife and two children moved in with Barbara at Boxhorn Farm to cut costs, and Virginia was expected to live a quiet life with them. Such a claustrophobic arrangement was tolerable only for so long, however, and she was soon applying for jobs. After seven months stuck at home, in August 1931 Virginia was impatiently on her way to a clerk's job in the American embassy in Warsaw. It paid two thousand dollars a year, a respectable salary and a third higher than the median household income of mid-Depression America when many families were on the breadline. She had also finally broken out of Baltimore and into the ranks of the State Department. But for all her studying and high expectations it was as a secretary, just like her mother.

Virginia nevertheless made an instant impression, conducting her duties – coding and decoding telegrams, dealing with the post, processing diplomatic visas and dispatching reports back to Washington on the increasingly tense political situation – with notable intelligence and initiative. Warsaw was a vibrant city with the largest Jewish population in Europe but Poland, an independent state only since the end of the Great War, was precariously squeezed between the two muscular powers of Germany and Russia and its future was uncertain. It was an instructive time and place, and her sympathies for the Poles were no doubt heightened by memories of her love affair with Emil. It may also be that in having been trained in coding she got her first intriguing glimpse of the intelligence world. She certainly felt her extensive studies and experience were being wasted behind a typewriter. So a year later she asked for and received her bosses' backing – including that of Elbridge Durbrow, who was now her vice-consul – to apply to retake the diplomatic corps entrance exam. She was particularly confident about the oral test, in which she had proved herself an outstanding candidate, scoring 100 per cent the first time round. Virginia knew she was at her most compelling and impressive in person. Yet mysteriously the oral paper questions never turned up and so she missed the deadline for the application. Just as she thought she was finally about to be accepted into the core of the State Department, she was cast out again.

In her frustration she applied seven months later to transfer to Smyrna (now Izmir) in Turkey – a perfect posting for someone with her love of the outdoor life because of its proximity to the lagoons and salt marshes of the Gediz Delta, famous for their pelicans and flamingos. Her official duties when she arrived in April 1933 were no more exalted than in Warsaw, and indeed politically Smyrna was of less strategic interest. It was in this unlikely spot, however, that an adventurous if perhaps still naive young woman was forged into a figure of exceptional fortitude; it was here that fate dealt Virginia a hand that would change her life. What happened here, where the Gediz River flows into the sparkling Aegean Sea, would help shape a distant nation's future in a war that was still six years away.

Soon after her arrival Virginia began organising groups of friends for snipe-shooting expeditions in the marshes. Friday 8 December dawned clear and mild as she prepared for another day of sport, taking the treasured 12-bore shotgun she had been given by her late father. There were plenty of the party's long-billed quarry that day and there was high excitement amongst the group, although snipe were always difficult birds to shoot on the wing because of their erratic pattern of flight. Ever competitive, perhaps it was Virginia's eagerness to be the first to bag one of the famously well-camouflaged birds that distracted her and also persuaded her not to apply the safety catch. Either way, it was as she climbed over a wire fence running through the tall reeds of the wetlands that Virginia stumbled. As she fell her gun slipped off her shoulder and got caught in her ankle-length coat. She reached out to grab it but in doing so fired a round at point-blank range into her left foot.

A creeping slick of blood stained the muddy delta waters around her as she collapsed into unconsciousness. The injury was serious – the round she had fired was large, blunt and full of spherical lead pellets now embedded deep in her flesh. Her friends desperately sought to staunch the bleeding with an improvised tourniquet while they carried her to the car and dashed to the hospital back in town. The doctors in Smyrna acted quickly and for the next three weeks she appeared to rally and recover. Her friends – and the State Department headquarters in Washington – were relieved to be told that Virginia would be back to normal within a couple of months. What the local medics did not yet realise was that a virulent infection was seeping into the open wounds. Just before Christmas, her condition began to deteriorate rapidly and the head of the American hospital in Istanbul was urgently summoned, along with two American nurses. By the time they arrived after a twenty-four-hour train journey, her foot was swelling up and turning black; the putrid flesh had begun to stink and her whole body was racked with waves of ferocious pain. Instantly the American team realised that it was the worst possible outcome: gangrene had taken hold and was fast spreading up her lower leg. In the days before antibiotics there was no effective medical treatment and Virginia's organs were in danger of shutting down. She was on the brink of death when, on Christmas Day, surgeons sawed off her left leg below the knee in a last-ditch bid to save her.[4] She was twenty-seven.

The amputation had gone well, given the circumstances, but when she came round nothing would assuage Virginia's grief for her old life. The Izmir consulate cabled Washington that 'Clerk Hall' was 'resting very comfortably' and was expected to recover her health within two or three weeks, although a return to duty would take a lot longer. But often in those early days Virginia could not foresee a future for herself that she could bear. Her life had contracted to a hospital bed and, worst of all, the pity of others. And how could she break the news to her mother, who had never wanted her to go so far away and who had already lost her darling Ned? Virginia was to relive her actions that fateful day again and again for the rest of her life, through a kaleidoscope of mental images of blood and suffering, all the while punishing herself for her carelessness.

The American consul, Perry George, cabled Washington to ask for a senior official to inform Mrs Hall about the accident 'as tactfully as possible'. As Virginia feared, Barbara was inconsolable at receiving the devastating news about her daughter. Soon the tragedy was reported in the press, but the consequent public sympathy did little to help Barbara, paralysed with fear that she could still lose her youngest child. Not until 6 January did she receive word from Izmir that Virginia was now thought out of danger. The American doctor finally returned to Istanbul, relieved that his patient had made it.

Eleven days later, alarm bells rang again. A new infection had set in, which appears to have been sepsis, a potentially lethal poisoning of the blood. Frantically battling for Virginia's life once more, the local doctors injected mysterious serums into her knee to try to save it, all the while consulting the Americans in Istanbul by phone every hour. Even today, her condition would have been critical; back then her chances were slim. The daily pain of having the pus-soaked bandages on her stump changed by the nurses was almost unbearable, and often her heart raced uncontrollably.

One night, delirious from the infection racing around her body, Virginia was galvanised by what she would describe as a vision. Although her remaining family were thousands of miles away, Virginia's late father appeared at her bedside bearing a simple message: she must not give up. Ned told her that 'it was her duty to survive', but if she genuinely could not bear her suffering, he would come back for her. Although not religious in any formal sense, Virginia truly believed that Ned had spoken to her. His words remained with her as a powerful force, and she talked often over the years about how he had urged her to fight to live.[5] And so she waged the first, but not the last, great battle for her life, alone save for a ghost. If she were spared after such appalling torment, she felt she could surely endure anything else life threw at her. She would not let her great mistake get in her way, for her father's sake.

Virginia did indeed miraculously pull through and Perry George, who devotedly visited her every day in hospital, came away astonished by her resilience. She was eventually transferred to a more modern hospital in Istanbul to convalesce. Throughout the long, slow weeks of her recovery, she determined that she would not be treated as an invalid. In May 1934 she insisted, against her doctors' and employers' advice, on returning to work the day after her discharge from hospital. It was a terrible decision. The doctors could supply only the most rudimentary and ill-fitting wooden leg so she was reliant on crutches; after months lying in bed even walking the shortest distances was exhausting. There was little follow-up medical attention back in Smyrna and the pain from her wound was still crushing. For once she felt bereft, so far from home. The result was a swift physical and emotional breakdown. 'This is a situation which I foresaw and tried to avoid, but Miss Hall did not understand the difficulties that were before her,' Perry cabled the State Department in Washington. 'The experiment has been painful for us all.'[6]

Within a few days Virginia was on a ship back to the United States, and a month later, on 21 June, she arrived in New York, where her family met her at the pier and watched her limp gingerly towards them. She was admitted to hospital for a series of what were called 'repair operations', almost certainly involving the cutting away of more of her leg to avoid flesh-eating infections, and to be fitted with a new prosthesis. Although modern by 1930s standards, it was clunky and held in place by leather straps and corsetry round her waist.[7] In hot weather the leather chafed her skin and the stump blistered and bled. Despite being hollow, the painted wooden leg with an aluminium foot weighed in at a hefty eight pounds. Simply getting around was a test of endurance, and her beloved field sports were surely now out of reach. Pain would be her unceasing companion for the rest of her days.

Over the summer months at Boxhorn Farm, Virginia taught herself to walk again, while still battling niggling infections and the constant spectre of depression. She enjoyed sitting on the veranda, and helping to feed the sheep, horses and goats. But by November 1934 she was itching to return to work and secured a new posting in Europe, this time in Venice, where she hoped conditions would be better than in Turkey, a country that held such bad memories she intended never to visit again.

She did not ask for – and was not granted – special dispensation regarding her workload. Only the occasional flashes of temper,[8] often the mark of someone facing intolerable frustrations, hinted to outsiders as to her anguish. She tried to disguise her disability with long strides, although even in the flat-heeled shoes she was now obliged to wear a rolling gait became more apparent when she was tired. Going up and down steps remained a particular challenge – and consequently Venice, as she was to discover, could scarcely have been less suitable for a new amputee.

La Serenissima was a walking city. Virginia gazed with horror at its slippery cobbled passages, and the four hundred hump-backed bridges, many with steps, over the city's 177 canals. She quickly devised an ingenious solution: her own gondola, emblazoned with a splendid golden lion, would be her carriage. A devoted local man, Angelo, would help her row and catch her when the 'sea was rough', making her 'foothold precarious'.[9] She was developing a knack of recruiting people who would go out of their way to help her, smitten by her charm and obvious courage in adversity.

Virginia set up home in an historic palazzo with a sweeping view from her apartment balcony over the Grand Canal. She started entertaining again, making good use of the Hall family's fine china and silver. She also invited her mother over to stay for several months in the early days when she still felt she might need some extra help, particularly as her stump 'suffered greatly' in the sticky Venetian heat. Perhaps it was in part their renewed disagreements over Virginia's decision to work once again so far away from home that made life with her anxious mother in constant attendance uncomfortable. In any case, it seems that Barbara, however much the two women genuinely loved each other, was never to travel to see her daughter in Europe again.

Despite these trials, Virginia once again impressed her superiors at the American consulate, where the staff dealt with the visas, passports and repatriations of American tourists as well as customs arrangements for businessmen. Desperate to prove her worth, she was soon handling the more complex or delicate tasks typically the preserve of career diplomats rather than clerks and even standing in for the vice-consul when he was away. Keeping busy, she discovered, was the best way to keep her darkest thoughts at bay. The consul noted that Virginia rarely took a day off, even at weekends, and never allowed her disability to get in the way of her work. Now assuming she would never marry, her career meant more than ever and she took pains to keep abreast of political developments. Horrified by the tide of fascism rising all around her she craved to be involved in the diplomatic efforts to stop it.

At this time of mass unemployment and grinding poverty, only the dictators seizing power across Europe seemed to offer hope. Hitler, until quite recently the butt of complacent laughter by commentators who said he would come to nothing, was now Chancellor of Germany and worshipped by millions; Virginia's host country, Italy, was effectively a one-party fascist state under Mussolini, upheld by gangs of blackshirt thugs known as *squad-risti*; in Russia Stalin ruled by murderous diktat. Such extremism (on the left and right) seemed to be on the march everywhere, on the back of propaganda, sloganeering and ruthless media manipulation.

In what became known as the decade of lies, truth and trust were falling victim to fear, racism, and hatred. Virginia found herself in a ringside seat as the increasingly fragile ideal of democracy failed to find champions with alternative answers. A rare exception was her home country, where President Franklin Roosevelt's New Deal offered programmes of emergency relief combined with the creation of properly paid jobs in giant schemes of public works. Virginia was a natural Roosevelt supporter and had been taught at Barnard by one of his chief advisers, Professor Raymond Moley. But to her frustration America, still wary of getting involved in what it saw as interminable European squabbles, was shutting its eyes to menacing developments in the rest of the world. However aesthetically glorious her surroundings, against such a global backdrop her clerical work in Venice felt like a stifling irrelevance.

In late 1936, Virginia decided to have another crack at becoming a diplomat. After five years' overseas service as a State Department clerk the rules stated that she was no longer required to sit the written exam and an interview would suffice. Confident that this would play to her strengths at last, she sailed back to the United States in January 1937 to pursue her application with the blessing of her bosses in Venice and a feeling of optimism. Now thirty and having served in three different legations, she had much to offer in local political knowledge. Yet her application was rejected out of hand, this time citing an obscure rule barring amputees from diplomacy. Initially she thought it merely a temporary hurdle and demanded a series of meetings at the State Department to prove that her work was in no way affected. It was a valiant – but doomed – campaign and she returned to Venice with her spirits crushed and a growing contempt for rules and their enforcers.

Secretary of State Cordell Hull had issued the verdict himself but Virginia's supporters were not content to let his treatment of her pass without a fight. After a number of months and a flurry of correspondence between various powerful family friends, one of them, Colonel E. M. House, took it upon himself to lobby his old friend in the Oval Office. Virginia, he told President Roosevelt, was a 'gentlewoman of great intelligence' and a 'credit to our country' who was the victim of an 'injustice'. Despite her injury she lived an active life, including rowing, swimming and riding and had 'kept up her work', but had been told that she could never progress to the diplomatic corps. On 4 February 1938 Roosevelt asked for a briefing from Hull, who appears to have taken umbrage at this special lobbying on her behalf. Virginia's disability hampered her performance, the president was told, and she was not up to the demands of a diplomatic position. Hull, apparently ignoring the glowing reports from the consulate in Venice, agreed she might make a 'fine career girl',[10] but only by remaining in the clerical grades. FDR had overcome his own semi-paralysis from polio to reach the highest office of all. Yet, with some irony, he saw no reason to pursue the matter further.

In what seems to have been a deliberate punishment for her impudence, Virginia was soon after ordered to leave Venice and to report for duty at the American legation in Tallinn, the far-flung capital of the increasingly authoritarian Baltic state of Estonia. When she requested to route through Paris – only slightly out of her way – so that she could seek urgent repairs to her prosthetic leg, she was curtly instructed that her costs would not be reimbursed. It was equally insulting that her successor in Venice – a man – was granted vice-consul status and higher pay. Increasingly living up to her rebellious reputation, Virginia decided to travel under her own steam to the French capital and pick up again with old friends at her leisure.

Few in Paris, even if they perhaps wondered why she always wore thick stockings in the spring sunshine, knew that she had suffered an accident. They certainly had no idea that the special hosiery helped to disguise the prosthesis and cushion her stump to minimise pain and bleeding. Although she described herself as Episcopalian, Virginia's mother's family hailed from the stoic traditions of the Pennsylvania Dutch, descendants of early German settlers linked to the Amish. She had been brought up never to discuss money, feelings or health and to hold back a little from the crowd. Keeping her problems – and her secrets – secret thus came naturally. She may not have been married to an indifferent husband, but a different form of silent suffering was now part of her life.

Virginia finally arrived in Tallinn at the end of June, and started work on the same two-thousand-dollar salary, never having had a pay rise during seven years of service. The one compensation was the bounty on offer in the vast, virgin forests of Estonia and Virginia wasted no time in securing licences to shoot capercaillie, grouse and pheasant. She determined that her accident would not deprive her of the sport of firing a gun, despite the challenging, marshy terrain. The low-grade work, however, bored her. She was answering the phone and filing papers while Europe was spinning towards war, watching with horror as Neville Chamberlain met Hitler in Munich in September 1938 and talked of 'peace for our time'. In Estonia, Virginia found a similar story to much of the rest of Europe: a nationalist fever had taken hold here too. Political parties were banned, the press was censored and all potentially foreign names were recharacterised to sound Estonian. Fearful of the future, all hopes of promotion dashed, pigeon-holed as a disabled woman of no importance, she resigned from the State Department in March 1939. For all her hopes at the start, her career had proved little more faithful or rewarding than the old-fashioned marriage she had once spurned.

After seven years of living under the shadow of fascism, she decided she could do more to wake up the public back home to what she described as its 'false thinking', 'corruption' and 'terrible deceptions' by selling articles to American newspapers. She had of course studied the press at the Akademie in Vienna, but writing was never really her forte. It is doubtful whether she was very successful or her voice heard. No published articles from this time have been found, although her passport proves that she stayed on in Tallinn for some months after leaving the consulate. Writing was in any case never going to satisfy her for long. She wanted to act, not just report.

On 1 September 1939 Germany launched a sudden and brutal attack on Poland, and two days later Britain and France responded with a declaration of war. It was well known that Estonia's neighbour Russia had similar expansionist designs and at the end of October Virginia decided to leave before it was too late, on a last-minute ship to London. She had already had another idea. She would abandon her typewriter and volunteer for the Auxiliary Territorial Service, the women's branch of the British army, but when she turned up at the recruitment office the sergeants took one look at her passport and declared that foreigners were not welcome. It was yet another rejection.

Most in her position might well have opted at this point to give up and return to the safety of the United States – but for Virginia such a move would have been an unthinkable admission of failure. She sailed back to Paris and with gritty persistence finally tracked down the one active role she could take up to help the fight against fascism. To avoid a row she deliberately kept it from her mother when she signed up in February 1940 with the French Ninth Artillery regiment to drive ambulances for the Service de Santé des Armées. She had no medical skills but did have a driving licence and the service was one of the few military corps open to women volunteers – and also to foreigners. To her joy, they snapped her up (perhaps unaware of her disability) and gave her an intensive course in first aid. Finally, she had the chance to play her part.

On 6 May, after her induction course, Virginia reported for duty just outside Metz on France's north-eastern border, close to the Maginot Line of concrete fortifications built as a supposedly impregnable barrier to future German aggression. There was little to do in those last days of what became known as the Phoney War. Soldiers lolled around at a loose end and their guns remained idle. As gently as she could, she took the chance to break the news of her new role to Barbara, insisting that while she was 'weary and grubby' she was 'well taken care of' in a cottage 'with plenty of good food'.[11] Her mother was hardly taken in. She told a reporter from the *Baltimore Sun* researching a story headlined MARYLAND WOMAN IS DRIVING AMBULANCE FOR FRENCH ARMY[12] that Virginia's words were 'well-intentioned but they afford me little consolation, for in her characteristic manner she is trying to make things sound better for me'. Why was her daughter, she asked herself, running away from a comfortable life at home towards more hardship, more guns and more horror?

That was the last that was heard from Virginia for some time. On 10 May the Germans mounted a deadly attack, simply bypassing the whole of the Maginot Line to burst into France via the undefended wooded highlands of the Belgian Ardennes. Panzer divisions swarmed over the border catching complacent elderly French generals on the hop and scattering their ill-prepared troops, some of whom Virginia had spotted from her ambulance. The French were locked in an outdated defensive mentality, sitting behind walls and sending messages to one another by carrier pigeon. They had little chance against the devastating brilliance of the Nazi forces with their frightening speed, flamethrowers and lightning waves of aerial bombardment. The negligent apathy – and in some cases venality – of the old French elite allowed a world power to descend into a subject people in just six weeks. The politicians and military had, as one French patriot of the time put it, fooled their people with an 'hallucination of strength and invulnerability' that when tested by the Germans rapidly turned out to be a 'criminal deception'.[13] Official posters had repeatedly boasted 'We shall win the war because we are the strongest!' No one in the French government or high command had ventured the possibility of collapse, until it came.

Within little more than a fortnight, the remnants of the French and Belgian armies and large numbers of British troops were cut off by the German advance and waiting to be evacuated from the beaches of Dunkirk. It seemed as if nothing could stop Hitler sweeping victoriously across the whole of Europe. Virginia was dismayed to witness most of her ambulance unit panicking and abandoning the dying where they lay. But then their mayors, councillors and officers had also given up on their responsibilities and fled. The French government itself abandoned the capital on 10 June, making its way south to Bordeaux, where it too soon collapsed in disarray.

When the Germans poured, unchallenged, into Paris through the Porte de Vincennes at dawn four days later, Virginia was already on her way to Valençay, deep in the Loire Valley. Here she had heard that a determined French colonel was still collecting the wounded and driving them the two hundred miles to hospitals in the capital. As the army collapsed around him, he was in urgent need of help and Virginia responded to the call. For several weeks she relayed soldiers to Paris, where she had to apply for fuel coupons and passes from the Nazi authorities, newly installed under giant swastikas at the Hôtel Meurice. She noticed how as a nominally neutral American she was permitted greater freedoms than the French she worked alongside. A thought began to form in her head.

The new hard-right French leader, Marshal Philippe Pétain, had already seized control and on 22 June signed an armistice with Hitler in a railway carriage at Compiègne, signalling his country's capitulation to the Nazis. Virginia was formally demobilised a few weeks later but at least had somewhere to go in the chaos, looking up an old friend from her student days who lived in the avenue de Breteuil in Paris. She had already endured the terror of enemy fire out on the road but the strict curfew, the reprisal killings and the first rounds of arrests – or *rafles* – disturbed her. She also railed at the complicity of the French authorities in return for what was all too clearly peace at a price. It was French police who guarded the Nazis ensconced in the best Paris hotels and the French who were allowing camps to be built on their own soil for the thousands the Germans were taking prisoner.

Virginia knew that she wanted more than anything to help her beloved France reject the acquiescence of its rulers and fight to reclaim the old freedoms. Only this could give her that longed-for purpose and relief from her darkest thoughts. She was convinced it would not be long before the French rose up again and in the meantime she would return to London and wait. Meanwhile Britain was now standing alone against Hitler, but for how long could it survive without help? To Virginia's dismay, America refused to be drawn into the war to help her old allies: Congress would not countenance the loss of American lives for what were seen as only marginal national interests in a far-flung continent, particularly so soon after the last European war. Public opinion – even in the universities – was overwhelmingly against allying with Britain in another re-run of the Franco-German conflict. But she had seen the realities of fascism with her own eyes, and her country's isolationism did not preclude her from entering the fight on her own account. Even if diplomacy was a closed door, there must be another way for Virginia to prove her worth in what she saw as the battle of truth against tyranny. She only had to find it.

Chapter Two

Cometh the Hour

On a white-hot day at the end of August 1940, an undercover British agent called George Bellows was working the dusty Spanish border town of Irun, keeping watch on the frantic comings and goings at the railway station. Spain was ruled by another fascist dictator, Generalissimo Franco, and teeming with Nazi sympathisers and narks, but was officially neutral. Every day hundreds or even thousands of refugees were pouring over the border from France, some of whom might have vital information on what was going on under the heel of the Third Reich. Since Hitler's invasion and the evacuation at Dunkirk, British intelligence had lost virtually all contact with its closest continental neighbour. Its once extensive network of agents across France had either escaped, been killed or were deemed unreliable. London was left dependent on the vagaries of aerial reconnaissance and sketchy reports from neutral diplomats and reporters when a Nazi invasion from across the Channel appeared to be imminent. Britain was fighting for its very survival, but was doing so almost blind.

Bellows's eyes were drawn by a glamorous American making enquiries in the ticket office under the sinister glare of the banner portraits of Hitler, Mussolini and Franco. Intrigued, he drew closer and struck up a conversation with the young woman who had just arrived from France and wished to take a train to Portugal, and continue on from there to Britain by ship. He introduced himself as a salesman experienced in the challenges of wartime travel and offered to help her secure her passage. As they got talking, Virginia recounted her extraordinary story to this reassuring companion (although as ever she was selective in what she revealed). Bellows heard about her ambulance-driving under fire, and how she had travelled the length of a France reeling from the humiliation of capitulation to Nazi Germany. And how she had had to cross the heavily patrolled demarcation line (broadly following the course of the Loire) that now divided the country into two distinct zones. She relayed in matter-of-fact detail how conditions were rapidly deteriorating in the south, the so-called Free or Non-Occupied Zone, nominally run from Vichy by Pétain. The Occupied Zone (the north and west of France) was under direct control of the Germans stationed in Paris and she angrily described the curfews and food shortages, the widespread arrests and the incident at a Renault factory when workers protesting about working conditions had been lined up against the wall and shot.

As he listened to her sharp yet impassioned account, Bellows was astonished by Virginia's courage, powers of observation and, most of all, her unqualified desire to help the French fight back. Trusting his instincts, he took the most important decision of his life, one that was to help revive dashed hopes of an eventual Allied victory in France. When he bade Virginia farewell, he slipped her the phone number of a 'friend' in London who could help find her a worthwhile new role and urged her to call him on her arrival. Even if the State Department did not appreciate her qualities, Bellows knew he had just encountered an exceptional force.

Bellows did not give anything away, and judging by her visa application Virginia seems to have assumed she would most likely be driving ambulances again once she reached England. In fact, the number belonged to Nicolas Bodington, a senior officer in the independent French or F Section of a new and controversial British secret service. Special Operations Executive had been set up on 19 July 1940, the day that Hitler had made a triumphant speech at the Reichstag in Berlin, boasting of his victories. In response, Winston Churchill had personally ordered SOE to set 'Europe ablaze' through an unprecedented onslaught of sabotage, subversion and spying. He wanted SOE agents – in reality, more special forces than spies – to find the way to light the flame of resistance, prove to the French and other subject nations that they were not alone, and prepare them to rise up against their Nazi occupiers. Through a new form of irregular warfare, as yet undefined and untested, they needed to prepare for the distant day when Britain could land its forces on the continent again. If this new paramilitary version of fifth columnists violated the old Queensberry rules of international conflict (involving codes of conduct, ranks and uniforms), then the Nazis had given them no choice.

To serve in SOE, Churchill believed, would require a character able to pursue a noble cause with piratical flair. Now a month old, SOE was, unsurprisingly, struggling to find men with the guile and guts it took to be secretly infiltrated into France without backup if things went wrong. No one had really thought of considering women for such potentially suicidal work. Yet Bellows believed the American he had found in Irun station could be exactly what SOE needed.

Virginia soon forgot about the phone number, though, because uncharacteristically she had a change of heart. Upon her arrival in London on 1 September she felt reluctant to put her mother through any more angst, perhaps also doubting that she really could make herself useful. She presented herself at the American embassy as a former State Department employee and asked for a temporary job while she waited to be repatriated. Virginia was not initially made welcome; after all, she had resigned before from the service. True, her up-to-date knowledge of France was invaluable and she obligingly wrote a detailed report on matters such as the curfew, food shortages – and the way that, in her view, the 'French were continuing to conduct themselves with dignity with the exception of prostitutes', whom she believed were shamelessly consorting with the Germans.[1] The State Department took more notice, however, of her linguistic and typing skills. The military attaché needed a secretary. Within a fortnight she was behind a typewriter again.

The weeks wore on, her nights largely sleepless as London braved the Blitz. Mrs Hall urged her daughter to speed up her return and shortly before Christmas Virginia agreed to book the passage home she thought due to her as a former State Department staffer. But she was informed she was too late: she had allowed more than a year to elapse since her resignation and was no longer eligible for an official ticket, and others were all but impossible to come by. Unexpectedly stuck in London alone, she dug out the telephone number she had been given in Irun. Nicolas Bodington, a former Paris correspondent for Reuters, invited her to dinner in the new year at his smart white-stucco house at 20 Charles Street in Mayfair, not far from where Virginia was staying.

Although his big round glasses lent him a scholarly air, Bodington could be a dilatory and even controversial character, and was known for his brutal lack of tact. Behind the blackout curtains that bitter winter's evening, however, Bodington was at his most entertaining and he and his American wife Elizabeth put Virginia at her ease by banking up the fire and laying on as fine a meal as wartime conditions allowed. She had no idea of her host's real war job – or his exasperation at F Section's continued failure to infiltrate a single agent after six months of trying – but soon she had him gripped by talk of her own plans. Now that she could not go home to America she wanted to return to France. Speaking about her trip as breezily as if she were embarking on a holiday, and seemingly unfazed by the dangers or obstacles, she told him how she had it all worked out, right down to how she would press her old contacts at the State Department to fast-track her application for a visa. She had also plotted her route via Barcelona, crossing the border on a train and then making for the French Riviera ostensibly to help the Quakers' refugee relief effort, but also taking the chance to report for newspapers back home. After all, as she pointed out to her exultant host as they finished their meal, as a neutral American she could travel into and around France quite openly.

Early the next morning, 15 January 1941, Bodington rushed to the top-secret SOE offices at 64 Baker Street[2] in a state of considerable excitement. He took the notoriously wobbly lift up to the fifth floor and dictated an urgent memo to the head of his section, known internally as F. 'It strikes me that this lady, a native of Baltimore,' he informed F, 'might well be used for a mission and that we might facilitate her voyage there and back, and stand her expenses on her trip in exchange for what service she could render us.'[3] The more Bodington thought about Virginia, the more exceptional the opportunity she appeared to offer SOE, now under intense pressure to justify its existence through action. As she was American there was no need for the sort of challenging clandestine sea landing or parachute drop that had so far proved beyond them. Neither did her accented French count as a problem as she could operate under the cover of working as an American journalist, which would also explain her need to travel around and ask probing questions.

Such was his certainty of the value of the idea, Bodington had already instructed a Captain Strong of MI5 to conduct a positive vetting of her, a rigorous screening process then known as 'putting her through the cards' or PTC. The PTC involved searching for traces of German connections in the vast vaults of cross-referenced paper files kept on undesirables of every sort. It was a lengthy process, and F swiftly agreed that Virginia was such a catch they could not wait. Well before her 'clean' verdict was finally returned on 17 February, Virginia had been offered a job. This time it was not typing that anyone had in mind.

Luckily, money was hardly the motivation as the five hundred pounds a year on offer was barely more than she had been paid for sitting at a State Department desk. But how could Virginia, lover of adventure, otherwise stuck in a dead-end job in what she considered a dead-end life, resist entering France as a secret liaison officer (Class A)? She would be the first female F Section agent and the first liaison officer of either sex. Tasked with coordinating the work of local Resistance leaders and future SOE agents, her appointment was an outstanding act of faith in her abilities, which had for so long been belittled or ignored. She resigned again from the State Department, and on 1 April 1941 started work on preparing for her secret mission without anyone understanding quite what it would involve.

What did become clear was that SOE's new, most 'ungentle-manly' brand of warfare would draw in large part on the terror waged against the British by Irish republican paramilitaries. In the Anglo-Irish war of 1919–21, the British had observed how regular troops could be defeated by a hostile population whose will had been stiffened by a few resolute gunmen. Now SOE agents would be expected to act as these Irish terrorist leaders had done, inspiring, controlling and assisting the French to rise up against their oppressors when the time was right and to eliminate without mercy those who got in the way. There was, however, a lot of groundwork to do before SOE had any hope of sparking what was in effect another French revolution.

Advertising for recruits for such subversive work was obviously out of the question – the government never mentioned Special Operations Executive in public and if asked would deny its very existence. Traditionally, British secret services had drawn from a shallow gene pool of posh boys raised on imperial adventure stories, but this regard for breeding over intellect was scarcely a match for the ruthless barbarism of the Third Reich. MI6 operatives were accustomed to lying low and patiently gathering intelligence while avoiding direct action themselves. SOE agents would be different. They would observe, yes, but also recruit and train guerrilla forces to agitate, spread propaganda and ultimately kill and destroy. As one intelligence writer has put it: if MI6 officers spotted enemy troops crossing a bridge they would observe them from a distance and estimate their number, whereas SOE would simply demolish the bridge. The old-style spies were outraged by what they deemed to be a 'high strategy low tactics' approach – branding it 'amateur, dangerous and bogus' and tried to thwart SOE's very inception.

Unsurprisingly, Hugh Dalton, the pugnacious Labour minister whom Churchill had chosen to put in charge of SOE, found the search for a new type of rule-breaking recruit capable of 'absolute secrecy' and 'fanatical enthusiasm'[4] exceedingly tough going. Dyed-in-the-wool military types, obsessed with what they termed ethics, had to be kept away, as indeed did most government

ministers. The devout Anglo-Catholic Foreign Secretary Lord
Halifax was excluded from SOE meetings, for instance, because
he did not have what it took to 'make a gangster'.[5]

Yet such was Britain's plight as she braced herself for invasion
that the highest hopes were placed on SOE by Churchill himself.
Others also saw it as an imaginative, if desperate, alternative to
the 'frontal slogging matches' of the First World War. Perhaps
through cunning and courage it could help break Nazi power
while Britain worked flat out to build up the military might
needed for an eventual return to the continent. And although no
one could yet predict when that might be, any future attempted
landing was always expected to be in France (the largest and
nearest country in western Europe), making it the pivotal military theatre in the Western Hemisphere. Yet there was still
no detailed plan or tested technique for stoking this rebellion.
Virginia was joining what remained a Cinderella secret service,
whose early days were marked by repeated failure. A boat carrying three agents to the coast of northern France had turned back
when it had run into a German convoy. Another agent had been
set to parachute in, but became terror-struck at the last minute
and refused to jump. Most recruits had not even got that far,
pulling out horrified the minute they discovered what they were
expected to do; others were ejected once found to be mad, sad
or bad. In London, the whole of F Section numbered only eight
people. The entire SOE had just ten phone lines.

It was a huge gamble in so many ways. Even if Virginia could
make it safely into France, did the desk clerk from Baltimore
really have what it took to succeed? Was there any real hope of
creating a Free France anyway, or was resistance just a fable? Early
on, Dalton had promised that by the end of 1940 the 'slave lands'
overrun by Germany would 'rise up in rebellion, causing Nazi
occupation to dissolve like snow in the spring'.[6] Certainly, that

had not happened. One prominent French patriot, for instance, had not been able to recruit more than five volunteers to form a fledgling Resistance group after three desperate months of trying. So was there any support at all for Britain continuing the fight? Could the French people be transformed into effective paramilitaries, or would they simply become hostile servants of the Third Reich? Could a British-controlled agent even survive long enough in France to report back? SOE had no answers to these questions.

The prospect of SOE service in the field was undoubtedly terrifying. So many backed out that SOE would later set up a 'cooler', a remote country house in the wilds of Scotland where quitters would be forcibly confined until what knowledge they had gleaned of SOE was of no use. As of July 1941, F Section had just ten people in training – of whom Virginia was the only woman. And the only one with a disability.

Yet there is no mention of Virginia's prosthesis in her files. SOE seems to have been unbothered. Her superiors already knew she could drive from her time with the French ambulances. When she was asked whether she could ride a horse, sail a boat, shoot, climb mountains, ski or ride a bicycle she answered Yes, Yes, Yes, Yes, Yes, Yes. True, she admitted she could not box, or – most importantly for a secret agent – run.[7] But for Virginia this was the first time since her accident that she was not defined by it. *She was not going to give up.*

Yet a frustrating series of events kept delaying her departure. It was as if the State Department (almost certainly unaware of the true reason for her trip to France) was deliberately holding her back even now, refusing to allow its London embassy to help push through her visas on the grounds that 'no special assistance'[8] should be given to 'Miss Hall'. Unwilling to promote her within their own ranks, State Department officials seemed equally reluctant to allow her to plough her own furrow elsewhere. Perhaps her name was noted down in a file somewhere as having asked for special treatment before, over her application to join the Diplomatic Service.

In the meantime, in May 1941, SOE had finally successfully parachuted two agents, both French, into France. The aristocratic Pierre de Vomécourt (or *Lucas*) was SOE's first network organiser and Georges Bégué its first wireless operator, and therefore its sole direct communications link with France. (Wireless operators were vital for sending intelligence and receiving orders.) Both were to become exceptional officers in different ways but they could scarcely cover the entire country of a quarter of a million square miles by themselves. The need for Virginia's presence was thus more urgent than ever, but now there were problems with her journalistic cover. SOE had used a go-between to approach Ralph Ingersoll, owner of the American magazine *PM*, to take her on as a stringer. 'We are not asking Miss Hall to do anything more than keep her eyes and ears open,'[9] Ingersoll was told. He said no. SOE had more luck with an 'extremely cordial' George Backer, publisher of the *New York Post*, who agreed to arrange for Virginia to become his accredited correspondent. Backer was 'obviously aware' of the 'ulterior motive'[10] although he knew to pretend otherwise, a delighted SOE operative reported back.

There were, as ever in Virginia's life, further obstacles. Churchill's Cabinet had forbidden women from front-line service of any sort. Government lawyers advised that women were particularly vulnerable if caught, as they were not recognised as combatants and therefore not protected by international laws on war. Within SOE itself, old-fashioned attitudes were also widespread. There was 'considerable hostility'[11] at every level to the idea of a woman in any other than supporting roles such as decoder, typist and courier. Also, as Virginia was American, could she be trusted? It was standard intelligence policy only to recruit

British citizens. Her country, in those pre-Pearl Harbor days, was not at war with Germany and was suspiciously friendly with the Vichy regime, which was proving deeply hostile to Britain. 'I have raised this question with CD [the SOE chief] and the Sections concerned and I do not consider that she can be qualified as an intelligence agent,'[12] a senior security officer argued a few days after she joined the service. It seemed as if her disability was now the only thing *not* to count against her.

In the end, Virginia's supporters won the day, persuading the doubters that the nationality of recruits was unimportant as long as they were loyal to the anti-Nazi cause and the British war effort. SOE would perforce need to be multinational; there could be no room for nationalism of any sort. And when the need to infiltrate agents into France was so urgent, the fact that one of the very few plausible candidates was a woman would simply have to be overlooked. Indeed, SOE decided in its desperation that it must and would be ready to work with 'any man or woman or institution, whether Roman Catholic or masonic, Trotskyist or liberal, syndicalist or capitalist, rationalist or chauvinist, radical or conservative, Stalinist or anarchist, gentile or Jew, that would help it beat the Nazis'.[13]

So SOE's urgency became Virginia's breakthrough. In true SOE style the rule book (such as there was) was discarded and her mission confirmed as 'Liaison and Intelligence in Vichy France' – although almost uniquely in SOE she was not granted the recognition of an equivalent military rank, perhaps because her disability would have prevented her from passing a pre-commissioning medical test. It was an omission that would dog her for rest of the war, but for now plain Miss Hall was given orders to report generally on operating conditions and to help other agents who would follow her in. Now, finally, what SOE termed her 'special' training could begin.

Despite the wide-ranging scope of her mission, the induction was perfunctory and nothing like the extensive preparation given to later recruits. Over a few days locked away in a heavily guarded modern villa hidden in the New Forest, she learned the basics of coding and clandestine warfare and security: how to disseminate pro-British propaganda; how to use only covernames or codenames in the field; and the importance of 'looking natural and ordinary' while doing 'unnatural and extraordinary things'.[14] During days that started at six and went on long into the evening, she learned how to spot a follower (look in a window) – and lose him (double back). She picked up when to change an address, how to make secret inks (urine comes up brilliantly when subjected to heat) and even how to conceal her personality (through altering a distinctive laugh, gesture or demeanour). She was shown how to seal microfilm documents (equivalent to nine sheets of A4 paper) in tiny containers and insert them in her navel or rectum – or, as she discovered, a handy little slot in her metal heel. She learned how to rifle files and go through a desk leaving no trace, even replacing dust on a smooth surface, and how to approach a guarded house noiselessly. A retired burglar came in to demonstrate how to pick locks. Staff dressed in German uniforms probably put her through the standard drill of a simulated Gestapo interrogation or *Verhör*, waking her up in the middle of the night with rifle butts, blazing lights and shouts of '*Raus, du Schweinehund!*'

She was obviously already familiar with handling a gun, but was now taken through her paces on how to use one in anger. She may have been allowed to practise in the firing range under Baker Street Tube station, belonging to the London Transport Rifle Club. (Although in 1941 Britain was so short of ammunition it is possible that she was allowed only to load and unload the favoured new Sten gun rather than fire it. Most trainees

had to practise with the 'dreadful old Tommy gun' instead.[15])
She was trained to fire a range of weapons at SOE's disposal,
although most agents – probably Virginia included – were in the
first instance issued with an easily concealable Colt .32 revolver.
But owing to the almost total lack of up-to-date intelligence on
conditions in France, none of this training could truly prepare
agents for the dangers in the field. Virtually the sole source of
maps, for instance, was an old Michelin holiday guide from a
London travel agency.

SOE staffers were just guessing at 'the sort of things they were
instructing us on', another agent, Francis Cammaerts, remarked.
'They were trying to teach us something that they themselves
didn't know.' Indeed, there was very little to say about the core
business of building up a Resistance network from scratch in a
foreign land behind enemy lines – because no one had really done
it. With their privileged former lives in journalism and business,
and as citizens of an island nation that had not been invaded for
nearly a millennium, SOE staff officers in London had little concept of how ruthless an occupier could be. 'At the start, it must
be confessed, we all thought of the whole business as a game,'
recalled one early agent, who rapidly realised otherwise. 'A serious, deadly one, but a game nevertheless. There was amusement,
excitement and adventure.'[16] But the Germans never saw it as a
game and Virginia was to be a pioneer in a whole new type of
warfare; an amateur and improviser pitted against the brutality
of the Gestapo and Vichy police. No records remain – or were
perhaps ever made – of how she performed in training. It was
generally accepted that in the field she would either learn fast or
die. In any case, most of her colleagues thought all women incapable of such a demanding and dangerous job. It was up to her to
survive and prove them wrong.

Virginia's final briefing took place in the F Section flat at

6 Orchard Court, just behind Selfridges department store, in
Portman Square. Arthur Park, a gold-toothed former doorman
from the Paris branch of the National Westminster Bank, welcomed her into the thickly carpeted hallway by her field name of
Germaine Lecontre. Although the flat was luxuriously furnished,
agents often found their final memories of London were dominated by the bizarrely macabre bathroom which had a black tub,
black tiles and a black basin with gleaming chrome taps.

An SOE conducting officer instructed Virginia to tell her
mother that she was going 'somewhere in Europe'. She was then
briefed on when she could exercise her licence to kill – in SOE-
speak, 'accident' her enemies – and how. Her preferred method
was to use one of the range of tablets supplied by the SOE labo-
ratories. What she called *the* pills were probably the L or Lethal
tablets – tiny rubber balls containing potassium cyanide also
intended for her own use if she were being tortured and could
no longer bear it. Their coating was insoluble and if swallowed
whole, the pill could pass through the body without causing
harm. But if chewed or the capsule broken and the contents added
to food, death would come within forty-five seconds. Under SOE's
own brand of morality – and where it departed from terrorism –
she was instructed to kill French citizens only when her own or
her comrades' security was in immediate danger. Her first 'elim-
ination', they said, would be the hardest.

Another sort of tablet produced a high fever and other symptoms of typhoid, and would be useful if a hospital visit could
facilitate an escape. The morphine-based K pills could knock
out someone such as a guard for four hours. Most widely used,
though, were the bitter-tasting blue Benzedrine tablets. Sleep in
the field would be a luxury yet the mistakes made in tiredness
were often fatal. Most took a couple of dozen of these amphetamines with them and quickly asked for more. Now ready to go,

on Saturday 23 August 1941 Virginia left her old life behind her and headed for the ship to Lisbon and on into the unknown with barely a backward glance.

No one in London gave Agent 3844 more than a fifty-fifty chance of surviving even the first few days. For all Virginia's qualities, dispatching a one-legged thirty-five-year-old desk clerk on a blind mission into France was, on paper, an almost insane gamble. Her mission, codenamed Operation *Geologist 5*, would expose her to grinding fear and the perpetual likelihood of a grisly death. There was no reception committee to welcome her or ready network for her to join but she was permitted – even obliged – to commit a range of crimes, from subversion to murder. To survive she must lead her double life to perfection and avoid capture at all costs. Her disability might help protect her, in that she made such an unlikely agent, but at the same time it rendered her more conspicuous.

It was two years to the day since the war started when she strode purposefully towards the modest Hôtel de la Paix in Vichy. Thunderstorms growled ominously in the distance and the heat was suffocating after a long summer drought but dozens of pairs of eyes fixed on this statuesque flame-haired newcomer with her aristocratic bearing as she climbed the steps into the lobby. Anyone out of the ordinary was ripe for denunciation to the Germans or their Vichy underlings. The financial rewards were generous.

The next day, 4 September 1941, Virginia registered her arrival at the gendarmerie under her real name, telling them she was a special envoy for the *New York Post*. As proof she pointed to the fact that she had already filed a story via Western Union cable, headlined 'EXCLUSIVE: BATHROOM OFFICES IN VICHY: Reporter finds capital crowded'. Its publication was an early measure of her calm efficiency – and cause for an outbreak of joy in Baker Street. Virginia had not only made it through her first hours but had already established contact. There was at last a connection with the political heart of France after silence for so long.

The article was ostensibly about how Pétain's administration was commandeering every inch of space in its new home town, including hotel bathrooms. But what enthralled London was her reportage on the lack of taxis and how her newly acquired ration book allowed her only ten ounces of meat a week, ten ounces of bread a day, but no rice, spaghetti or chocolate. 'I haven't yet seen any butter and there is little milk [and] women are no longer entitled to buy cigarettes'[17] was noted down word for word. These tiny threads of information could make the difference between life and death, and initially London sought such intelligence above all else as it stepped up its efforts to infiltrate more agents into France.[18] One operative walked into trouble, for instance, by not knowing that French cafés were forbidden to sell alcohol on alternate days. His ignorance immediately marked him out as an impostor, and he had had to run for his life when the proprietor called the police. As letters were censored and the Germans listened in to phone conversations, what Virginia could safely tell her controllers was limited to her published articles. Some contained pre-agreed words as coded messages, but mostly she was making her points *en clair*. She gave warning to Baker Street that even family postcards sent across the demarcation line were routinely checked, with the apparently innocent observation that 'one is not inclined to write at length [on them] or air any grievances'.[19] London had no direct way of contacting her.

Virginia's status as a journalist was her sole protection, so establishing her cover had been Virginia's priority in her first few days. Combining a beatific smile with her genuine love of France, she cultivated senior Vichy bureaucrats and policemen and soon had them eating out of her hand by appealing to their patriotism and pride. In time, some would risk their own positions to save her life and help protect many others. As one historian has noted, 'she seems to have totally bewitched everybody who knew her'.[20]

She also presented herself to the American ambassador, Admiral William Leahy, but he proved more resistant to her magic. American isolationism remained a formidable force and Washington had recognised Pétain's totalitarian regime despite its evident accommodation with the Nazis. But President Roosevelt had plucked one of his old friends out of retirement as his envoy to handle relations with Vichy, precisely because he was (privately) worried that France would in some way help the Axis powers defeat Britain. Despite the public policy of non-intervention, America had already sent food and aid to the French specifically to try to wean them off German support and win their allegiance. Leahy, so punctual when arriving and leaving work that a local luggage shop set its clock by his movements, thus saw it as his overriding duty to maintain courteous relations with the marshal even as the Vichy government adopted some of the worst excesses of Nazi ideology under the banner of a new moral order for France. Pétain's repression of Jews, or 'immigrants', as he referred to them, was to become, in some ways, more draconian early on than Hitler's (including a wider definition of who was Jewish and the summary imprisonment of foreign Jews). In the circumstances, some of Leahy's more liberal colleagues worried that his 'sympathy for the Vichy regime often seemed warmer than considerations of diplomatic and strategic expediency could account for'.[21]

Leahy made it clear he did not want his staff, or other Americans, to associate themselves with any espionage activities in case it messed up his careful diplomatic choreography. He had already noticed this 'girl reporter' in an otherwise male press pack, with her independent attitude and thirst for knowledge, and soon harboured suspicions. It was clear that she was winning over key French officials and extracting far more information from them than her peers. Suzanne Bertillon, chief censor of the foreign press in Vichy's Ministry of Information, was just one who went out of her way to help Virginia. There was something about this woman that commanded Bertillon's trust and the two became friends. The fiercely Gaullist Bertillon not only avoided censoring Virginia's articles but set up a network of ninety contacts across France (such as mayors, farmers and industrialists) to supply her every week with information that proved vital for the British war effort. Virginia was thus able to collect intelligence on the location of ammunition and fuel depots, German troop movements, industrial production and a Nazi submarine base under construction in Marseille, which was later destroyed before its completion by Allied bombs.[22] Indeed, Virginia became so knowledgeable on the state of France that Leahy's staff surmised that she must be working for British intelligence. Soon she persuaded some of them to help her, even if they risked their careers to do so, and all had to be careful to cooperate out of the sight of the ambassador. Prominent among them was the defence attaché Robert Schow, who was, unknown to his boss, in contact with early members of the Resistance. Later on, there is evidence that an African American official called Johnny Nicholas was also directly involved.[23] It is more than likely they met, but there are no records of any meetings with Virginia for good reason. Any intelligence role was a bold proposition for him as no safehouses or false identity papers would have been available in case of trouble. The Nazis held a pathological hatred for black people, still a comparative rarity in Europe. Whenever they took control of an area they set about rounding them up.[24]

Despite her progress with making contacts, Virginia faced formidable obstacles in those early days. She soon found that Vichy, a faded spa with an operetta atmosphere, was too small and claus-trophobic for her to lead a full double life as reporter-cum-spy. Despite Leahy's friendliness to the French regime, his embassy was under constant surveillance;[25] in fact, the town was crawling with undercover Gestapo who were increasingly predatory. The so-called Free Zone may have been spared mass Nazi occupation, but its 'freedom' was a pretence. The truth was, as one historian has put it, that Vichy France was firmly 'under German control once removed'.[26]

Pétain was eighty-five by this time and almost certainly senile. He was kept alert by morning injections of amphetamines, although when these wore off in the afternoon he was often dif-ficult to rouse or simply incoherent. And yet he was still revered, despite shocking many supporters across France by his handshake with Hitler at Montoire, south of Paris, in October 1940 and by his espousal of collaboration with the Nazis. His actions had per-versely had the effect of making many believe that to resist the Germans was to commit a crime. The marshal was seen by most French as the embodiment of whatever honour France had left; to go against a First World War military hero for most of a nation still stunned by the speed and ignominy of its capitulation was tantamount to treason. Also seen in the south as the final hedge against full-scale German occupation (and equally the feared Reds of Russia), he rationalised defeat into an opportunity for the power he had long craved. Pictures of him were plastered on classroom walls and shop windows; his likeness was on coins and stamps.

In the face of such a powerful cult of personality, sustained by vicious muzzling of the independent press, Virginia discovered with dismay that there was precious little appetite to rejoin the fight. Pétain – subverting the legacy of French heroes such as Joan of Arc and Napoleon – had persuaded, or at least allowed, the French to believe that honour could be found in defeat. He would brook no opposition to his alliance with the Germans or his rejection of democracy; his diktats against internal enemies were enforced by arrest, internment and, when necessary, execution squads. Opposition had been and still was fragmented and weak. Not one major political party had stood united against the dissolution of parliament or in favour of resistance to the Germans – and now they were dispensed with. One prefect of the Eure-et-Loir *département*, Jean Moulin, slit his throat in a bid to take his own life rather than agree to sign a pro-German declaration under torture, but at the time he was an isolated figure. A junior French general and former under-secretary of defence called Charles de Gaulle had also had the courage to proclaim that he did not accept the surrender. The day before Churchill founded SOE, the Frenchman had invited those of his compatriots who agreed with him to join him in fighting on. 'Whatever happens,' he had proclaimed in a shaky voice on 18 June 1940 over the BBC from exile in London, 'the flame of French resistance must not and shall not die.' Pétain had duly responded by having de Gaulle tried for treason and sentenced to death *in absentia*. His call had in any case gone largely unheard – and for the most part the French simply accepted the price of defeat.

After a month in Vichy Virginia moved to what she believed to be more promising pastures in the city of Lyon, seventy miles to the south-east and out of sight of Ambassador Leahy. Lyon's bourgeois façade belied a seditious past and what she heard could be stirrings of a rebellious future. Its craft guilds rose up against the clergy in the thirteenth century and during the 1789 revolution its citizens had stood their ground against the Jacobins in Paris. Since then secret societies such as the Freemasons had thrived; it remained a difficult city for outsiders to crack.

Lyon's proximity to the border with neutral Switzerland (just

eighty miles away) could open up a new channel of communications as Virginia remained without a wireless operator. The city's
dramatic topography and confusing layout was another factor in
making it a natural birthplace for an underground movement.
Divided into discrete areas, the heart of the town was a penin-
sula washed by two rivers, the Rhône and the Saône, which were
straddled by seventeen bridges and surrounded by wooded hills.
Behind the place des Terreaux, with its seventeenth-century city
hall, were the Croix-Rousse heights. Here, hundreds of steep
stone steps led up to Vieux Lyon, with its impenetrable network
of *traboules*, or interconnecting passages, through buildings and
between streets, 'much like an above-ground sewer system, and
almost as dirty and evil-smelling'.[27] Only the locals knew their
way around the labyrinth, as the Gestapo had discovered. Further
out of town were vast floodplains, ideal for parachute drops of
agents and supplies.

Word had reached Virginia that a few uncommonly tough
Lyonnais were gathering in smoke-filled *bouchons* – the city's
famously homely little bistros – to plan and to plot. Some were
publishing the first tentative anti-Nazi tracts, using tiny primitive presses, such as *Les petites ailes de France* (The Little Wings of
France) and *Le Coq enchaîné* (The Chained Cockerel). There were
a handful who 'preferred death to accepting German domina-
tion'[28] and their spirit was just beginning to inspire a change of
mood from craven acceptance. The fact that more than a million
French husbands, sons and brothers had still not come home from
prisoner-of-war camps in Germany was prompting a quiet but
seething anger; groups of Lyonnais also bridled at exhortations
to improve themselves as Christians, soldiers or obedient wives
under Vichy's new moral order. They scorned Pétain's vows to
rid France of the Third Republic, which had hosted an exceptional literary and artistic flowering, but which he denounced as

'overrun by homosexuals and women'. They felt betrayed by the way in which he sought to destroy the ideas of *liberté*, *égalité* and *fraternité* from the French Revolution and replace them with the *travail, famille, patrie* (work, family, country) slogan of the new *État Français*. French communists had been particularly fired up since the Reich had attacked the Soviet Union in June, breaking a non-aggression pact.

For the first time since the armistice, therefore, and for conflicting reasons, there was a faint muttering on the streets of Lyon amongst shopkeepers, doctors, factory workers, railwaymen and industrialists. But no one, however they felt, had so far been able to join the 'resistance', because until now so such organisation had really come to exist. There was no blueprint imposed from above and membership relied for the most part on haphazard encounters. The focus was still on talk rather than action; there were no guns nor explosives, nor the skills to use them. Help from London remained unreachable; genuine information was equally elusive because Vichy propaganda had long since drowned out real news. And with denunciation by neighbours, colleagues or even family a constant threat, there was a fierce suspicion of outsiders.

When Virginia arrived at Lyon's Gare de Perrache she had more immediate concerns. The place was heaving. Some two hundred thousand refugees had descended on a city with a population of 570,000. Every hotel and guesthouse was fit to burst, there were no apartments to rent, and she had no friends to turn to. Later that day, an exhausted Virginia dragged herself up the verdant hillside high above the Saône to La Mulatière, where she knocked on the door of the Sainte Elisabeth convent. Fortunately, the cloistered sisters, unused as they were to receiving visitors, took pity and offered her a bed in a tiny room in a tower where she had the 'undivided attention of a strong north wind'[29] The one condition was that she returned by half past six in the evening, when they locked the gates – she admitted it was all 'certainly a change' from her heady pre-war existence in Paris. The nuns, who wore a 'quaint headdress – a white dutch cap with wings' fed her with produce from their own farm. Despite their otherworldliness, they became not only her first shelter in Lyon, but also her earliest recruits. Thanks to Virginia's lateral thinking, F Section had just secured one of the best safehouses in early Vichy France.

As soon as a room became available, however, she booked into the Grand Nouvel Hôtel on rue Grolée to be in the centre of town. It was ideal as her PC, or *poste de commande*: the hotel had several entrances (vital for a quick getaway); easy access to the number 3 tram (handy for getting about); and most importantly it was close to the American consulate on place de la Bourse. Virginia registered as *Brigitte Lecontre* with her false papers supplied by SOE, printed up by a friendly forger on the Kingston bypass just outside London (another of SOE's underworld contacts) and then stamped on and chewed up until they looked appropriately tatty. *Brigitte* quickly settled into a routine, going out early in the morning and coming back at six in the evening, when she had a glass of wine at the bar while reading any messages left for her in reception.

Afterwards she sometimes dined in a little restaurant near the hotel, where the Greek patron, who stocked up on the black market, treated this good-looking woman 'like a loving daughter'. He refused to take her food coupons but plied her with plates of macaroni, her favourite cocktail of gin and It (similar to a martini, composed of gin and sweet vermouth) and much-prized English cigarettes despite the bar on women buying anything to smoke.[30] He was another early recruit.

As Virginia she took greatest care to inveigle herself with the American consulate, visiting almost every day as the correspondent from the *New York Post*. Gone were the red tresses of Vichy's Miss Hall, however. She had learned to become less conspicuous than the striking figure who had caught the eye of George Bellows in Spain, dyeing her hair light brown and drawing it tightly into a bun to reveal the 'features of a cavalier' and 'beautifully calm eyes' that 'twinkled in friendly circumstances'.[31]

She had also abandoned her pre-war Parisian wardrobe, avoiding the flamboyant look that Vichy propaganda termed *'virago juive et bolchévique'*[32] in favour of the quiet tweed suits of the petite bourgeoisie. Wearing her beloved trousers was now out of the question as Vichy blamed them for the female emancipation that had enthralled Virginia in pre-war Paris but which Pétainists equated to a dangerous 'moral turpitude'.[33] Now those freedoms had been lost, and women dressed demurely to avoid attention from the French police or their German masters. The upside was that in those early months such regressive views meant that most men struggled to believe that women could be involved in subversion.

Drawing on her love of drama and dressing up at school, she learned how to change her appearance within minutes depending on whom she was meeting. Altering her hairstyle, wearing a wide-brimmed hat, putting on glasses, changing her make-up, wearing different gloves to hide her hands or even inserting slivers of rubber into her mouth to puff out her cheeks: it all worked surprisingly well. With a little improvisation she could be three or four different women – Brigitte, Virginia, Marie or Germaine – within the space of an afternoon. Always moving, always changing, it made her difficult to pin down.

In place de la Bourse, the vice-consul George Whittinghill received her warmly as Virginia. Although he had to remain outwardly neutral, she quickly assessed Whittinghill's sympathies correctly and recruited him as one of her most important helpers. It was not long before the pair had set up a reliable method of smuggling her messages out of France to the American embassy in Berne via the diplomatic pouch. From the Swiss capital, the military attaché Colonel Barnwell Legge – who declared Virginia an 'excellent type and a most reliable worker'[34] – would faithfully send the reports on to London. He forwarded replies and cash from Baker Street to Lyon in sealed envelopes marked 'Marie c/o Lion', *Lion* being Whittinghill's codename. Virginia now had an enviably reliable – if not speedy – channel of communication.

Yet what she really needed was a wireless operator. It was virtually impossible to organise parachute drops of new agents or supplies, for instance, without instant communication. SOE had so far managed to dispatch only two working operators into the whole of the Free Zone. The first, Georges Bégué, was overworked and monopolised by *Lucas* nearly two hundred miles away in Châteauroux. The only other Free Zone operator, Gilbert Turck, whose codename was *Christophe*, had been parachuted in in August but had immediately been imprisoned by the French police after being knocked unconscious on landing. His future had looked ominous until news came of his 'amazing escape' thanks to a mysterious intervention by the Vichy high command, the first hint of the SOE wipeout that was to come.

September 1941 was a busy month for SOE, which was rapidly gearing up its operations in France. Virginia was standing by to make contact with the dozen or so new agents coming in by parachute or via the Mediterranean coast. Among the jumpers on the night of 6 September were George Langelaan, a former *New York Times* correspondent; Michael Trotobas, a charismatic young English chef; Victor Gerson, or *Vic*, a Jewish textiles businessman; and a supremely brave Lancashire engineer, Ben Cowburn. On 19 September, several more F Section men arrived on board a converted freighter, including Georges Duboudin, or *Alain*, who headed to Lyon to join Virginia, and Francis Basin (*Olive*), who remained on the Riviera.

Just as Virginia was settling into the Grand Nouvel Hôtel, four more dropped during the night of Friday 10 October, near Bergerac in the Dordogne, along with the first SOE air delivery of money, explosives and weapons. One arrival was particularly welcome, as Lieutenant Jean-Philippe Le Harivel had orders to travel to Lyon to act as Virginia's wireless operator. He and the others were welcomed by a reception committee led by the former socialist deputy Jean Pierre-Bloch and his wife Gaby, who hurried to hide the materiel and sweep up the men into a safe-house. But one newcomer could not be found. In the confusion, he had been dropped four miles off course – together with most of the supplies – and had blacked out after landing on a rock. When the Vichy police picked him up the following morning they found in his pocket a piece of paper London had carelessly provided to all its outgoing agents. It was a map showing the location of an SOE safehouse, a gated residence in Marseille with a large verdant garden, called the Villa des Bois, where *Christophe* had been holed up since his release. It was just one of a number of leads now in police possession that all led to that address on the outskirts of the French port.

After recent outbreaks of violence against the occupying army in Paris and elsewhere, the Vichy authorities and their German masters were in the process of a brutal clampdown with wholesale arrests and bloody reprisals. The assassination of a German colonel in Nantes had, for instance, led to the shooting of forty-eight citizens in revenge. The French police were as eager as the Nazis to stamp out further trouble and 'bully the dissidents into submission'.[35] SOE may have been unaware of Vichy's 'efficiency and ruthlessness' against the Resistance, and failed in its duty to warn its agents.[36] But soon they were to learn to fear them more than the Gestapo because of the skill of the Vichy security services in laying traps and infiltrating their ranks.[37] The French authorities were doing a highly competent job on the Nazis' behalf.

In some ways, the Nantes shootings played into Virginia's hands as she began to establish herself in Lyon and plan for the future. They galvanised opinion against the Germans and their Vichy supporters and helped to spark the very first thoughts of a national resistance movement. She reported back to London how the Nantes tragedy, while unconnected to SOE, highlighted the need for strategy, training and supplies to be properly coordinated across France. It was also clear that the Resistance could never pose a real threat to the occupiers until it had multiple and reliable radio links with the only free nation in Europe continuing the fight. Less obvious was how Virginia was to build up the necessary manpower for a fighting force. Although officially still only a liaison officer she now embarked on setting up her own network, codenamed *Heckler*, but had started with virtually nothing, let alone guidance on how to recruit supporters on the ground. The going in those early days in Lyon was extremely tough. Even those rare souls she had found with the will to fight would have to be exceptionally patient. Their job at this point was merely to exist, to form the nucleus of a secret army that would one day rise up to attack the Germans from within when the Allies finally came back. In the meantime, however tempting, assassinations or spectacular acts of sabotage that could be attributed to 'deliberate interference' were strictly forbidden by Baker Street. Virginia would have to stop hotheads from having a go at glory until the right time; she must prevent her people from engaging in more unplanned and ultimately pointless exercises like the one in Nantes. 'Fires might mysteriously light themselves', engine bearings might suddenly 'run hot', or perhaps a German car seize up from sugar in the tank. 'But things must not "go bang in the night",'[38] was how one SOE report put it. 'Premature explosion of French resistance was our worst danger,' explained a future F Section boss, 'as there could at that time be no prospect of an early landing of Allied troops to sustain such a movement.'[39] Virginia knew it was vital to have everything in place for when the time came for action, but until then her mission to recruit would have to tread a delicate path and avoid unnecessary sacrifice.

A list of nine names provided before her departure by Baker Street, largely based on pre-armistice information, was neither safe (it was no longer certain where their true sympathies lay) nor sufficient. She in any case preferred to make her own contacts, ones she knew she could trust, as after years of unhelpful or hostile reaction to her disability she felt she had become a shrewd judge of character. She needed couriers to carry messages, money and arms; more safehouses to hide incoming agents and out-going escapees; and 'letter boxes' – people who would take delivery of secret parcels and messages without asking questions. She needed false identity papers, driving permits and ration cards. And she needed them fast. The fact was, though, that a newly arrived lone agent such as Virginia was in great danger of discovery or betrayal because in her haste or ignorance her very first whispered enquiries might reach the Gestapo, who could arrest someone on the merest rumour from an informant. It would have been all too easy for an indiscreet word or a momentary lapse to lead to disaster. She urgently needed some safe introductions to get going.

That same sense of desperate urgency saw the self-effacing Bégué, who although French had studied engineering at Hull University, frantically transmitting to London from a small hotel room in Châteauroux. Five fledgling SOE circuits relied on him, but none thought to offer him protection though it was evident he was in danger. Vichy and the Germans had started deploying radio detection cars, which, through a system of triangulation, could track down the source of clandestine radio signals.[40] The only active SOE radio operator in southern France, Bégué was staying on air far too long and the days were ticking down until he was inevitably caught.

'Feeling the breath of the police hot on his neck',[41] Bégué decided to get in contact with the only other Free Zone wireless operator known to be at liberty. *Christophe* responded by issuing an invitation to all agents in southern France to meet at the villa in Marseille – a stark contravention of basic security rules. Why he did so was soon to become a subject of violent debate; the tragedy was that by then so many had responded. Some came for camaraderie, finding it even harder in the field than they had expected; others, so short of money they were virtually starving, came to pick up cash from the recent parachute drop. Many of them had been stripped of their own money by reception com mittees composed of unscrupulous locals who somehow thought it their due.[42] The problem was in large part that SOE agents and individual *résistants* were still operating alone with no clear direction or back-up, locally or in London. The need for a commanding figure in the field could not have been more urgent.

Virginia, waiting in Lyon for Le Harivel to show up, was feeling isolated. After seven weeks alone, she too felt the lack of guidance or support. Yet some sixth sense seemingly stopped her from joining this mass gathering of the SOE clan. She had also long ago discovered the benefits of self-dependency and was far older than her years.

By contrast one Lieutenant Marc Jumeau, a tall bushy-haired technical adviser who had parachuted in on 10 October, was in search of friendly company in a frightening world. The first to arrive at the Villa des Bois, he ignored the fact that no one had answered when he had phoned the house several times earlier. He brushed aside the concerns of a female neighbour about *Christophe*'s suspicious behaviour. He failed to notice anything untoward in the thickly planted garden, blithely walking the twenty yards up the path to the front door past a number of concealed policemen. Instead of being met by his fellow SOE agent, three inspectors of the French counter-terrorism force, the fearsome Sûreté, opened the door from inside and arrested him.

A dozen agents, including Le Harivel and Langelaan, were picked up soon after. Five more were pulled in at the villa, including Jean and Gaby Pierre-Bloch, (who were carrying the five million francs sent from London wrapped in a towel, and who were both Jewish). This led to further arrests in Châteauroux and Antibes. Finally, as darkness fell on 24 October, Georges Bégué walked up the road to the villa's front gates to discover the house all closed up. At least he had followed security protocol to the letter, having phoned half an hour beforehand to take soundings. A man with a voice exactly like *Christophe* had assured him that everything was 'normal'.[43] But when he rang the bell and waited to be admitted, six Sûreté officers nabbed Bégué too and took him to join the others in the cells, where interrogators were in the habit of spending the nights blow-torching the soles of prisoners' feet. Bégué believed that *Christophe*, never a popular figure, had knowingly allowed himself to be trailed and the Villa des Bois to be used as a mousetrap. Others[44] were convinced he had bought his freedom by actively luring his colleagues into disaster. *Christophe*, the only one still at liberty, continued to plead innocence. But whether treachery or not, the fact was that in one swoop French – rather than German – police had practically cleaned out SOE in the Free Zone. Virtually all its most promising agents, and both of its Free Zone wireless operators, were behind bars and facing the prospect of weeks of torture followed by a firing squad. Most had not even started their secret work.

A few days later, André Bloch, who had been transmitting from the Occupied Zone, also vanished after being denounced by a French neighbour for simply looking like a Jew. No one had properly considered the extra dangers this presented. He was tortured by the Gestapo, who gleefully discovered his radio, but courageous to the last Bloch faced the firing squad without giving anyone away. Now there was not a single working SOE radio operator at liberty in the whole of France.

F Section entered what was seen as a new 'dark age'[45] and was deafened by the silence from its agents. After fifteen months of intense activity involving the recruitment, training and infiltration of nearly two dozen agents, London was left 'with little else in the field except Miss Virginia Hall'.[46] Only she had means of contacting Baker Street. Only she had a growing network uncontaminated by the arrests. Only she was supplying vital information on Vichy and the Nazi occupiers. The future of Allied intelligence in France now rested on a solitary woman who had been written off for most of her adult life.

Chapter Three

My Tart Friends

The Villa des Bois disaster knocked SOE badly. Heads rolled in London amid allegations of appalling amateurishness, just as the rivals at MI6 had predicted. Several staff were cracking under the strain and within a few months the SOE chief known internally as CD – the one-time MP Frank Nelson – would retire because his health had irretrievably broken down. In the meantime, a new F Section chief, by the name of Maurice Buckmaster, was appointed to raise standards, but he also had little or no training or experience in either clandestine or regular warfare. A former Ford Motor Company manager in France, he was said to have 'brought the optimism of a sales director' to Baker Street. But sometimes the Old Etonian's cheeriness was actually naivety, and his superiors hired him only because 'there was nobody else'.[1] Soon Virginia's new forty-one-year-old boss was working eighteen-hour days, cycling home to Chelsea in the middle of the night, but all – for a painfully long time – without news of his agents. The Villa des Bois and Bloch's death marked a turning point for SOE and meant that no one in Baker Street now thought of their work as a game. 'The complete silence from France was a strain on our nerves and a dam to our progress,' Buckmaster recalled. 'There was nothing we could do but wait.'[2] Puffing frantically on his pipe, Buckmaster relied on Virginia somehow surviving, finding out what had happened and finally reporting back. But while they were exhorted to keep cheerful at all times, staff officers in London were left with a lurking fear that they could have done more to safeguard their prize agents – if only they knew how.

SOE could now count on one hand the number of other surviving agents in the Free Zone: Philippe de Vomécourt (*Gauthier*), who had been recruited by his brother *Lucas*, Francis Basin (*Olive*) on the Côte d'Azur, and Georges Duboudin (*Alain*) in Lyon with Virginia. It was a skeleton operation and Virginia was the one on whom others depended, above all because she had the sole reliable means of communicating with London. Each message sent via the diplomatic pouch, though, took several days to come through, and without a radio operator SOE's toehold in France was not sustainable for long.

The need for Virginia to reboot the whole French operation could not have been more acute. There was barely an hour in the day, let alone days in the week when she was not working to retrieve lost ground. But just as more were prompted by Vichy and German brutality into wanting to join the Resistance, so it was in danger of being snuffed out. Emboldened by successes such as the Villa des Bois, the Vichy authorities and their German masters swooped in on anyone they suspected of harbouring pro-Resistance views. Many dissidents made it too easy; to Virginia's continual dismay they met in public, talked loudly and proudly, did not check out new recruits, used their own names and fought with rival groups. Despite the events in Nantes, they continued to make futile gestures, often leading to terrible reprisals for little or no gain. As a mere liaison officer, she had no control over the actions of other groups, but when it came to recruiting her own people she sought to create a more secure and disciplined system of small, discrete cells of hand-picked members prepared to follow orders. They also had to understand the penalty of careless behaviour. She could not allow a Villa des Bois to happen again.

Lyon offered some comfort to refugees for now, but the city was watched closely by the German security services. Both the Gestapo, the Nazis' secret police, and the Abwehr (military intelligence) ran undercover operations and competed to outdo each other and to press the French authorities to do more too. They were helped by the fact that the *mairie* was run by collaborators who took their lead from the Nazis in Paris. Everyone feared their neighbours' ears – there were more than fifteen hundred denunciations every day – and most were frightened to open their mouths or break the law. Virginia was disappointed that so few considered it their duty to put themselves in peril to try to free their country – but perhaps it was hardly surprising.

The fact that the British were simply not trusted to continue the fight also posed a considerable problem. Pétain had pointedly blamed them for the French defeat. Dunkirk may have been spun by Winston Churchill as a type of miracle, but to the French (encouraged by a barrage of Vichy propaganda) it had represented a treacherous act of desertion. Now British prestige had been wrecked once again by military reverses such as the humiliating loss of the battleship HMS *Hood* and the bungled Battle of Crete, which resulted in the forced evacuation of thousands of troops. London had been expected to follow Paris, quickly caving in and negotiating for peace. Even though that had not happened, with the exception of Russia where victory was still elusive, Germany was winning battle after battle. What was the point of risking torture and death in pursuit of a lost cause? As an agent of a secret service run by the mistrusted Brits, how could Virginia find those willing to take her orders and help?

The British were seen not only as weak but, aided by centuries of mutual distrust, specifically anti-French. Vichy controlled the press and radio in the south, as did the Germans in the north, and so truth was an early casualty of Pétain's collaboration, and widespread hatred, hunger and disease the result. Most French were led to believe that a British blockade was the chief cause of shortages of food, wine and fuel. Virginia knew that that was a lie. Systematic plundering by the Nazis had stripped France of much of its coal and a large share of its plentiful produce such as meat, vegetables, fruit and fish. And Vichy was complicit in the bulk shipping of such bounty back to the Fatherland. No wonder, then, that Virginia soon sought instructions from London on how to spoil food bound for Berlin. The best way was to insert 'a small piece of putrefied meat' in a carcass, make a pinhole in tinned provisions, place salt water in sugar or allow vegetables and cereals simply to get damp.[3]

In one of her New York Post articles, Virginia told how the famously French crimes passionelles had given way to petty theft – desperate people were snatching food out of shopping baskets or tearing down fences for firewood. Even scrawny pigeons in town squares and rabbits bred on apartment balconies were prized for their meat. People were on average a stone lighter than before the war, and many lost teeth and nails to malnutrition.[4] Children were so hungry their growth was stunted, and many died from common illnesses. Poor diet led to epidemics of scarlet fever, diphtheria, tuberculosis, typhoid, boils and impetigo. Virginia herself, although she ate when she could in her favourite bistro, could barely afford to lose more weight.

In one dispatch – which, like many, was not published but sent straight to SOE – Virginia reported that thirty people had been hospitalised in Lyon with famine oedema, a swelling up of the body caused by starvation.[5] As winter approached (the worst since the Napoleonic Wars) everyone's health was made still worse by the intense cold. Clothes were hard to buy – especially bras, because of the labour and multiple components involved. Leather stocks had been requisitioned by the German military so there was a desperate shortage of normal shoes. The rudimentary footwear sometimes still on sale in the shops had wooden soles that clacked loudly as their wearers walked down the street – a wartime phenomenon that became the soundtrack to Nazi rule.

This, then, was hardly fertile ground for growing a London-controlled network. It was Virginia's good fortune that George Whittinghill at the American consulate introduced her to an RAF pilot who visited him almost every day. Gravely burnt by a fire in his bomber over Belgium on the first day of the blitzkrieg back in May 1940, William Simpson had spent months in hospital wrapped in greased bandages and was now awaiting repatriation to Britain while such humanitarian arrangements were still allowed by France. Once handsome, his face was now scarred and blotched, and part of his nose and his left eyelid were missing. His fingers had been amputated and he could not lower his flies without help, so he always required someone to help him to urinate. His left foot and knee were badly burned and he limped painfully, even with the help of a stick, steeling himself to deal with the inevitable horrified or pitying looks. Simpson went out of his way to reward her understanding, while grabbing the chance to make himself feel useful again. They developed an instant rapport.

Simpson thought he might have the answer to her urgent need for reliable recruits. He offered to introduce Virginia to one of

Lyon's most fêted residents. His French friend had already risked her life to help him find shelter in Lyon, and was doing her bit to fight the Nazis on an ad hoc basis almost entirely on her own (like many *résistants* at that point). It would be up to Virginia to win her trust – if she could – and enlist her to help create a Resistance operation answering to SOE. Simpson believed if anyone could do it, Virginia could. He found her different from other women; she possessed what he deemed, in the thinking of the day, to be a masculine 'courage and a strength of purpose' in contrast to her 'essentially feminine appearance'.[6]

Simpson's favourite Lyonnaise (whom he said had given him back his 'sense of manhood') was nobody's idea of a typical *résistante*. A thirty-seven-year-old 'burning brunette' with 'animal sexual magnetism', Germaine Guérin was part-owner of one of Lyon's most successful brothels. Exuding a 'gypsy warmth', she liked to wrap herself in jewels, silks and furs at the evening salons she held in the apartment above her business, surrounded by a collection of black cats – one of her kittens would even follow her devotedly down the street. Outside, the building looked like an ordinary tenement on a dowdy backstreet (now replaced by modern offices for the French National Treasury), but inside her home was a treasure-house of tapestries, wooden chests full of gold coins and wardrobes stuffed with Paris couture. Wealthy and powerful men came here to pay court and in return for her favours were happy to do her bidding for the cause.

In the *maison close* downstairs, the lustrous Germaine separately welcomed German officers, French police, Vichy officials and industrialists. She supplied them with black-market Scotch and prime steaks at exorbitant prices but kept some aside for her friends. Her clients never thought to doubt her motives, let alone search the premises. They took pleasure in supplying her with otherwise unobtainable petrol (never suspecting she would use her car to transport agents and escapees), plus coal (an almost impossible luxury that winter). Germaine 'moved in sordid surroundings and her morals were irregular', Simpson recalled, although he also recognised her underlying virtue: 'She had . . . the shining cleanliness of a sealion.'[7]

When Virginia met Germaine for the first time, both were wary. The Frenchwoman was proud and fiercely patriotic; she baulked at joining a formal network and especially the idea of taking orders from a foreigner. Virginia already had the nuns at La Mulatière as her devoted helpers but now she found herself recruiting from the other end of the morality spectrum. Even her thirst for adventure had never previously led her into a world so removed from her strait-laced home life, one where the female body was bought and sold for cash. Neither woman typically sought female intimacy, but despite obvious differences in background Simpson observed them discovering they had much in common: they were both happiest when flirting with danger; they enjoyed a wicked sense of humour; they could both 'make something out of nothing'; and they shared a 'disdain for their own sensations of fear'.[8] Germaine seems to have been yet another won over by Virginia's evident integrity and courage, and understood that the London connection would hugely advance her desire for a free France. She quickly agreed to make parts of her brothel and three other flats available as safehouses (heated by her illicit coal), although both women initially pretended Germaine had no idea why they were needed. Germaine was to become an unlikely pillar of Virginia's entire Lyon operation and one of its most heroic agents, even if Virginia also immediately recognised that she would have to manage her new friend and try to teach her at least the basics of security. As Simpson had warned her, Germaine's artistic swagger was beguiling to man and woman alike but she could also be 'careless' in her courage and 'ridiculously rash'.[9]

Nevertheless, Germaine became a 'rallying point'[10] for many SOE agents coming through Lyon, as well as Jews fleeing the Occupied Zone, Poles on their way to fight, and escapees making their way south to Spain. She said she wanted to help the 'revolution against the German occupiers', to recreate what she called a 'virile France', so she found them all somewhere to hide, supplied them with food, clothes and false papers, and sent them on their way to freedom. The risks she took seemed to amuse her, but for all her apparent insouciance Germaine's enrolment marked an entirely new stage in Virginia's mission. Her *Heckler* network was now viewed by SOE as 'solidly established',[11] with a roster of exceptionally useful and committed recruits, at the centre of which was this unlikely pair of women.

Germaine's powers over well-placed Frenchmen proved extraordinary and opened all sorts of doors. She recruited some of her most devoted admirers to help Virginia. One was a wealthy Lyonnais engineer called Eugène Jeunet, a widower with three children, who had a much prized pass to cross the heavily patrolled demarcation line between the two French zones. He offered to shuttle Virginia's messages to and from underground groups in Paris and beyond, offering her the chance to extend her network to the capital. He was also to provide transport, petrol, accommodation and food for agents as well as hiding places at his business for arms, explosives and radios. Most fortuitously, Jeunet's brother-in-law was the local police chief, who was persuaded not to look too closely into what Virginia was doing and to tip her off when his officers were about to mount a raid or make an arrest. His well-timed warnings were to save Virginia from capture on many an occasion, as well as a number of her most important agents.

It was Germaine's 'girls', though, who were to take perhaps the greatest risks of all to provide Virginia with intelligence. With

their madam's encouragement, they spiked their clients' drinks
to loosen their tongues and rifled their pockets for interesting
papers to photograph when they slept. A year earlier, in her
report to the American embassy in London, Virginia had reserved
particular contempt for prostitutes entertaining German clients,
but now she affectionately dubbed such women her 'tart friends'.
Thanks to their 'Jerry bed companions', as she put it, they knew
'a hell of a lot!'[12] and passed on what they knew to her. Some went
even further, using heroin smuggled over from London in the
American diplomatic bag as part of the fight. Drunken German
clients would be lured in with the offer of 'just a little sniff' of the
drug 'to see what happens'. If all went according to plan, the men
would soon become hooked and rendered mysteriously incapable
of work; some of the pilots found their eyesight was affected and
were grounded from their planes. It was a perilous and unorthodox form of warfare, but effective nonetheless.[13]

Germaine also introduced Virginia to another vital figure with
links to the demi-monde. Dr Jean Rousset was chubby-faced and
jovial, with a rakish moustache, and much loved by the city's
filles de joie, whom he visited most weeks on a professional basis
as their gynaecologist. His 'many a devilish idea for the discomfi-
ture of the German clients'[14] appear to have included infecting as
many as possible with syphilis or gonorrhea. He doled out white
cards denoting a girl was free of infection when she was nothing
of the sort. One or two appear to have spread their condition to
a dozen or so of the enemy – Germans were actively encouraged
to visit brothels in the belief it would increase their motivation to
fight – before quickly seeking treatment for themselves. Others
put itching powder in their clients' clothes to maximise their distress. It is fortunate that the good doctor had an uncanny knack
of talking himself out of awkward situations – a talent that would
eventually save his life.

Rousset ran his gynaecology and dermatology surgery behind imposing wooden doors at 7 place Antonin-Poncet. The old honey-coloured stone building soon became Virginia's private *poste de commande*, a convenient location as she could attribute her visits to seeking medical advice for a genuine rash. Dr Rousset looked after injured or ill agents, received messages and introduced her to dozens of other useful contacts. He also set up a fake lunatic asylum on an upper floor as a further safehouse – Germans were unlikely to come looking as they were taught to fear mental illness. An army reservist, Rousset had already sheltered Jews and escaped prisoners of war since being demobilised in 1940. His heavy consulting-room furniture hid a stock of underground literature and he had been waiting for the chance to do more for the Allied cause in any way he could. Now finally here was someone from London who could organise and supply the Resistance with outside help. When Virginia encountered Rousset for the first time she liked his optimism, energy and vast network of similarly minded friends. In turn he, like so many others, was bowled over by her force of character. There was something infallibly wholesome about her, no matter what she was doing or where she found herself. Her authority, competence and charisma were obvious, but so was her selflessness. Both of them recognised that in wartime, nobility could be found in unexpected places. But to Vichy and the Germans, they and their colleagues would be classed as terrorists.

Rousset saw no reason not to take orders from this woman, even if to do so was to risk his neck. She was, after all, putting her life on the line for his country when so many of his compatriots were not. His willingness was all the more exceptional given that the reactionary New Order regime expected women to stay at home, get married and have a minimum of four children as their patriotic duty. Abortion was illegal and punishable by guillotine.

(No wonder the birth rate in the Rhône *département* around Lyon had risen by 35 per cent in little more than a year.[15]) The backlash against the emancipated metropolitan women of the 1930s had been decisive and extreme. Females were now vassals who still could not vote, were legally bound to obey their husbands and, declared Vichy, 'had their nerves upset by strident noises'.[16] Yet Rousset ignored all such strictures and devoted himself to becoming Virginia's 'very most valuable assistant'.[17] She codenamed him *Pépin*, meaning 'pip', and appointed him her chief lieutenant.

Virginia was also introduced to Robert Leprevost, a former French intelligence officer and another key player who had already helped a number of downed RAF pilots to escape France via Marseille. As luck would have it, he had become expert at smuggling out British officers who did not speak or look French. They ate, drank and even walked differently from their Gallic hosts. They also tended to be taller, broader, paler and have larger feet – which posed problems for Virginia and others when trying to fit them with non-military footwear. Just appearing in the street posed a danger to them, and more still to those helping them. Later, when America entered the war, the challenge became even greater. Gum-chewing had to be specifically banned and bow-legged Texans painstakingly taught how to move like Europeans and to avoid putting their hands in their pockets, which was seen as a 'Yankee' peccadillo. Leprevost's expertise was a skill that would serve them well.

George Whittinghill also secretly joined Virginia's efforts to help escapees. He dug into his own pocket on many an occasion to help exfiltrate through Spain some hundred RAF pilots over the course of the war and another twenty British and Belgian agents. Within weeks of Virginia's arrival in France, British airmen were being advised that if they were shot down they should head for the American consulate in Lyon and declare themselves to be 'a friend of *Olivier*'. This was the password to be put in touch with *Marie Monin*, Virginia's *nom de guerre*. With the help of Germaine and friends, she was able to hide and feed scores of them and then organise their escape from France. Word began circulating far and wide of the miracle-working *Marie of Lyon*.

Virginia's days were long and a whirl of activity, with barely a moment to dwell on her own troubles. She had set up the core of her network with Rousset and Germaine, but now she wanted to expand, initially across Lyon and then into the rest of southern France and beyond. As liaison officer, her job was ostensibly to coordinate rather than lead different circuits of agents but SOE's desperation for progress, combined with her energy and ability to unite French from all sorts of backgrounds, saw her going far beyond her original brief. She recruited a fifty-year-old scent manufacturer, Joseph Marchand, who provided a safehouse in Lyon and would go on to head an SOE circuit; a pair of valiant elderly spinsters, the Mesdemoiselles Fellot, who stored supplies for the Resistance in the basement of their antique shop while housing agents on the run in their apartment; the owner of the Lyon underwear shop La Lingerie Pratique, France Pejot,* who stored weapons under piles of lacy bras and hosted sweaty Resistance meetings in her back room; and several hairdressers who sheltered escapees and helped *résistants* on the run to change their looks. Mme Alberte took in messages from different Resistance leaders at her laundry, signalling she had something to collect if she placed two mended stockings close together in the window. If they were far apart, nothing had come in. Friends from Virginia's college days in Boston, Jean and Marie-Louise Joulian, now

---

* Later mother of the French musician Jean-Michel Jarre and mother-in-law of the actress Charlotte Rampling.

factory owners in Le Puy, hid escapees in the mountains of the Haute-Loire and lent money to Virginia when none had come through from London. She also recruited a brilliant forger, a highly respectable engraver in an upmarket shopping arcade called the Passage de l'Hôtel-Dieu. Monsieur Chambrillard became expert at creating official papers that fooled even the most eagle-eyed inspectors. He, like all her other supporters, knew that the likely price of capture was death.

To act effectively against the enemy, SOE recognised before the French themselves that the disparate strands of resistance had to be welded together into disciplined secret armies. Most groups knew nothing of one another and struggled to operate effectively with no cohesive plan set down by a central figure. Virginia left no potentially useful contact untouched and travelled extensively to establish the necessary links under the SOE umbrella, and most of all to promise outside help and hope for the future. She worked out the logistics for how different types of *résistant* (adult, youth, Catholic, Protestant, Jew, non-believer, man, woman) would be able to work together, with her liaising between them. Through a combination of personal recommendation and judicious approaches to strangers, she recruited more and more to the cause. By giving a tiny bit away of her own feelings about the war, and her burning desire for a free France, she had a way of making people open up to her. But she also made it clear that only by signing up to her network and following her orders could she guarantee subsequent deliveries of arms, explosives, food, money and medicines. Only SOE could and would eventually provide thousands of tons of supplies – but her recruits had to keep to their side of the bargain. The problem was that many people were still more interested in their own factional struggles – between communists, radicals, ex-army officers, aristocrats and increasing numbers of supporters of General de

Gaulle – than in accepting command from London on how to serve the Allied cause.

Virginia ploughed on, refusing to take sides. She presented herself as a unifying force, interested in anyone genuinely willing to put winning the war first, whatever their secondary allegiances. To make it work she travelled to Marseille to build up the escape lines with Robert Leprevost; to Avignon to recruit local women as couriers and set up a safehouse for a future radio operator; and again to Le Puy, where she signed up a haulier called Eugène Labourier to provide lorries to pick up supplies from parachute drops, and store them in his warehouse. (Deliveries of arms and explosives began modestly in autumn 1941.) She visited *Olive* in Antibes to help his embryo circuit on the Côte d'Azur, which was ideally placed to welcome new agents arriving or leaving by boat, and other contacts in Perpignan near the Spanish border to set up escape lines over the Pyrenees. She approached sympathetic lawyers, who passed on information about Allied prisoners and the strength of the case against them. She targeted friendly hoteliers who would provide rooms, town-hall clerks with access to official stamps for false papers, farmers with barns for storage. And, of course, she regularly returned to Vichy to visit the embassy and pick up on political intelligence from her contacts in Pétain's administration.

Perhaps her biggest coup, however, was infiltrating the Sûreté – the 'ersatz-Gestapo'[18] that had laid the trap at the Villa des Bois and which through its 'snoop ears'[19] operations expertly tracked down secret radio signals. She identified and recruited an idealistic and handsome thirty-year-old Corsican officer called Marcel Leccia, who was based in Limoges, and then, incredibly, proceeded to enlist both his assistant (Elisée Allard) and boss (Léon Guth). Now she would most likely be warned of future similar traps and could hope that the Sûreté would be more lenient with any of her agents that they did happen to catch.

Meanwhile, many French – factory foremen, railway workers, police officers, government officials and housewives – started to pluck up the courage to approach the good-looking woman with the strong American accent and offer her help, spurred on by the fact she came from a country that was in those dark days a beacon of freedom and liberal democracy. 'She was in a good position to help for, as an American, people talked to her openly about their feelings,' noted an impressed Ben Cowburn, whom Virginia rated as SOE's most brilliant agent. Although in France only on a temporary mission, he visited her often and observed with amazement how these unsolicited approaches from French locals were providing her with a steadily growing raft of useful contacts.[20] She had recruited more people in better places than anyone else; from nowhere she now had her finger in virtually every significant French pie. Glamorous but also authoritative and decisive, there could not be a better ambassador for the British cause or champion for the Resistance. The Allied presence in France had been transformed.

The constant travel through sleet, snow and slush as winter set in was, however, in Virginia's own words, a 'grim undertaking not to be embarked upon lightly. It is devastating for the weak and exhausting even for the strong.'[21] The Germans had requisitioned the modern rolling stock from the railways, leaving behind only antiquated locomotives that were slow, dirty, unheated and often broke down. It could take all day to travel just a couple of hundred miles. The timetable was much reduced from its pre-war levels, and few people were able to procure petrol for their cars. So the carriages were, Virginia reported, 'crowded beyond belief and looked like a Walt Disney brainstorm'[22] with people pressed up against the windows and holding on to the entrance platforms so that the doors could not shut properly. Virginia herself sometimes found herself stuck in the doorway, narrowly avoiding death (or

what she called the 'void') for up to two hours at a time by clench-
ing the hand of a complete stranger just inside the carriage. Some
women took to putting a cushion under their clothes in the hope
that fellow passengers would take pity on a pregnant woman
and surrender their seat, but even that ploy often did not work as
'the atmosphere was charged with chilly gloom and suspicion.
Nobody talked.'[23] Sometimes only a couple of Benzedrine from
her fast-dwindling supply would give her the strength to go on.

Virginia took full advantage of her journalistic status and
informal police protection, in Lyon at least, to explain her travel
and irregular hours. She continued to write articles as often as
possible to maintain her cover, and indeed so pleased her editors
at the newspaper that she was given a thousand-franc bonus.
The more sensitive articles on political news were not published
but merely sent straight to SOE to avoid attracting attention to
her. One exception, though, appeared in the *New York Post* on 24
November, datelined Lyon, and told the world about the growing
threat from Vichy's repression of Jews.

For her own safety, Virginia avoided editorialising but was
finding it harder to disguise her anger over the treatment of Jews,
who were now excluded from virtually any prestigious or influ-
ential profession. They were banned from working as bankers,
stockbrokers, publicity agents, merchants or estate agents, or
even in the theatre, movies or press. She quoted a 'particularly
qualified government official' as saying 'it is better to prevent
than suppress' and warning that more restrictive laws were
on the way.

Despite the caution in her writing, Virginia's perennial roaming was inevitably risky. Trains were subject to snap police
controls, sometimes backed up by Gestapo, particularly the *rapide*
down to Marseille. The safest option while travelling was to keep
incriminating papers (containing messages too long to commit

to memory, or perhaps technical details of potential sabotage targets) in one hand. This meant they could easily be pushed down between the seat cushions, thrown out onto the track or even eaten if necessary. Some agents held up tiny mirrors next to the window at each station to see who was about to board, to be forewarned of approaching trouble. Virginia observed that the security police took more interest in the cheapest seats so she made sure to book in first class. She memorised the address of where she was going rather than writing it down and always had a plausible reason for going there worked out and rehearsed. Even so, every journey presented a mortal danger – and her wooden leg precluded the last-ditch option of throwing herself off the train and running for cover. At every meeting contacts might turn out to be double agents or traitors or they might have been caught and tortured so that the Sûreté or Gestapo turned up instead.

Perhaps the worst moment of all, though, was finally returning to her hotel room in Lyon. Winter came early that year and the temperature outside plummeted to fifteen degrees below zero; with no heating Virginia's room was little better and she had to resort to blocking the draughts from the windows with old rags and lining her clothes with newspapers (which made a crackling noise when she moved) to keep warm. There was a drop of hot water, but only on Sunday mornings. Fortunately, her school years at Roland Park Country had prepared her for enduring the cold. Far worse for her was the absence of soap for herself or her clothes and sheets, so everything felt not only chilly but grubby. After a while she decided that wearing dark clothes made sense as the dirt did not show, but it went against her naturally fastidious nature. 'If you could ever send me a piece of soap,' she wrote to London via the diplomatic pouch, 'I should be both very happy and much cleaner.'[24] She would also have been better protected from the first epidemic of scabies for more than a century – travelling crammed in with other under-nourished, under-washed passengers on the trains meant the disease was rife and most people just could not stop scratching. Perhaps the biggest challenge of all was running out of special medical socks for her stump, without which her hair-raising journeys on the trains were even more of an endurance test.

Time alone in their rooms was when agents had to confront their fears, ears pricked for the slightest suspicious sound. Despite Virginia's friendly relations with the local police, her unusual gait made the 'Limping Lady' or *la dame qui boite*, as some now called her, a conspicuous figure. 'Fear never abated,' recalled one candid French resister. 'Fear for oneself; fear of being denounced; fear of being followed without knowing it; fear that it will be "them" when at dawn one hears or thinks one hears a door slam shut or someone coming up the stairs . . . Fear, finally, of being afraid and of not being able to surmount it.'[25] Resistance called for a 'lonely courage, for men and women who could fight on their own'.[26] But the solitude was an eternal strain. One agent took to eating dinner in front of the mirror. No one except a reflection could be entirely trusted. Behind enemy lines, loyalty had a different meaning, and in the end it was to an ideal rather than to a person or people. Virginia knew all too well that dropping her guard, even with other agents or helpers over a meal or a drink, could be fatal. Everyone experienced loneliness and an urge to share thoughts and fears, but survival depended on holding back. For Virginia, though, since she had lost her leg hiding her emotions and rigid self-reliance had become second nature. And all the terror and turmoil was better than feeling dead inside. She was doing a vital job, and doing it well. She had a role. Although capture was a real prospect every minute of the day, she had never felt so free.

*

It was clear that Virginia had made an impressive start. In fact, SOE considered her 'amazingly successful' and rated her work and fieldcraft as 'inspired'.[27] But not everyone was pleased with her progress. *Alain*, or Georges Duboudin, was one of the few other SOE agents who had avoided the Marseille mousetrap and was based near her in Lyon. A year younger than Virginia, he was French but married to a British woman and had worked for the Crédit Lyonnais bank in London before the war. He had been trained by Kim Philby, then working for SOE,* and had been lauded in London as 'an exceptionally superior type' and a 'natural leader'.[28] *Alain* had been formally appointed chief (or organiser) of his own fledgling circuit and therefore was technically superior in rank to Virginia. He thought it only proper that he – and certainly not a woman with a disability – should take overall charge of SOE operations.

Alain informed an ecstatic Baker Street that he had enlisted some ten thousand men ready to launch a giant sabotage campaign when the time came. But even if London, desperate for good news, wanted to believe it Virginia knew differently. On his arrival in the city she had set him up with the Resistance group publishing *Le Coq enchaîné* and put him in touch with others collecting arms for future missions and producing false papers. She had done what she could to get him going. Yet *Alain* was struggling; he failed to turn up to important meetings and seemed unable to recruit helpers, or keep them if he did. Virginia saw that he was unsettled by his clandestine life and detested the hyper-alert solitude it demanded. Denied the easy companionship regular soldiers found in their platoons, he sought to steady himself with booze and the company of a variety of women, none of whom was his wife. Nor were these girlfriends discreet or

---

* Later exposed as one of the Cambridge ring of Cold War Soviet spies.

even sympathetic. While he swaggered around playing at being a secret agent Virginia worried that his bravado was becoming a major security problem for her and the entire SOE edifice. 'One was most afraid of one's own people,' another pioneering officer recalled. They knew too much about you.[29]

What she would not do, therefore, was put *Alain* in touch with her own network, let alone allow him to take it over – a refusal he clearly resented. These were her personal contacts, who trusted her alone, and she repeatedly warned Baker Street to 'lay off'[30] when they suggested *Alain* should take over command. From her brief time in the field Virginia understood all too well, even if London did not, the need for Communist-style self-contained cells of a handful of people, each one recommended by an existing member and knowing only their immediate superior. She knew the dangers of a single weak link in the chain, having lost most of her colleagues at the Villa des Bois. The saga had perversely saved her. It had forced her to recognise from the first weeks that isolation and self-reliance – including, it would seem, refraining from taking a lover – had to be the first rule if she was going to stay free and survive. She had learned from her own life the terrible price of carelessness. She therefore spent her nights alone and did not struggle to keep a secret. Her disability further widened the distance she felt obliged to keep from others. Her challenge was to ensure her contacts did the same, or to limit the damage if they did not by keeping them in separate, clearly defined groups who knew little about each other or her beyond one of her several different codenames. She insisted they kept in touch only by leaving messages at a safe letter box or through a cut-out such as Madame Alberte's laundry. But *Alain* was an emotionally needy amateur and had to be kept out of it.

Yet such was her own success at making reliable contacts and solving problems that *Marie Monin* was a legend beyond the city of Lyon. Her networks had become so large and successful that she was no longer able to select every member herself, as she had liked to do at the beginning. Being so good at her job had made her, in SOE eyes, the 'universal aunt to all our people in trouble and anyone in difficulties immediately called upon her'.[31] Sorting out so many others was, however, inevitably drawing attention to herself.

The bar at the Grand Nouvel Hôtel, which she still regularly visited to pick up her messages, was now known far and wide as the place to go for help. In fact, London fretted that it could be what they termed *brûlé*, or burnt – SOE-speak for compromised. Virginia was happy to rely on her police contacts to warn of any problems, and the fact that the bar had multiple exits. Yet it could hardly be secure when practically every agent[32] in France continued to turn up to ask for money, safe refuge, false papers, escape routes – and, in the absence of any radio operators, to send or receive messages from London through her contacts at the consulate. New arrivals headed straight to her for help to find their feet or effect introductions. They needed tickets for food, tobacco and wine; coupons for clothes, shoes and soap. In truth, Virginia was perhaps too willing to help others even though, or perhaps because, there had been no one to give such support to her. It was a joy to be valued.

New agents were now somewhat better prepared than Virginia had been. Since Villa des Bois, greater attention had been given to false names and identities, perfect French and security train-ing, in large part thanks to Virginia's critical reports. Yet most still felt uncomfortably conspicuous in their first days. 'You almost imagine that neon lights are blinking from your forehead and proclaiming, on and off, "Made in England",'[33] recalled Peter Churchill, a thirty-two-year-old former ice hockey international who left London that December to travel to the south of France

by submarine. He, like almost all the others, found himself heading to Lyon in search of Virginia, turning up at the bar of the
Grand Nouvel Hôtel, where he hoped to find her. He returned
several times that day and into the evening to look for her, each
time walking past the Carlton Hôtel, the Gestapo headquarters
guarded by ranks of Vichy police. He had not eaten for twenty-
six hours as supplies of food coupons promised by others had
failed to materialise, and at one point spent two hungry hours
kicking his heels in the bar. Churchill finally gave up, following
Baker Street's instructions to leave a note for her in reception,
making sure to use the words '*nouvelles de Marie*' in the text and
sign it *Raoul* with four letters underlined.[34]

It seems that Virginia's non-appearance may have been a way
of testing Churchill's bona fides. For as soon as he returned to
his room at the Hôtel Verdun – where he had been warned to
hide his precious soap from the chambermaid – he almost immediately received a call from her. He offered news of her 'sister'
Suzanne – another password – and she invited him to dinner.
They ate at her favourite restaurant, where she fed him up and
furnished him with all the food coupons he could possibly need,
courtesy of a friend of hers in the food administration. Churchill
was amazed at the quality of the meal – they both opened with a
dozen oysters – but she told him it came only at an exceedingly
high price and such privileged diners had to be introduced by a
well-known customer first.

As they chatted away in French, she was friendly, charming and
complimentary, and put Churchill at his ease – until he uttered
the word *Angleterre*. She interrupted him mid-sentence to explain
that he should never 'name that place when we wish to speak of
it. Instead we say "chez nous" – at home. The other word is apt
to attract attention.'[35] She delivered her rebuke in the same calm
tone to avoid alerting the neighbouring diners but there was no

mistaking her seriousness. Churchill could not help noticing the smile had gone and that there was a telling weariness in her eyes.

Virginia knew that trivial errors could cost agents their lives – and hers. One colleague was captured by a keen-eyed Gestapo officer after walking out in front of a car, having forgotten for a moment that the French drove on the other side of the road. Virginia reminded newcomers to eat like Frenchmen – gustily using bread to wipe up their gravy, not leaving a speck of food on the plate and certainly not neatly aligning their cutlery at half-past six at the end of a meal like a well-brought up Brit. And as they were no longer in England they should desist in always carrying a raincoat.

Virginia tried to think of everything. Banned from buying her 'boys' cigarettes to soothe what they all called 'attacks of the jitters', she collected stubs from the floors of cafés for them to smoke instead. It also helped them blend in. Stub-snatching had become a national – and respectable – pastime and was thought a better bet than the other popular alternative of rolling cigarettes using autumn leaves. That habit had made the streets of Lyon smell of bonfires and was often the cause of a persistent hacking cough.

Yet for all her own fieldcraft, it was apparent even to newly arrived agents such as Peter Churchill that *Alain*'s irresponsible conduct was making her vulnerable. Losing her at this point, he realised, could be even more damaging than the fiasco at the Villa des Bois. Yet it was also evident that *Alain* was constantly trying to undermine Virginia and would not accept her help, when the truth was that he was a failure. When he returned to London a few weeks later, Churchill informed F Section of Virginia's frustration with *Alain*, who was a bully, and even suggested he should be recalled before he caused any more damage. At the same time, Churchill could not be more complimentary about *her*, suggesting that London should make her life easier – and reflect reality on the ground – by making it clear that she was in charge.

Virginia was considered the true 'executive out there', he explained. She was 'known as *le champion américain* in Lyon and gets all the best done for her'. She was, he added, 'a walking encyclopaedia, knows everyone, is in with everyone, liked by everyone'.[36] Liked, certainly, but she was also slightly feared. Her willingness to help others was matched by burgeoning ruthlessness. She made sure to hone her shooting skills on regular hunting trips in the hills outside Lyon (assuring London that she was keeping Cuthbert, her pet name for her leg, well out of the way). And with steely calm she informed Churchill that her 'chaps' would 'dispose' of a contact suspected of giving away information to unfriendly French police.[37] Yet formalising her position as chief or giving her clear authority to take command in the field was a step too far for a woman, even in SOE. It seemed that whatever she achieved in establishing SOE's sole solid foothold in France, and however unsubstantiated his claims about his own progress turned out to be, *Alain's* word was taken more seriously in London than hers. There was growing irritation at her refusal to take orders from him and hand over her networks to his control.

The ebullient Peter Churchill was also a star in Baker Street. He rather than Virginia had been tasked with the top-priority mission of establishing what had happened to the dozen agents arrested at Villa des Bois. He was finding it harder than he had expected. After leaving Lyon, Churchill travelled to Marseille (where he thought the men were being held) to follow up what sounded like a promising lead. He was carrying with him a vast quantity of cash – and a stash of soap – to extract information.

Virginia was to assist him as a guide, so she met him from his train under the vaulting arches of Marseille's Gare Saint-Charles and escorted him down the platform towards the exit. Spotting a throng of Gestapo at the ticket barrier she ushered him swiftly away into the crowded station buffet and out of an unmonitored side door without being seen or saying a single word. By the time they had hastened down the station's famously grand flights of stone steps into the teeming backstreets Churchill considered Virginia 'a woman who could overcome any obstacle'. He was so astounded at the pace she kept up through the crowds of under-fed and ragged Marseillais clacking through the town's ochre-coloured streets that he felt obliged to break the silence to ask whether the rumours about her false leg were true. She confirmed them – and later she would laughingly remove Cuthbert and knock it against the table so that he could hear it was hollow. Yet she never liked to tell how she had lost it: many in SOE believed a cock-and-bull story about her falling from a bus. She preferred to let any such rumours fly rather than reveal too much of herself. Just as she kept her guard, so she alerted Churchill to do the same. She warned him that Marseille was a dangerous place and he should avoid the Gestapo V-men – or informants – patrolling the Corniche and especially the bands of toughs down by the Vieux Port.

Churchill set off, this time on his own, to see a government lawyer he believed would help him in freeing the Villa des Bois men. The meeting did not go at all to plan, however, despite him offering a million francs as an inducement. In fact it was so tense that Churchill thought he might have walked into a trap himself and possibly even made the prisoners' plight worse. Virginia surmised he had bad news when Churchill joined her afterwards at a café table where she was writing postcards. 'You look like a crowd I once saw when they heard they'd lost the Ashes,' she told him,[38] * referring to the ferocity of Anglo-Australian cricket rivalry. Virginia offered to intervene, suggesting she approach one of her own contacts, Madame Germaine Poinso-Chapuis, who indeed proved considerably more useful than any of Churchill's. Madame soon reported back that the men were not in Marseille but were being held in a forbidding fortress of a prison two hundred miles away at Périgueux. Virginia tried to pay her contact for the information but the woman refused, despite the fact that she was walking around in rags.

This was the first firm indication for three long months that the men were still alive. There was hope at last that some of SOE's finest agents could be saved. But time was short and Churchill was soon to return to London. All too many prisoners at Périgueux either perished from the freezing, rat-infested conditions and pitifully meagre diet or were lined up against a wall early one morning and shot. Without the protection afforded to regular forces by the Geneva Convention, they were unlikely to survive capture. (Indeed, only fifteen or one in eight of the 119 London-based SOE agents who were arrested in France during the war ever came home.[39]) It was clear they had to be freed urgently but the task was re-assigned to *Olive* and so Churchill handed the million francs in bribe money over to him. Soon after, another French SOE contact, codenamed *Carte*, chipped in with the welcome news that his own sources expected the men to be released imminently. A loquacious painter without even a basic grasp of security, he assured a still-impressionable Churchill that he personally would be attending to the whole matter and that no one else, including Virginia, need get involved. Baker Street

* Her jokey remark reveals Virginia's impressive grasp of the cultural significance of the Ashes to her English colleagues, as well as her considerable talent for winning people over.

lapped up *Carte*'s talk of commanding a secret army of three hundred thousand, but he was yet another fantasist who promised big and delivered practically nothing. The inaction constantly nibbled at the corners of Virginia's mind, however much else she had to get on with. She quietly began to prepare shelters and escape lines for the agents in jail, just in case she could help.

Churchill and Virginia planned to meet one last time in Marseille before he headed back to England, exhausted from his short time in the field. Against Virginia's advice, he was taking a shortcut to the rendezvous café through the foul-smelling passages of the Vieux Port when his way was barred by two men, one of whom was wearing the official white armband of the Vichy police responsible for tackling black marketeers. They asked for his papers, and as Churchill looked down one of them pushed something forward under his overcoat as if it were a gun. When Churchill reached into his pocket the men spotted his bulging wallet and threatened to ship him out to Germany as slave labour unless he handed it over. A few minutes later the SOE man walked away free, if shaken, and twenty-five thousand francs poorer.

Virginia was meanwhile finishing a meeting with *Olive* at another café nearby. As they rose to leave there was a blur of noise and commotion, with whistles and screams and shouts and dozens of armed policemen running in and ordering the customers to line up against the wall. Standing next to *Olive*, Virginia realised they had fallen into a dangerous trap. The police were rounding up innocent people to be deported to Germany to satisfy the monstrous Nazi appetite for slave labour in their factories (just as Churchill's assailants had threatened). Vichy had previously agreed to send thousands of volunteers to the Fatherland, promising good food, good pay, concerts and free holidays. But few had been taken in and the numbers had fallen far short of

Nazi demands. Now Vichy had secretly agreed to forced expatriations and ordered round-ups in several target cities. Marseille had to have three hundred workers on their way to Germany within three days or it would be forced to bundle its own policemen onto the trains going east instead. Virginia and *Olive* were in the wrong place at the wrong time and would be dispatched under armed guard that night without a chance to say goodbye or pack a bag. The police had blocked off the entire street. There was no escape.

Virginia was frantically trying to think of a way out when the District Police Commissioner marched in and inspected his prey, many of whom were beginning to cry. An inspector followed him in, at which point *Olive* linked his arm with hers, which she thought was a welcome gesture of comfort but which was actually a quick-thinking signal that they were together. The inspector noticed too and pointed to *Olive* and Virginia, tersely ordering one of his men to lock them into a back room, where he would deal with them privately.

A few streets away, Churchill was hurrying from the scene of his unpleasant ordeal to his rendezvous with Virginia. He was surprised and disappointed that she was not already at the café, as she had promised. She was so reliable, it was not like her to be late. And nothing, he felt, was quite so bad when she was around. He sat down facing the door, ordered a Cinzano, lit one of his last cigarettes and pretended to read a newspaper to calm his nerves. Still Virginia did not turn up, and he wondered why the place was empty. He sensed tension in the air. He finished his drink and ordered a second to give himself time to think.

Virginia and *Olive* heard the door lock behind them and thought their fate sealed. But to their joy they realised the room contained a small window that opened on to an alleyway. As their fellow customers were shoved screaming into trucks at the front of the café, they silently climbed up and squeezed one after the other through the narrow opening. Virginia looped her good leg over the ledge and just managed to pull Cuthbert through before easing herself down on the other side. She kept up with *Olive* as well as she could as they scrabbled to get away and fetch Churchill.

Finally, after what seemed an interminable wait, *Olive* came striding in to Churchill's café. 'Let's go,' he said quietly, taking the Englishman's arm. Catching sight of Virginia just inside the entrance, keeping watch on the street, Churchill knew that something must be very wrong and that the three of them needed to act quickly. He threw down one of his remaining notes onto the table and followed Virginia outside. *Olive* hurried them up another side street, while they kept looking behind them. 'They're raiding the cafés,' he explained to Churchill as he led them quickly up a flight of stairs to a safehouse flat and locked the door. He also related, with a grin, that he had been friends with the police inspector before the war; he had recognised *Olive* and deliberately given them the chance to escape. It had been a close call.

Their immediate instinct was to get out of town right away. Virginia advised waiting until the morning, however, as more round-ups were likely and the station would be a 'humming hive of hatred'. Churchill spent his last night in Marseille being told by Virginia that it had been Mafia gangsters impersonating Vichy police who had conned him into surrendering the twenty-five thousand francs, and that another racket involved selling suspected *résistants* to the Germans in return for cash or their victims' possessions. Suddenly feeling crushed by the multiple dangers confronting him, Churchill felt more in awe and in need of her than ever.

Perhaps it was his vulnerable state that prompted a rare moment of softness in Virginia during those anxious hours while they waited to escape. 'We age very quickly out here, and with age comes wisdom,' she counselled him. She admitted that, facing fear all the time, she felt 'a hundred years old' and after such narrow escapes as they had both experienced that day, none of them would ever be 'quite the same again'. She also predicted that on his return to Britain Churchill would find himself comparing his 'life of companionship' in Baker Street 'with the solitary life we lead [here]'.[40]

'When you get home it'll look different from a distance,' she teased him with a smile as she stopped to light a cigarette. 'You'll forget how cold you were – except to bring warmer clothes next time; you'll forget all the frights you've had and you'll only remember the excitement.'[41]

Chapter Four

Goodbye to Dindy

The *New York Post's* George Backer cabled Virginia to urge her to come home.[1] The surprise attack by Japanese bombers on the US naval base at Pearl Harbor at breakfast time a week earlier, on 7 December 1941, had been described by President Roosevelt as a date that would 'live in infamy'. It had brought America crashing into the war against Japan, and then a few days later against Germany and Italy. Backer knew that as an American, Virginia was now in far greater danger, and thought she should reconsider her mission. France was to remain nominally neutral but her journalist cover offered little if any protection from now on in what was in reality a puppet Nazi state.

Pétain was obliging his German masters by engaging in yet another crackdown on the Resistance. Vichy police handed over dozens if not hundreds of prisoners to the Nazis for mass shootings but guillotined others themselves on rows of purpose-built scaffolds. Over in London, General de Gaulle, relying on little more than force of character and British funding, remained for many *résistants* merely a voice on the radio, far away from the mortal dangers of their everyday lives. Even those who had secretly listened to his BBC broadcasts – to do so was strictly forbidden – were unsure as to whether to believe them. Enlightened souls such as the former prefect Jean Moulin, now a Resistance leader working out of Lyon, recognised the six foot five diehard as a vital rallying point for the entire Free French movement. But Virginia knew that de Gaulle remained a divisive figure. Most of his compatriots still felt alone, abandoned and without hope.

That feeling was exacerbated by the French media, which was more tightly controlled than ever and vehemently opposed to the Anglo-American alliance, portraying it as kowtowing to Stalin's dreaded Russian communists. London, the French were repeatedly told, had in any case been destroyed in the Blitz and a full Nazi invasion of Britain was surely imminent. Paul Marion, the Minister of Information, was tasked with enforcing press censorship and the constant dissemination of Vichy propaganda with the aim of ensuring a coherent fictional reality and ultimately 'the uniformity of opinion against democracy and its Jewish supporters'.[2] The same false messages were pressed home again and again until they were almost universally believed, even when flying in the face of incontrovertible facts. To deny, dissent or deviate had become treason. The newspapers did not reveal, however, just how far Vichy was actively supporting the German war effort, including supplying five thousand tons of petrol and fleets of trucks to Field Marshal Rommel's army in North Africa.[3] Believing in Hitler's victory, France was aligning itself more and more closely with the Third Reich and was more determined than ever to crush those in its way. Yet despite the winds of war blowing against her Virginia refused to leave. Her sole major concession was to dateline her articles for the *Post* with the vague 'Somewhere in France'. George Backer's call for her to abandon her post as the fight intensified made her all the more inclined to stay.

Early 1942 saw Virginia in an uncharacteristically gloomy state of mind, however. Agents, especially those with wives and children, treasured every snippet of news from home and relied on them to get through the darkest moments. But for Virginia there had not really been a sweetheart since Emil, the Polish officer in Vienna fourteen years earlier. And since Pearl Harbor all letters from her family in America had stopped, apart from a telegram from her mother at Christmas passed through the normal diplomatic route by SOE. What particularly upset her was that a homemade fruitcake sent by Mrs Hall had never arrived. 'We never despair,' she wrote to Nicolas Bodington back in Baker Street on 5 January, 'but we doubt the arrival of such interesting delicacies . . . it seems unfair.'[4]

Lonely and no doubt fearful, Virginia let down her guard in an acutely personal letter to 'My dear Nic', typewritten on her hotel bed on the bleak rue Grolée while the sleet outside flecked her windows. Despite her determination to stay, she confessed that her health was suffering and she had a cold and an 'ache in the thorax' caused by the persistent 'snow, rain and slush . . . The dark days are fairly abysmal.' Virginia sought comfort wherever she could find it, writing: 'Great excitement. It looks . . . quietly possible to have some butter . . . Base low mind – ever victuals.' She knew that those living in relative comfort in London had no real concept of the sacrifices she was making and thought her mad for fantasising about food in this way, but 'Some day . . . even you may comprehend . . . Everything revolves about, first, stomach, second, inability to purchase shoes.' Yet for all her toughing it out in a man's world, her upbringing still held her back from swearing even now. The word to describe her mood, she explained, was 'purest anglosaxon' and 'written -h--'.

'I get so "fedup",' she then sighed, pleading with Baker Street staffers to write to her in the absence of letters from home. 'I resent this dearth of mail, and this barren desert in which I exist. Gosh, and gosh durn, I do!' Then, in a cry from the heart, she added: 'I hate war and politics and frontiers ... In fact, I am feeling very sour.' She ended, though, with the typically upbeat message that she would 'get over it'. She sent her love to the office, signing off with a British valediction and her family nickname: 'Cheers, Dindy'.

It was an endearing note and probably the last such message from the Virginia of old. In truth, the enigmatic Bodington was never likely to provide the comfort she sought. The war had also moved into an even more brutal phase, and if *Marie* was to survive she could not display such vulnerability again. Aggression was what was needed; aggression had to be drummed into herself every hour of the day. She must 'eat with it, sleep with it, live with it' and focus on every chance to 'harm the enemy'.[5] Dindy had to be left far behind.

The hard winter meant that no more agents – let alone wireless operators – had been dropped into France to replace the keenly missed Villa des Bois prisoners, who continued to rot in jail. Without modern navigation aids, pilots relied on moonlight to identify landmarks such as lakes or hills to guide them as daytime sorties were considered too dangerous. This meant that there were only a handful of opportunities for successful parachute drops in any one month, which could easily be lost to bad weather. Freezing temperatures, winds of over twenty miles an hour or thick cloud cover all kept the planes at home. After weeks of radio silence F Section was thus still dependent on Virginia's slow message route via the American consulate to communicate with its agents. Such a situation was intolerable for ambitious

circuit organisers such as *Lucas*, based in Paris, who had worked
with Virginia since her first days in France. He deduced that
there must be other radio operators transmitting to Britain independent of SOE. He set about finding one – inexorably drawing
Virginia into the Nazi maw in the process.

The first she knew of trouble was when an unshaven figure in
stiff and heavily stained clothing came knocking frantically on
her door late one February afternoon. Ben Cowburn, on another
of his short missions into France, was clearly on the point of
half-starved exhaustion and she quickly ushered him in before
he attracted unwanted attention. Cowburn had travelled for
five sleepless nights across the length of France, dicing with the
Gestapo and French police, to warn her she was in great danger.
As the result of a disastrous betrayal by a female double agent
he bitterly referred to as the 'lady virus', Virginia's existence and
whereabouts were most likely known to the Germans. It was
only a matter of time before they came for her. Cowburn pleaded
with her to leave Lyon at once to save herself – after all, she had
already been in France for six months and that was normally
considered the advisable limit for any mission. Cowburn himself
restricted his time in the field to avoid detection or excessive
fatigue. But Virginia focused on arranging for him to have his
first bath for a week and a clean pair of pyjamas. In the meantime
she sent word to her contacts in Marseille to organise an escape
line for him over the Pyrenees into Spain. Seemingly unmoved
by Cowburn's warnings, Virginia would make up her mind about
her own situation once she had heard his whole story. This was
her first real test and she would not crumple. Her sangfroid at
this moment astonished Cowburn and marked her out from the
others; it seemed as if the greater the peril she faced the more
calm and resolute Virginia became.

Cowburn related how a few weeks earlier, on Boxing Day

1941, *Lucas* had met up with Mathilde Carré, a dark-haired Frenchwoman nicknamed La Chatte (The Cat), in a café on the Champs Elysées in the desperate hope that she had access to a radio. A woman of voracious sexual appetites and curiously tilted green eyes, she was the mistress of the head of a Polish intelligence network called Interallié. Wearing her trademark red hat, she confirmed that she still had access to her lover's transmitter even though he had been arrested. She offered to send London a message on his behalf, and when she did so soon afterwards both *Lucas* and Baker Street were delighted finally to re-establish contact.

Seduced by La Chatte's coquettish charms, *Lucas* had not asked enough questions or apparently wondered why she was free when her lover was not. In fact, La Chatte (codename *Victoire*) had been living for the past six weeks with a non-commissioned officer in the Abwehr and was passing all *Lucas*'s radio messages to and from SOE through him. Sergeant Hugo Bleicher's beguiling charm – he would win his prisoners' trust by convincingly proclaiming himself an enemy of Hitler as well as of his rivals in the Gestapo – belied a frightening cunning and a mission to conquer. He had been a modest office clerk in Hamburg before joining the Abwehr, but as a private soldier in the First War had escaped from prisoner-of-war camps an astonishing four times. Now he was already proving himself one of Germany's counter-espionage aces. With Allied schedules, codes and security checks provided by La Chatte he was using the captured Polish radio to transmit misleading reports to London – including one that had helped trick the British Admiralty into allowing two German battleships to make their famous 'Channel dash' right under their noses. The *Scharnhorst* and the *Gneisenau* avoided detection for more than twelve hours, and managed to reach Germany from Brest in north-western France to the huge embarrassment of Britain and its intelligence agencies.[6] Now, in what the Germans

called *Funkspiel* or 'radio game', Bleicher could also read and
decode *Lucas*'s messages to F Section and their replies. Methodical
and persistent, he began to piece together details on *Lucas*'s
fellow SOE agents across France. He was especially intrigued by
how they revolved around a hitherto undetected figure in the
area around the Rhône. Thanks to *Lucas*'s impatience and lust,
Bleicher was now hot on Virginia's trail.

By the time *Lucas* became suspicious – after a couple of weeks –
the damage was done: Bleicher had already compiled a number
of key names and addresses. Lucas confronted La Chatte, and she
broke down and confessed that she was indeed a double agent.
It was true she had been working for the Allies and had been the
mistress of the Polish network chief. But when Interallié's leaders
had been caught in November 1941 she had been offered a way
to save her life and also make six thousand francs a month as an
informant. It had taken her no time at all to betray seventy of
her former comrades-in-arms. Apparently without remorse, she
had watched one after the other being carted off, most of them
to their deaths. After a celebratory feast of pâté and champagne
with Bleicher, La Chatte had become his lover.

At this point, *Lucas* should have eliminated La Chatte, gone
into hiding and immediately contacted Virginia to let her know
she was at best compromised, at worst about to be arrested.
Instead, he sought to save his own skin with a high-risk plan.
He would turn La Chatte into a triple agent (retransferring her
loyalties to the Allies while staying in touch with the Germans),
take her with him to London for interrogation and persuade
Baker Street to use the wireless link to turn the tables on Bleicher
by sending him misleading information with a *Funkspiel* of their
own. La Chatte knew the penalty if she did not cooperate – but
Lucas recklessly left his fellow agent Virginia entirely in the dark
about the consequences for her.

La Chatte was so adept at lying that it was comparatively easy for her to persuade Bleicher that she should be allowed to go to London with *Lucas*. The bait was that she would be an Abwehr spy at the heart of SOE (an increasingly feared opponent). The Germans, exasperated by the number of spies now successfully moving in and out of France under their noses, could also observe how an agent pick-up was conducted. Excited by such a prospect, Bleicher agreed and, posing as *Lucas*, arranged via the Polish transmitter for the SOE agent and a VIP companion to be picked up by boat. *Lucas* was unable to warn London that the Germans were involved or that they would be observing the entire exercise – or indeed that La Chatte was not to be trusted. When London unwittingly agreed, the stakes could not have been higher.

Late on the bitter moonless night of Thursday 12 February, *Lucas*, La Chatte (in her red hat and a fur coat) and Ben Cowburn duly made their way to a remote, little-defended cove near the Breton resort of Locquirec. La Chatte told Bleicher that Cowburn was coming merely to help get them away and would himself remain behind in France. In fact, although Cowburn was sceptical about the whole scheme, he knew that the Germans were planning to arrest him immediately afterwards and so intended to jump into the boat at the last minute. After they all arrived at the beach at midnight, a group of Abwehr took up their observation positions behind the rocks just as a British motor gun boat appeared with Bodington's white coat clearly visible on the bridge. As two small launches approached through the surf *Lucas* was dismayed to pick out a Royal Navy officer in uniform and two much longed-for new SOE radio operators, all heading for a trap that he had himself created. Perhaps in his desperation *Lucas* simply had not anticipated London using the operation to infiltrate more agents, but then Baker Street was unaware of the dangers and wanted to exploit the mission to the full. As the officer and agents stepped onto the sand along with the two seamen who had rowed them in, *Lucas* whispered a warning to all five that they were surrounded by Germans. The enemy would not touch La Chatte and him as part of the agreed mission to take her to England, but the incomers would be rounded up. The naval officer desperately flash-signalled his ship for help but then realised he should not draw yet more people into danger.

Undeterred, La Chatte tried to clamber aboard one of the dinghies, but the flimsy boat was swamped by the pounding waves, leaving her drenched and her suitcase lost in the sea. After an hour of struggling in the foam the two seamen abandoned trying to pick up their new passengers and rowed back to the ship just as the Germans started to emerge from their hiding places. The last the group on the beach saw was the gun boat turning round to race home to Britain before daybreak. Realising it was hopeless, the stranded naval officer gave himself up, knowing that his uniform meant he would be comparatively well treated as a prisoner of war. The two SOE agents had already made a run for it inland, but were caught the next day after a farmer betrayed them for money, and quite likely shot.

After the abortive mission, *Lucas*, La Chatte and Cowburn set off for Paris with German minders in tow to signal London and rearrange for another night. But Cowburn knew that he had a duty to warn Virginia that the Abwehr had penetrated *Lucas*'s network and that her life was in peril. *Lucas*'s closest followers knew of her and where she was based. If they were caught and tortured, as was now to be expected, soon the Abwehr would too. Like Peter Churchill, Cowburn recognised that her loss would be the biggest SOE calamity of all. No one else had her contacts, her communication route or her resolve. He also had to find a way of informing SOE that the radio was in German hands and that they must stop sending more agents to near-certain death. Without a working wireless transmitter, his only option was to reach Virginia's friendly military attaché at the American embassy in Vichy and persuade him to transmit the warning. He would then travel on to Lyon and an unsuspecting Virginia.

So as not to alert the Germans assigned to watch them, Cowburn joined the others on the train to Paris, but when he got the chance at Le Mans he quietly peeled off and took the painfully slow service to Tours. La Chatte was told to inform their rather gullible minders that he was merely going off to plan another possible exit route in case it was needed. Despite his best attempts to pose as a Frenchman, he struck a conspicuous figure and when a man began making clumsy attempts at conversation with him he realised he was still being followed. So at Tours he mingled in the crowds outside the station, and then slipped back in to board a train to Bordeaux. He had lost his tail, but just in case of further trouble he stayed up again all night, still in stained shoes and clothes stiffened by dried sea water. He jumped out in the early hours at Angoulême station, from where he sneaked past the armed patrols on the demarcation line and took several buses to Limoges. After an epic journey over five nights of nail-biting tension, he finally arrived in Vichy and dashed past the Gestapo surveillance team into the now skeleton American embassy to beg them to wire London with the news (since entering the war after Pearl Harbor a far more fraught exercise). Finally, dishevelled and exhausted, he took yet another train to Lyon and Virginia's new apartment (where she had moved from the rue Grolée).[7]

But despite Cowburn's pleas to heed his warnings, Virginia decided to stay put. Her work in France was not done and she would not leave until it was. The fact that the Germans were on to her made her more determined to prove her worth. There would be no more displays of weakness to Bodington or anyone else. As her father had told her in her dream all those years ago in the hospital in Turkey, she had a duty to survive but also to make sense of why, against all the odds, her life had been saved.

Thanks to Cowburn's efforts Baker Street was fully alerted before the successful exfiltration of La Chatte and *Lucas* on a flat-calm night two weeks later. Buckmaster himself met the pair on arrival at the cosy Devon coastal village of Kingswear and they travelled on to London without further hitch. Once briefed by *Lucas* as to her true identity, SOE immediately put La Chatte under surveillance and bugged her room. They took a particular interest in her red hat, believing it was possibly a sign to her Nazi masters. When they no longer had use for her, she was sent to prison for the rest of the war.

Lucas, meanwhile, was itching to get back into France to try to rescue his circuit, despite the obvious dangers to himself and (especially if he contacted her again) Virginia. He took the basic precaution of changing his field name to *Sylvain* when he returned on 1 April but still faced the intractable problem of not having a wireless operator. Incredibly, after just a fortnight *Sylvain* put security to one side and sent two couriers to Virginia with messages for her to transmit via the diplomatic bag as if nothing had happened. One got through to her safely but the other messenger was stopped on the demarcation line by an army control and tortured for three days. The papers he was carrying were sent to Bleicher, who did not recognise the name *Sylvain* but was all too familiar with his handwriting. Knowing his prey to be back in France, Bleicher exacted a ruthless revenge for the trick played on him through La Chatte. A brilliant manhunter, he wasted no time in sending in the Gestapo to round up *Sylvain*'s entire circuit, using the details he had acquired through the radio and subsequent interrogations. On 25 April they arrested *Sylvain* himself in a Paris café. During his interrogation the horrified Frenchman tried to commit suicide with morphine but failed, then managed to talk his way to Colditz rather than the firing squad. Once again, for want of a radio operator disaster had struck. Once again, Virginia was the one to find out about the arrests through her contacts and was the bearer of the bad news to London. Once again, the recklessness of another presented the greatest threat to her life.

Indeed, Bleicher would now focus his deadly genius on hunting down the intended recipient of *Sylvain*'s messages. Who was it in the Free Zone whom *Sylvain* was trying to reach and who obviously had reliable access to London? The Abwehr now knew all about SOE and F Section's Maurice Buckmaster, but who in France was keeping things going despite all the arrests? The intelligence pointed towards a key figure operating out of Lyon. Whoever this resourceful 'man' was, 'he' was clearly the lynchpin of Allied intelligence; his F Section networks were regarded in Berlin as the 'number one enemy' to its own internal security.[8] This elusive and dangerous agent must be tracked down and neutralised.

Even *Sylvain*'s arrest failed to put off the indomitable Virginia. Report after report in Baker Street noted how she was effectively running operations across the entire Free Zone, with some help down on the coast from *Olive*. In SOE's official history, M. R. D. Foot noted that without her work, 'one can say that half of F Section's early operations in France could never have been carried out at all'.[9] Indeed, her name appears more than virtually any other in SOE's surviving war diaries, reflecting the way in which she was constantly expanding the frontiers of her role beyond anything originally envisaged in Baker Street; her work was so vital and varied it was described after the war as of 'universal character'.[10] Despite the mounting dangers, she was collecting details of the political situation in France; the scope and effect of Vichy propaganda; the use of dummy wooden aircraft to fool British aerial reconnaissance; the identity and movements of German regiments; the warring factions within the French Resistance; the installation of machine-gun nests on the flat roofs of Paris; and lists of possible sites for future sabotage attacks that would reduce the need for aerial bombing raids, with their inherent dangers of civilian deaths. Through what she called her 'political information service' (composed of the serving and former officials she had cultivated) she was able to provide London with vital intelligence on Vichy's relations with the Axis powers. These included reports on the top-secret meetings between Pétain and Hermann Göring (Hitler's deputy), and Count Ciano (Mussolini's son-in-law) with Admiral François Darlan (Pétain's deputy), intelligence almost certainly sent to Winston Churchill himself. She reported back on the 'temper' of the French people, notably how many were dismayed by Britain's humiliating surrender to the Japanese in Singapore in February and the fiasco of the escaped 'Channel dash' German battleships (as we now know, in part thanks to Bleicher). The French are 'still hoping for their victory and many, many of them are willing to help,' she noted, 'but they would appreciate seeing something concrete besides retreating'.[11]

There were some small signs of hope, however, including the stirrings of dissent where once there had been compliance. Workers in factories all over France were slowing down war production by striking in protest at lack of food and fuel, or simply by losing important documents or transposing labels on goods. In March, in one of the first mass acts of public resistance, a crowd stopped people attending a concert in Lyon by the Berlin Philharmonic Orchestra, ensuring the auditorium was virtually empty. More and more police were switching sides and passing information to Virginia, including the welcome news that recent RAF bombardments of Renault factories making lorries and tanks for the German army had been spectacularly successful.

Virginia's industry had established her as the eyes and ears of the Allies across most of France – and Lyon as the crucible of French underground activity. Even without a direct radio link to London, her presence proved that the Allies were still in the game and prepared to lay down their lives for France. Meanwhile, Dr Rousset and Germaine continued to work tirelessly for their *chef*, recruiting helpers and finding new safehouses. Rousset's popularity ran far and wide, and a request from him was something that most people were eager to oblige. Indeed, 'I've come on behalf of the Doctor' became the standard SOE password in much of southern France. There was also no shortage of those prepared to come to Germaine's aid; she was never shy in exhorting her compatriots to be more 'virile' for their country and for her they often obliged. Together the trio formed a permanent framework for SOE that spawned several new circuits reaching south to the coast and east to the Swiss border, with recruits coming from as far afield as Paris. Virginia could now call on the support of hundreds of men and women from Lille to Perpignan and in dozens of professions – from doctors to prison officers to train drivers. Here, then, was the genuine nucleus of a secret army for when the time came – if only they could have a transmitter to talk to London in real time to make plans and take orders.

When the gallant Cowburn returned to France in June 1942 on an another in-and-out mission to attack railway lines near Tours, he found that not only had Virginia ignored his warnings to leave but also her apartment had become 'the centre of all Resistance'[12] in France. Virginia's fame meant that she took what Buckmaster described as 'insane and incredible' risks by recruiting so many different people to the cause. But she was no fool. She changed her field name from *Marie* to *Isabelle* and later to *Philomène*. She took care to vary her routes home, to check constantly if she was being followed, never to approach a house or café without walking around the block first, to avoid going to the same place every day, and frequently to alter her appearance. She also acquired a new driver's licence so that she could avoid taking so many trains. Her survival had in effect become a Homeric battle of wits.

Yet the dangers of betrayal and infiltration were mounting. Her luck, fieldcraft and police protectors could not protect her for ever. Bleicher's obsessive interest in a shadowy figure in Lyon since *Sylvain*'s arrest had come to the notice of the Gestapo. One evening a young man Virginia did not know and had never heard of had turned up at her door claiming to be an SOE parachutist. He was persistent and in some ways plausible, but her sixth sense detected trouble and, feigning innocence, she turned him away. It had been a close call. She heard soon after that a number of German *agents provocateurs* had been trying to infiltrate themselves into her network. The Abwehr and Gestapo were now hellbent – separately and in tandem – on hunting down this notorious agent they knew to be somewhere in the city. Bleicher was an urbane figure who preferred to outwit his enemies rather than torture them. The Gestapo had no such qualms.

Sensing the mounting danger Virginia stepped up her security. She moved to a new three-roomed apartment at 3 place Ollier, an elegant square of solidly bourgeois six-storey houses, the sort of place where well-heeled dentists or lawyers would in normal times lead unexciting lives. Virginia's corner building had several useful exits, including a discreet doorway at the back. When there was a flower pot behind the ornamental ironwork at her front window, it meant it was safe to knock on the door and Cowburn was astonished at the constant and varied stream of supplicants from across the whole country as if she were some sort of fairy godmother. 'If you sit in [her] kitchen long enough you will see most people pass through with one sort of trouble or another which [she] promptly deals with,' Cowburn reported, concerned that she was acting as 'mother figure' to so many different people. She was providing them with contacts but also even doing their washing and donating her own food and soap. Her welfare work ran to distributing cash to the families of *résistants* in prison,[13] as well as arranging for the Red Cross to send food parcels to the Villa des Bois men in Périgueux jail. When people asked for help, Virginia found the greatest pleasure in being the one able to provide it. 'She was paying the price of having a strong, reliable personality: everybody brought their troubles to her,' Cowburn observed.[14] There was, indeed, never a dull moment but that was exactly how she liked it. In fact, she was now developing a new line of work breaking agents out of prison – what she called her 'unofficial releases'. No one else seemed to be doing it, allowing some of SOE's greatest talents simply to waste away in French jails apparently without hope. Thanks to her contacts in the police, hospitals and prisons, she relished the chance to make a truly major contribution to the war.

One evening in March 1942 a man knocked at her door, clutching his stomach and delirious from pain. She had been expecting him. A senior F Section agent called Gerry Morel, he was a French-born insurance broker who described himself as 'wartime British' and had been the first to be infiltrated by Lysander, a tiny three-seater plane able to land and take off almost anywhere. He had, however, lasted just six weeks in his home country before a contact betrayed him to the authorities. It was his good fortune that the officers who had arrested him reported to Léon Guth, regional chief of the Sûreté based in Limoges and one of Virginia's devotees. Thanks to her persuasive powers, Guth knew to call his inspectors off if they were on the track of British agents, as long as they had a plausible story to write down in their notebooks. Some even offered friendly advice on obtaining better forged identity cards or how to carry pistols less conspicuously. But Morel had been picked up by two new officers with German accents, and for their benefit Guth had had to put on a show of 'grilling [him], trying to terrify him by threats and shouting'. After an appropriate interval, Guth then 'quietened down completely [and] said . . . everything would be alright'.[15]

Not even Guth could overlook, however, what was a major SOE blunder. It was discovered that Morel's ration card cited a non-existent address and so his case was taken out of Guth's hands. Vichy itself took direct charge of what they deemed to be an 'especially important' and 'extremely dangerous'[16] British agent once they found out he had landed in a 'Lizzie'.* Morel was placed in solitary confinement in Périgueux jail, where the Villa des Bois prisoners remained in chains.

On hearing the news, Virginia swung into action. She and Guth enjoyed 'very cordial'[17] relations and whenever she travelled the two hundred and fifty miles to Limoges she stayed with him and his wife. Indeed, it would not be long before she called his subordinates Marcel Leccia and Elisée Allard her 'nephews' (although only a few years younger than her they showed great respect and gratitude to their 'aunt') and Guth himself her 'most special friend'.[18] Virginia told Guth that, whatever the difficulties, he had to help her save Morel and the pair hatched a meticulous plan that gave her a blueprint for what was to come. She would

---

* The flimsy-looking but nimble Lysander was to become a great boon for SOE as it could take off and land in a forest clearing or smallish field with up to three passengers.

not leave him to die, the fate she feared for the men from the Villa des Bois.

Morel deliberately stopped eating and his health rapidly worsened, almost certainly with help from SOE's famous sickness tablets smuggled in by Virginia (which caused symptoms similar to typhoid, including stomach cramps and a high fever). Friendly prison wardens were able to have him moved to a prison hospital near Guth's offices for an abdominal procedure. After the operation, Morel was transferred from a hospital cell guarded by heavily armed military patrols to an annexe monitored by a single policeman. The surgeon, also one of Virginia's recruits, signed a statement that it would be impossible for Morel to walk in his post-operative condition and the officer outside his room equally obligingly dozed off. A pre-warned Morel crept out of his bed, slipped on a doctor's white coat and with the aid of a sympathetic nurse scaled the hospital perimeter wall. Yet another helper was waiting on the other side with a suit, shoes, sugar and some rum. Morel then travelled through a snowstorm to one of Virginia's safehouses outside Limoges where he gathered his strength before pushing on to her apartment in Lyon. To spring one of Vichy's most prized prisoners was, by any measure, a spectacular coup. It showed what Virginia could now do.

After a few days nursing him back to health, she escorted Morel on the train down to Marseille despite the dangers of accompanying the subject of a national manhunt on a service typically bristling with Gestapo. They were to pick up the escape line that she had helped to set up, which left from Perpignan to cross over the eastern edge of the Pyrenees to Barcelona. Codenamed the Vic line – in honour of its chief Victor Gerson – it would see hundreds of agents and airmen to safety thanks to guides, or *passeurs*, supplied by a general from the remnants of the Catalan Republican Army. As Gerson was a Jew, as were most of his lieutenants, they were all taking a greater risk in the field but were also driven by intense personal anti-Nazi motivation. Against the odds, the Vic line shepherded the still-poorly Morel over the mountains into Spain. Back in London there was 'stupefaction'[19] at Virginia's success and Morel also marvelled at what Virginia had done for him. 'Her amazing personality, integrity and enthusiasm was an example and inspiration for us all,' he reported. 'No task was too great or too small for her; and whatever she undertook she put into it all her energy, sparing herself nothing.'[20] For Virginia the escape was really the first time that she was not preparing, helping or supporting others but directing an operation herself. She had proved she could take charge in spectacular style. Morel, though, was merely the warm-up.

When the Germans made mass arrests of *résistants* it never stopped there. Torture extracted more names, carelessness led to more leads and more arrests. At times it felt as if the whole of SOE would be wiped out. As an inquiry into F Section at the end of the war concluded, 'that the sweep was not complete was due in no small measure to the inspired activities'[21] of Virginia alone. One particular act, in February 1942 – just as *Lucas* was dealing with La Chatte's betrayal – was judged to have saved the 'whole set-up' in the Unoccupied Zone from 'premature extinction'.

SOE had certainly not been ignoring the desperate calls for a new radio operator to replace those arrested. It was months now since the F Section agents had been deprived of that crucial link with London. That was why SOE had landed two operators on the beach that stormy February night in Brittany with La Chatte. With considerable irony, a radioman had at the same time been in a desperate search for *Lucas* to offer his services. *Georges 35* (wireless operators were now codenamed *Georges* and a number, in Bégué's honour) had been dropped at the end of January at Vaas in the Sarthe *département*, some 150 miles from *Lucas*'s Paris head-quarters. The new arrival (real name Donald Dunton) had never reached *Lucas* because he had landed in a vineyard twenty-five miles from the designated spot, narrowly missing being impaled in the dark on a row of sharp stakes. 'It really isn't good enough!'[22] Virginia protested in relation to the pilot's inaccurate navigation. Since *Georges 35*'s reception committee were at the original landing place, he was met instead by an attentive and noisy farm dog. Fearing the imminent arrival of the police he had hastily buried his radio with his parachute and set off on foot.

After a month fruitlessly roaming around France trying to make contact with anyone in SOE – and without the necessary tickets to buy food – he eventually made for Marseille, where he thought he might be able to find help to leave the country and head home. It was here on 24 February that, thanks to her vast network of contacts, Virginia heard of his arrival and quickly moved to prevent him from leaving. A wireless operator was simply too precious to lose, and she devised an ingenious solution to his lack of radio. Georges Bégué must have hidden his set in Châteauroux the previous October, before he headed to the Villa des Bois. She dispatched *Georges 35* to see whether he could find it. He came back grinning a few days later. Thanks to her initiative, Virginia had finally re-established radio communications with London. She had by now gone way beyond her original liaison brief. Along with her other duties, she had become problem-solver in chief.

The return to government in April 1942 of Pierre Laval – a particularly vicious Nazi collaborator known as 'Black Peter' – sparked another hardening of the political climate in France. Pétain had dismissed him in December 1940, in part for being *too* pro-Nazi, and now his renaissance had 'caused the rise of a lovely tide of hate and [the Marshal's] stock has slumped very sharply,' Virginia reported in one of her dispatches to London. 'But there is so much apathy and fear in the country that there has been no decided reaction.'[23] Even government instructions not to shake hands with Jews or use their first names or titles but to address them simply as '*le Juif*' or '*la Juive*' caused only a ripple. Public opinion began to turn only in June when Laval called for German victory in the war and the Vichy police chief, René Bousquet, accepted Nazi demands to round up ten thousand Jews for deportation from the supposedly Free Zone. When the numbers fell short of the requirements of the Final Solution, the Nazi plan to exterminate Jews agreed at the Wannsee Conference in January 1942, Laval overrode German exemptions for children under sixteen and insisted on sending them as well. That summer the first goods wagons packed with whole families could be seen pulling out of the station in Lyon; Vichy did not bother to hide what was happening, let alone try to stop it. Constrained in what she could safely report in her articles, Virginia nevertheless broke the news in the *New York Post* on 22 June that Jews in Paris were now obliged to wear a yellow star. SOE's Jewish agents continued their perilous work regardless, but her time as a journalist was of necessity coming to a close for fear of drawing more attention to herself.

Virginia continued to be held back by some of her colleagues. As an official circuit chief, it was *Alain*'s rather than Virginia's responsibility to implement Baker Street's new orders to start building up and training groups of men as future paramilitary forces and to coordinate parachute drops of arms, ammunition and explosives. He gave every impression of activity, bombarding London with talk of his many friends among the police, press and gangster circles of Lyon, and his grandiose plans for blowing up railways. London believed the spin and sent him half a million francs to fund his impressive-sounding operations. Only later did SOE come to realise that 'not even her energy and finesse could get satisfactory work'[24] out of him.

Virginia was not one to hold her tongue for too long. She thought it her duty to point out that, in her opinion, *Alain* was actually timid and lazy. Far from having built up a large, well-trained and cohesive force, he was simply wasting opportunities (and volunteers) that she was sending him and doing very little. Despite his claims, he had virtually no men, and certainly none properly trained or armed. Again and again she was approached by factory workers or railwaymen offering to put machinery or trains quietly out of action if only they could be supplied with equipment and training. She alerted *Alain* but he ignored her. 'A good executive and organizer would be greatly appreciated,' she wrote pointedly to Nicolas Bodington in March. She had made so many contacts and researched suitable sabotage targets, 'but they need following up and organizing, none of which has been done'.

The nature of SOE was attracting some sizeable egos. but in Virginia's opinion, 'A different type is needed to exploit the situation, a type both *travailleur* [hard-working] and punctual. Please ask [*Olive*] about this as I hate the thought of telling tales – only I do despair at times.' With most of the better agents such as Cowburn and Churchill simply dropping in and out on short missions (and with the Villa des Bois agents still languishing in Périgueux), she was carrying too much of the load on her own. The other SOE agent in the area – Philippe de Vomécourt, or *Gauthier* – was a big shot in the Resistance like his two brothers (*Lucas* and yet another de Vomécourt sibling called *Constantin*, or Jean, who operated near the Swiss border) but was hardly of much use to Virginia. Baker Street later conceded that he too was 'slapdash' and 'most difficult' towards her. Perhaps it was

simply professional jealousy that led him to insinuate that she was
sleeping with some of the men and that she had a bad reputation
in London, but it was an underhand ploy. *Gauthier* made equally
spurious claims about the size of his following (boasting of two
thousand men when the truth was more like half a dozen) and
failed to fulfil his promises to receive a number of newly arrived
SOE agents who otherwise had nowhere to go. He left one pair
waiting in a Lyon café for seventeen days; they had to spend their
nights in ditches. 'We could use about six clever chaps,' sighed
Virginia, 'perfectly and utterly reliable persons – persons from
"home".'[25] In the meantime, she fought on alone.

Perhaps the arrival in Lyon of his own and long-awaited permanent wireless operator (or pianist in SOE parlance) would help
galvanise *Alain* into action. When Edward Zeff, a 'man of nerve
and resource',[26] arrived by submarine in April, Virginia was overjoyed. Zeff, who normally ran a Paris haberdashery, was soon
transmitting for as many as six hours a day organising drops of
arms for *Alain*'s supposedly huge army on zones just outside Lyon.

Alain soon received plastic explosives, fuses, denotators, time
pencils, Sten guns, Colt pistols. There were also cigarettes, chocolate and packets of tea (a favourite comfort of Virginia's) and
itching powder (no doubt for Germaine's girls). It was an impressive stash and *Alain* passed on the munitions to a small band of his
favourite contacts at *Le Coq enchaîné*. He did not, however, share
his training in their storage or use. Despite the high risks for the
aircrews running them into France, the guns were left to rust
in damp conditions or were simply abandoned. The explosives
were also largely wasted on 'irritating acts with no real value'[27]
such as blowing up newspaper kiosks: hardly in Virginia's view
a worthy precursor to what would have to become at the right
time a disciplined and focused guerrilla war. Perhaps overlooking

the usefulness of these adventures for distracting the enemy and boosting morale, Virginia raged at the waste and incompetence. She argued that in future only properly trained SOE operatives should take receipt of arms and explosives (rather than amateur French *résistants* unfamiliar with both). But still ranked as a mere liaison officer, she was not officially chief. Without London's backing, there was nothing she could do.

Virginia's fury brought her conflict with *Alain* to the boil. Aware that she had already complained about him, *Alain* cabled London as a retaliatory action.[28] 'I am sorry I clashed with *Marie* but I protest against her behaviour,' he said. 'I do not doubt she was helpful to you, but I did my work without her help.' He accused her of claiming credit for all his (unspecified) achievements. 'I know my job, *Marie* is of no use to me and if somebody has to give orders I shall, not her.' He demanded enormous expenses of sixty thousand francs a month – despite claiming to have lost seventy thousand francs he had previously been given – and put himself forward for promotion by suggesting 'what about that third pip!' To make matters even more heated, Zeff contacted London to complain about both of them: *Alain* for lacking leadership and Virginia for being too brusque. London hardly made the situation any clearer when it responded a week later by informing *Alain*, Zeff and Virginia that they were all doing 'first class work', but they were not there to squabble.

Zeff was right about *Alain* but also may have had a point on Virginia. It was true that after months in the field the pressure was taking its toll. Her messages to London had once reflected her chatty, cheery manner, but if she had become more dictatorial, arguably it was necessary. It was difficult to stay pleasant if Zeff frequently ignored her instructions and constantly demanded more money. She started to worry that he and other agents were salting SOE cash away for themselves. 'Why the hell should I pay him?' she complained to Baker Street. It was not just Zeff. As more agents came in, so did other prickly characters. Her position was made all the more difficult by her lack of military rank, making her authority easier to question. 'What happens to soldiers who refuse to obey orders?' she asked in one dispatch. 'What do you recommend for men sent by you who flatly refuse to obey orders received from you? Have I authority to deal with such cases as I see fit?'[29] Eventually London tired of Zeff's moaning. He was informed that his 'opinion of Marie was totally unfounded: he was kindly to settle down and work calmly'.[30] But it was hardly sufficient. Even *Gauthier* deplored the fact that SOE had created a situation 'leaving dangerous doubts in our minds about who was responsible and who was subordinate in the field'.

One night in June, a British bomber on SOE duty dropped a load of containers three kilometres short of its target near Montbrison. *Alain*, with his usual disregard for security, had assembled a team of seventeen garrulous *résistants* to pick up the supplies. As they noisily rushed about gathering the containers they were easily spotted in the moonlight and rounded up by the police. Only *Alain* was released, but he then made his second major blunder. He bragged publicly about the police officer who had agreed to let him go, leading to the secret Resistance sympathiser being arrested and tortured for forty-eight hours. 'This has not made him exactly popular,' noted Ben Cowburn, who said he 'steered clear of *Alain*' as 'everyone [was] after his hide'. The latest in a long line of mistresses, Germaine Jouve, had accompanied *Alain* that night, against SOE rules forbidding personal attachments. Now she was fuming in jail, where she was sharing a cell with the wife of a well-known collaborator. This was a serious matter, as Jouve's sympathies were unclear (she had previously been the lover of an Italian spy) and thanks to *Alain* she knew most of the leading agents in Lyon and the locations of their caches of arms. Even worse, in Germaine Jouve's absence *Alain*, who was exploiting to the full the pulling power of being a secret agent, had brazenly started to squire another woman, a Mademoiselle Pradel. 'If Germaine hears about this,' one recently arrived agent reported back, 'the effects will be disastrous.'[31] A livid Virginia awaited Jouve's release from prison – expected in six weeks – with alarm.

It was not just *Alain* who was distracted by a frantic love life. Perhaps it was down to the fact that Benzedrine often caused a dramatic rush of libido. In any case, several male agents were playing around with dozens of different women who posed obvious risks to Virginia and the entire SOE operation. When Charles Hayes, a dental mechanic, arrived in May 1942 to scope power stations for future sabotage attacks, he was horrified at the 'serious lack of security' of such constantly shifting liaisons. Many of the women were loose-tongued; a few were actual Nazi sympathisers. It was all part of a *chercher la femme* bravado and endemic carelessness. One agent was overheard leaving a bar crowing about what fun the full moon would give them all that night, giving away the fact that they were expecting a parachute drop. He was arrested shortly afterwards, as were two of his companions. A courier took a wireless set to a football match on his bicycle and boasted about it while watching the game. The police later followed him on his delivery and broke into the room where the radio's owner had just begun transmitting, taking him prisoner with nine bullets inside him. Yet another giveaway was groups of men looking furtive while going in and out of bars carrying packages, especially if they were wearing what had become the unofficial uniform of the *résistant* – a *Canadienne* (or fur-collared leather jacket) and sunglasses. And time and time again – despite all the warnings – so many captured agents were found to have lists of their contacts' addresses on them, leading to the fall of their entire circuits directly afterwards.[32] Too often the fear felt at the beginning of a mission dissolved into complacency when nothing happened during the first few weeks. The Germans would watch a suspect patiently until he made a mistake or could not account for his movements, and then pounced. Each loss of a life took its toll on Virginia and the others who remained; the effect was cumulative and shattering.

Living a secret life meant never relaxing for a moment, and always having an explanation worked out. Those who survived for any time were naturally wily, with a highly developed sixth sense. When entering a building Virginia could feel danger just by looking at the concierge, and she knew to listen at the door for unexpected voices before she went in. A single mistake made in tiredness or haste could result in disaster, as too many agents found out. One experienced hand ignored the danger signal of closed shutters when rushing to a contact's house, only to find the Gestapo waiting for him inside.

Virginia's police contacts were extraordinarily well-informed, even on the movements of their German counterparts. Thanks to a stream of tip-offs, she moved one contact no fewer than thirty-two times to keep him one step ahead of the Gestapo. She also found out when the police had obtained a detailed description of Charles Hayes and arranged for his escape before officers came to arrest him. One of Dr Rousset's most trusted recruits believed that her intelligence was so good that she must have had allies within the Gestapo itself.[33] However impressive her personal connections or however tight she tried to make her own security habits, being so well-known still meant she was vulnerable to the flaws in anyone else's.

*

Denis Rake was a pudgy, bespectacled forty-year-old music hall artiste who had been brought up in a circus as a child tumbler when his opera-singer mother abandoned him at the age of three. As a bewildered boy during the First World War, he had been in Brussels when the Germans occupied the city and had found himself assisting the legendary nurse Edith Cavell, who was later shot for assisting some two hundred Allied soldiers to escape. As a young man he had been kept in luxury by a prince in Athens, who eventually broke off the then-illicit liaison because he feared a political scandal. Perhaps because of his tumultuous youth, Rake was 'scared to death'[34] of bangs and parachutes and refused to handle a gun. Resembling an old-fashioned grocer, he struck many as one of the more eccentric SOE appointments. But he volunteered, he said, because as he had neither parents nor wife he had 'nothing to lose'[35] and his rootless upbringing had made him unusually self-reliant. Despite others' misgivings Buckmaster rated him, astutely noting that he had the 'courage to conquer his fears' and recognising that sometimes the most unlikely candidates, as with Virginia herself, made the very best agents. Rake himself confessed that he had much to prove to himself – as well as to others – and that he relied on muttering to himself the phrase 'Pull yourself together, duckie'[36] at the most challenging moments.

Rake's arrival at Antibes one night in May by felucca – a small but swift sardine-fishing boat crewed by recklessly brave Poles – was not much less challenging than dropping down from a plane. The local police (some friendly, some not) took turns to watch landings, conveniently illuminated by the moon, from their windows and new arrivals had no more than a system of different-coloured flashing lights from colleagues on the shore to advise them of their likely reception. A long red flash meant that the coast seemed clear, a white flash meant wait and a series of blue flashes warned of imminent danger. After the red flash, Rake rowed the last few hundred yards in a collapsible dinghy.

Once he negotiated himself safely ashore, Rake soon moved up to Lyon to help Zeff with his immense workload. Zeff was in desperate need of a break after transmitting for many hours at a stretch several days a week. He was not supposed to spend more than five minutes on air at a time, and no more than twenty minutes in total in a day, but sometimes messages would have to be painstakingly re-transmitted because they had become mutilated and the receiving officers in Britain could not decode them, even after hundreds of attempts. Every minute extra Zeff spent tapping out his Morse-code messages exponentially increased the likelihood of his signals being detected and their source located by the enemy. Each and every moment he had his radio set – a coiled mass of wires, dials and plugs – in front of him while he waited for a reply, the higher the chances of being caught red-handed.

Yet nothing could be rushed. Even once one of the rows of young women with headphones, pencils and paper in the four receiving stations across Britain had picked up the rapid insect-like chirps of his signals, taken them to the cipher clerks to be decoded, waited for the text to be read by Baker Street and its answer encoded to be transmitted back, at best he would have been waiting for at least seventy minutes for a reply. A weak signal or mistakes in the Morse – virtually every operator made either their dashes a little too short or their dots a touch long, their 'fist' or style considered as individual as a fingerprint – only added to the whole laborious process. During what seemed like an eternity, he would sit there with his eyes on the road outside, looking for suspect vehicles, his Colt pistol next to his hand, his poison capsule in his mouth, his ears straining for any usual noise. Once he had finally finished for the day, he rushed to fold up his aerial and ground wire, took out the tiny quartz crystal that set his frequency, removed his headphones and hid the battered leather radio case as well as he could. The fact that it was bulky and weighed forty-five pounds made moving location hazardous and likely to arouse suspicion.

Zeff had not left his room for weeks at a time for fear of being seen or captured, spending the intervals between transmitting obsessively pacing his room while nursing severe and debilitating stomach butterflies known as somatic anxiety. He knew that the Germans were tracking every signal sent on frequencies not used by their own radio operators. Each one of his signals might well be picked up by their panoramic receivers, showing up as brilliant green dots on banks of cathode-ray screens in a vast room in Paris. Immediately work would begin on locating the source. The Germans were fast improving their direction-finding techniques and getting quicker and quicker at precisely locating clandestine radios. Zeff and his fellow radio operators knew that the more they transmitted, the closer the enemy would be to tracking them down via a methodical process of triangulation that could eventually pinpoint a signal to within two hundred metres. The Nazis were determined to silence the messages weaving their way across space and keeping the dream of liberation alive. An appalling death would certainly follow capture, but with so few working radiomen in the field the work just piled up and up. Nervous depression was unsurprisingly common, and several buckled under the strain. Zeff was clearly at risk of the same, and Virginia was all too aware of the dangers presented by not having a direct link to London.

The well-meaning Rake would, however, unwittingly add to Virginia's woes. At first he was of great use, taking over some of Zeff's transmissions during the day while singing cabaret in the evenings at the La Cicogne club to establish his cover. After putting him up in her apartment, where Virginia made him 'very comfortable, very happy'[37] she moved him to the heavily perfumed home of one of Germaine Guérin's *filles de joie*, who alarmed him with numerous offers to provide her services to her lodger free of charge.[38] Rake was, very unusually for those times, semi-openly gay, and eventually persuaded her that neither she nor any other woman was qualified to 'console' him.

Once again, there was a careless lapse in security. Rake's companion on the felucca had discussed his arrival with an aunt, who turned out to be a strident Pétainist and who had promptly reported her own nephew to the police. Many families and even married couples were similarly riven between collaborators and *résistants*. Thanks to Virginia and Germaine's spider's web of contacts, however, they quickly found out that the nephew had talked under interrogation and that the police were hunting down Rake. This was bitter news. Virginia knew she had to distance herself from him immediately; he knew far too much about her location, contacts and operations. She urged him to flee to Spain and made the necessary arrangements, but Rake – later described by Maurice Buckmaster as the most 'coldly courageous' man he had ever met – refused to go. Intent on remaining in the field to serve rather than going home at the first sniff of danger, he took up her alternative offer of joining Ben Cowburn on a new mission in Paris after another wireless operator had refused point-blank to enter the Occupied Zone.

First he had the challenge of crossing the demarcation line, which stretched from a point twenty-five miles inland from Hendaye on the Spanish border up to Tours on the Loire and then across to the Swiss frontier near Geneva. Rake tried to cross at Montceau-les-Mines but was betrayed and arrested by German soldiers who recognised him from a description given by his arrested colleague. He tried to flush incriminating papers down the lavatory and when that did not work had to scoop them up from the pan 'with a silent prayer'[39] and eat them. He endured several interrogations and was imprisoned in a Nazi-run jail in Dijon before managing to escape in a stinking refuse bin with the help of a priest. He then headed up to Paris where, incredibly, he lived in domestic bliss with an aristocratic German officer whom he had met in a bar and who risked his own life by becoming Rake's lover. Rake was not to be distracted for long, however. He was determined to return to work and knew that to do so he had to head back to Lyon to fetch a new radio and identity papers. This time he avoided further problems on the demarcation line by hiding in the fuse box of an electric train that he had boarded when it slowed down to go around a bend. But by the time he arrived he was barely able to walk because of acute dysentery. He was a marked man. He was being hunted by the police and the Gestapo all over France. They had a detailed description of him and knew of his links to Lyon. Even to be seen near him was to invite destruction. There was, however, only one person in France he knew would not let him down and he made his way to her door. But it was now clear to Baker Street – if not Virginia herself – that she must be gravely compromised. Her own time in the field was surely fast running out.

Summer 1942 in Lyon was as hot as the winter had been cold. For all its handsome houses and fine streets, the city's sanitation left much to be desired, with most lavatories 'no more than holes in the ground. And in the warm evenings and the muggy nights . . . the mosquitoes came out in mass sorties.'[40] It was breezier up on the Croix Rousse hill – although for Virginia the hundreds of uneven steps to get up there in the heat made the pain from her stump almost unbearable. And the wafts of cooler air barely penetrated the dark shadowy *traboules* where *résistants* ran to give the Gestapo the slip, or the jumble of crumbling old houses where wireless operators sat sweating for hours at their sets.

What had been a comparatively safe refuge for the pianists was now a priority target. In the summer of 1942 the Funkabwehr – the German counter-intelligence service dedicated to tracking down radio signals – moved in a large operation to a spot across the river from the *traboules* at Fort St Irénée, on the heights of Fourvière. It was all part of the special attention paid to Lyon, now marked down as the centre of Allied transmissions as well as Resistance activity. The Germans installed highly sophisticated new tracker equipment at the Fort and brought in a fleet of eighty grey-green detector vans. Fortunately, Virginia had managed to procure from her French police friends a list of their registration plates and the knowledge that they should be easy to spot because they had no roof to avoid interfering with the signal. They looked from the outside like motor caravans with unusually large aerials.

From the instant they heard a clandestine radio operator tap on his keys to London it was now often less than thirty minutes before the Funkabwehr or Gestapo screeched up in their black Citroëns and sent men fanning out across the network of *traboules* to pounce on their prey. Another method was to switch off the power district by district and when the signals stopped they knew to lock down that part of the city. No wonder the attrition rate was high, and Zeff and the other radiomen now working in France were suffering. Although SOE was sending in more operators, none was now officially expected to survive more than three months.

The perennial shortage of safehouses caused most if not all operators in the Free Zone to end up at Virginia's apartment on place Ollier, which was protected for now by her friends in the police. Indeed, there were so many transmitting from her home that the hallway started to resemble a bird's nest of different aerials, some up to seventy feet long tacked back and forth across the walls. Cowburn considered this arrangement extremely insecure even for her; Virginia saw it as a matter of whoever could offer protection to a pianist also had power over communications to London. And if she did not help the radio operators, then who would?

It was in June that Virginia became genuinely rattled, but not by Rake's troubles, nor *Alain*'s obstructiveness or even the activities of the Funkabwehr and Gestapo. Buckmaster asked her to return to London for a 'personal discussion' about F Section's plans. The request became an order when Baker Street was informed that the American consul, Marshall Vance, had been interrogated by the Sûreté as to whether he knew Virginia. He denied categorically that he did, but on a visit to Berne soon after he took the opportunity to warn an MI6 agent there that Virginia was clearly a target and her 'outfit completely compromised'.[41] While her own integrity was not in doubt, too many around her were careless.

Now deeply alarmed, Baker Street cabled George Backer at the *New York Post* on 28 June to ask him to summon her back via Lisbon for urgent consultations in the United States (although her real destination would be London). He obliged and even took responsibility for persuading the State Department to 'turn up the heat' on Vichy to accelerate her visas. A recall by her newspaper was a plausible explanation for her sudden departure, which might otherwise put her Lyon contacts in danger. Baker Street informed Virginia that her work had been appreciated, but that now it was time to discuss her future. The curt wording outraged her. Had she not kept herself – and so many others – out of trouble since the earliest days with no practical help from London? What else could she do to show that she could handle her own future except survive in the field for nine long months? Surely it was up to her to judge whether or not her security was compromised? Had she not built up well-placed contacts in the police who protected her? In her opinion, she was 'singed' rather than *brûlée* and therefore still 'all right'. Worst of all, if she suddenly left the field she would surely never be able to return. As Baker Street knew all too well, Virginia harboured a rebellious streak and a forceful belief in her own abilities. She 'did not submit easily to discipline,' as Buckmaster once put it, and had 'the habit of making up her own mind without regard to others' point of view'.[42] For all the grinding fear, she had never been so happy. For all the frustrations, she had never been so fulfilled. For all the traitors and collaborators, she desired more than anything to help the good people of France. She would not meekly obey a recall to return to the confines of her old life without a fight.

Virginia knew she had to play it tactically. She blamed bad atmospheric conditions for making transmitting difficult and thus delaying her response to orders. Secondly, she converted a colleague into a powerful ally and supporter. Ben Cowburn, who before had urged her to leave, now sent in a report 'urging the importance' of Virginia's work, emphasising the 'difficulty of passing her connections to others' and insisting that 'No one . . . was capable of replacing her'.[43] Virginia promised to scale down her operations, to move apartment again and to see only a handful of her most security-minded contacts. As for the others, such as *Gauthier*, she would 'cease to exist'.[44] She never came home and never intended to. It became clear a few days later what Virginia had been working on, and why she could not be spared.

Chapter Five

Twelve Minutes, Twelve Men

The prison at Périgueux was a freezing and sombre fortress with stinking dungeons and damp coursing down the walls. The twelve SOE agents from the Villa des Bois trap – half British, the other half French – had been left to fester for some six months amongst the filth and morale was low. One of them, Lieutenant Marc Jumeau, described the experience as 'degrading and humiliating to the last degree'.[1] They had endured a long winter without heating and were allowed only ten minutes a day outside, where the sole tap had frozen solid so they were unable to wash. Neither Peter Churchill nor *Olive*, nor his successor *Carte*, seemed to have made progress towards their release or been able to offer hope for the future. The men, collectively known within SOE as *Clan Cameron*, were still awaiting trial with no date set, or any certainty that as trophy Allied prisoners they would not be handed over to the Nazis or face a firing squad. Baker Street was increasingly impatient to rescue its star agents – experts in wireless transmitting, weapons and sabotage – who were urgently needed back in the field. It was shameful to have them languish in chains, apparently beyond its capability to help. Virginia had never forgotten them and at least her occasional food parcels gave them some glimmer of comfort. To her continued frustration, however, she did not have authority to do more.

Meanwhile, it had been the twelve's good fortune that the wife of the former French deputy Jean Pierre-Bloch, who had been arrested with them in Marseille, had subsequently been released. Gaby Bloch, a woman of a similar age to Virginia, had spent much of her time since January visiting her husband in prison and trying to drum up support for him outside. She had already lobbied ministers in Vichy to no avail and her options were running out. She and the *Camerons* had lost faith in SOE's sporadic efforts but they had heard that Gerry Morel, who had crossed paths with them in Périgueux, had managed to escape thanks in large part to Virginia. At her husband's request, Gaby made her way to Lyon and the bar at the Grand Nouvel Hôtel to ask *Marie* for help. On her arrival Virginia could not fail to be impressed by the courage of this petite Frenchwoman who was acting entirely on her own. All the more so because of the incredible dangers she faced as a Jew under Pétain's increasingly repressive regime.

Georges Bégué had also found a way of smuggling out a letter to Virginia. One of two *Camerons* facing the serious charge of 'Attempt against the Security of the State', he could hardly write openly about needing help to escape. Constantly worried that he might otherwise endanger[2] her if the letter were discovered, he wrote that the men were well and sympathetically treated, and that morale was excellent.[3] No doubt he hoped that she would read between the lines – and indeed the letter almost certainly contained coded messages. In any case, Gaby made all too clear the reality of Périgueux: the beatings, the dark, the disease and the daily diet of one bowl of greasy liquid and precisely 250 grams of bread; how vermin gnawed at the bodies of the ill and the weak and how the place crawled with lice; and how by spring 1942 the *Camerons'* strength and spirits were plummeting fast. Gaby insisted that Virginia was their last hope.

Virginia appreciated all too well the scale of the problem. An impenetrable stronghold of high walls and iron gates, no one escaped from Périgueux. After all these months of watching others fail, though, this desperate plea was surely Virginia's chance to prove what she could do. She drew up a two-pronged plan and promised Baker Street, who in the absence of any other progress finally gave her authority to have a go, that 'if they cannot come out officially, they will come out unofficially'.[4] There seems to have been little faith in London that Virginia could do any better – and indeed she was still expected back in Britain very shortly – but she secretly determined to team up with Gaby to make it work.

Soon afterwards Virginia dashed down to Vichy for an appointment with Admiral Leahy at the American embassy. Even now that the United States was at war with Germany, the ambassador continued to wield some influence with Pétain's administration. If only he would lobby on *Clan Cameron*'s behalf, she thought, they might at least have a chance. But because of his disapproval of Allied intelligence-gathering on his patch, she could hardly reveal that they were secret agents who faced the prospect of execution. And nor were they American citizens with a right to his protection. So Virginia appealed to his sense of universal humanity. She argued that they were symbolically important prisoners and that since Pearl Harbor surely the Americans were on the same side as the British, while their French companions had done nothing wrong. Perhaps Leahy was worried about potentially negative coverage in the press back home if he ignored her pleas. Perhaps

Virginia was simply at her most beguiling and persuasive. Leahy agreed to see what he could do through diplomatic back channels.

The response came quicker than she dared hope, but it dashed any prospect of an early release. A telegram on 14 March announced that the *Camerons* were to be moved out of Périgueux – but straight into the confines of the Vichy-run internment camp at Mauzac, near Bergerac. Conditions in the countryside were considerably better but their future would remain uncertain. So Virginia began to plan to spring them during the twenty-five-mile transfer between the two prisons, only to discover that after months of maltreatment the *Camerons* were too weak to run. Even worse, she heard that they were to be put in chains for the journey and that the guards had orders to shoot any who tried to break free. The operation would have to wait.

It was dark when the men arrived, exhausted, at Mauzac. In the morning they discovered that the camp contained six hundred political prisoners (mostly de Gaulle supporters) and was surrounded by two barbed wire fences, armed guards and a series of watchtowers. But at least it was in the open air, the men were housed together in large huts, they were permitted to cook for themselves using food brought in by Gaby and the Red Cross (arranged by Virginia), and even shower once a week. They could also see through the fencing to the outside world. Already in better spirits, the men set up their own parliament and choir to pass the time and focused on rebuilding their strength.

It was clear that Mauzac offered the best possible chance of a break-out and Virginia and Gaby began work immediately on drafting in an army of helpers to seize the moment before the men were moved on elsewhere. The *Camerons* began their own preparations from the inside. They considered digging a tunnel, but no one thought they had the technical skills and so they plumped instead for finding a way through the barbed wire. The athletic young English chef Michael Trotobas then began intense physical training drills every morning. He was particularly keen to practise a strange low style of crawling – which would come in useful later – but in the afternoons the group played the more leisurely game of *boules*. Throwing the balls in pre-selected directions gave them cover for calculating the time needed to cross between the barracks and the fencing, detecting blind spots from the watchtowers, finding hard sun-baked ground where they would leave no tell-tale tracks, and noting the timings of patrols.

Bégué, a skilled handyman in civilian life as well as a car salesman, drew up a list of necessary tools. The problem was how to communicate his needs to Virginia and Gaby on the outside – and equally how to deliver him what he needed without being found out. Virginia was too well-known to be seen near the camp, so drilled Gaby in detail on how to recruit some of the guards as messengers. Leaving her small children at home, Gaby now made the thirty-five-mile trip to the camp three times a week, sometimes staying at the Hôtel de Mauzac, where she knew several camp wardens drank at the bar. Many were Pétainists who foresaw their whole future under German control and who might very well report her as acting suspiciously. But Virginia supplied Gaby with plenty of money and advised her on how to identify potential helpers, without putting herself at unnecessary risk. She duly chatted in the bar as casually as possible, just as Virginia had instructed her, about how an eventual Allied victory was a certainty. She added, to anyone who seemed genuinely interested, that there were ways that it could be speeded up by helping right now, and that there might be handsome rewards in return. At first it seemed that no one would take the bait but finally one guard who overheard her made himself amenable, but was careless and soon sacked on suspicion of smuggling in messages to the prisoners.[5] Another two also seemed intrigued, but ultimately backed out. The last guard she befriended, Jose Sevilla, stayed the course, merely asking by way of payment to be taken back to London so that he could join the Free French gathering in ever greater numbers around General de Gaulle.[6]

Sevilla turned out to be extremely useful. His first contribution was to persuade the camp commandant that Watchtower Five – the nearest to the *Camerons'* hut – should not be manned at night. Showing considerable initiative, Sevilla convincingly claimed that it swayed in the wind, making the ladder to the platform unsafe in the dark. When he could he also passed on word from the men, but this proved more difficult as he rarely had access to the *Camerons* directly. Virginia needed to come up with another more reliable means of smuggling messages out and vital supplies in.

Soon afterwards Gaby started taking Jean a supply of clean clothes, books and, most notably, large quantities of food on every one of her permitted visits. Virginia gave her money to buy a list of carefully selected black-market groceries so that it looked as if she was merely a devoted wife wanting to feed up her husband. Such largesse was of course noticed and Gaby was denounced to the police on several occasions, possibly by jealous neighbours, and her house searched. She was searched again while carrying the parcels of food to the camp. The police found nothing. Yet inside one of the jars of jam was concealed a tiny file, and in a pile of fresh laundry a pair of wire cutters; hollowed-out books accommodated a small screwdriver and hammer; and tins of top-quality sardines in tomato sauce had been chosen for the best possible re-usable metal. Jumeau was just one of the *Camerons* who marvelled at Gaby's resolve, knowing that discovery of these items on her person would almost certainly, as a Jew, lead to her torture and death. He recalled how many male friends had refused to get involved because of the incalculable risks – ones that Gaby undertook without hesitation. Her extraordinary courage and

Virginia's ingenuity meant that Bégué soon had all he needed to make a key for the door of the barracks, using bread from the prison canteen to take a mould of the lock. Every evening from now on the *Camerons'* choir bellowed out the most obscene[7] songs to drown out the noise of the filing and hammering.

At the same time, Virginia was hard at work on plans for immediately after the men had left Mauzac. She drafted in *Vic*, the chief of the eponymous escape line, to find safehouses and organise the *Camerons'* eventual passage over the Pyrenees to Spain. Together they recruited a getaway driver and arranged for twelve sets of papers, ration cards and train tickets. Most importantly, they found a hideaway not too far from the camp for those nailbiting first few hours and days of freedom when the danger of recapture was at its highest. There were countless details to arrange for such a bold undertaking, requiring all of Virginia's field skills and resourcefulness. Indeed, this had been the chief reason she had been so dismayed when she had received the recall orders from London. She could not abandon her closest team – Germaine Guérin, Dr Rousset and his new wireless operator André Courvoisier (a likeable former French army man) – who were working the networks to the full on her behalf. A more direct and speedy way of contacting all the men to finalise plans remained the most stubbornly difficult problem, however. Gaby's visits and Sevilla's efforts were not enough. Together Virginia and her supporters came up with a breath-takingly bold solution.

A few days later a jovial seventy-year-old French priest, an army veteran who had lost his legs in action in the First World War, started a series of pastoral visits to the *Camerons*. He was good at lifting their morale and seems to have arranged for the men to be allowed a few pots of paint to spruce up their hut. One day, when they had finished, he asked to be lifted up the steps into their barracks in his wheelchair to see their efforts at interior decoration. Once inside, the priest wheeled himself to the middle of the room and quickly beckoned the men to gather round. 'I have a little present for you,' he whispered, while his eyes darted excitedly. 'But first post a sentry or two at the door and window ... Now, one of you look under my cassock ... where my legs should be.' One of them duly lifted up the robe to a collective gasp. 'Great Scott! It's a piano!' exclaimed Bégué, no doubt guessing who must have arranged for a transmitter to be smuggled in in such an ingenious fashion. 'Yes,' the priest replied. 'I was given to understand that you can get plenty of music out of it. It has been nicely tuned ... Hide it and, of course, forget how it got here.'[8]

A couple of nights later, taking advantage of the absence of sentries in Watchtower Five, Bégué ran seventy feet of aerial out of sight under the eaves of the hut. Within a week he was transmitting his first message to Baker Street, in which he reported the names of those with him and that ten of them intended to 'form escaping party and reach safe country hideouts' with a possible four more hangers-on. F Section was astonished to hear from its celebrated pianist from inside a French prison camp. Almost incredibly, there was now a direct line in and out of Mauzac. Knowing that Virginia was directing the operation, although kept unaware of the details in case of interceptions, London responded with instructions on how the *Camerons* could contact her in person at the Grand Nouvel Hôtel as soon as they reached Lyon. They should give the following code phrase: 'I am coming to ask you how many eggs I should put to one side for you.' Her reply would be: 'Keep ten for me, unless you have four more.' Yet even now there was still general scepticism that the agents could actually break free.

Bégué became so adept at transmitting from the hut that he was even able to pass on useful intelligence gleaned from a garrulous guard. After signalling details of the new German shells and explosives factory in Bergerac that the warder had been talking about, the *Camerons* were delighted to hear RAF bombers roaring over them a couple of nights later and see the sky glow red as heavy explosions shook the ground and 'sent clouds of sparks into the night'.[9] It was more than gratifying to overhear the same guard the following day discussing the destruction of the plant. They were, incredibly, playing a role in the war even while still behind barbed wire.

Bégué sent so many messages that the signals soon attracted the attention of a radio detector van, seen passing the camp on at least one occasion. He was confident that the police would never think to look inside the camp, however, and he was proved right when they learned that several nearby houses and farms had been thoroughly searched instead. It was also perhaps via the radio that a solution was devised for a tricky problem with one of the other prisoners. Old Père Fleuret, a garage-owner from Châteauroux and one of the first locals to be recruited by SOE, was threatening to inform the guards if the *Camerons* actually went ahead with their plans. No one wanted to harm him, as he had been a brave and loyal supporter of Bégué's from the earliest days, but his fears that the escape would endanger his wife and daughter imperilled the entire operation. Some time in June, just as Virginia was fighting to stay at her post, the camp doctor called George Langelaan into his surgery and made it clear he had been briefed on a certain forthcoming event. The doctor – very likely a contact of Dr Rousset's – handed over a tiny phial of what he said was a harmless sleeping draught, and which he suggested might come in useful. It could, he explained, be slipped into coffee or beer (but not tea) without altering the taste. 'I'm thinking of taking a few days' rest but I do not exactly know when,' the doctor added with a knowing look. 'Would you be good enough to tell me when you think it might be a good time? You see, there are times when I would sooner be far away.'[10]

The escape plans were now almost complete. But when they tested the key in the lock it did not turn. This was a disaster. The escape had to take place during the new moon period between 8 and 15 July. After that, the nights would be too bright and their escape too obvious so time was running out. Bégué worked frantically at reshaping the key while the 'interminable sing songs' started up again. An anxious Virginia and Gaby were warned of the delay via another ingenious means of communication. They had started slipping messages to the men into tubes of aspirin brought in by another friendly guard. Now the men wrote to them about the glitch with the key by tossing the tube back over the fence to a sympathetic middleman (another warder). When the key worked properly, after a couple more nights, they were able to relate the good news in the same way. As arranged, the warder passed on the message to the colleague he knew to be in direct contact with Gaby by slipping the tube into the pocket of his jacket hanging up in the mess. But she never received it, and when she arrived at the camp two days later the mess sergeant announced he wanted to speak to her.

With heart pounding she stepped into his office preparing for the worst. To her horror, their plans had been discovered: the warder had mistakenly put the tube in the mess sergeant's jacket rather than the one belonging to the guard. Gaby denied any knowledge of what he was talking about, but it must have been clear she was lying. To her great relief, however, the mess sergeant suddenly changed tack, telling her that he too would help in return for the princely sum of fifty thousand francs.[11] Virginia, of course, swiftly supplied it.

Thanks to the food parcels and their exercise sessions the men were feeling physically stronger, which was just as well. For the escape to succeed they would need to be in peak condition. First they would sprint from the hut to a dark spot shielded by another building from the bright arc lights on the towers. From there they would run to an exact point in the barbed wire fencing (located during the countless sessions of *boules*), out of sight of the manned watchtowers and relatively dimly lit. Here the wire would be held slightly apart by trestle tables built by Bégué (as part of their supposed redecoration of their hut) from old planks of wood. A piece of old carpet would be thrown down to stop their stomachs from being torn to shreds as they crawled through in the near-flat style taught them by Trotobas. But it would still be a huge challenge to run to the fence in two stages, then work their way through several yards of barbed wire fencing, all in the dark, all in no more than a minute. The entire process had been timed to the split second to avoid the regular rounds of the guards; a single delay could wreck the whole operation. And the patrols might at any time spot the open door of the barracks so the more artistic among them painted a false door on sackcloth, which could be pinned up in seconds once the real door had been unlocked.

Gaby brought the children to see Jean on Bastille Day, 14 July, and could not stop crying about the dangers that lay ahead for them all. The following night – the last possible – had been set for the escape and the next day was the longest that most of them had ever known.[12] Shortly after four on the afternoon of the 15th they waited for the final signal from Virginia that all was ready. Sure enough, an old lady passed by the camp at the appointed time with three children in her wake. If it had been an old man, that would have meant that the operation had been called off. At dinner that night, the prisoners tried to act normally as one of them slipped the doctor's sleeping potion into Fleuret's beer, which had been brought in specially by Gaby. The other men grew increasingly twitchy as they ate, noticing that the normally fretful Fleuret seemed uncharacteristically chirpy. Usually one of the first to go to bed, this evening he showed no signs of being remotely sleepy. He stood at the window and whistled for some time, while the others constantly checked their watches and frantically wondered whether the sleeping potion was a dud. At last, he went over to his bed, all eyes upon him for signs of winding down, but he defied their hopes by starting to whistle again. Only when he started to undress did Fleuret mercifully keel over and begin to snore.

Meanwhile, Sevilla had a friend bring in two litres of white wine to the guardroom, and at around midnight started a drinking session with his chief. As soon as they had settled in and started singing, it had been arranged that another friendly warder, called Conrad, would mount Watchtower Seven and give an all-clear signal to the *Camerons* with his cigarette lighter. In their locked hut, the men were stuffing rags to create dummies under their bedclothes to make them look slept in, drawing lots as to who was to go out first and taking up positions at the window. The hours passed, the sliver of moon rose, and still there was no signal. Perhaps it was all a trap, or maybe the guard had been found out. Sevilla was also waiting and waiting for Conrad to climb the Watchtower Seven ladder, but he had got cold feet and never did.

Finally, at three o'clock, with no one able to wait any longer, Sevilla slipped away from his inebriated chief and scrambled up into the watchtower himself, and with shaky hands managed to light his pipe. Relieved beyond measure Bégué inserted the key in the lock, turned it and opened the door. It creaked painfully – despite being oiled the previous day – but within seconds he had pinned up the painted sackcloth and Trotobas rushed through to the wire with the carpet and unrolled a ball of string as a signal line. One tug meant it was all clear, three short tugs signalled danger. One by one the men ran across to the hut and then to the fence and wriggled through the wire as quickly as they could. Langelaan was one of the last to throw himself on to the carpet, but then a guard suddenly loomed over him. Trotobas was about to leap on him from behind, putting his SOE silent killing training into action, when the guard whispered, 'Is it the English?' Trotobas answered: 'Yes.' 'Well, don't make so much noise,' the guard responded, before walking away. Within a few more seconds Trotobas had seen Bégué, Jumeau, Pierre-Bloch, Garel, JB Hayes, Le Harivel, Langelaan, Liewer, Robert Lyon and Roche through the wire, as well as Sevilla, while the mess sergeant met them outside. The whole exquisite exercise had taken twelve minutes – a minute a man.

A couple of miles away, well beyond the lights of the camp, a curly-haired Corsican called Albert Rigoulet was waiting in an old Citroën lorry parked in a leafy hollow. As soon as they were all out, the men sprinted through the darkened woods in twos and threes, jumped in the truck and Rigoulet drove them away into the night unseen and unheard. Only at daybreak did one of the remaining prisoners start shouting about his fellow inmates having disappeared in the night, swearing (just as he had been instructed) that he had noticed nothing unusual until then. He had also re-locked the door and discarded the key so that the remaining guards were completely nonplussed as to how the *Camerons* had escaped from their hut. Immediately the alarm was sounded vast numbers of police swarmed in to mount an unprecedented manhunt. All road traffic within a hundred miles was checked, all roads, bridges, railways, river boats and stations either closed or put under twenty-four-hour surveillance. Photographs of the prisoners were circulated to controls and checkpoints and local houses, farms and countryside were systematically combed by the police. Some of the Mauzac guards were savagely beaten and imprisoned for failing to stop the escape – whether they had helped or known or not – and under German orders security at other camps and prisons was tightened up. As expected, Gaby was promptly arrested but Virginia had advised her to create a cast-iron alibi well in advance. She was able to name witnesses to testify that she had been on her way back from meetings with officials in Vichy – where she had again been pleading for her husband – at the time.

Gaby was released but both the Germans and Vichy knew full well that the Allies had pulled off a spectacular escape and a major propaganda coup. The break-out acquired a legendary status far beyond Mauzac. It was feverishly discussed in bars and shops and amongst the passengers squashed together on buses and trains. 'A dozen men were picked up in a field by an RAF bomber,' the locals informed each other in considerable awe. Little did they know that it was Virginia's friendly local prostitutes, doctors and hairdressers who had deliberately started the rumours. She wanted the police to believe that the men were already back in England.

In fact, Rigoulet had driven a mere twenty miles before he dropped them off in a swathe of springy wild heather clothed in a light morning mist. They lay down in the heavy dew for around an hour while he disposed of the lorry. Then he reappeared and led them on foot across a landscape of folding hills densely shaded by walnut and sweet chestnut trees, pressing on until they were well out of the reach of any vehicles at the heart of the forest. Jean Pierre-Bloch recalled finally arriving at 'a dilapidated, abandoned house and barn' around noon and being thrilled to discover that 'with admirable organisation someone had prepared for our visit'.[13] The cupboards were stocked with biscuits, jam, razors and even soap – a nice Virginia-style touch that went down very well.

For a fortnight the *Camerons* hunkered down, sleeping during the day and taking only a brief silent walk outside at night, tuning their ears to any unfamiliar sound and scouring the dark for movement. Finally, the fuss started to die down. Virginia's informants reported that the police had decided that the escapees must by now have fled the country. The manhunt was called off – but the men's faces were now uncomfortably well-known. It was nevertheless time for them to leave and continue their journey on to Lyon. They would simply have to find a way of avoiding attention and getting through. Some took the train, others travelled by truck. All made their way as instructed to the Grand Nouvel Hôtel, where they knew Virginia would be waiting to prepare them for their passage to Spain. Some took much longer than others to reach Lyon, after a number of close calls with their French and German pursuers. Even when they arrived the atmosphere was jumpy – the Mauzac escape was still on everyone's lips – and so she quickly dispersed them to different safehouses to avoid them drawing attention as a group. Two stayed with one of the city's legendary Resistance hairdressers, others were put up by Germaine, possibly at her brothel. On 11 August *Vic* cabled London: 'All *Clan Cameron* repeat *Clan Cameron* safely transferred to Lyon repeat Lyon. First party leave next week.'[14] For the first time in a long while, there was quite a celebration in Baker Street.

It took some *Camerons* longer than others to reach London, and around half of them spent time in a Spanish prison on the way. But thanks to Virginia and Gaby's ingenuity, with the help of *Vic* and a cast of others, the escape released Bégué to be F Section's future signals officer. Four others – Hayes, Liewer, Lyon and Trotobas – became distinguished circuit heads. Trotobas's exploits on his return to France earned him a recommendation for the Victoria Cross. Although it is astonishingly little-known, M. R. D. Foot, the official SOE historian, acknowledged the Mauzac jailbreak as 'one of the war's most useful operations of the kind'.[15] Such was the scale and daring of the escape it was inevitable that at the time many claimed and were given credit for it to a greater or lesser degree. At this stage of the war, Virginia's role was in the background and she was reticent about pushing herself forward. Many of the *Camerons* themselves were unaware of the full extent of her role. But her closest lieutenants, such as Courvoisier in Lyon,[16] and later her superiors in London, saw just how much of the operation's success was down to her. How Virginia Hall and Madame Bloch inspired, led and drove forward to the very end such a 'daring rescue operation . . . [right] under the noses of the guards' eventually became an SOE legend, noted the historian E. H. Cookridge. Virginia was the lynchpin, Foot decreed after researching the Mauzac events in detail. Many of SOE's greatest triumphs have remained 'quite unknown' to anyone, he explained, 'except to the people who were concerned in them'.[17] Morel also officially recorded later that 'She was personally responsible for a number of escapes from prison, and in many cases the organisation of those escapes was entirely her own work.'[18]

In recognition of Gaby Bloch's extraordinary valour, SOE pulled out all the stops to bring her and the children to Britain to rejoin her husband. Both went on to serve the French security services in London and later received the Légion d'honneur, and she was recommended for a King's Medal for Courage in the Cause of Freedom. Enthralled by the Mauzac operation, SOE put Virginia forward for one of Britain's highest civilian honours. Indeed, she may have been the only F Section field agent to be considered eligible as a Commander of the Order of the British Empire while still active in enemy territory. And as such her citation could not include operational details and hardly did her justice: 'She has devoted herself whole-heartedly to our work without regard to the dangerous position in which her activities would place her if they were realised by the Vichy authorities. She has been indefatigable in her constant support and assistance for our agents, combining a high degree of organising ability with a clear-sighted appreciation of our needs ... Her services for us cannot be too highly praised.'[19] She was turned down.

Later, after the liberation of France, Baker Street finally acknowledged the true extent of her contribution to a 'very great number'[20] of escapes, but most of all Mauzac. An internal F Section memorandum, written on 21 November 1944, recorded for posterity that 'many of our men owe their liberty and even their lives' to Virginia Hall. But the world outside never knew.

Chapter Six

Honeycomb of Spies

Virginia's daring break-out of the Mauzac 'terrorists' caused uproar at Nazi High Command and led Hitler to unleash a brutal crackdown in France. It made clear that the Resistance was now a significant threat and that French semi-autonomous rule in the southern zone was no longer sustainable. Repeated attacks on factories, railway trucks, German cars, power lines and a Lyon recruitment office also proved to Berlin that Pétain's adminis-tration, for all its promises, could not be trusted to destroy the enemy within. So the Third Reich would now lay the ground-work for a full occupation, ordering Vichy to issue five hundred French identity cards to the Gestapo to help them infiltrate secret Allied networks across the Free Zone.[1] Under Operation Donar, named after the Germanic god of thunder, the Nazis planned to honeycomb the cities of the south with double agents to root out and eliminate the remaining terrorist cells. The terms of the 1940 armistice stated that the Gestapo were to intervene only in the presence of French police, but the Germans now just arrested and tortured virtually at will. Lyon was their primary target. 'The pot was simmering,' as one SOE historian has put it, 'and it would soon boil over.'[2]

They made it an urgent priority to track down those responsible for Mauzac as well as the notable recent upswing in the effectiveness and frequency of sabotage. Both the Gestapo and the Abwehr now harboured suspicions about the American consulate in Lyon and kept it under close surveillance. The two security services of the Reich were bitter rivals, however, and competed against each other in pursuit of the greatest prizes. For now its success with breaking SOE codes – thanks to Sergeant Bleicher and La Chatte – put the Abwehr in pole position. It had deduced that the target was either English or Canadian and a woman; a woman with a limp – *la dame qui boite* or *Die Frau die hinkt* – called *Marie Monin*. But the Abwehr favoured a methodical approach over the Gestapo's preference for wholesale arrest. Bleicher would not move in until he was sure who she was and who she was working with. He would also wait until he could get his hands on one of her wireless transmitters, so that he could play *Funkspiel* with London in her name. By the beginning of August he had a plan to bring her down – and disrupt the British war effort – and just the man to carry it out. It was to be a pivotal month.

Meanwhile the Gestapo's most notorious investigator – who would within a year be awarded the Iron Cross (reputedly by Hitler himself) for torturing and slaughtering thousands of *résistants* – was also taking a personal interest in Virginia. Hauptsturmführer Klaus Barbie, reared by an abusive father who had been severely mentally and physically damaged in fighting the French at Verdun in 1916, was not yet based full-time in Lyon. But he was already consumed by an obsessive desire to crush SOE, seen by the Germans as the backbone of the whole underground threat. Dozens of Gestapo officers were intercepting

suspect signals coming out of Lyon and conducting waves of
arrests and constant day-and-night raids from a plushly carpeted
suite of offices on the third floor of the cavernous Hôtel Terminus
next to Perrache station. They knew they were fast moving in
on the centre of the terrorist cell. Someone would break down
under torture; Barbie would make sure of it. The Limping Lady
of Lyon was becoming the Nazis' most wanted Allied agent in
the whole of France.

Unaware of the dark forces closing in on her, Virginia's health
was better and her spirits higher that August than they had been
for some time. The Mauzac triumph had cheered her and at the
beginning of the month Nicolas Bodington came to Lyon for
discussions about her future. She made a convincing case for
continuing in her post, insisting that her high-placed friends
would keep her out of danger and that she had plenty of work to
do in freeing more agents, recruiting others, and helping to step
up the sabotage campaign. Bodington gave in and recommended
to London that it should cancel Virginia's recall. After all, he had
been the one to take a gamble on her and it had certainly paid
off. Baker Street agreed and asked the *New York Post* to confirm
her position and commission more articles to maintain her cover.
Virginia was sent three-quarters of a million francs through the
American military attaché in Vichy to continue her work. It was
a useful addition to the ten thousand francs a month she received
from SOE, paid to her secretly via the unorthodox route of the
bank account of Germaine Guérin's brothel, where it was wired
from London in the name of the burned RAF pilot William
Simpson.[3] Bodington also sought to calm the rivalries between
the SOE agents in Lyon and to make it clear who was commander-
in-chief. Perhaps he thought it politically expedient to have a
Frenchman in charge to assuage wounded national pride. Maybe

F Section still simply baulked at promoting a woman. To many *résistants'* horror and Virginia's dismay, the position went to *Alain*.

It was almost a year since Virginia had gone behind enemy lines, and she had been the only woman dispatched by F Section for all of that time. At first, it had been an advantage to be a woman working undercover, particularly a handsome one who could use her charms to distract or deceive. Most Germans, fed propaganda on how women's lives should revolve around *Kinder, Kirche, Küche* (children, church, kitchen), had assumed that these fragile vessels would hardly get involved in something as dirty and dangerous as the Resistance. But as Virginia was fully aware, the party line had changed dramatically. The Gestapo had discovered that more and more local women were playing an active role, many as couriers ferrying money, messages or weapons between agents. One weighed down her baby's pram with ninety pounds of firearms so that the springs scraped the wheels and the whole contraption nearly collapsed. Couriers often carried incriminating items, heavy and light, but they also kept a lot in their heads, including agents' names and addresses. If caught, women were therefore deliberately subjected to some of the worst forms of torture the Nazi mindset could devise.

Rumours had no doubt reached Virginia of the sort of treatment she could expect if she were finally found out. A favoured technique was wrenching off women's nipples with pliers, or pressing down on the raw nerve of a smashed tooth, pulling out fingernails or burning skin with cigarettes or soldering irons or acid. Others were sexually assaulted or raped – one of Barbie's favoured techniques would reputedly involve the use of a dog. Later on, the bathtub method of torture – a forerunner of waterboarding – came into favour. The prisoner was immersed, naked, in icy water, her hands manacled behind her back and her head held under until she was on the point of drowning. If she fainted she was dragged out of the water by her hair. If she still refused to talk she would be pushed under again. Sometimes, on the point of death, she would be offered a coffee or tea, but if she still did not cooperate the process started all over again.[4] Occasionally, if the women were Jewish, Barbie would simply crush their faces with the heel of his jackboot.

Not that such barbarity was exclusive to the Germans. Some agents felt even more fear of the French authorities because of a perverse competition to impress their Gestapo masters by setting new standards in cruelty. One particularly pernicious method of breaking down captives was to threaten to harm their family. At least one captured courier was faced with the prospect of watching her baby's head being smashed against a wall unless she talked. Vichy was also pouring resources into beefing up its own police, not only the number of men but an explosion of different elaborately uniformed forces, each watching another and together ultimately 'succeeding in weighing the whole country down under the oppression of an army of spies'.[5] The aim was to cleanse the country of dissidents for good.

Despite reports of these atrocities, Virginia's success opened the gates to more women agents. It is no exaggeration that this 'gallant lady', as SOE called her, changed the course of history for women in Allied intelligence. Her track record had finally overcome considerable hostility to the very idea of female officers in the field. Just as the position for women became particularly dangerous, F Section was thus ready that August to dispatch the first of thirty-eight more female officers. 'We were destined to be surprised to find that even in jobs ... originally deemed to be men's prerogatives, they showed great enthusiasm and skill,' said Maurice Buckmaster. 'For certain jobs, women were superior to men' in part because of 'their ability to focus on a single objective'.[6] While they did indeed go on to play what Buckmaster dubbed an extremely important role, they would pay a high price. Thirteen, or one in three, of the thirty-nine women SOE sent in to France never came home. That compared to one in four of the four hundred or so male agents. The higher attrition rate for female spies was due in part to the fact that many took the particularly dangerous roles of courier (which involved constantly passing through patrols with incriminating materials) or, later on, of wireless operator. Thousands of French *résistantes* would also pay with their lives. Their typical role of staying in one place to provide safehouses won them no glory but made them particularly vulnerable to betrayal. A fifth of the women who took in people or supplies were executed for their trouble.[7]

Such was the urgent need to send more agents into action, though, that some were recruited without being let in on the secret. A bilingual secretary who found herself unwittingly on an intense SOE training course waited several weeks before finally venturing to ask one of her fellow trainees whether she knew why they were there. Some were more knowing, but bought into the idea that a clandestine life was somehow glamorous, rather than a death-battle for survival. Upon arrival by ship on the Riviera one SOE woman's first thought was to demand from Virginia where to find the best local hairdresser. Virginia had no truck with such vanities and made her displeasure clear by sending another recruit straight back to the boat because it was obvious she had permed her hair just before leaving London, a luxury not easily available in France. The woman could have been caught at once, posing a mortal danger to them all.[8] One of the first new women to arrive, a fortyish French-born receptionist in a West End hotel, had, however, been a different commodity. Yvonne Rudellat's 'cheerful, fluffy manner'[9] belied a steady nerve and a lot of common sense. She headed up to Tours to start work as a courier, for which she would be recommended for the Military Cross (but denied it as the medal was not then awarded to women). A month later, the twenty-year-old Andrée Borrel became the first woman to be parachuted in, to work as a courier with Francis Suttill, a half-English barrister and organiser of the extensive *Prosper* circuit. Although a profoundly courageous man, Suttill was perhaps naive as to how to recruit local helpers. He and Borrel picked up the circuit's future second-in-command by choosing a Paris nightclub to demonstrate Sten guns – the Resistance weapon of choice – to an 'interested mixed audience'.[10] It was not a good start, nor did it end well. Suttill and both women were eventually to die. Suttill was executed at Sachsenhausen concentration camp near Berlin in March 1945, eight months after Borrel had been injected with phenol and while still alive dragged into the crematorium at Natzweiler concentration camp in the Vosges mountains of eastern France. An emaciated Rudellat died from typhus in 1945, just after liberation from Belsen.

Virginia herself just kept going. She was, however, in desperate need of the right sort of back-up. Having been given a reprieve by Bodington, she was busier than ever. Baker Street felt compelled to warn her not to spend time helping other Allied intelligence agencies, such as the Poles, Belgians and indeed even MI6, as it feared they were trading 'on her kind heart'.[11] But she could not resist the many opportunities for intelligence-gathering and network-building that came her way. And some of the biggest legends of the Resistance – including *Gauthier* – were still proving of little practical help. 'There is too much stress on grandiloquent plans, too many words and far too little grubbing,' Virginia complained.

She repeated her request for a permanent envoy to help her exploit her contacts to the full. But she also made it clear that London could keep him (apparently not entertaining the thought of another woman) 'unless he was a first class man, experienced, authoritative, willing to take responsibility and lead an unpleasant life' and, most of all, 'not complain'.[12] After bailing out one agent who lost nearly thirty thousand francs and his papers on a train, and another whose cheques for nearly forty thousand francs bounced in a casino, she was tired of playing mother to men behaving like unruly children. Peter Churchill compared the half-dozen 'aces' such as Virginia, who did all the work for the 'privilege of half-starving . . . to death in this no-man's land', with those who were 'sloppy and gutless and come whining and groaning' and could not hold their drink.[13] All agents were scared. Most suffered from chronic insomnia. 'There are endless nightmares of uncertainty,' said one. 'The tensions, the nerve strain and fatigue, the all-demanding alertness of living a lie, these are [the agent's] to meet, accept, and control. They are never, really, conquered.'[14] But even if not vanquished, the fear had to be controlled without the prop of alcohol, gambling or sleeping around. Agents had to find the strength to go on from within themselves, but there were precious few who could do so.

Ben Cowburn returned to Lyon to carry out a number of strategic sabotage operations. As usual, he headed straight to Virginia's apartment to prepare for his mission, which included persuading friendly workers at a local aircraft factory to introduce abrasives into the machinery, and blowing up high-tension lines around a power station. Virginia could never let anyone come too close to her, let alone allow herself to confide in them. But as a reassuring figure with an endearingly impish grin, who had gone out of his way to warn her about the La Chatte saga, Cowburn was special to her. She welcomed his arrival early one morning by making him lie down to rest while she prepared breakfast for them both. But for all her solicitude during this brief domestic moment, Cowburn was afraid for her. Each round of arrests was drawing ever closer to Virginia. One of the strongest SOE advocates of her remaining in France, he was nevertheless aghast at the risks she continued to take. Cowburn pleaded with her to stop relying on her powerful protectors, urging her to save herself by leading a 'mouselike' life instead. That approach worked well for him on his short, comparatively well-defined missions, and with rest periods back in London in between. But it was hardly realistic for Virginia, whose role was both permanent and all-encompassing. It was her job – and her nature – to be available at all times to whoever needed her. During August alone she worked with twenty-five SOE-trained organisers and six pianists in the Non-Occupied Zone, and eight different circuits across the whole of France. She helped them with sabotage, parachute drops, intelligence-gathering and receiving two thousand pounds of supplies delivered by sea.[15]

Even now Virginia continued to extend her sphere of influence, particularly within Paris. She was taking a grave risk. The capital was the target of the most brutal Gestapo raids, and the Resistance there was constantly decimated by mass arrests, known as *coups durs* or hard kicks. But her reputation and contacts allowed her to pick up a number of outstanding high-society recruits such as Vera Leigh, an expert shot and the glitzy director of the haute couture house of Reboux. Virginia summoned her to Lyon to help with the escape lines to Spain and Switzerland. Two wealthy Jewish businessmen, Jean Worms and Jacques Weil, who had been running their own independent war against the Nazis since 1940 with a group of like-minded friends, also approached her. They had consistently refused to join French-run resistance organisations because they neither trusted nor respected them but they had heard nothing but praise for her work. Another valuable contact was the champion racing driver Robert Benoist who teamed up with his old British rival William Grover-Williams (who had already joined SOE). The pair ran small sabotage missions and parachute drops south-west of the capital. Virginia's contacts had thus come good, but connecting with such high-profile figures also redoubled the threat of discovery. Her renown in Paris would indeed cost her – and many others – very dear.

On 14 August Denis Rake slipped out of Virginia's apartment in Lyon, where she had nursed him back to health and hidden him from his many pursuers. By the following day he was eating breakfast in the café of the Hôtel des Faisans in Limoges. With both the police and the Gestapo still after him, he had had to brave the dangers of taking a train and booking into a hotel, and was sweating from a combination of fear and summer heat. But he had arranged to meet two other SOE agents, Ernest Wilkinson and Richard Heslop, and he would not let them down. Virginia had been sheltering them too, and had got the three together to agree to set up a new circuit in Angers, with Rake as wireless operator. She had supplied them, as Rake put it, in her 'wonderful way',[16] with false papers, money and even a radio (a new, lighter model) from London. She alerted Baker Street to expect Rake to be transmitting from Angers within a few days.

Yet the airwaves were silent and all three simply vanished. A day or so later Virginia felt 'stricken with grief' when she found an unsigned note for her at the American consulate, warning that they had been arrested in Limoges. Through what Cowburn termed her 'remarkable grapevine'[17] she discovered that an Inspector Morel of the Sûreté had spotted the suspiciously nervous Rake at the hotel and decided to search him. He found in Rake's pocket the huge sum of sixty-five thousand francs, which he tried (but failed) to explain away by claiming to earn an implausible eight thousand francs a month as a shirtmaker.[18]

The inspector – a subordinate of Virginia's Sûreté contact Commissaire Guth – promptly arrested him on suspicion of spying and when the other two agents arrived they were also rounded up despite claiming they had only just met. Their story fell apart when it was discovered that the wads of thousand-franc SOE-printed notes that Virginia had provided them all had consecutive serial numbers – a bad mistake on the part of Baker Street that she had apparently failed to notice. Rake was also carrying three identity cards, all purporting to be from different towns but bearing the same handwriting. For all SOE's ingenuity in printing French money and documents, such mistakes were nevertheless all too common.

Inspector Morel had no choice but to escort them to the police station. Fortunately, once it was established they were British not German, Guth's most sympathetic officers obligingly burned the fake money and hid the automatic weapon found in one of their rooms as well as the radio. Inspector Morel himself flushed Rake's superfluous identity cards down the lavatory. Without these incriminating items, there was every confidence that the charges against them would be minor. Virginia's influence over Guth was once again proving a lifesaver and she rushed over to Limoges, where the trio were now held in the central prison, and smuggled in a food parcel containing tinned meat, chocolate, condensed milk and cigarettes. She assured London she would 'get them out fairly quickly with a bit of assistance from her friends'.[19]

As usual, the chunky blond-haired Guth appeared willing to help. He prolonged the interrogations of the three agents so that they should not be sent away from Limoges. He even allowed Rake to transmit messages from his home, and provided food, wine and books in the jail. But Virginia was frustrated that he was otherwise 'slow in doing anything'[20] actually to get them out. It was soon to become clear why.

At this point, Rake's dysentery came back with a vengeance, although this at least provided Virginia with an opportunity. She immediately enlisted Dr Rousset to help extract Rake from the hospital in Limoges, so he could be hidden in the fake 'mental asylum' above the Lyon surgery until he had recovered. The following day a junior doctor provided Rake with a white coat and some cash and instructed him to leave the hospital right away. But Rake, also now suffering from an abscess on his face, was too weak to move quickly. On his way slowly down the stairs from the ward he bumped into the only one of his nurses not involved in the plot, who was on her way back up from lunch. She shouted to raise the alarm and not long after Rake found himself back in Limoges prison.

Meanwhile Virginia had received the dreaded news that Wilkinson and Heslop were to be sent on from Limoges to an isolated fortress called Castres, a well-known transit jail for the Nazi camps at Dachau and Buchenwald in Germany. Even worse, the normally gung-ho Guth suddenly claimed he was powerless to help them. Virginia was astonished. Only later did it transpire that the Gestapo had threatened reprisals against his family if he 'lost' any more prisoners, let alone appeared to be helping them.[21] Even the most careful and devoted supporters could be brutally brought into line in this way and the escape of Gerry Morel, now followed by Rake's foiled attempt, had roused unhelpful suspicions. Without the time to ponder Guth's odd behaviour, however, Virginia urgently turned to his sharp-witted subordinate Marcel Leccia. She ordered him to arrange a gang of toughs to jump the guards as they prepared to transfer the SOE men to Castres, some fifty miles from Toulouse. Leccia was proving resourceful and valiant – the nearest she had to a fellow spirit in the loneliness of waging a secret war – and eager to oblige. But then Guth found out about the plan and to Virginia's

furious disbelief deliberately increased the number of warders
to make it impossible. 'I've been to see the police in L[imoges],' a
perplexed Virginia signalled London. 'I can't make heads or tails
of it.'[22] Virginia devised yet another scheme for Leccia, who was
disgusted at what he now considered to be cowardice on Guth's
part and caring nothing for his own safety. He boarded the train
taking Wilkinson and Heslop to Castres, and pushed his way
through the crowded carriages to where they were standing in
a corridor shackled together. He somehow managed to slip an
eighteen-inch file into Heslop's hand, and in the crush Heslop was
able to slide it up his sleeve without being noticed. But the prisoners never had the chance to use it as the obviously edgy guards
accompanying them did not relinquish their close watch again for
a second and they arrived as planned in Castres (where Rake was
shortly to join them) still in chains. Undaunted, Virginia started
work on a new escape operation. 'I hope you don't mind if the
evasion of the three does blow relations [with Guth]', she cabled
London, hinting she was planning another of her spectaculars.
He 'really deserve[s] it for lack of moral courage'. One of her chief
protectors, though, had now become yet another potential threat.

To most people in the summer of 1942, it was quite clear which
side was winning the war. The German offensive in Russia had
reached as far as the Volga River, and General Erwin Rommel
was advancing on the gates of Cairo. There were some small signs
that the tide was beginning to turn, however. The United States
was shifting its focus to the Western Theatre from the Pacific
conflict with Japan and in June had set up its own version of SOE
called the Office of Strategic Services (OSS). The Americans and
British were finally gearing up for their first joint mass offensive
as an eventual launching pad for invading Europe. SOE knew
that this would probably come within weeks, in the form of an

Anglo-American landing in Vichy-held North Africa – known as Operation Torch – and that these would be critical days for its agents in southern France. They also knew that the offensive was likely to be the trigger for Hitler to send his armies across the demarcation line to place the entire country under formal Nazi control. At that point even Virginia's well-placed friends would be powerless to protect her.

Yet there was so much to do before then. SOE had decided it was time to hit the Free Zone, while it still existed; to move on from the niggling small-scale attacks they had so far organised to detonate carefully selected 'big bangs'. Virginia was soon ordered to dispatch Cowburn to sabotage the entire railway network around Lothiers in central France, using the specially equipped groups of men they had spent months training. She also took delivery of two hundred thousand francs to arm and instruct teams for, when the time came, taking control of Lyon Perrache station and a nearby aerodrome, as well as blowing up a power station.[23]

Parachute drops of arms and explosives were generally being stepped up, when clear skies and light winds permitted. New agents came in with dozens of false-bottomed suitcases, with warm clothing for the forthcoming winter on top and explosives hidden below. SOE boffins based at the Thatched Barn, a former hotel on the Barnet bypass north of London, had secretly designed a range of ingenious explosive devices to cause maximum impact in the most challenging situations. The real-life forerunners of James Bond's Q had come up with milk bottles that exploded if the cap was removed; loaves of bread that would 'cause devastation' when cut in half, and fountain pens that squirted poison. Perhaps the most popular was fake horse dung that exploded if driven over – but there were also tiny but lethal charges that could be inserted into cigarettes, matchboxes, bicycle pumps, fountain pens or hair brushes, and perhaps most usefully railway engines and fuel tanks.[24] On a larger scale, for the first time, there was even talk of moving on from sabotaging industrial sites to identifying 'A'-class or military targets to hinder the German counter-attack in a future Allied invasion. Virginia's months of slog and preparation appeared to be leading to real action. Finally, it seemed as if SOE had the critical mass and the direction needed to do something truly significant, and she wanted more than anything to see it through.

It was also clear that she had to free the remaining imprisoned SOE agents before it was too late and they fell into unfettered Nazi control. There were so many good people relying on her alone for their very survival. The calls on her time were dizzying and expectations of her immense. 'I am doing too much,' she told London, 'and find it hard to swing round the circuit fast enough.'[25] She felt particularly responsible for *Olive*, her colleague on the Riviera, who had saved her from the police *rafle* in Marseille. He had formed an impressive thirty sabotage cells along the Côte d'Azur that had successfully wrecked a number of trucks as well as fuel reservoirs, power lines and railway trucks. He had also collected vital intelligence on Axis defences in the Mediterranean and was delighted to have enlisted a new courier, a clerk at the Swiss consulate-general in Marseille, who used his diplomatic status to carry highly sensitive material across the border into Switzerland, where he handed it over to a British intelligence officer at La Chaux-des-Fonds. But around the same time as the arrests in Limoges, the courier was denounced and apprehended by German and Italian military police. They tore open the sealed diplomatic valise he was carrying to discover microfilms on the coastal defences in Sicily, which the Allies planned to attack the following spring. The courier insisted he knew nothing about the photos, but finally after days of torture gave *Olive* away. He was captured on 18 August.

Virginia found out that *Olive* was to be escorted by police two weeks later from Nice to Montluc prison in Lyon. She knew that few who went in to the German-run fortress jail ever came out – they either died there or were deported – so she urgently arranged for the now returned Peter Churchill and a band of helpers to spring him during transit. But when they tracked him down in a crowded carriage just north of Nice they found that (the married) *Olive*'s new mistress, a Mademoiselle Menier, was accompanying him. *Olive* spotted Churchill but signalled that he did not want the men to free him while she was there. 'So now O. is nothing but a gone gosling,' Churchill reported to London. 'What beats me is, why, if they must have a pancake on the premises, our lads always select some dizzy dame instead of a serious and helpful partner.'[26]

Mlle Menier was a worry. Virginia's informants had warned her that this 'passionate and dangerous redhead' was 'fed up' and intended to sell all she knew to the Gestapo. Virginia immediately messaged Baker Street that what she called a 'weak line' on Menier 'would make matters worse'. 'The logical solution was unpleasant,' she warned, but she needed to move fast. London replied that she could try to buy her off, but that if this proved impossible, she had 'full authority'. This, then, was Virginia's licence to eliminate the wayward mistress of a foolish colleague. A few days later she was impatiently demanding 'Where are the pills?', to be reassured that the poison capsules were on their way. Meanwhile, *Olive*, still hopelessly in thrall to Mlle Menier, was languishing in a dark cell in Montluc, apparently without hope. Virginia had to come up with another plan for him.[27]

As if one rogue girlfriend was not enough, around this time *Alain*'s former amour Germaine Jouve was released after six weeks in the same prison. As feared, she was consumed with fury at finding him in the arms of a younger woman – the sister-in-law of another leader of *Le Coq enchaîné*. It cannot be a coincidence that soon after twenty-four members of the group were arrested and some were clearly talking. The fear now was that Jouve was also in a position to sell SOE agents including Virginia herself so she urgently asked for more pills from London, but Jouve disappeared before she could eliminate her.[28] The threats on all sides had driven Virginia to become a battle-hardened assassin, a far cry from the Virginia of January who could not even bring herself to swear in her letter to Bodington. 'I have not been able to touch Germaine,' she gravely warned London on 30 September. This new version of Virginia understood it was now a case of killing others to survive.

Alain was soon off the scene for a different reason. F Section finally realised his womanising, boasting and boozing – and lack of any significant achievement – made him a threat to himself and others. Baker Street re-evaluated him as 'a bluffer, vain and boastful'[29] and recalled him to London. He tried to bring his new mistress, before other agents intervened and sent her packing, pushing *Alain* onto the plane alone. 'We are all vastly relieved . . . that A has departed,' Virginia reported, but she demanded guidance from London on what to do with all the weapons supplied to him by SOE. She feared that if she lost control of them a bloody anarchy could break out between rival resistance organisations. 'I don't know how or where it will all end,' she warned. London would have been saved a lot of trouble if it had listened to Virginia from the start.

Virginia now constantly sensed she was being watched. There were a handful of faces she felt she saw too often to be a coincidence. The sound of footsteps behind her gave her shivers; the sight of the dreaded black Gestapo Citroëns was becoming too frequent. She took to the backstreets, melting into the *traboules*, clinging to the shadows, constantly glancing up at the windows above her in case of sudden movements, hoping to render herself almost invisible. Yet the intense heat merely added to the sickening fear that the Gestapo were rapidly closing in. One sweltering August afternoon a regular guest was at work in a spacious flat on the Quai Perrache belonging to Joseph Marchand. Marchand, a valiant long-term *résistant*, was sitting with his wife and two other SOE agents as one of Virginia's wireless operators, *Grégoire*, tapped away at his set, having already put in several hours of transmitting and receiving. Intelligence from Lyon was highly prized and on this occasion the former American Express employee had just sent London important news about the SS chief Heinrich Himmler secretly planning to visit Toulouse. The message led to leaflets being printed up and dropped by the RAF over the city that very night, warning its inhabitants. Fearful for his safety, an enraged Himmler would be forced to cancel his visit.

Finally, *Grégoire* lifted off his earphones and began to take down his aerial, believing he had finished for the day. His face and body were running with sweat from the concentration of his work and the stifling lack of air. Suddenly there was a shriek of tyres from the road outside, followed by car doors banging and the sound of people shouting. Madame Marchand leaped to the window, only to see what they had been dreading. Three black Citroëns and the classic grey-green radio detector van of the Funkabwehr were blocking the street. Further down the road a military-style truck was hurtling in their direction. '*Bon Dieu!*' she exclaimed as six men in civilian clothes yelling in German stormed into the building while another four uniformed troops, sub-machine guns at the ready, took up positions at the entrance to the flats.

Virginia wanted to catch *Grégoire* with some last-minute messages before he finished for the day so she was at that moment hurrying towards the Marchands' apartment block. She was about to turn the corner, straight into the mêlée, when she paused for a moment before veering off into a newsagent's to make sure that no one was following her. She asked for a newspaper, and as the shopkeeper gave her her change he leant towards her and whispered, 'Don't go up, the police are there.' She turned and vanished – but it had been another close call.

Virginia was relieved to hear later that *Grégoire* had managed to hide his set on the top of a kitchen cupboard and that the five of them had pretended to be in the midst of a game of cards. The Germans had in any case thought the signals must be coming from higher up in the block. But the flat was now another safe-house that was *brûlé* and there were precious few addresses that were still uncompromised. Shortly afterwards, the Gestapo descended on Edward Zeff. He too had just finished transmitting when there was loud banging at the door of his block of flats and shouts of 'Police, open up!' He raced to the entrance to be the one to open it, and was asked: 'On which floor is the Englishman?' 'On the second floor,' he replied, 'but I saw him go out not ten minutes ago – that way.' They went roaring off, allowing Zeff to collect his set and 'make his getaway, before like maddened bulls they were back for him'.[30] Step by step the Germans were tightening the net.

Brian Stonehouse or *Célestin*, a twenty-four-year-old fashion illustrator for *Vogue* blessed with model good looks and a gentle soul, was another of Virginia's protégés. He had parachuted in in June to act as wireless operator to Philippe de Vomécourt, or *Gauthier*. As usual, *Gauthier* showed no regard for the new arrival's safety – and had not bothered to show up at the landing ground. *Célestin*'s set had become tangled in a tree and he had been left to sleep alone in a wood for five nights while he tried to get it down.

Even when he had managed to make contact with *Gauthier*, the ragged-looking French aristocrat had not provided *Célestin* with anywhere to live or work, or indeed any protection while he was transmitting. *Célestin* had to make do with the flimsy cover of being a dress designer and hiding his wireless set, the size of a small suitcase, under a bundle of fashion drawings. *Gauthier*'s stance was that 'all this security stuff is overdone by London'[31] and that *Célestin* was acting as if in need of a nanny by asking for passwords and safehouses. (Responsible circuit chiefs, by contrast, deployed lookouts for their wireless operators, primed to raise the alarm at the first sight of a black Citroën or men in black leather jackets and felt hats, the plain-clothes choice of the Gestapo.) *Célestin* was under intolerable strain and became seriously ill with dysentery, so Dr Rousset sheltered him for a while in his clinic. But then he once again had nowhere to go and had also lost his identity papers. Whatever the dangers, Virginia simply could not abandon him, so she took him home, but it was clear his presence was making her existence even more perilous. There had been yet another round of arrests, including of *Constantin*, the brother of *Gauthier* and *Sylvain*. Virginia was ordered to isolate herself completely from anyone connected to any of them. No one knew who would be next.

Meanwhile, a job advertisement appeared in the Lyon press for a wholesale groceries representative. New positions were rare – and many were desperate to feed their families somehow – and so it was not surprising to see a crush of applicants waiting for interview at a recruitment bureau's offices. Some of them were particularly friendly, immediately striking up conversation with their neighbours. Those who came over as sympathetic to the German cause were invited to go on to a café afterwards to continue the conversation over a beer. Not until this point did it become clear that the whole set-up was a Gestapo front. An enormous offer of twenty thousand francs a month was made, with a possible fifteen-thousand-franc bonus for outstanding work. The task was simple: to denounce anyone connected with the Resistance, or who might simply sympathise with the Allies, or who even uttered an anti-German sentiment.[32] Many found it an attractive proposition. The new recruits soon spread out across the whole of the city. They got to work in the streets, cafés, shops and stations, and there were certain figures they were specifically instructed to look out for, including a woman who limped.

On 4 August – the day before Virginia's recall to London was officially cancelled – a youngish priest in long black robes rapped on the high wooden double doors leading to Dr Rousset's surgery at 7 place Antonin-Poncet. The inner courtyard was as busy as ever, but when he was admitted, the priest demanded to see *Pépin* himself, explaining that he was the new courier from the *WOL* circuit in Paris. The priest handed over a number of microfilms in an envelope marked *Marie Monin* for dispatch to London, just as the previous courier had done. The doctor had never seen the man before, but was happy to take the parcel as he knew from Virginia that *WOL*'s intelligence was highly regarded in London. A good Catholic, he was reassured by the visitor's religious calling and of course the fact he knew the protocol, such as *Marie*'s name on the envelope, his own field name of *Pépin*, and the right password for a representative of *WOL*. The priest asked for the two hundred thousand francs that was due for his circuit's expenses – only to be told that *Marie* had not known he was coming so had not left it at the surgery. Would he care to wait? The priest would not, but said he would be back in a week.

As it turned out, it was three weeks before he made another appearance on 25 August. This time he was insistent on meeting

Marie in person as he had important news to impart. Rousset was relieved to see him again and happy to fetch his chief so that she could hand over the money herself. He scurried over the Pont de l'Université to place Ollier, checked that the flower pot was on the windowsill to signal the all-clear, and knocked softly on Virginia's door. When she answered, *Pépin* told her that the WOL courier had finally returned from Paris and she was required urgently. She grabbed an envelope stuffed with cash from behind a cupboard and followed the doctor back to his surgery at a safe distance. She then slipped past the waiting patients into a private side room. Inside, her eyes immediately fell on a powerfully built clergyman in a black cassock, with piercing blue eyes, tight mouth and prominent dimpled chin. She noted that Abbé Robert Alesch stared at her and appeared slightly ill at ease when he asked if she were *Marie Monin*. But it was Virginia who froze with horror at the unmistakable sound of a heavy German accent, right in the heart of her network's headquarters. Registering her reaction, he explained that he came from the border region of Alsace, which had been annexed by Germany in 1940, but that he was currently a priest in suburban Paris, in a parish called La Varenne-Saint-Hilaire. He apologised that his colleagues in the WOL circuit had not warned her that he was coming. But he had had to insist to Dr Rousset that he see her in person.

WOL, one of the most active circuits in Paris, was another part of Virginia's kingdom. Since its wireless operator had been arrested in March, it had been bringing her vital intelligence on German coastal defences to transmit back to London. The information was of such quality she had been authorised to pay a hundred thousand francs a month in expenses to the joint circuit chief Jacques Legrand. He was yet another Parisian who had asked her for help after hearing of her good work through the capital's Resistance grapevine. She agreed, even though WOL was not part of SOE – although it was backed by MI6, and Legrand himself had once worked for *Sylvain*. Virginia had also taken comfort from the fact that its other joint chief was Gabrielle Picabia,* who had served with her in the French ambulance corps in 1940. Other leading lights were Samuel Beckett and the anthropologist Germaine Tillion, so it all seemed above board.

Back in July Legrand had handed her another 109 photographs and maps (dutifully gathered by his network of Scout masters and youth leaders) but explained that this visit would have to be his last. It was too dangerous for him to continue coming as he believed the Gestapo were on to him, so he would send someone else to deliver the microfilms in future. Alesch's first visit had been shortly after.

On the occasion of 25 August, however, Alesch had come empty-handed, blaming the need to lie low following the arrest of a *WOL* colleague with a list of agents in his pocket. He smiled and expressed grave concern for her own safety, warning *Marie* that Lyon was 'extremely menaced and that great prudence should be observed'. He then made an unexpected request. He urged her to provide him with a radio set, which he said would come in useful for the resistance group in Paris and cut out the risk of travelling down to Lyon. Perhaps he registered her surprise at his asking so soon for such a valuable item, as he immediately switched to talk of how closely he was working with his chief. As if to prove it, he gave her a handwritten note from Legrand, reminding her of something they had previously discussed. Reassured, Virginia gave the abbé the envelope of money and wished him 'God speed'.[33] He stowed the cash in his bag, put on his beret and left.

Alesch had gone out of his way to prove his credentials, including the fact that his own father had been shot by the Germans.

---

* The daughter of the Dadaist painter Francis Picabia.

He had spouted trenchant anti-Nazi rhetoric during their meeting and had on his previous visit delivered what appeared to be extremely useful intelligence on the Atlantic Wall, the massive but as yet uncompleted coastal fortifications that Hitler hoped would prevent an Allied landing in France. He had also known *Pépin*'s address and both their codenames. Even if Virginia harboured a gnawing doubt, Dr Rousset was impressed by the fact that Alesch was a man of the cloth and he had heard that he denounced the Third Reich in his sermons. And while the hierarchy of the Roman Catholic Church supported Vichy, both he and Virginia knew that many of its parish priests secretly backed the Resistance. The abbé had also given her the note from Jacques Legrand, which she could see was legitimate because she recognised the handwriting. True, Baker Street had sounded a slight warning about Virginia working with MI6's circuits, which they could not vet for themselves, rather than sticking only to SOE's. But it was possible that F Section was merely perpetuating the turf war with its intelligence service rivals. Virginia and Dr Rousset discussed the abbé and what he could do for them, and decided to welcome him into the fold. They gave him the codename *Bishop*.

Over the following week, however, Virginia suffered a crisis of confidence. One of her best couriers, just back from Marseille, hurried to inform her that *WOL* had been devastated by arrests in mid-August, with both Legrand and Germaine Tillion in the hands of the Gestapo. In other words, Alesch had come to see her after that disaster and not even mentioned it. Then her trusted Marseille courier had suddenly been arrested too and disappeared. Finally, on 1 September, an MI6 agent codenamed *Blanchet* turned up at the surgery, giving Alesch's name as a reference. He claimed the abbé owed him seventy-five thousand francs and he demanded repayment as well as a pistol to help him escape to Spain. Luckily, Virginia did not see him personally but signalled London for instructions, and was warned to cut *Blanchet* loose as he was now considered a traitor (and was in fact working for Bleicher). 'At no price are you to have contact with or help this very dangerous man: if he persists in bothering you, you are fully authorised to treat the problem as neatly as possible.' Virginia again had a licence to kill.[34] 'Certain friends' duly executed him in a villa on the Corniche in Marseille.

Virginia confessed to London that all this made her increasingly uneasy. When Alesch reappeared on 2 September she confronted him, but he was quick to explain himself. He had also been worried, he said, about not hearing from Legrand, but had not wanted to alarm Virginia until he knew for certain what had happened. As for Germaine Tillion, he had only recently heard that she had been rounded up too. He had, however, managed to track down Gabrielle Picabia and had handed over *Marie*'s money to her, but had since lost contact with her as well. When Virginia asked him to describe Picabia, he said she was tall and blonde whereas she was in fact a petite brunette.[35] Perhaps realising he had made a mistake Alesch, seeming suddenly unsure of himself, meekly asked for her instructions and advice. He did what he had rightly observed worked best in winning over a woman who so desperately needed to be needed; he asked Virginia for her support.

Even so, Virginia remained chilled by his insistence on being put in contact with other members of her circuit in case she 'disappeared over night'. For what possible reason could he need to know other names? What made him think she might disappear? She was too canny, of course, to agree to everything demanded by the man she now referred to as her 'problem child'. But she was rattled enough to seek advice. 'Can you check on him and give me instructions?' she asked Baker Street two days later. 'I can't believe he's a phoney,'[36] she added, not least because of his familiarity with intimate details of her work with *WOL*. And yet neither could she entirely banish such thoughts. Baker Street agreed to put Alesch through the cards but came up with nothing. They nevertheless encouraged Virginia to have no more to do with him, just to be safe.

Perhaps her exhaustion after so long in the field had worn her down. Perhaps she had become too confident in her own precautions. Or maybe she simply saw the material provided by *WOL* as too valuable to lose. And in any case Rousset, whose judgement she valued, continued to believe in the priest. She had grown used to harbouring doubts about just about everyone; after all, complete trust in the secret war was impossible and dangerous. She also considered herself an astute judge of character – so she decided she could handle Alesch. When she saw him again on 1 October he supplied her with another apparently exceptional haul of films, papers and maps for transmission to London. He was really turning into a golden informant. With Baker Street's blessing she handed him a hundred thousand francs and even a newly arrived radio set. In return, she instructed him to obtain specific military information that would assist future Allied plans – and also revealed what they might be. There were lingering doubts in London and in Virginia's mind, but they both allowed the apparent quality of Alesch's material to quell them. And once she had put her faith in the abbé, her vast army of supporters thought it safe to do the same.

It was an error on Baker Street and Virginia's part that was to have devastating consequences. Alesch had not misremembered Picabia's appearance because he had never met her, let alone given her the money. He had already spent a large part of it on living a high life with two parishioners who served as his mistresses and whom he paid lavishly. He was drinking fine wines in the cabarets of Montmartre and was about to move into a gilded eight-room apartment in the chic sixteenth *arrondissement* at 46 rue Spontini, decorated with fine works of art bought with SOE cash. His father had not been killed by the Germans, but was very much alive. Alesch – or rather Agent *Axel* of the Abwehr, code number GV7162 – had succeeded beyond his wildest expectations. Driven by personal ambition, he had railed at missing out on a plum priest's job at the fashionable Saint-Joseph's church in rue La Fayette in Paris, and having to make do with a living in an unglamorous backwater. In reality a native of Luxembourg, he had soon worked out that he needed German backing if he were to achieve his aims – and make a fortune in the process. In late 1941 he had become a naturalised German and approached the Abwehr with an offer to spy for them. They immediately saw his potential.

First he allowed his charisma, and habit of handing out photographs of General de Gaulle at mass, to win his parishioners' confidence. After hearing his violently anti-Nazi pronouncements in church, local youths soon came to confide in him about their work for the Resistance. When he thundered about their arrests from the pulpit some time later – after betraying them to his German masters – he won the admiration of his unsuspecting flock. So when he heard of WOL, and approached them with the idea of getting involved they saw him as someone they could trust. And when Legrand could no longer travel to Lyon for security reasons, it made sense to send Alesch in his place. He could hide the matchbox containing microfilm in his cassock and use the travel pass that came with his job to cross the demarcation line without trouble. WOL gave him Dr Rousset's address, the relevant codenames and passwords, and the package for *Marie Monin*. From that moment her fate was sealed.

The Abwehr were obviously delighted to have finally tracked

down this woman. They were even more thrilled when Alesch duly opened the package given him by *WOL* and showed them the intelligence on the Atlantic Wall – giving Nazi High Command a valuable glimpse of Allied intentions. The Germans then cleverly doctored the material before Alesch took it down to Lyon.

On 12 August *WOL* asked Alesch to travel to Lyon again. This time they gave him the letter to Virginia from Legrand and urged him to see the woman the *résistants* described as 'la personne principale',[37] *Marie*. They also arranged to give him another package, which they said was extremely important. Alesch's Nazi paymasters once again looked at the explosive contents, recognised their exceptional accuracy, and decided it was time to draft in the Gestapo to liquidate the whole *WOL* circuit. Plain-clothes officers trailed Alesch to the Café des Voutes in place de la Bastille, where he had arranged to meet Germaine Tillion and another key *WOL* member, supposedly to finalise his plans. All three were then followed to the Gare du Lyon and as he went through the ticket barrier onto the platform unhindered, the Gestapo seized Tillion and her partner. They were last seen being pushed into a black Citroën on their way to the interrogation chambers at Gestapo headquarters in rue des Saussaies.

The package contained photographs and plans of the coastal defences of Dieppe in extraordinary and exact detail. The Abwehr understood its probable significance and tipped off Nazi High Command that they should prepare for an attack on the Channel port. When the Allied commando raid took place just a week later, on 19 August, deprived of the crucial element of surprise it came up against unexpectedly fierce counter-fire from well-prepared German forces. Fatally, the raiding force had had to rely on old holiday snapshots and was unaware of gun positions on the surrounding cliffs. The men were soon kettled under fire on the beach and well over half – or nearly four thousand men, most of them Canadians – were killed, captured or wounded. Without the vital *WOL* intelligence, the assault had been an appallingly expensive failure.

Following Alesch's directions the Gestapo had meanwhile also arrested Jacques Legrand, taken his papers and tortured him without mercy before deporting him to Mauthausen camp in Austria, where he died. They had then rounded up another sixty members of *WOL*. Many were never seen again. One of London's best sources of intelligence was snuffed out for ever. The fact was that Alesch had not kept his appointment in Lyon on 11 August because he had been too busy helping the Gestapo in Paris. And yet when he finally met Virginia on 25 August he was able to behave as if nothing had ever happened.

Alesch made a couple of later trips to Virginia and continued to provide her with what looked like similarly useful intelligence, but which was in fact almost useless. Virginia was now at the centre of a vicious Nazi game; she was truly being played. Such was his triumph that the Abwehr was only too happy to pay Alesch up to twenty-five thousand francs a month for his efforts – and offered him fine art they had looted from museums as bonuses. But the biggest prizes of all were the large sums of cash given to him in good faith by the many people he had betrayed – likely to have totalled nearer one million francs. Now he was a rich man, and a celebrated one at the Abwehr's Paris headquarters at the art deco Hôtel Lutetia on the Left Bank, which he regularly visited in layman's clothes. His Abwehr paymasters, Captain Karl Schaeffer and Colonel Reile, had waited for a long time to track down *Marie Monin* and now they finally had her in their sights. They were also delighted to be able to play *Funkspiel* with London again, by sending misleading radio messages purporting to come from one of Virginia's best contacts. Schaeffer and Reile were pleased with the abbé, whom they considered to have done '*bon*

travail' on *'l'affaire de* Miss Mary'.[38] The Abwehr had now penetrated Virginia's network to the extent that they could intercept
and break many of her coded messages. By early October they
even knew that she suspected Alesch of being a German agent.
They would therefore use him only sparingly from now on.[39]
And they would move in on Virginia when the time was right
and she was no longer so useful. Or if the Gestapo looked like
getting there first.

Chapter Seven

Cruel Mountain

After all the recent arrests, but especially those of Rake, *Constantin* and *Olive*, Virginia had a dramatic change of heart. Although unaware of the Abwehr penetration, she finally conceded that she had no choice but to leave before the Germans took over the Free Zone. On 21 September she asked London to arrange her ticket for a Clipper* flight from Lisbon so that she could apply for the necessary visas and 'clear out if necessary'. 'I think my time has come,' she reported regretfully. 'My address has been given to Vichy, although not my name, but it wouldn't be hard to guess.' Peter Churchill also picked up that Virginia was definitely in the frame. 'The old spotlight is playing round and round,' he warned London, 'and the colour of this light is very red indeed. In fact, the heat is positively on.'[1] Virginia wanted to leave openly as the *New York Post* correspondent, fearing that an unexplained departure

---

* The Clipper, made by Boeing, was a long-range flying boat and one of the largest aircraft of the time.

would create problems for those she left behind. Also, to help her successors she started to hand her equipment, such as official stamps for making false papers, to a former Mayfair hairdresser codenamed *Nicolas*. She considered him competent if 'very quiet' but as he was the most senior remaining agent, she had no choice but to entrust him with these precious items now.

Virginia warned London that she could no longer shelter *Célestin*, however. 'I am sorry to say that I shall have to drop him again now as I may be watched, or at least my house may be supervised,' she signalled London. 'However, I hope he will get a place to live soon.' And for once she was not going to be able to mount a rescue attempt for *Olive*. 'On account of the above I am afraid that it will be impossible for me to do much,' she said, before tartly suggesting someone else might take on at least some of the 'escape business': 'I do think they might tend to their own knitting on the coast.' Yet Virginia being Virginia, she did not keep to her detached position for long. Despite the obvious dangers, Peter Churchill persuaded her that she was *Olive*'s last chance and a week later was reporting gleefully to London that he had 'new hopes' for his beleaguered colleague now that she was 'going through the hospital routine'.[2] In case that failed, she also opened negotiations via an intermediary (a friendly French army colonel she had cultivated) with the commandant of Montluc prison over the size of the bribe necessary to secure *Olive*'s release. She could never resist the call to help others, for all the peril she was in herself and so she told London to delay her departure once again. Not knowing, of course, that the Abwehr were listening in to virtually every word.

Germaine Guérin lent Virginia an apartment near her brothel on rue Garibaldi from the beginning of October, because 'astounding personages'[3] had been turning up day and night at place Ollier asking her to send them to England. Virginia's new residence was more tucked away, not least because it was on the sixth floor and the lift was broken. With Cuthbert it was a hard climb, but its inaccessibility would help cut down on visitors and the concierge was a loyal member of the Resistance who would look out for her. Evidently Virginia believed moving house would buy her time. 'I may postpone my departure if I can't get [the prisoners] out before, or if things look all right and I can be useful,' she informed London. She even found time to do her expenses, sending Baker Street her receipts since 1 August and showing that much of the money had gone on arranging various escapes. 'But as I am not very good at keeping accounts they may seem a bit strange. I trust you will sort them out.'[4]

With Virginia's help, *Célestin* had found new quarters as well, in the attics of the sixteenth-century Hurlevent château, just south of Lyon at Feyzin. Zeff had by now taken time off to recover his health, and so *Célestin*'s workload was intense. By the morning of 24 October he had been at his set for almost forty-eight hours straight, mostly organising parachute drops of arms and explosives. Suddenly the power went off – the agreed danger signal from the château's owners Monsieur and Madame Jourdan. *Célestin* jumped to the window to see that a ring of black Citroëns had already encircled the property. It was too late to escape. He and his assistant tried to hide his radio and papers in the cellar via a lift shaft, but despite their frantic efforts there was no time to lower everything out of sight. Plainclothes Gestapo were already running up the stairs, and burst into the room with guns trained on their prey. *Célestin* was one of the first – but by no means the last – radio operator to fall to Operation Donar.

The Gestapo had moved in as soon as they were sure of the source of the signals picked up by a radio detector van. Now they seized *Célestin*'s wireless and papers, handcuffed him and drove him to Lyon for interrogation. To his horror, the Gestapo found what they had most wanted in his pocket. It was an old decoded message from *Gauthier* that contained an obvious clue that his real name was Philippe de Vomécourt. It also gave the actual address of one of his assistants in Lyon, J. M. Aron, a senior Citroën executive and one of the fiercest critics of what he called Virginia's nanny-style security. Worst of all, the message referred to a *Marie* as the leader of an SOE circuit called *Heckler*.[5] *Célestin* admitted to being the owner of the radio, but even under extreme duress refused to answer any further questions.

Aron was arrested soon after at Lyon station, as were the half-dozen other *résistants* who came unwittingly to his *poste de commande*, as well as another connected group in Marseille. For all his bravado, Aron cracked under torture and gave away *Gauthier* (who was arrested a fortnight later) and the location of SOE's stores of arms and explosives. A diary found in the stash led to a further flurry of arrests. It was lucky in the extreme that earlier in the summer Virginia had distanced herself from both Aron and *Gauthier* and their information on her was now out of date. That was not, of course, the case with *Célestin*, whom she had seen very recently. Yet despite the unimaginable treatment he suffered at the hands of the Gestapo, the fashion illustrator's heroic silence bought Virginia a few more days. Again and again they asked him about *Marie* or 'that terrorist'. They got no answer. But the Gestapo smelled blood.

Within hours of the arrests dozens of SOE couriers were dispatched to raise the alarm right across the Free Zone. Some were instructed to wear a specific colour of clothing or to make a certain sign while walking past a particular building at a particular time. This signalled to those who knew to look: 'Caution! Lie low until you receive instructions.' One young woman was ordered to take a crowded train to the town where her elderly relatives lived, a hundred kilometres away. On her arrival she was to visit a certain café at precisely 9.45 in the evening and order a black coffee and three aspirins. She never knew the reason or even noticed that a man playing dominoes on a neighbouring table heard the phrase and hurried off to warn his colleagues that the 'heat was on'.

Understandably, news of *Célestin*'s arrest made Virginia nervy. Two days later she was badgering London for her Clipper ticket, which had not yet arrived. She was told that she needed to provide her passport details so she signalled them over on 4 November and the next day Nicolas Bodington instructed SOE's New York office to arrange the visas and ticket from Lisbon 'as soon as possible'. Her departure could not be more urgent.

Despite the furore, Virginia was busy finalising audacious new plans for the Castres men, who had now been joined by *Célestin*. Intelligence officers often talk about sharing a creed of protecting their colleagues and the trauma of leaving fellow agents behind.[6] There was no way she was not going to see this through as a matter of duty and, yes, pride. She had carefully worked out every detail based on her unrivalled record of similarly daredevil operations. A vehicle that could pass as a German staff car had already been appropriated complete with authentic number plates and an SS uniform for the driver. Two of her trusted agents (Henry and Alfred Newton) would dress up as gendarmes and two others would pose as plainclothes Gestapo officers in polo-neck jumpers, dark green riding breeches and polished jackboots. Virginia drilled them on how they should sign the log book on arrival at the prison and then produce four 'prisoner transfer forms' (from one of her army of expert counterfeiters) with orders to move the British prisoners to another jail. When the prisoners were brought out, the 'Gestapo' should bundle them into the waiting vehicle, followed by the 'gendarmes', and then drive off at speed. If the warders became suspicious at any time, the 'Gestapo' should press the alarm bells as a decoy, seize the phones to prevent calls for help and shoot it out with anyone in pursuit of the car.[7]

Sourcing the gendarme uniforms had proved difficult, however. Finding them in the right size was almost impossible. The Newtons – acrobats in a variety troupe who had toured Europe's theatres before the war as the Boorn Brothers – were simply too beefy and the tightly stretched outfits made them look more matador than policeman.[8] So Virginia decided to recruit two genuine gendarmes who were 'willing to desert and do the job'.[9] This too was to prove challenging as it would place the officers and their families in grave danger. They would need to be shipped out of France immediately afterwards, and their families put under the protection of the Resistance. The Newtons were especially eager to help solve the problem. Both were driven by a hatred of the Third Reich after the unimaginable tragedy of losing their parents, wives and children in September 1941 when a U-boat torpedoed the SS *Avoceta*, the passenger ship taking them home from Lisbon to Liverpool. So the brothers took it upon themselves to approach several contacts in the gendarmerie at Le Puy, and at the end of October got lucky.

Greatly relieved, Virginia rushed over to her collaborators in Limoges. She was particularly grateful for the devoted support of the perennially cheerful and obliging Marcel Leccia, whose presence never failed to raise her spirits. He was, she generously told London, doing most of the work in putting 'the final touches to the plans for the "Castres" party'. Guth was obviously kept out of it but the Newtons – affectionately known as the Twins although they were actually nine years apart in age – would escort the volunteer gendarmes to Lyon for a final briefing on 11

November before carrying out the operation in the early hours of the following day. Now realistic about her future, Virginia warned them that if there were an occupation she would have to leave immediately, so they should not be surprised at any abrupt departure. Just in case, she gave them thirty thousand francs to cover expenses, and fulsome instructions including how to find help afterwards to cross the Pyrenees into Spain.

Shortly after her return from Limoges on Saturday 7 November, the American consulate contacted her with news of Operation Torch from its few remaining colleagues at the embassy in Vichy. The invasion of North Africa was imminent, meaning that full German occupation was too. She must leave, they told her, or suffer the consequences. Even now Virginia wanted to resist the inevitable, still fervently hoping to see the Castres operation succeed. Nevertheless, she began to liquidate all her affairs, arranging a wireless operator for the Twins and destroying the papers at her flat. She gave *Nicolas* the last of her seals for false documents and a number of blank ration cards, and left two hundred thousand francs with the Mesdemoiselles Fellot to distribute to the Twins, *Vic* of the escape line and Edward Zeff, who was on his way back to work again in Lyon. She found a safehouse for a female courier on the run with the friendly nuns up at La Mulatière. And perhaps most importantly, she made one last contact with the commandant at Montluc to finalise the release of *Olive*.

Early the next morning, a hundred thousand Allied troops under the command of the American major-general Dwight Eisenhower landed in Vichy-held North Africa at Algiers, Oran and Casablanca in the first joint mass Allied offensive of the war. Marshal Pétain ignored pleas, even from some of his own ministers, to fly to Algiers and declare himself on the Anglo-American side. Instead he ordered French troops to fight back against the

Allies, although such resistance soon petered out. He also broke off diplomatic relations with America and interned the most senior officer at the United States embassy, the chargé d'affaires Pinkney Tuck, along with his staff. (Admiral Leahy had already been recalled to Washington.[10]) Nothing would now stop Hitler from tearing up the armistice agreement and flooding Pétain's domain in southern France with his troops and tanks. Any attempt by the Allies to attack Hitler's territory from their new base on the other side of the Mediterranean would be met with the Wehrmacht's iron fist. Within hours Virginia's friends and protectors would become powerless in a full Nazi state where German terror would be unbridled. The Resistance would be crushed, with no holds barred. How could she stay and hope to survive?

Virginia rose early and on hearing the news, ever conscientious, dashed off to tie up loose ends. While hurrying through the eerily empty streets she bumped into an ex-agent of the French secret service, the Deuxième Bureau, who had been helpful in the past. He heartily advised her to leave at once. She would not go, however, before seeing the Twins, who had gone to meet a friendly gendarme about the Castres operation and were due to report back to her apartment at six that evening. She returned to rue Garibaldi to receive them but they never came. She nervously waited even longer for *Nicolas* to arrive as he had promised, so she could give him further instructions. But he too did not turn up. 'I decided they were nervous about coming to the flat or else took it for granted that I had left,' she reported to London. Virginia went out again at nine in the evening to track down the French intelligence agent for further news, but he pleaded with her to disappear immediately as her life depended on it. No French protector, no American diplomat, no cover as a journalist could help her now. The Germans knew all about her and would come for her without mercy. He had even had word that an advance guard was expected in Lyon – its first target city – some time between midnight and the morning. Virginia made one final visit to her apartment, packed the rest of her money and a bag of clothes and lugged it as quickly as she could, Cuthbert permitting, along the two-mile walk to the station. She made the last train south out of Lyon, which left at eleven o'clock, by the skin of her teeth.

Virginia had told no one, not even Rousset or Germaine, that she was bound for Perpignan, three hundred miles away. It was a long night. The track meandered painfully through the factories, silk warehouses and oil refineries of southern Lyon to Marseille, where she had to change train under the tense and watchful eyes of knots of Gestapo officers. By now she assumed that the Germans would most likely be in Lyon and intent on bringing her in. She did not yet know that Alesch had provided his new masters in the Gestapo – he worked for whoever was willing to pay – an accurate description of her appearance, but no doubt she had donned one of her disguises to get her through the snap controls.

After a sleepless night she arrived safely at Perpignan, twenty miles from the Spanish border near the eastern edge of the Pyrenees. It was a rebellious old French Catalan town with an edgy atmosphere, but one she had got to know well having used it as a base to help so many others to escape. She checked in at the Hôtel de la Cloche, where the owners were sympathisers, and stayed out of sight in her room until the afternoon, when she knew that a contact, *Gilbert*, spent an hour on the square every day between two and three. *Gilbert* immediately spotted the tall, striking American woman he knew as *Germaine* hovering half out of sight behind the trees. He had done business with her before and he signalled for her to follow him down a side street where they could talk. The biting north wind cut through them even down here on the coastal plain, and the November air smelt of snow. But Virginia's only chance of escape lay over one of the

Virginia spent idyllic childhood summers at Boxhorn, the family farm in Maryland. The house was spacious and elegant, but lacked central heating and pumped water from a stream. Her mother Barbara had greater social ambitions.

The young Virginia loved country life and dressing in tomboy clothes. Dindy, as her family called her, was fearless and proud and revelled in being unlike her less adventurous female peers.

Virginia and her more conservative elder brother John were close growing up together on the farm but held very different outlooks on life. Later on, John did not always approve of his sister's 'modern' ways.

Virginia adored her eternally dapper father Ned, who similarly doted on his unusual daughter and indulged her yearning for travel and adventure. His early death was devastating.

From an early age Virginia had an empathy with animals that would prove unexpectedly useful during the war. Here she is in her teens wearing pigeons as a hat, and on another occasion she wore snakes as a bracelet into school.

Virginia was posted to Tallinn in the late 1930s and loved hunting in the huge forests of Estonia, but otherwise her life was a series of cruel rejections. Her lifelong ambition to become a diplomat was repeatedly thwarted, and she was frustrated by the limits of her role as a State Department clerk.

The loneliness and fear of operating behind enemy lines was a heavy burden. Some agents found they could trust no one except their own reflections. Undated self-portrait.

(Left) Virginia's striking good looks made her a conspicuous figure during the war, especially after her face appeared on WANTED posters. On her return to the field, she adopted a disguise created by Hollywood make-up artists and refugee tailors operating an atelier behind Oxford Circus. It fooled practically everyone. *(Middle)* Frustrated by the restrictions of Prohibition-era America, Virginia crossed the Atlantic when she was only twenty for the freedoms of Paris. Its literary, artistic and music scene engendered a fierce love of France and later a determination to fight the growing threat of European fascism. *(Right)* Virginia had style and was brought up in the expectation of an advantageous marriage. She had several suitors, but held most expressions of male ardour in contempt. Her ambitions were much greater.

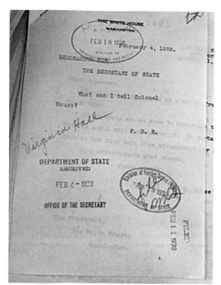

President Roosevelt himself became embroiled in the row over Virginia being banned from the Diplomatic Service.

The *Baltimore Sun* ran a story in January 1934 on Virginia's hunting accident in Turkey. The rest of her life became a mission to prove what she could still do.

Virginia came up with an ingenious way of bypassing the hundreds of challenging bridges of Venice.

Virginia's way with farm animals would later enable her to collect vital intelligence for the Allied offensive after D-Day.

A painting by Jeff Bass of Virginia urgently transmitting messages from Léa Lebrat's farm in the Haute-Loire, July 1944, with Edmond Lebrat providing the power with an adapted bicycle. The original is in the CIA Fine Arts Collection.

Virginia organised one of the most successful prison breaks of the war, from Mauzac prison camp in the Dordogne. Twelve SOE agents, shown here with other helpers, were whisked off to safety, but few knew the full extent of her role.

Virginia managed to have the SOE men moved from Périgueux fortress jail to Mauzac, where she knew they had a much better chance of escape. She found ingenious ways of smuggling in messages, tools and even a radio transmitter.

Virginia proved her exceptional courage under fire in 1940 by volunteering to drive ambulances on the front line for the French army's SAA, or Service de Santé des Armées.

The abbé Robert Alesch was one of the most deadly German double agents of the war.

Henry and Alfred Newton (shown here in 1938) had been entertainers before the war but lost their entire family when a passenger ship taking them home was torpedoed by the Germans. They became valiant supporters of Virginia, but were caught and tortured by the Gestapo.

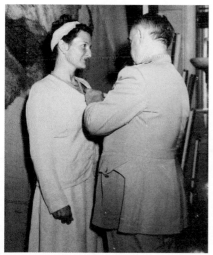

Virginia was the only civilian woman in the Second World War to be awarded the Distinguished Service Cross, for extraordinary heroism against the enemy. She received the medal in Washington, DC from 'Wild Bill' Donovan in a low-key ceremony on 27 September 1945.

Only Virginia's mother Barbara accompanied her when she went to receive her decoration. Donovan, director of the OSS, was one of her greatest admirers and regaled most of Washington with tales of her heroism.

Virginia's strategic sabotage campaign was devastatingly effective. The railway bridge at Chamalières was blown up on 2 August 1944 and a locomotive driven at high speed into the breach.

German forces surrender at Estivareilles on 22 August 1944 after a successful guerrilla offensive. In large part thanks to Virginia, the Haute-Loire was one of the first *départements* of France to be liberated outside Normandy.

A solitary maquisard on patrol near St-Clément on the Haute-Loire plateau.

(*Left*) 'Bob' or Raoul le Boulicat, one of Virginia's most devoted helpers on the plateau. He died in 1946, aged twenty-six, from his war injuries. (*Middle*) Virginia called the ever-grinning Gabriel Eyraud her *chouchou*, or pet. An orphan, he saw Virginia and the Maquis as family. He died in 2017, the last of the *Diane* Irregulars. (*Right*) Virginia rated Ben Cowburn, an engineer from Lancashire with an impish grin, as the greatest SOE agent in France. The admiration was mutual.

(*Left*) Maurice Buckmaster, a former Ford Motor Company manager in France, brought 'the optimism of a sales director' into SOE but some saw his cheeriness as naivety. (*Middle*) Virginia fought bitterly with *Alain*, or Georges Duboudin, over his womanising and boozing. She considered him a security risk. (*Right*) The dashing Marcel Leccia was Virginia's closest comrade-in-arms and a heroic figure. He never failed her but he paid a bitter price.

(*Left*) Brian Stonehouse, or *Célestin*, was a fashion illustrator for *Vogue* in civilian life but proved the bravest of agents. He refused to reveal Virginia's name or whereabouts, despite the most horrific torture. (*Middle*) Denis Rake was one of the most colourful and courageous characters in SOE and possibly the most coldly courageous – despite hating loud bangs. He dubbed Virginia the greatest female agent of the war. (*Right*) Pierre Fayol, a leading Maquis commander, initially resented Viginia's authority and actively tried to undermine her, calling her the Ginger Witch. Later he became a devotee.

Virginia with her boys at the commandeered château at Roissiat. Paul (on her far left) became her lover. Henry Riley is holding the dog, with Lieutenant Aimart in the centre.

Virginia with Paul in their latter years at home in America. He was shorter and younger than her, but 'lightened her life'.

Saying a poignant and final goodbye to the *Diane* Irregulars on the balcony of the Roissiat château. As commander, Virginia stands at the centre. On her left is Gabriel, but for once his grin is missing.

cruellest mountain passes in the Pyrenees, eight thousand feet above them past the glaciers and sharp flanks of the Canigou Massif. Treacherous and sometimes impassable even in the summer months, few would expect an escapee to try negotiating the narrow, rocky trail where the snow could reach waist height in winter and the freezing wind called the *tramontane* stole the breath from your lungs. But there was now no other way to leave France – it was too late for an exit by boat or plane, the trains across the border would be heavily patrolled and her pursuers would be checking all the easier routes over the mountains into Spain.

Gilbert agreed to try to find a *passeur* willing to take her but he warned her that he was unlikely to succeed as the stakes were so high. The guides did not like taking women in any conditions, let alone in winter. And with the news from North Africa there would also be more gendarmes in town and patrols in the mountains, all tense, and accompanied by sniffer dogs trained to follow tracks in the snow or find a discarded piece of clothing such as a glove. Crossing the mountains in the so-called forbidden zone was strictly illegal without a special pass; anyone spotted would be stopped and arrested.

Passeurs were a hardbitten bunch, often smugglers by trade who would not risk their own lives by taking on someone they thought might slow them down, give up halfway or get them caught. Stories abounded of *passeurs* shooting laggards, pushing them over ravines or just leaving them to die at the mercy of Germans, or the bears and wolves that roamed the mountains. Others, too reduced to go on, had simply lain down in the snow and invited death to take them. Plenty of fit, able-bodied young men had never been seen again; although sometimes escape parties would come across a frozen corpse, occasionally in an upright position, gazing forward with a fixed stare. *Gilbert* explained that, in the circumstances, the rate Virginia would need to pay would be very high to have any chance at all, as much as twenty thousand francs a head (nearly twenty times the previous rate). And to make it worthwhile for the guide she would need to take two other escapees with her – two men she did not know but who had been waiting for some time. They did not yet have the money and so she would have to be patient. There was no question of a delay, she replied. She herself would pay fifty-five thousand francs for all of them. No doubt surprised at her insistence, *Gilbert* promised to be in touch as soon as he had news. He did not know about Cuthbert, and at all costs Virginia had to prevent him and especially the *passeur* from finding out. Any last hope of escape would be dashed if they did.

They parted and Virginia hurried back to the Hôtel de la Cloche but no one came to see her that night. She could do nothing but wait, knowing that the clock was ticking and the Germans would be closing in by the minute. In London the next day, 10 November, Winston Churchill was celebrating British victory at El Alamein and the apparent success of Operation Torch. In his speech at the Lord Mayor's luncheon at Mansion House, the prime minister uplifted his war-weary audience with the words: 'Now this is not the end. It is not even the beginning of the end. But it is, perhaps, the end of the beginning.' But there were no such crumbs of comfort for Virginia. Just a long lonely wait, all day and another night in her hotel room feeling trapped.

At seven the following morning the full might of the Wehrmacht stormed over the demarcation line into the Free Zone. The French offered no resistance. It would now be only a matter of hours before the troops and the tanks arrived in Perpignan, depriving Virginia of her last bid for freedom. Back in the Hôtel Terminus in Lyon, Klaus Barbie was stroking his beloved pet cat and seething with rage. Under his command,

Lyon had more Gestapo officers relative to its size than any other city, including Paris. Full Nazi occupation had also brought him the support of heavily armed troops and the black-uniformed elite officers of the SS, sporting their death's-head badges. A large reward was on offer for anyone with information leading to the arrest of *Marie Monin*. Yet no one knew where Virginia was, and Barbie was still unsure even of her nationality. Some time later the Butcher of Lyon, as he was soon to become known, was heard screaming 'I'd give anything to get my hands on that limping Canadian bitch!'[11] Now redoubling his campaign to track her down, he ordered thousands of WANTED!' posters to be issued right across France, with a large lifelike drawing of Virginia. Splashed in enormous letters across the bottom were the words 'THE ENEMY'S MOST DANGEROUS SPY: WE MUST FIND AND DESTROY HER!'

Still in hiding at the hotel, Virginia finally received a note around midday that someone would come to see her late in the afternoon. A *passeur* duly arrived after nightfall, and with huge relief she slipped into the front of his van in the darkness without anyone seeing. She handed him half the money with the promise that the balance would be paid on the other side of the frontier. She could just make out two men huddled on the floor at the back of the vehicle. They introduced themselves as Leon Guttman, a Polish Jew who had emigrated to Australia before the war, and an Anglo-Frenchman by the name of Jean Alibert. As the van pulled out of Perpignan onto the mountain road, the men expressed their gratitude to her for paying their way. Virginia, ever on the lookout for good recruits, started wondering whether she could use them on a future mission. She was, even now, determined that there would be one.[12]

At that same moment another train was arriving at Lyon Perrache jammed with German troops. Tanks and trucks bearing more men, weapons and ammunition were not far behind. Fleets of the Gestapo's Citroëns were whizzing through the city's streets. German officers were pushing pedestrians off the pavements. Swastikas were being raised above public buildings, and the clocks were being reset to German time. Some of the shops started advertising their Aryan credentials to woo a Wehrmacht clientele; the station bookshop now sold only Nazi or Vichy tracts, including an anti-British rant by a French naval officer. Meanwhile, the remnants of *Alain*'s paper army – which he had once led Baker Street to believe was a mammoth fighting force – did nothing. Most were 'seized by panic' and 'chicken-heartedness' and threw their remaining arms in the river. 'At the first sight of danger their bluff had been called,' an official report later found.[13] There was no longer a Free Zone, and France no longer had an army, an empire or even a fleet – what remained of its navy was shortly to be scuttled by its own officers in Toulon. In Vichy, Pétain's quaint government hotels were taken over for billeting German soldiers. For such total humiliation, Hitler was extracting from the French treasury five hundred million francs a day and his thugs were seizing valuable assets, from farm machinery to Old Masters.

The Twins had descended on a town in tumult as the full horror of events was just beginning to sink in. They had brought the gendarmes for the Castres operation with them, but left the men at the corner of rue Garibaldi while they made for Virginia's apartment building to receive her final orders. As Henry Newton entered the hallway, he had an 'uncanny sense' that something was wrong.[14] He leapt up the stairs to the sixth floor, but the all-clear sign was missing from her front door. He decided it was best not to knock. Hurtling back down to the ground floor, he asked the concierge, whom he knew to be trustworthy, what had happened to Virginia. The woman told him that she had left in a rush, with no time to finish all her projects. As the Twins left the building, a priest approached them, giving his codename as *Bishop*. They were reluctant to talk and tried to press on, but he persisted, saying that he was sorry *Marie* was away as he worked for her. At the mention of her name, they paused to listen. The priest continued, in his strong German accent, that he had a 'number of people photographing the pill boxes on the coast' and claimed he was owed seventy-five thousand francs to continue funding them, so did they know where *Marie* was? The conversation was brief; just long enough for Alesch to work out who they were.[15]

The van turned off onto a road with sharp hairpin bends before slowing down to take a steeply climbing rocky track. It drew to a halt outside an unlit barn not far from the walled mountain village of Villefranche-de-Conflent, in the foothills of the Pyrenees to the west of Perpignan. The party of three were told to sleep there for several hours, with the sound of rushing rivers either side and the Canigou Massif towering over them.[16] While she was trying to rest on the straw, Virginia could not take her mind away from the boys she had had to leave behind in prison. She felt particularly heartbroken[17] at not being able to finish the Castres operation, but hoped that it had gone ahead smoothly just as she had planned, particularly for Rake. The minute she reached the American consulate in Barcelona, she decided, she would attempt to find out.

What she did not know was that Rake was already free and at that moment also looking for her in Lyon, only to find her gone. He and his two companions had been extremely fortunate in that they had been transferred to a prisoner-of-war camp where the pro-Allied commandant had decided to release them before the Nazis got hold of them – even supplying them with civilian clothes, chocolate and cigarettes. Now Rake would have to follow her to Spain on his own. Nor had she heard that *Olive* was hiding at Madame Gilbert's hairdressing salon on the rue de la République in Lyon, having been let go as a result of Virginia's last-minute intervention with the prison governor. It would have infuriated her to know that he continued to fool himself that Mademoiselle Menier was the one to credit.

The morning mist hung like gauze over the iridescent pink marble houses of Villefranche when Virginia's party left on foot at first light. They headed south along the path carved through steep snowy mountainsides by the turbulent Rotja river. At first the climb was fairly gradual, the route rising five hundred feet over two miles as they made for the valley of Corneilla-de-Conflent, where the party skirted the village to avoid attracting attention. Virginia was carrying her heavy bag on her right side to try to disguise her limp, but after several more hours of increasingly steep terrain, and as the snow grew heavier and slippier, the pain in her stump began to tell. Yet she could not fall behind; she must keep up because she knew there was much harder terrain still to come and fifty miles to go. On they climbed, past the hot water springs at Vernet-les-Bains and then a long gruelling ascent to the tiny settlement of Py, seemingly clinging for its life to the white slopes of the Canigou. Even this was nothing on the misery of the next twelve miles. After months of semi-starvation enforced by wartime conditions in France, she now had to climb five thousand feet in the cruellest of winter conditions; each sideways step jarred her hip as she dragged her false leg up the vertiginous slope with the weight of her bag tearing at her shoulder and cutting into her frozen hand. On one side of her yawned a precipice several hundred feet deep and on the other a steep slab of mountain with virtually nothing to hold on to or grant her shelter from the fierce mountain gale. The snow was three yards deep in places, but she had no snow shoes to help her, or even a stick. Her face was contorted with agony as the sharp icy wind hammered into her; the air so thinned that her chest strained for oxygen in short, rapid breaths; her head pounded with the effort and she felt dizzy; and blood started to seep out of the top of her prosthesis where her stump was now an open, oozing sore. But she had no choice but to keep up with the men. Step by step she pushed on, up and up. 'The climb is endless,' recalled Chuck Yeager, an American pilot who made a similar crossing later in the war. 'A bitch of bitches.'[18] Indeed it was here that many of those who had passed before her had been overwhelmed by frostbite or vertigo – or simply the desire to die. Once again Virginia drew on her father's words in the dream about her duty to survive, but nothing else in all the hardships of the war came even close to the agony and fear of these long hours of endurance – and now Cuthbert was crumbling beneath her, its rivets slowly working loose under the strain as she fought for the will to go on.

Not until they finally reached the Mantet pass at six thousand feet did the guide let them rest in a shepherd's hut and eat some of the sparse provisions they had brought with them (probably just sugar cubes and biscuits). They huddled together to keep warm but even here she had to hide her prosthetic leg and her blood-drenched sock. It is likely that it was at this point that she sent a now legendary message to London, perhaps with one of the new, lighter radios hidden in her bag, or maybe a set that had been stowed away in the hut. It read: 'Cuthbert is being tiresome, but I can cope.' The duty officer who took her message in the receiving station in a large country house near Sevenoaks in Kent had no idea to whom she was referring. 'If Cuthbert is tiresome,' he signalled back, 'have him eliminated.'

The next day, Friday the 13th, started very early again. The path was now even steeper and the mountains rose up as a seemingly impregnable barrier between them and Spain. Climbing up and up in single file to eight thousand feet, they finally reached the top of the pass near the rocky cone of Pic de la Dona at midday. From here they looked on in wonder at Spain unfolding below them, offering the tantalising prospect of freedom. So far they had come across no one except a few wild animals, and now they were to be left completely alone as the *passeur* took the rest of Virginia's money and turned back. There was no time to rest, however, as they still had another twenty miles to go and stories were rife of wolves and bears picking off escapees along this stretch. There would, in fact, be no more breaks during the afternoon or the long, bitter night that followed. They trudged the long winding path past the first Spanish mountain village of Setcases, a windswept spot where the winter temperature regularly falls to minus twenty degrees centigrade, down the steep course of the Ter river to Camprodon and finally to San Juan de las Abadesas in the valley. Their limbs now heavy as lead, the thought of taking the morning train to Barcelona and making the consulate in a couple of hours, just in time for lunch, kept them going, step after step. Virginia urged her companions to push on through the pain, although finding the energy even to talk was now a struggle. It was almost more than they could bear to raise their heads to look at the lights in the distance, the lights that signalled the end of their ordeal. She took care to walk in a way she thought might hold Cuthbert together until the end, but it was even more slippery going downhill and keeping her balance was proving almost impossible because the lack of flexibility in her false ankle meant she had to lean unnaturally far forward. For hour after hour she feared falling into the void.

It was an astonishing achievement on Virginia's part to have scaled the pass – or in the words of an official report at the end of the war, 'a record all by itself'.[19] Somehow this trio persevered and they reached San Juan before dawn, making their way to the station to catch the 5.45 service. Once aboard the train they knew they were safe, as police controls were almost unknown at that hour, so it was merely a question of waiting a short while and trying to keep warm and out of sight until it arrived.

It was still dark when a Civil Guard patrol bristling with guns came onto the platform. Members of the much-feared paramilitary police force, they searched the station thoroughly and all too easily found Virginia and her companions in a state of virtual physical collapse. Barely capable of speaking, the two men stuttered out some excuses but Virginia, more comfortable in Spanish, explained that she was American and claimed she had merely been enjoying the mountains. The Civil Guard looked at their filthy clothes and considered them all highly suspicious. They promptly arrested them as 'undocumented and destitute refugees',[20] and pushed them into the patrol car to take them to the police station and then on to the prison in Figueres. From there Guttman and Alibert were transferred to the notorious concentration camp at Miranda de Ebro.[21]

Virginia had escaped France, the Gestapo and the Abwehr; she had battled through the snow and wind over an eight-thousand-foot pass; she had helped countless others escape from custody; and she was within an hour of catching a train to safety, a warm bath and a hot meal. But now she was behind bars. Would the flame of resistance itself be snuffed out?

Chapter Eight

Agent Most Wanted

Before dawn on that Friday, 13 November, Dr Rousset was awoken by a violent banging on the doors of his surgery on place Poncet-Antonin. As Virginia was about to scale the final heights of the mountains on her way to Spain, Gestapo and SS officers swarmed into the courtyard and arrested him in his nightclothes on charges of spying and terrorism. Thanks to intercepts of Virginia's transmissions and their brutal interrogations, the Gestapo had penetrated the heart of secret Allied operations within forty-eight hours of taking full control of the Unoccupied Zone. They knew Virginia's codename, her headquarters and the identities and addresses of many of her networks. They just did not know where she was.

Pépin was hauled off in handcuffs and the Gestapo guards sat on top of him in the back of the usual black Citroën so that he could not escape and had to gasp for breath. Over the next days and weeks, they subjected him to barbaric torture, leaving his body shattered but his spirit defiant. Where is the Limping Lady?

they screamed. Where is *Marie Monin*? Days and nights passed in a blur of agony and exhaustion but he refused to give her away, acknowledging he knew her but insisting that he was merely her doctor and had no idea who she really was or where she had gone. It was a bitter irony that the very same day of his arrest, now that the Allies had a strategic foothold in North Africa, London had sent out new orders to its agents. The years of planning were finally over and the preparations for a landing in Europe could begin. The new command was to cause 'maximum disruption' and 'attack all planned targets!' with 'any means available!'[1] It was the day they had long been waiting for, but neither Virginia nor Rousset was there to see it.

Pépin was taken to the notorious fortress-prison at Fresnes on the outskirts of Paris, where he was subjected to further 'treatment' and kept in solitary confinement in secret cell number 282 for twelve months. Throughout 1943 he waited alone to find out whether he was to be deported to a death camp or executed on home turf. Perhaps he clung on to the vanishing hope that Virginia might somehow rescue her most loyal lieutenant. But no one knew where he was, and she was gone and surely could not come back. And there was no one else with the audacity or skill to pull off such a feat.

Back in Lyon, Alesch redoubled his efforts to track down *Marie*, and the even greater Abwehr riches that her capture could bestow on him. The day after Rousset's arrest he made his way to the surgery, where the doctor's housekeeper, Eugénie, answered the door. Having seen the priest in conversation with her boss she felt able to reveal that the doctor had been arrested. Livid that the Gestapo had moved in on his rightful quarry without involving him, Alesch demanded to know the whereabouts of the 'Englishwoman' to claim her for himself. Eugénie, who knew nothing of her employer's clandestine life or that Virginia was anything but a patient called *Marie Monin*, replied that she had disappeared. Boiling with rage, the abbé ordered her to give him information on *Marie*'s closest friends, insisting that it was vital for him to contact her. Fatefully, the flustered Eugénie handed over the names and addresses of Germaine Guérin and the Joulians, Virginia's contacts in Le Puy.

Alesch moved swiftly to ingratiate himself with Germaine. With Virginia gone and Rousset arrested she had by necessity become the hub of SOE's Lyon operation, but no doubt was still surprised to receive the insistent attentions of Virginia's pet priest. Rousset had always declared Germaine to be 'one of our best agents',[2] but she was only too pleased for someone to share the burden now that she had lost both her chiefs. The abbé was, after all, effusive in his praise for Virginia and so knowledgeable about her work. He knew how to reassure Germaine (that he was on her side) while simultaneously playing on her fears (that she was not qualified for the role in which she now unexpectedly found herself). All too quickly she came to trust and depend on him, and introduced him to one of her favourite admirers, Eugène Jeunet, the engineer who had been so helpful to the cause. Germaine dined with them both several times over the next few weeks at Lyon's top black-market restaurants and even took Alesch in at her private flat above the brothel on rue Garibaldi. It was here that many agents, couriers and helpers of all sorts – including Virginia's beloved 'nephew' Marcel Leccia (now an accomplished saboteur) – came to visit Germaine for instructions from London or just companionship now that Virginia had gone. One by one, in good faith, she introduced them to Alesch, who lay in wait in her kitchen, almost as if he had become family, to observe the comings and goings. Thus with appalling ease much of the remnants of Virginia's operation became known to him. When *Nicolas* dropped by, Alesch even dared to demand yet more money – although his request for 275,000 francs was firmly refused by an increasingly suspicious London.[3] Even so, *Nicolas* let slip that Virginia was now in Spain, a fact Alesch quickly passed on to Colonel Reile in Paris, who tipped off his Abwehr colleagues south of the border. Alesch meanwhile sold the Gestapo the names and descriptions of Germaine's visitors. Then, around Christmas, he disappeared.

Lyon was paying the highest price for its defiance, and there was now no restraint on its oppressors. As one visiting SOE agent, George Millar, recalled, 'there was hatred and revenge and battle in the air'.[4] No one was spared: even children were stopped and searched on the streets and the cold nights were punctuated by the 'screech of tyres as Gestapo cars swerved round the corner on their way to arrest more people'.[5] *Grégoire*, Virginia's radio operator who had narrowly avoided capture at the Marchands' flat, was another to fall. The lookout at his safehouse panicked on seeing a Gestapo car and had run away, leaving *Grégoire* to be caught at his set red-handed.

In such harrowing conditions, Germaine was trying to hold the fragments of Virginia's networks together, constantly running between agents, hoping to stay one step ahead of the Germans. The loss of *Marie*'s resourcefulness and courage had left a gaping void even the Swiss consul in Lyon cabled the State Department in Washington to say he would 'appreciate any information ... regarding her whereabouts'.[6] Edward Zeff was also desperately searching for Virginia. He had returned to Lyon for a rendezvous with her on 14 November. Her disappearance left him with no money or anywhere to go, although he was sheltered by *Nicolas* for a while, until the Gestapo caught up with him again. In truth, anyone connected to Virginia was now in mortal danger, and in one frantic chase through the *traboules* a Gestapo officer actually caught hold of Zeff's foot but he managed to pull free, leaving his shoe in the German's hand.[7] Completely *brûlé*, he made a dash for Spain in February 1943 but was betrayed by his *passeur* in exchange for the large reward on offer for a Jew. Immediately handed over to the Gestapo, he was beaten and water-tortured over a period of three months as they tried to flesh out what they had heard from Alesch about Virginia's whereabouts. He gave nothing away and was finally deported to the Mauthausen death camp in Austria, where somehow he managed to avoid execution. Even as the weeks passed without sign of her, Virginia remained a key target for the Gestapo; they would never give up until they had her. Many would pay the price.

Germaine recognised the mounting dangers and frequently altered her route between her various properties, where she continued to shelter SOE assets. But none of these security precautions – nor her connections, wits or impossibly good looks – could save her now. In seeking to protect herself and her fellow agents by working with Alesch, she was unwittingly to introduce disaster to them all. At ten o'clock on the evening of 8 January, Germaine let herself in to a comfortably furnished flat in rue Boileau that she had once lent to Virginia but was now being used by Alfred and Henry Newton. The Twins had warned Germaine about Alesch, whom they had disliked ever since bumping into him outside Virginia's apartment on the night of the occupation on 11 November. He came over to them as too nervous, too insistent and with the cold, hard eyes of a man who feels he is owed something. To their horror they had seen him again a couple of weeks later in Germaine's apartment, where he had listened in to their discussions and learned their codenames of *Auguste* and *Artus*. They had considered eliminating him on the spot but their plans were disrupted by the arrival of other *résistants* and Alesch had grabbed the opportunity to escape. But now he knew that they too were closely linked to Virginia – and even where they lived.

Germaine kept up her usual cheery manner as she handed the Twins supplies of food and newspapers. She had placed a jaunty hat, decorated with two birds of paradise, on her dark curls, but this time there was no sign of the wild black kitten that habitually followed her. Even her impeccable make-up could not disguise the fear in her eyes, but as she recounted news of yet more arrests Henry Newton interrupted her. The three of them held their breath as they listened to heavy footsteps marching past the apartment on the outside staircase and coming to a halt on the floor above. A gun butt hammered on the door and a voice bellowed: '*Aufmachen! Polizei!*' Another German yelled that they must have the wrong floor. A mêlée of Gestapo, SS and Vichy police immediately stampeded down the stairs to kick at Germaine's door while screaming 'Open up or we shoot!'

Henry pushed open the kitchen window and dropped soundlessly into the back yard, then Alfred dragged Germaine with him by the hand. He put his arms around her to lift her down to his brother waiting below, but she tore herself free. 'On your way, boys,' she said with a twisted smile. 'You're not taking me. I'm a Frenchwoman and I can handle these babies.' She began to peel off her coat and hat, and the brothers realised she was preparing to sacrifice herself so that they could get away. What her friends admiringly called her 'fiery love and shame for France'[8] came first and foremost; she positively embodied the courage she felt so many of her countrymen lacked. The brothers pleaded with her to escape while she could, but her face was set in steely determination. One brother briefly considered knocking her out and carrying her to safety unconscious. But they would have to clear several walls and more than likely shoot their way to freedom. So with the final seconds ticking away until the door was battered down they did as she asked. Alfred's last sight of Germaine was of her stripping down to her underwear and calling out sleepily:

'Allo! Who's there? What do you want at this time of night?'[9] Proud and dignified, she pulled on a robe and opened the door.

The Newtons returned to rue Boileau two nights later, disguised as gas engineers to, as they put it, 'get some Gestapo'. Although the lights were still burning, the Germans and Germaine had gone. In shocked silence they looked around the empty apartment, which had been turned upside down. Chairs, tables and lamps had been thrown and smashed, and the wallpaper hung down in shreds. An alarm clock, a silver lighter, cigarettes and all the food in the larder had been taken. Most chilling of all were the bloodstains on the carpet. The brothers retrieved some papers from under a placemat in the kitchen and fled.

Around the same time, Alesch reappeared in Lyon and visited Jeunet, who was distraught at the news. Pretending he knew nothing of what had happened, the abbé offered the fact he had contacts in the Gestapo, claiming they might be able to get her released if he was given enough money to oil the wheels. Enormously grateful, Jeunet gave him tens of thousands of francs from his own pocket and confided in Alesch that Germaine had many millions more in gold coins at her own apartment. Could the priest ensure that they were put somewhere safe? Also, could he pass on some food parcels to Germaine in her cell?

It was likely that very same evening that Alesch began plundering Germaine's possessions while enjoying the black-market provisions intended for her in prison. Under the pretext of removing her possessions to safety, he loaded up the chests brimming with gold coins, the furs, the couture and the jewels and ripped down the prized tapestries (which he later sold for a small fortune to a Paris dealer). Even the fixtures and fittings were stripped back to the bare plaster.[10] Inevitably Jeunet himself was arrested a few days later and also sent to Fresnes, where he was seen by another *résistant* with his arms tightly manacled and his wrists pouring with blood. Soon after he was deported to the death camp at Buchenwald with 150 other prisoners, packed into a cattle truck where he died of suffocation.

Of course, Alesch did nothing for Germaine despite promising several other of her friends that he was working tirelessly for her freedom while extracting cash from them too. He did visit her in Fresnes, but merely to inveigle more information about Virginia and other *résistants* that he claimed was necessary to organise her liberation or to protect her comrades. The tragedy was that while Germaine refused to reveal anything to her interrogators, Alesch tricked her into betraying some of those she had fought hardest to save. When she was no longer of use Germaine was transported from the Gare de l'Est in Paris to Ravensbrück, the concentration camp for women north of Berlin, where her head and pubic hair was shaved. She was given prisoner number 39280 and the camp uniform of a rough blue-and-white striped cotton dress and wooden shoes. Later, as the killing was stepped up, she was assigned to a sub-camp handily placed next to the gas chambers.[11]

In the absence of Virginia, the desire for her helpers' blood continued. Couriers, wireless operators, safehouse keepers and contacts of every sort were rounded up, beaten up and deported. On 28 February, it was the turn of the radio operator André Courvoisier, who had helped on the Mauzac operation and many others, and who had fortunately just hidden his set. He was taken to the torture suite at the Gestapo HQ in the Hôtel Terminus. A half-crazed Klaus Barbie arrived in jodhpurs and riding boots, wielding a swagger stick, demanding information on the 'Englishwoman' and threatening him with the firing squad. Courvoisier held out and said nothing until he too was sent to a camp in Germany.

The net was also tightening around the Newtons, who were blowing up radio detector vans (London's current priority) whenever they could. Knowing that their appearance was too well known, they had one of SOE's friendly hairdressers wave their hair and darken their moustaches with mascara, brush their eyebrows the wrong way and dress them in horn-rimmed spectacles and heavy-soled French shoes that made them seem taller but gave their wide British feet excruciating blisters.

The brothers were haunted by Germaine's self-sacrifice on their behalf so Alfred, or *Auguste*, was delighted to hear from another of her devoted boyfriends, the wealthy and married Monsieur Dubois, to say he had news of his mistress from a French police officer. Dubois offered to meet Alfred at a black-market restaurant and he agreed now that he felt more confident in his new disguise. On his arrival he spotted Dubois by the bar and walked up to him unrecognised. Cheered by the success of his new look he identified himself to Dubois, only for the Frenchman immediately to introduce him to another hitherto unnoticed figure in a business suit. To Alfred's horror, it was the ubiquitous Alesch, unusually attired in civilian clothes. The abbé had duped the normally astute Dubois into believing he was a friend of *Marie's* and inveigled himself into the rendezvous. Dubois blurted out, 'Don't you recognise our friend here? It's *Auguste!*' 'By the Holy Trinity!' Alesch replied delightedly. 'So it is. You fooled me all right.' Alfred was cold with 'blind rage' at Dubois's stupidity and reached for the Colt secreted in his pocket, only to realise he had, most unusually, left the revolver behind. Alesch watched the futile move, smiled mockingly, mumbled excuses about another meeting and left. Alfred knew he would go straight to the nearest telephone to alert his superiors.

Shortly afterwards Alfred himself exited the restaurant and sensed he was being followed. As he rounded a corner he spotted two figures in the darkness. Nearest to him was a flashily dressed youth, one of the despised French stooges working for the

Gestapo. The other was in a familiar double-breasted gabardine trench coat and trilby pulled low over his eyes – Alesch himself was on his trail. Alfred vanished into the *traboules*, believing he had given his tail the slip. Then he heard click-clack footsteps behind him once more. He speeded up, grateful for having put rubber pads onto his soles to avoid making a noise (as his SOE training had taught him). Alfred turned a corner and stepped back into a dark doorway, which reeked of cats, and where he could just make out the undulating sound of radio jamming coming from inside the house: a *résistant* must have been trying to listen to the banned BBC. The footsteps came closer and closer in the pitch dark, slowed, stopped, and then restarted. A figure suddenly loomed up in the mist and Alfred pressed his back hard against the door. Then as the man drew level he pounced with all his force. This, finally, was his chance to stop the betrayals, the arrests, the torture; his time to exact revenge for losing his family to the hated Reich and, for all he knew, Germaine and Virginia and Rousset too. Once he had been a devoted and gentle family man who loved nothing better than to grow flowers and present them to his wife and mother. Yet the horrors of war and unfathomable loss had changed him for ever.

Fired up with fury, he jumped on the traitor like a wild animal, one hand smothering his mouth and the other arm rounding his neck. The man struggled frantically, making a muffled gurgling sound until at last his limbs flopped and resistance ceased. Alfred could hear a baby crying as he rammed his victim's head against the wall until it made a 'peculiar sound like wet cloth flapping in the breeze'. Finally, he let the body slide down to the ground, still and lifeless. As the man's hat rolled off into the dirt, Alfred was hit by a whiff of eau de Cologne that made him retch. Then, as his eyes adjusted to the dark, came the appalling realisation: it was not Alesch. He had killed the wrong man.

At that very moment, there was the ear-splitting crunch of a nearby bomb explosion, followed by the crash of glass. In the seconds afterwards Alfred heard a repeated two-note whistle, which became ever more frantic. The youth was calling and calling the man in the gabardine mac, wondering where his companion had gone. Alfred hastily melted back into the *traboules* and hurried away. Bangs and explosions were commonplace now, as the Resistance made their presence felt, but Germans would be on the spot in minutes and then the body would be found. He did not dare run, but after ten minutes of fast walking he tore off his bloodied gloves and pushed them down through a grating into the sewers.

Later, he rejoined his brother at their safehouse above a factory in rue du Docteur-Crestin, but the bare one-room dwelling felt like a trap. Badly shaken, the Newtons rarely went outside for the next few weeks, for fear of being recognised again. One attempt left them running halfway across the city with the Gestapo in pursuit, firing shots at them. They were lucky to get away. Finally, at the beginning of April, a courier brought news that they were to leave for Spain the next day via a safehouse in the country. That evening the brothers held a little party for their French friends including Alphonse and Marie-Fortunée Besson, who had risked everything to shelter them. The wine was flowing when the doorbell rang. No one else was expected. No one knew that the courier had been followed.

One of the company looked out of the window just as trucks of Gestapo and steel-helmeted German soldiers trained their machine guns towards them. Henry yelled to his brother to jump down and shoot their way out. But it was too late, and with heavily armed troops surrounding them they stood no chance. The first group of Gestapo were already running up the stairs yelling 'Hands up, *Auguste* and *Artus*, this time you won't get away!' Klaus Barbie then walked into the room delightedly shouting *'Heil Hitler!'*

As they walked up the stairs of the dreaded Hôtel Terminus soon afterwards, both brothers knew what lay ahead. Some time later, Alfred dashed to a third-floor window and threw himself out. If he escaped he would come back to rescue his brother; if he died at least he had given nothing away. He somehow sustained only a fractured shoulder and broken fingers, but was recaptured immediately. He was thrown into a cell while his younger brother was beaten unconscious in another room by Barbie and his thugs. They stood in a circle and kept Henry bouncing between their punches for hours until one of his eyes dangled out of its socket. Barbie beat the soles of Henry's feet and the palms of his hands to a pulp, placed electric nodes in his wounds and watched his writhing agony as the current was dialled up. In another room he repeatedly hit Alfred's head with a truncheon, crushed a cigarette in his face and battered his broken shoulder. Both brothers later recalled their assailant's piercing deep-set blue 'serpent eyes' and thin, knife-edge smile as he demanded again and again and again: 'Do you know Marie?' No. 'Virginia Hall?' No. 'Do you know that dangerous terrorist woman?' No. The Butcher of Lyon screamed at his men to hold the prisoners' heads under freezing water until they choked and then shoved intercepts of Virginia's messages in their faces. There now could be no doubt that Barbie knew her real name, but he wanted to know where she was. Twice he sent the brothers out to be liquidated by firing squad when they refused to say, only to change his mind each time at the eleventh hour.

Over the next few days more of Virginia's *résistants*, every one identified by Alesch, were rounded up. Over in Le Puy, on 6 April it was the turn of the Joulians to be taken and tortured. Marie-Louise Joulian had her front teeth knocked out and her arm broken. She told the Gestapo nothing. After two months the Germans released her when a doctor said she could not possibly have long to live. She nevertheless hurried to Paris, where she believed her husband was being held, and bribed a German official to destroy the most incriminating papers in Jean's file, although he was still deported to Austria to work as slave labour. Their few friends still at liberty set out to hunt down Alesch (now widely suspected to be the chief source of the whole disaster) and execute him. But knowing Virginia was beyond his reach, he had vanished from Lyon for good. Still wearing his cassock, he was beginning new work for the Abwehr up in Normandy.

The decimation of SOE's networks in Lyon and elsewhere – deemed in London to constitute 'an immediate and serious threat' to British security – led to frantic soul-searching in Whitehall. A Top Secret inquiry in April 1943 blamed the success of double agents but also the Germans' highly developed radio detection operations. Radio operators were the sole and slender link with occupied countries such as France, and their sets considered the most meaningful and emotionally charged objects of the war. These brave men and, later, women were particularly vulnerable to capture and their commanders acknowledged their life expectancy in the field was becoming intolerably brief.[12] Their courage in transmitting in such conditions kept whole circuits alive, a fact for which they themselves were too often paying with their death.

From the police station in San Juan de las Abadesas, Virginia had been taken to a filthy, flea-ridden cell in Figueres, crammed with a motley group of women. Even as an American journalist she knew full well that the Franco government would most likely agree to requests from their German counterparts to take her into their custody. It was only a matter of time before the Gestapo or Abwehr tracked her down. Although weak, gaunt and tormented by an infected rash across her back, she spent the long hours and sleepless nights trying to plot her escape. The situation was unpromising even for a seasoned jail-breaker: she was locked up in an eighteenth-century military fortress with thick stone walls* and was struggling to walk as Cuthbert was in tatters from the rigours of the crossing. After a couple of weeks, however, came her chance and she seized it.

One of her cellmates – a prostitute from Barcelona – was coming to the end of her term. Virginia befriended her and asked her to smuggle out a coded letter for the American consulate. This she dutifully did as soon as she was released. Addressed to 'Dear Nic', the letter's apparently innocent chatter about her health and friends concealed secret messages about Virginia's whereabouts and demands for urgent action to secure her release. She signed off 'Best to you all. I've got my fingers crossed and, as usual, chin up and tail over the dashboard. V.H.'[13] Once decoded, the American diplomats were quick to react. Thanks to their concerted interventions with the Spanish authorities (probably involving exchanges of money), Virginia was released on parole a week later as she was about to be transferred to another prison – or *maison de retraite*, as she jokingly called it.[14]

Finally ensconced in the safety of the Barcelona consulate, Virginia had a hot bath, slept in a blissful clean bed and made sure her mother, who had been starved of news for months, knew she was safe. After allowing herself two days to recover she snapped back into action. She cabled the *New York Post* to send her five hundred dollars (swiftly reimbursed by Baker Street) plus a visa and emergency passport to travel to England. She composed a long report for SOE via the diplomatic bag that included

---

* Still used for dissidents today, including two Catalan independence leaders in 2018.

painstaking arrangements for the people and supplies she had left behind in Lyon – unaware of course of all the arrests. And she pressed London to secure the release of her Pyrenees companions Guttman and Alibert from the camp at Miranda de Ebro, stating she wanted to work with them in future. Her principal aim, she said firmly, was to return to the field 'as soon as possible' – if London would just help her change her appearance 'a little'.[15] Being Virginia, she had it already planned out.

Baker Street was overjoyed to hear from her. They sent congratulations on her release but, to her dismay, administrative hitches meant that it was more than a month before Virginia made it to Lisbon and nearly two before she could rejoin them in London. In the meantime she had to lie low. There was little she could do in a city widely considered a vipers' nest of spies to prevent Lisbon's security chiefs informing the Abwehr that on 19 January 1943 she had taken the BOAC Clipper flight to London. On her arrival in England she was picked up in a polished Humber limousine, driven up to London and through the arch to the entrance of Orchard Court. She climbed the two flights of stairs to No. 6 where Park opened the door exclaiming 'Oh, *comme ça fait plaisir*' before the gangly figure of Maurice Buckmaster hove into view, enveloped in a cloud of pipe smoke.[16]

He, Nicolas Bodington and F Section's new key player, Intelligence Officer Vera Atkins (who by extraordinary coincidence had met Virginia before through their mutual State Department friend Elbridge Durbrow), gave her a rapturous reception. Their exceptional American had survived longer in the field than any other agent. She had avoided capture by the Germans and impeccably maintained her cover as a journalist. She had set up vast networks, rescued numerous officers, provided top-grade intelligence and kept the SOE flag flying through all the tumult. She almost alone had laid the foundations of discipline and hope for the great Resistance battles that were to come. She had even crossed the Pyrenees in the winter snows with a wooden leg. Against all the odds, F Section's high-risk gamble had paid off and a legend had been born (within the tight confines of SOE at least).

It was not an entirely comfortable landing for Virginia, however. Many agents on their return from a country overrun by Nazis found the atmosphere in England strangely complacent even though only two days earlier another huge air raid on London had left whole streets in piles of rubble. Churchill and Roosevelt had just met in Casablanca to discuss their war plans and issued a rousing declaration that they would accept nothing less than unconditional surrender from the Germans. Yet after the febrile daily fight for survival in France, Virginia's return to headquarters was almost inevitably an anticlimax. Of course, she finally had the time to recover properly physically and take Cuthbert to the specialist prosthetic unit at Queen Mary's Hospital in Roehampton to be fixed and the rivets re-done. William Simpson accompanied her as he was having a false hand fitted, and as they talked he marvelled at what she had achieved. 'For the life of me I cannot conceive how it was possible,' he exclaimed about her escape over the Pyrenees. Yet she was 'a picture of health and abounding good spirits'.[17]

Virginia was extensively debriefed and able to give her thoughts on good agents (Rousset) and bad agents (*Alain* and *Carte*), plus the constant and dangerous lack of radio operators and sets. She was also questioned more than once about Alesch, as London belatedly pieced together evidence suggesting he could be one of the deadliest double agents of the war. What dominated her thoughts, though, was not her good fortune to be free but the fate of her friends. As news came in to Baker Street over the next few weeks of one arrest after another, she became increasingly tormented. Was she to blame for their downfall by recruiting them in the first place and then allowing the abbé access to the network? Should she have left them to fend for themselves when she had taken the chance to flee? Even in Virginia's darkest moments she could not have imagined that so many of those who had helped her survive would themselves be betrayed. Whatever the risks, she now knew she had to go back. She owed it to them all to continue the fight.

Despite the brutality it unleashed, there were many in London who welcomed the Germans' occupation of southern France. It stretched Nazi resources to the limit and acted as a recruiting sergeant for the Resistance. With enemy tanks, trucks and troops on streets right across France, no longer could people in the old Free Zone delude themselves that the war was not their direct concern. It touched everything. If someone was caught harbouring Allied operatives his or her entire family might be summarily shot – whether they had known about it or not. Sometimes all the inhabitants of a block of flats in which an agent had been sheltered (unbeknownst to them) paid the ultimate price. Winston Churchill saw such acts of Nazi savagery as directly helping the war effort: 'The blood of the martyrs,' he told a meeting of the Cabinet Defence Committee later that year, 'was the seed of the Church.'[18]

The true colours of Vichy were also apparent, even to those who had initially supported Pétain. No more was he seen as national saviour. Opinion cooled even further when French police connived in the all-too-visible 'public hygiene' deportation of up to ten thousand Jews a week, including children, women and the elderly. The predatory Milice – Vichy's version of the Gestapo, created in January 1943 – sowed further dissent by using local knowledge to infiltrate, repress and torture fellow countrymen.

Its chief was a French member of the Waffen-SS and its black-shirted members (mostly would-be gangsters or wealthy young hardline royalists) swaggered around with newly acquired weapons; their thuggish barbarity disgusted even some Germans. Incredibly, one in six Miliciens was a woman.[19]

At the beginning of 1943, pro-Allied French youths started to display their allegiances by ostentatiously reading *All Quiet on the Western Front** or carrying two fishing rods – *deux gaules* sounding like de Gaulle.[20] Such modest gestures turned into mass civil disobedience in March 1943 when the ad hoc seizure of French people as slave labour for the German war industry, such as the raid narrowly escaped by Virginia and *Olive* in Marseille, turned into a French-run systematic transport of young men and sometimes women. The Nazis were demanding 1.5 million French workers to replace their own people who had either died, been taken prisoner or been wounded in battle. For the French, it was no longer foreigners or strangers who were at risk, but every son, brother, husband and father aged between nineteen and thirty-two who was obliged to leave for Germany. The only option to avoid the Service du Travail Obligatoire, or STO, was to go into hiding. Young men in the south disappeared into the maquis, a Corsican term for the dense and stunted mountain undergrowth common on the island. Within a month of the STO's introduction, 'taking to the maquis' became a common phrase across most of France, no longer just meaning running off into wild terrain but referring to bands of men hiding anywhere and forming groups of resistance. The most rule-abiding French became habitual lawbreakers. Tens of thousands secretly gathered in mountain huts and caves, forests and remote plateaux, some preparing for the

---

* Erich Maria Remarque's novel of the First World War, *Im Westen nichts Neues*, was feared by the Nazis because of its pacifist message.

day when they could take on their occupiers in combat. France was finally reacting. National pride began to grow again. The line from the 'Marseillaise' sung with particular gusto was *'Aux armes, citoyens! Formez vos bataillons!'* (To arms, citizens, form your battalions!)

Over the next few months, sporadic fighting broke out between the Maquis and the Germans, along with their supporters in the Vichy police, across south-east France and the Massif Central. The outlaws, although lacking leadership, training, money, arms, ammunition and even strategy or food, were spurred on by the turning of Allied fortunes elsewhere. The end of the war was not yet in sight but no longer were the Germans seen as invincible. In February the Red Army had annihilated the Wehrmacht at Stalingrad after a five-month siege, and by late August the Soviets were repelling the Germans from Russian soil following victory at the Battle of Kursk. In May the Allies had laid claim to the Middle East, following on from the successes in North Africa. This led to the key advance into Europe when the Allies landed in Sicily in July and Mussolini was ousted soon after. Hitler was already fighting on several fronts when the build-up of Allied forces in Britain began in preparation for the long-awaited invasion of France. Feverish rumours suggested that it could take place as early as the autumn.

Yet France was now an even more dangerous place than in the first years of the war. The Reich was now under threat and on the defensive. Klaus Barbie's regime of institutionalised terror was continuing to crush what Resistance remained in Lyon. Three French underground organisations had merged to create the Armée Secrète in January but six months later their inspirational leader, Jean Moulin, was captured in the city and tortured by Barbie for a fortnight until he was dead. Soon after Moulin died – with his secrets intact – quite separately, the Gestapo arrested Francis Suttill, head of SOE's largest network, leading to a thousand more arrests and the seizure of arms caches throughout northern and central France. Suttill's disregard for security, which had of course seen him demonstrate his gun skills in a Paris nightclub, also led to the Germans acquiring two more SOE wireless sets. Despite warnings that the entire *Prosper* network was destroyed and no element should be touched, Baker Street refused to believe one of the sets was under German control when it started sending messages a few days later, even though vital security checks were missing. Eventually Buckmaster realised what had happened, but continued to transmit orders and even deliver more agents and arms into the area. This apparent insouciance led some to accuse Baker Street of lethal carelessness.

What seems likely is that there was an attitude that sacrifices were simply the necessary price of a bigger prize. Brigadier Colin Gubbins, veteran of the First War and the Troubles in Ireland (who had replaced Sir Charles Hambro as SOE chief) noted in a memo of the time: 'Strategically, France is by far the most important country in the Western Theatre of War. I think therefore that SOE should regard this theatre as one in which the suffering of heavy casualties is inevitable. But it will yield the highest possible dividends.'[21] As a result, many more agents were sent to the area around and to the south of Paris and ended up in Nazi custody within days of their arrival. Some were women urgently drafted in to fill gaps left by the relentless rounding up of wireless operators. Noor Inayat Khan, an Indian Muslim noblewoman, was sent out to what was clearly an already compromised network, and despite having been judged by her SOE trainers as temperamentally unsuited to clandestine work. She had crumbled under a mock Gestapo interrogation in training but, desperate for more radio operators, Buckmaster had dismissed warnings about her vulnerability as nonsense. She was captured and executed with three other SOE women at Dachau, courageous to the last.

Despite all the bloodshed, the Resistance was demonstrating remarkable resilience. Thanks to Virginia's long-haul campaign and genius for recruitment and organisation, F Section was simply too well-rooted across whole swathes of France, and the networks it sustained too widespread and numerous, to die. Baker Street was also finally heeding her warnings about its choice of agents and, in truth, becoming less naive. It now tested male recruits' suitability by targeting them with professional seducers during training to see how they behaved. A new assessment board of psychologists sought to weed out the uncontrolled egos that had so enthralled it in the early days. Virginia's professionalism in a world of amateurs had shown everyone what could be done and how to do it. She may have no longer been in the field herself, but her legacy lived on.

As 1943 wore on the remaining SOE networks in France conducted a sabotage campaign that was nothing short of striking. Factories, aircraft, railway tunnels, lock gates, electricity pylons and locomotives were repeatedly blown sky-high. This signalled the beginning of the guerrilla warfare for which Virginia had meticulously planned, and had helped to make possible. 'Our organisations in the field were [now finally] sufficiently virile to make themselves felt,' was how it was seen with delight in Baker Street.[22] 'For the first time,' as the official SOE historian would later conclude, 'SOE could claim that it was making the sort of impression on the enemy high command in France it had been set up to achieve.'[23] Lord Selborne, Winston Churchill's minister of Economic Warfare,* reported to the chiefs of staff on 24 April that

---

* Selborne had succeeded Hugh Dalton in 1942 as the minister directly responsible for SOE.

'the tide of resistance is mounting steadily in France. Sabotage is widespread and to a large extent under SOE control; there is no doubt that it is ... helping to rally people against the enemy ... [and] provided adequate supplies can be furnished, support of a very effective kind can be given to regular military operations.'[24] Even if there was perhaps a flick of wishful thinking in London's assessment, Virginia could only watch from her desk in London with growing dismay that she was no longer leading the charge.

On 17 May 1943 Virginia landed at a windswept aerodrome near Madrid with a new cover as foreign correspondent for the *Chicago Times*. The job was a sop to her frustration at not being at the centre of the action: it kept her away from the dangers of her pursuers in France but removed her from the dreaded office work she had been doing for the past few months in London. Her orders were to devote a couple of months to journalism to establish her bona fides before starting on her real task, which was to organise Spanish safehouses and escape routes for French Resistance refugees. Even though she spoke Spanish it was an odd appointment and perhaps one made only in the absence of any other obvious solution.

Madrid, according to the British ambassador, the former Foreign Secretary and one-time leading appeaser Sir Samuel Hoare, was crawling with German agents.[25] Operating in the city would make her face and name even better known to the enemy and the local Abwehr (whom Franco allowed to operate in Spain) were already on the lookout for her. Yet Virginia was instructed not to visit SOE's Spanish chief, known internally as H/X, in the seclusion of the British embassy, Hoare considering SOE agents 'more trouble than they were worth'.[26] Instead, she must await a pre-arranged meeting at H/X's convenience at one of the round of cocktail parties she was expected to attend in the stifling Madrid heat. Far from giving her the freedom to rely on her wits and run her own show as in France, she was told that she must thereafter seek his permission for every step she took. She must also be ready to undertake any task, however humble, including low-grade yet perilous and time-consuming courier work between Bilbao and Madrid. Incredibly, for all her triumphs in exfiltrating pilots, agents, *résistants* and refugees from France, H/X judged her unqualified to run an escape line in Spain herself, and capable merely of assisting others. Perhaps he felt threatened by her prowess or was simply incredulous of the reports of her exploits in the field. Either way, H/X was so dismissive of her talents that he considered that 'much of her usefulness' would revolve around the traditional feminine work of 'being able to give and accept entertainment' such as tea parties.[27] Most important of all, however, was that *DFV* (her new codename) should be tightly controlled. 'You will see . . . that we have done our best to tie DFV up so that she can have no excuse for undertaking any work without your prior knowledge and approval,' her immediate superior DF crowed to H/X. 'I do not envisage that you will have any trouble.'

There was an equally insulting showdown over money. Paid in dollars to support her cover as a *Chicago Times* employee, her new bosses deliberately sought to cut how much she received by forcing her to change most of her salary into pesetas on the black market. DF considered Virginia's modest $250 a month as 'out of proportion for any services' she appeared 'capable of rendering'. He suggested her take-home pay – which was little more than for an embassy typist – 'might be reduced'.[28]

It was a cruel disappointment. Although Virginia was not particularly interested in money for its own sake, she knew the row reflected how she was once again underrated by her employers. Worse still was the sense of exclusion. Where Virginia wanted to be, of course, was six hundred miles away in southern France, at the centre of the real action. But that wish had been blocked categorically by SOE's top brass. She was *brûlée*; she could never go back. No argument. Even her request to train as a radio operator was turned down; there was no need, she was informed, for one in Spain. Nor should she build alliances with her compatriots in Madrid; such 'inter-communication' with Americans (which had been life-saving in Lyon) was deemed undesirable by her rule-loving new chiefs. It was even more galling now that America was finally making its own contribution to the intelligence war. Indeed, the first American agent to be parachuted into France, E. F. Floege, arrived on 13 June to organise a sabotage circuit around Le Mans.

In the circumstances, news in July that she had been awarded an MBE – or Member of the Order of the British Empire, a lesser recognition than the CBE for which she had been turned down the previous year – was perhaps scant consolation. Baker Street sent 'heartiest congratulations' on her 'well-deserved honour' – although as she was still in the field there could be no public announcement or celebrations.

Virginia, as ever, tried to overcome obstacles – and perhaps also the resurgent depression of recent years – by throwing herself into her work. There was a steady stream of escapees coming over the Pyrenees now that summer had come. She would alert London to the arrival of a new batch with a message such as '*La chienne de Florence a reçu je dis reçu cinq chiots dont un est une petite chienne*' (Florence's dog has had five puppies, repeat five puppies, of which one is a girl – meaning that five more had made it over the mountains, of whom one was a woman). Virginia would then provide safehouses and papers to help them on their way back to Britain, either via Gibraltar or through Portugal. But, being a well-worn path, this was hardly taxing work.

She was delighted, however, to be able to help her 'nephews' – Marcel Leccia and Elisée Allard who had been so useful and brave in Limoges. The two men arrived in Madrid thin and exhausted after eight gruelling months in noisome Spanish prisons. Having left France a month after her, in December 1942, when 'things were becoming too hot',[29] they had been caught on a train without papers. Once released, the obvious thing to do was to make for Madrid, now that word had spread that she was helping escaped agents through Spain, to pay a visit to their ever-solicitous 'auntie'. Bored and disappointed with her posting, Virginia was delighted to be reunited with both of them, particularly Leccia, whose gallows humour she greatly enjoyed. She considered him one of her bravest recruits – and he and Allard were inseparable – and so she arranged for both of them to go to London to receive formal SOE training ahead of an eventual return to France. She furnished them with documents to exfiltrate them via Portugal to Baker Street, where they eventually arrived on 10 October.

Even so, this all hardly occupied her time and the idea of eating suckling pig and drinking champagne in Madrid's well-fuelled party scene while France was suffering under German occupation appalled her. She had arranged for her mother to send over her special skiing harness for Cuthbert – determined as ever to pursue her favourite sports – but of course she would have to wait for the winter snows before taking to the slopes. Eager to be useful in the months that stretched out ahead of her, she wrote to Maurice Buckmaster offering to monitor the French and German newspapers for her old colleagues in F Section.

By September, though, Virginia was done. She considered she had given her new job 'a good four months try' but that remaining in Madrid was 'a waste of time and money'. Meeting the nephews had reawakened her thoughts of returning to France, as she told F in a letter a few days later. 'I have had the luck to find two of my very own boys here and send them on to you. They want me to go back with them because we worked together before and our team work is good . . . I suggest I go back as their radio [operator].' She believed she could learn the ropes 'quickly enough in spite of scepticism in some quarters' and what was the sense of remaining in a backwater when there was so much to be done in France? 'When I came out here I thought that I would be able to help F Section people but I don't and can't . . . I am simply living pleasantly and wasting time. After all,' she added, 'my neck is my own' and she was 'willing to get a crick in it because there is a war on'. Pressing home her point about returning to France, she added: 'I think I can do a job for you along with my two boys. They think I can too and I trust that you will let us try, because we are all three very much in earnest about this bloody war.' She sent her regards to the office and said that she had got the 'boys to drape themselves in lemons' to give to Mrs Buckmaster on their arrival in London, where citrus fruits had become a rarity, signing off 'Yours truly DFV'.[30]

Buckmaster was at first affectionate in his response, and like other repressed Englishmen of his era dreamed up a nickname for a woman he found endearing if puzzling: 'Dearest Doodles, What a wonder you are!' But he swiftly became more stern: 'I know you could learn radio in no time; I know the boys would love to have you in the field; I know all about all the things you could do, and it is only because I honestly believe that the Gestapo would also know it in about a fortnight that I say no, dearest Doodles, no.' He warned her it would be impossible to 'escape detention for more than a few days', claiming that 'what was previously a picnic, comparatively speaking, is now real war'. Even if she could look after herself, her mere presence would put others in danger: 'The Boche is good at patiently following trails, and sooner or later he will unravel the whole skein if he has a chance. We do not want to give him even half a chance by sending in anyone as remarkable as yourself.' No doubt he could imagine her disappointment, so he tried to cushion the blow: 'I know your heart is in F Section, and I know that F Section has missed you greatly' and suggested she come back to London 'as a briefing officer for the boys'. Aware she would bridle at the prospect of another desk job, he held out the 'possible, repeat possible' chance of returning to the field when the Allies launched an invasion of Europe – whenever that might be. Finally, he promised to look after her nephews when they got to London, signing off with 'Love from all of us'.

Buckmaster was only doing his job and was right about her being fatally compromised. It was also true that the very qualities that rendered her a superb operative in the field could blind her to the realities of her position and that of SOE in this new phase of the war. Yet even he was unaware of just how much the Germans had found out about Virginia. Through torturing dozens of agents and intercepts of SOE messages they had pieced together a highly detailed picture of her, her work and her network of contacts. Even her old colleague Peter Churchill had confirmed her details to the Gestapo during interrogation in the torture chambers at 84 avenue Foch in Paris. Unwashed, without his glasses, starving and knowing his life was in the balance, he had broken down after six months in solitary confinement and having regularly been beaten unconscious. In any case he believed she was safely out of France and never coming back. Furthermore, when he had first been arrested in April (thanks again to Sergeant Hugo Bleicher of the Abwehr) Virginia's old phone number had been found in his pocket.[31] Neither did Buckmaster know that her real name and exact role in Lyon was shortly to be deliberately communicated to the Germans by MI6, again in the belief that it was inconceivable she would return to the field. The rival British intelligence service had seized a wireless from a German agent arrested in England and Virginia's details were nuggets of truth transmitted to his controllers to give validity to a mass of disinformation designed to mislead the Germans about the location and timing of the planned cross-Channel landings.[32] The result, by the end of 1943, was that Virginia's name, description and role were known across German intelligence and beyond. She remained a figure at the centre of the secret war in France, even if she did not know it.

When her bosses in Madrid heard of Virginia's desire to leave, they were not sorry to see her go. Her war record was an awkward reminder of their own comparative safety and leisure. Her preference for whirlwind activity sat uncomfortably with the slow wheels of officialdom and the underlying reluctance in some quarters to help agents at all. At times they were downright disobliging. Jean-Marie Regnier, one of Virginia's assets in Lyon, had managed to flee from the Gestapo into Spain by the skin of his teeth, only to be put up by the British embassy in a Madrid hotel owned by a notoriously dangerous double agent. It is fair to say that *résistants* needing to know they had a safe route out if necessary would miss Virginia's presence in Spain a great deal, even if others would not.

Virginia arrived back in London in time for Christmas and slotted in alongside Vera Atkins, whose job was to look after agents about to be dispatched on mission. The operation in Baker Street was fast expanding as preparations began to gear up for the landings in which the Resistance intended to take a major role. She kept busy debriefing returning agents and preparing departing ones but also found time to look up old friends, both British and American. London was teeming with her compatriots, drawn to the capital as the military planning hub for the Allied war effort in Europe. But she never relinquished her goal of training as a radio operator, knowing full well the urgent need for more pianists but also the appalling odds of extinction. She knew too that to be in direct contact with London granted agents a particular power in the field and she would not be held back again. If there was no other way, she would pay for the six-week course herself.[33]

Virginia duly started in the new year at SOE's wireless school at Thame Park in Oxfordshire, hoping to take advantage of the fact that the Allies would desperately need more wireless operators in France before they landed their invasion forces in the summer. Students were put through their paces on a variety of different sets including the new Type 3 Mark II, a lighter model at some twenty pounds, less than half the weight of the old ones. She was now expected to learn to transmit Morse at a minimum speed of twenty-five words a minute, practising her craft in the nearby countryside by rigging up her aerial over a tree. With her extensive track record in the field, Virginia was not like her peers. Specialist School 52 was unsure how to deal with her, not least because she had not been put through the cards just before her arrival, as was the normal procedure. The management cabled Baker Street for instructions on whether there were 'subjects which should not be discussed in her presence'. What also bothered them was that Virginia stated her wish to go to London every Saturday, whereas students were normally confined to the school's grounds until they had completed their course. No one at Thame Park knew why she wanted to visit London or whom she was seeing. It was all most irregular.[34]

It was after one of these mysterious trips to London in January 1944 that MI5 received an enquiry from the Office of Strategic Services, or OSS, about the American journalist Miss Virginia Hall. OSS had been set up by President Roosevelt in June 1942 as the American counterpart to SOE and MI6 and had a heavily guarded London office at 70 Grosvenor Street, a short walk from the American embassy. It had endured a difficult birth because of hostility from the United States military and even White House staff appalled at what they considered a sordid spy service composed of 'a scattershot collection of Wall Street brokers, Ivy League eggheads, soldiers of fortune, ad men, news men, stunt men, second-story men, and con men'.[35] (Indeed, apart from the support staff, they *were* mostly men.) America had no great spying tradition and a general distaste for professional espionage, as was summed up by War Secretary Henry Stimson's 1929 pronouncement that 'gentlemen don't read each other's mail'. Hitherto intelligence had consequently been gathered on an ad hoc basis – a fact some blamed for the devastating surprise attack on Pearl Harbor. The swashbuckling OSS director, General William 'Wild Bill' Donovan, who alternated his starched army uniform with a natty Savile Row suit, thought differently. Having taken advice from Commander Ian Fleming of British naval intelligence, Donovan had promised FDR ranks of 'calculatingly reckless' men of 'disciplined daring' who were 'trained for aggressive action'.[36] In return, the president granted him virtually unlimited government cash to splash on the names in his high-society contact book. But while well-connected recruits from America's East Coast elite were not in short supply (leading to the gag that OSS actually stood for Oh So Social) there were things that money could not buy – notably experience in the field. 'All those first OSS arrivals in London,' wrote Malcolm Muggeridge, who was then working for MI6, 'how well I remember them, arriving like *jeunes filles en fleur* . . . all fresh and innocent, to start work in our frosty old intelligence brothel.'[37]

OSS was wasting time and energy on fantasies such as introducing oestrogen into Hitler's food to remove his moustache or putting mustard gas in flower beds to make Nazi generals go blind. It was also still being babied by its (sometimes

condescending) British partners, while Donovan felt his access
to Roosevelt was being increasingly blocked by Admiral Leahy,
whom Virginia had known as ambassador to Vichy but who was
now back in Washington as FDR's top military aide.[38] Leahy continued to distrust the world of secret warfare and now Donovan
in particular. It did not help that OSS was yet to establish a single
circuit in France, compared with more than thirty run by SOE,[39]
and internal reports referred to a 'deterioration of morale'.

If OSS was to earn its spurs with the Brits, the American military and most of all the president, it needed to infiltrate seasoned
agents into the field to prepare for D-Day. They needed to be
ready and able to instigate and direct an unprecedented campaign
of guerrilla warfare designed to divert the enemy's resources
and sap its strength. Such a prospect made the adventure-loving
Donovan 'snort like a racehorse'[40] with excitement – but who
within its ranks was actually capable of such disciplined daring?
The pampered sons of Wall Street tycoons J. P. Morgan and
Andrew Mellon and the advertising executives from J. Walter
Thompson who staffed OSS headquarters and bought their field
kit from Abercrombie & Fitch were tyros, no match for the
'desperate sharpers ... of struggling, tortured Europe'[41] or the
'case-hardened double-crossers'[42] of the Gestapo and Milice. As
Wild Bill was realising, it was all very well for wealthy Princeton
types to dream of finding themselves fighting with French communist guerrillas and calling them comrade, but different people
were needed, people who knew how the Germans operated and
could dodge everything the Reich had to throw at them. Irregular
people who could wage irregular warfare. Power, at this point in
the secret war, was passing from the experienced but exhausted
hands of Britain to the strong but untested ones of America. The
OSS was desperately scrabbling around for American intelligence
officers who had already proved their worth in action. They

were few and far between but then one unexpectedly walked through the door.

MI5 meanwhile responded to OSS's inquiry on Virginia that it had 'no reason'[43] to doubt her reliability, without of course revealing that she was SOE Agent 3844 with an unparalleled track record behind enemy lines. OSS already knew that. That was precisely why they were asking.

Chapter Nine

Scores to Settle

On the moonless night of 21 March 1944, a small advance guard for the forthcoming Allied invasion of northern France was deposited on Beg-an-Fry beach in Brittany. The handpicked duo had dashed across the Channel in a Royal Navy motor gun boat after spending the previous night in a hotel near Torquay. One was an elderly peasant woman, bundled up in shawls like a Russian babushka and carrying a heavy suitcase. She was the first to land, silently manoeuvring herself out of the camouflaged dinghy onto the rocks and away from the rising tide. A male figure followed but twisted his knee in the dark and barely suppressed a loud yelp as the woman helped him to his feet. He complained all the way up a narrow path onto the headland and on through the gorse to the road for the long walk to the nearest railway station. Yet talking was supposedly forbidden for fear of alerting the Germans in the nearby pillbox, who could turn on their searchlights at any moment and start firing.

Grey-haired *Henri Lassot* had a pale face, thin moustache and round glasses and was a painter by profession and a grumbler by nature – although prized by his OSS commanders, who considered his air of aged fatigue a brilliant cover. Codenamed *Aramis*, at sixty-two the American was old enough to be his companion's father for she was actually coming up to only her thirty-eighth birthday. Virginia or *Diane*, as she was known in OSS, looked as if she were in her late sixties because she had gone to extraordinary lengths to change her appearance. In her youth, she had preferred dressing up as a dashing pirate but for this mission she had opted for something dowdier. She had dyed her hair a dirty grey and secured it with a wooden hairpin in a severe bun that sharpened her features; Hollywood make-up artists had taught her how to pencil in authentic-looking wrinkles round her eyes; baggy woollen blouses and several floor-length skirts with peplums bulked out her silhouette and concealed her Colt .32 automatic pistol; and she had had her fine, white American teeth ground down by a much-feared female London dentist to resemble those of a French countrywoman. At five foot eight she was tall for a peasant but her clothes had been made, distressed and rigorously checked by Jewish refugees in a secret atelier behind Oxford Circus to ensure they looked real, right down to the way the buttons were sewn on: the French favoured parallel threading while the British and Americans preferred a criss-cross pattern. She had even altered her famous gait by learning to shuffle.

The effect was startling but OSS judged that Virginia's disguise alone was not enough and that 'radical alteration of her features was indicated for her own safety'. She refused, however, to go under the surgeon's knife, perhaps because of the memories it brought back of the aftermath of her accident in Turkey. It was nevertheless a brave stance – and an unusual one. George Langelaan, one of the Mauzac escapees, was one of a handful of other compromised agents who all agreed to, or even requested, surgery before returning to the field. Two major operations had involved breaking Langelaan's pointed chin and making it smoother and rounder with a bone graft from his pelvis, a painful procedure he topped up with glasses, a different parting and a new moustache. After all that, even his closest relatives did not recognise him.

Virginia's refusal is all the more remarkable given that German officers across France were still on maximum alert for the Limping Lady sixteen months after her escape from Lyon. The Gestapo had given her the codename of *Artemis*, the Greek goddess of hunting, and for them tracking her down still represented a particularly gripping if sinister sport. Her pursuers knew she had returned to Britain via Portugal. Now they must at all costs be prevented from finding out she was back in France.

Even so, it was an unusual way to dress for the role she intended to take once in the field, one that went well beyond the orders given to her new circuit, codenamed *Saint*, which were surprisingly modest. Her official brief was to find safehouses for other agents and wireless operators on the run in central France south of Paris – crossing over the perilous area where the Germans had decimated the SOE *Prosper* circuit and which had become almost no-go territory for Allied agents. OSS headquarters were clear that *Aramis* would be her chief (and had given him a million francs to take with him as expenses) while *Diane* was his assistant and wireless operator (with half a million francs).[1] It was still felt in America to be controversial to send a woman on a paramilitary operation and inconceivable to put her in charge. In the United States military, which had been hurriedly expanded after Pearl Harbor, female recruits (who never got near the front line, let alone behind it) were branded by some male colleagues as prostitutes or the so-called 'lesbian threat'. Women were known to fly fighter aircraft, but only to and from the factories and never into combat; normally the nearest women got to the fighting was as nurses. However, taking orders in the field from the untested *Aramis* was hardly a situation that Virginia was likely to tolerate for long. Nor was she likely to stick to her restrictive support-role brief. From the off she had greater ambitions now that she was finally back in France, and scores to settle.

The country had suffered a great deal since her last mission and the mood had dramatically changed. Virginia had kept her eye on the big picture and had seen well before she arrived that the time had come to form guerrilla armies to attack, rather than set up circuits as before to observe or prepare. As one SOE officer put it, 'we had sown the wind for two and a half weary years. We were about to reap the whirlwind.'[2] Indeed, it was already obvious what could be done with the right leadership and equipment – but both were seriously lacking. Churchill had ordered the RAF to drop more than three thousand tons of weapons and supplies (including concentrated foods and vitamins) to French fighters over the first four months of the year. Even so, the majority remained unarmed, untrained and badly led – and often starving. Some, tired of waiting for rescue, were simply giving up on hopes of the Allies ever coming at all, no longer believing claims that help was on its way. The best-led and equipped groups had, however, already used their new riches to blow up munitions dumps and petrol tanks, derail trains and even attack individual Germans or small military units, demonstrating just what could be done. Most occupying Nazis now feared the Resistance as a genuine military threat rather than a mere subversive one. Field Marshal Gerd von Rundstedt, the commander-in-chief in France, was describing some regions as fomenting into a state of 'general revolt' and the lives of German troops as 'seriously menaced through shootings and bombings'.[3] The threat became more organised when the Resistance as a whole began to take orders from de Gaulle's Free French government. Hitler was thereby forced to deploy Gestapo and Waffen-SS divisions away from the front line to mount a counter-attack of the utmost brutality. Anxious to rid themselves of insurgents before the expected Allied invasion, they rounded up thousands of members of the Resistance over the early months of 1944. Many of them were executed by firing squad, some crying '*Vive la France!*' before they fell.

In March a Resistance stronghold on the Glières plateau in the Savoy Alps was the first to fight a pitched battle with regular Nazi forces. But dive-bombed by Stuka aircraft and encircled by a crack German mountain division more than twenty times its size – and without the desperately hoped-for Allied back-up – the result was a bloodbath. The Glières tragedy sent out a resounding message that the Resistance was actively engaged in the war but also accelerated France's descent into a furnace of bloody retribution. The SOE agent Francis Cammaerts had warned London before Virginia left about a 'reign of terror' in her target area of central France with 'farms burnt, shootings, and hangings'. 'These are very difficult days,' he added. 'The Germans are attacking everybody, even those who are only slightly suspected.' Virginia was well aware of the risks but the thought of the fate of her friends in Lyon drove her on. She believed that this was finally the ideal environment in which to gather a mighty force to fight back, to create a nation in arms. One way or another she too would have her revenge.

The first test of Virginia's disguise took place early the following evening as she and *Aramis* arrived at Gare Montparnasse in Paris. The ticket barriers were bristling with Gestapo officers scrutinising passengers and she knew if she were stopped she would be finished. Her suitcase was dragging painfully on her left arm but she had to make light of it and not arouse suspicion as it contained her wireless transmitter, and this particular new

version still weighed thirty pounds. Fortunately the Gestapo
took no interest in the shuffling old woman coming up from
the country, just one in a teeming crowd in the station. But now
that she was acting under cover every such occasion would be a
question of life or death.

Virginia was travelling under the new cover name of *Marcelle
Montagne*, only a few days after signing on with the special operations section of OSS. She was one of only a few field officers to
cross over from SOE during the entire war but she had hardly
been forthcoming about why she wanted to do so. 'I feel confident that the main reason she wishes to transfer . . . is one of
national loyalty,' suggested one of her recruiters, who seemed
unaware of SOE's ban on her returning to France. 'This lady . . .
comes from American parentage.'[4] In reality, the sideways move
was, of course, her (typically inventive) way of circumventing
Buckmaster's refusal to send her on another mission. She had
probably been looking to join the fledgling American service
ever since her frustrating time in a desk job in Madrid, as she
knew OSS was woefully short of experienced operatives. She
figured that the extreme exigencies of war meant that even a
one-legged woman stood a chance of breaking in – just as she had
done at SOE. As luck would have it, yet another old friend had
come in useful: William Grell, former manager of the opulent
Hotel Saint-Regis in New York, now worked as a captain for OSS
in London and she had met up with him several times on those
mysterious weekend trips from the radio school at Thame Park.
At first Virginia did not reveal that she was already working for
SOE, but Grell saw that her fluency in French and credentials as
a reporter in France might well be of use and arranged for her
to come in for an interview. Virginia wanted the job so badly
she quickly made it clear that she was no intelligence novice.
She had probably spent more time in enemy territory than the

rest of them put together and could also now operate a radio. Furthermore, she could continue to operate closely with her old SOE colleagues as the two agencies had agreed in January to operate jointly at a new Special Forces Headquarters (SFHQ) in London. Little was therefore changing except her pay cheque and freedom to return to France.

The first that Mrs Hall knew about Virginia's latest exploit was from her neighbours. Government officials arrived in town, knocking on doors and questioning as many people as they could find who knew her as part of her security clearance. Her mother was set on edge: Barbara had known she had been doing something dangerous before, though she had never been privy to what, exactly. The family waited for occasional clues in rare letters from Europe, following the war's progress on a world map in the living room and guessing where Virginia might be. They knew she had been resting in London for a while but now it was obvious from these brusque official visits that she was going somewhere dangerous.[5] Perhaps it was in part guilt for her mother's anxiety that led to Virginia arranging for almost all her OSS pay to be sent to Mrs Hall at Boxhorn Farm (or perhaps she wanted to benefit from Barbara's skills at playing the stock market). In either case, money was never Virginia's real motivation. OSS was struck that she never even asked how much she was to be paid, which at $336 a month comprised the salary and allowances of an unmarried army second lieutenant with no parachute pay (for obvious reasons). This was still a welcome 65 per cent increase on her SOE rate, but now that she had had her way in returning to the field her pay rate had ceased to be of such importance. Her life was supposed to have been insured for ten thousand dollars but she never signed the policy because of the rush to infiltrate her into France.[6] More significant was that although she would remain a civilian she was finally to be granted an equivalent military rank. That said, considering her record of command in the field becoming a second lieutenant – the lowest officer rank – was no doubt a disappointment. Would it give her the status she needed for the job she wanted to do?

The arrival of Virginia and *Aramis* brought the number of OSS agents in France to a mere five, but after such a slow start the Americans were determined to make up for lost time in the clandestine war. The SFHQ objective was for OSS and SOE to play a crucial part in D-Day by forming companies of maquisards and training and arming them to execute strategic sabotage operations, and, once the time came, hit-and-run attacks on German convoys. Above all, the plan was to direct these guerrilla bands to follow orders from Allied High Command rather than local chieftains who could do more harm than good by pursuing their own politically motived objectives. Such a task – never attempted before on this scale – would require military nous, diplomacy and sheer force of character from the agents. Such qualities were presumed to be exclusively found in men, it was up to Virginia to prove that she had them too.

So it was she rather than her male chief who immediately took charge on arrival in Paris, and led the way to one of her contacts. *Aramis* slowed her down, complaining constantly about his knee. Virginia became exasperated as now was not the time to attract attention. Paris had grown even more tense and downtrodden than on her last visit and everywhere was under surveillance. Schools had become barracks; cinemas, theatres and cafés had been taken over exclusively for Germans; the old dance halls and jazz clubs she had loved as a student had all been forcibly closed down; streets bearing Jewish names had been renamed after anti-Semites. And following years of anti-Allied propaganda on the radio and posted up on billboards, there was hostility in the air, particularly to Americans. When a USAF plane was shot down after an Allied bombing raid, there had reportedly been dancing in the streets.

Finally, they reached the home of Madame Long, recommended by one of Virginia's old student friends, who lived at 57 rue de Babylone, near Napoleon's last resting place at Les Invalides. Mme Long had provided a roof for Virginia before without asking questions but she took an instant dislike to *Aramis*. Not only did he break the basics of security by recounting how he had hurt his leg clambering out of a boat, but she found his absurd use of long words insufferably pompous. Quickly tiring of her guest, Mme Long insisted on driving him straight to a *pension* run by a Gaullist friend before he said any more. Virginia was welcome to use the entire apartment but Mme Long refused to allow the worryingly loquacious *Aramis* ever to come back.[7]

Everyone knew the Allied invasion was imminent, but OSS agents – Virginia included – did not know the precise date or location, to avoid potential leaks under duress. Another landing was due to take place some time afterwards on the Riviera, to form a two-pronged attack on the Germans. From the knowledge of France gleaned from her first mission Virginia had already identified an area in La Creuse, roughly equidistant between the Channel and Mediterranean coasts, as a strategically important battleground for the Resistance. Her instincts were well-founded. The country between Châteauroux and Limoges had been cited by Allied Supreme Command as a priority target for arming guerrilla groups so that they could attack enemy forces on the move, disrupt their supply lines and lower their morale. It was already familiar territory to her as she had operated there on her first mission. This fact also increased the risk of being recognised in an area thick with Germans and their informants, but such concerns did not stop Virginia setting off to La Creuse the next day with *Aramis* in tow. They alighted at a little town called

Saint-Sébastien, two hundred miles south-west of Paris, where she took note of the possibilities for sabotaging the train sheds and tracks for future reference.

Her local contacts immediately came into use, one of them driving the pair to meet a farmer called Eugène Lopinat at Maidou-sur-Crozant, a hamlet near the steep granite gorges of the Creuse river. Lopinat asked few questions but offered the use of a one-roomed hut by the side of the road without running water or electricity. It was perfect, as was Lopinat's rustic farmhouse at the other end of the hamlet, where Virginia (known here as *Madame Marcelle*) could transmit from the attic using the intermittent power supply, running her aerial over the back of the roof. She felt safer here than in a Paris overrun with Gestapo. Most importantly, she felt more useful. With the clock fast running down to D-Day, the area might be operationally vital but was also largely unconquered by the Resistance. The local Maquis, such as it was, was small and disorganised and almost entirely without guns or ammunition. Her priorities were to recruit, train and bring in weapons by air from Britain to form a functioning guerrilla unit. It had taken Virginia only a couple of days to move on from her original orders – with her admiring controllers' blessing – to conduct the sort of mission she had wanted.

Virginia's mother used to say that everything she learned in childhood would one day come in use, and indeed those long summers in Maryland helped her establish her cover as a milk-maid. 'I cooked for the farmer, his old mother and the hired hand over an open fire as there was no stove in the house,' she reported. 'I drove his cows to pasture, and in the process found several good fields for parachute drops.'[8] Such primitive conditions made for excellent intelligence-gathering but did not appeal to *Aramis*. He hastened back to Paris where he found more salubrious quarters with an old family friend called Madame Rabut. Effectively now operating solo, as she had hoped, Virginia saw her supposed chief only once a week, when he came to Maidou with updates on his progress in finding safehouses. Not one to complain about her own trials with Cuthbert or the fact she had to lug around a radio set, she was annoyed by *Aramis*'s grumbling about the travelling and his bizarre refusal to pick up anything heavy. 'In spite of his robust appearance he is not very strong,' she reported later. '[He] was ill for a few days after each strenuous trip.'

She also bridled at *Aramis*'s thin achievements in Paris and continued talkative habits. Infuriatingly, he refused to listen to her advice on security despite the fact that his regular visits could well invite unwanted attention to them both. '*Aramis* came ... with nothing to report except having found Madame Rabut,' she complained. 'He did not seem to understand using couriers or the advisability of so doing and fiercely resented any suggestions.' Her limited patience had now run out. Virginia decided she would find a way to cut him out and run her own mission in the way she saw fit. She began recruiting new members for the Resistance while delivering the milk on her daily rounds. Within days locals from the mayor's secretary to the village postman had signed up and word spread that someone was finally taking charge in the area. She was delighted to find 'farmers and farm hands willing and eager to help'[9] and set about transforming 'peasant squads' into organised guerrilla units. This was exactly what she had for so long wanted to do. In pretending to be a (most unlikely) French peasant woman, Virginia had found her true self. Despite the dangers, she once again felt free.

A week later another familiar and rather more welcome face appeared at her door. Elisée Allard, one of the 'nephews' whom she had known in Limoges, Lyon and latterly Madrid, had just parachuted in on the *Chat* drop zone a few kilometres away. She had always hoped that one day she would work with them again and now here he was at his 'auntie's' rustic hut, having returned to France with Leccia and a third SOE agent she knew and liked, the Belgian Pierre Geelen. No doubt he gasped when he saw *Madame Marcelle* in her peasant rags, but he knew that Virginia would go to almost any lengths to do her job. When he had heard local talk of an old lady with a strange accent creating a small band of guerrilla fighters he had known it must be her.

The three nephews were tasked with preparing for D-Day by blowing up the German naval headquarters near Angers and a railway marshalling yard outside Tours. They were a small part of a much larger three-pronged Allied operation: Plan Vert (destroying railway communications), Plan Tortue (organising roadblocks and ambushes) and Plan Violet (cutting telephone wires, forcing the Germans to use wireless signals that could, unlike phone calls, be intercepted). Allard asked if she could message London that the three agents had arrived safely and were starting work. Leccia himself was on a trip to the Nièvre *département* but would return shortly to see her too. It was as if she had never left SOE, which was joyful – but also, it would turn out, a serious problem.

Virginia stepped up her efforts to gather intelligence on the German troops in the area. She offered to help the farmer's mother make more cheese so that she could sell the surplus to the occupiers. Finding a small German convoy, she shuffled up to them to offer her produce, speaking in a feigned old lady's voice to try to conceal her accent. German officers across France had been issued with those 'WANTED!' posters bearing her likeness and warnings about the threat she posed to the Reich, yet no one seemed to find *Madame Marcelle* remotely suspicious. They innocently bought her cheeses, allowing her the chance to listen in to their conversations (using the German she had learned at the Konsular Akademie in Vienna) all to be radioed back to Britain that evening. In this way, she began to draw a picture of German military plans that was to have a dramatic effect on the progress of the war.

A few days later, she was folding up the aerial at the Lopinat farm after transmitting her messages back to London when she heard a truck pull up outside. She thought it might be *Aramis*, but she closed the radio's suitcase and slid it under the crates and old furniture stored up in the loft just in case. She climbed down the ladder and walked normally towards the door. Outside, it was not her American colleague but, to her horror, a group of German soldiers, fronted by an officer who demanded to know what she was doing alone in the cottage. Virginia, switching into character, replied in her practised raspy croak that she cooked for the farmer and tended his cows. Not satisfied with her response, he ordered three men to search inside. Virginia was desperately hoping she had hidden the radio sufficiently well. From within she could hear crashing sounds, and what sounded like furniture being pulled apart. Then came the scrape of the ladder against the trapdoor into the loft and she started to calculate how far she could get away before being shot. A better idea would be to stay in character and claim that, as an old woman, she never climbed ladders or knew what was upstairs. What was certain was that if she were taken in, they would discover Cuthbert and deduce her identity. Her fate would be certain: torture and death.

Virginia's heart was thumping as the soldiers continued to turn the cottage upside down. Then, at last, they marched out to their officer and handed him something she could not see. Nor could she quite hear what they were saying. She tried not to look but the officer finally came over and peered right into her face, his breath on her skin. Would he see through her disguise – under such intense scrutiny would he realise that her wrinkles were fake? Instead the officer recognised her as the old cheese-lady he had met out on the road, proclaimed her produce to be very good and helped himself to more, chucking a few coins at her feet as they drove away. Virginia remained still for a few moments, leaning against the door for support, but her mind was racing as to what had brought the 'wolves' to her door. Was it her accent? Had she been too brazen? A few days later she came across the severed heads of four friendly villagers; they had been spiked through the neck by the Nazis and left on display in the wild flowers beside the main road as a warning to others. Joining her in the Resistance carried a devastating price.[10]

Virginia suddenly felt very alone. She could not mention these horrifying incidents in her next message to London for fear of identifying herself if it were intercepted. Instead, she asked on 18 April for permission to move her base 'due [to] daily cutting electric current and travelling conditions'.[11] Before she left, however, Allard and Geelen returned with a 'biscuit box' – the nickname for a new, smaller radio that weighed just fourteen pounds – that Virginia had been asking for and which had arrived with another batch of agents. They also brought more bad news. The nephews' mission in the nearby Indre *département* was in trouble. Leccia had been able to find them hideouts thanks to his cousins – two doctors called Laurent and Joseph Leccia – but a wireless operator they had been using had been arrested. The whole place was 'teeming with Gestapo,' an agitated Allard told Virginia. Everybody was 'scared stiff' and now no one would work with them. Leccia had gone off to Paris 'to try to arrange something else'.

Five days later, on 1 May, came the disturbing news from London that Geelen was feared captured. His most recent radio transmission had not contained the proper security checks, and since then there had been silence. If Geelen cracked – and the Gestapo would surely subject him to the basest forms of torture – the Germans would know that their ultimate prey, *Artemis*, was back in France. Virginia barely stopped to pack before she fled on the next train to Paris. 'I left no address behind, of course,' she reported. Upset by the news about Geelen, she headed straight to Madame Long's apartment to think through her next step.

Clearly, she had made mistakes. She had allowed too many people to know where she lived, and to gossip about the way that she spoke. An impeccable command of French was almost as indispensable as ammunition for an undercover agent's survival, a fact that in OSS's haste to dispatch Virginia they seem to have overlooked. It had not mattered on her first mission, when she was operating as the American journalist Virginia Hall, but several of the ill-fated SOE *Prosper* circuit had died because they had voices that were detectably not French.

As ever, Virginia came up with a solution. She decided to take a major gamble on *Aramis*'s landlady, Madame Rabut, whom she judged after just a couple of days to be discreet and reliable. She asked her to travel with her and do the talking whenever needed. Despite the obvious risks Mme Rabut jumped at the chance to serve and became, reported Virginia, a 'very devoted and useful friend'.[12] There was no time to waste. Within forty-eight hours of Virginia's return to Paris the two women were on their way to another strategic crossing point in central France. She had now proved her mettle to OSS and with time running out before D-Day her controllers had granted her the roving brief that she had desperately wanted. Her new orders were far more to her taste, to 'examine the capabilities of the Resistance, in particular their manpower, and [to] establish their requirements'. As she had already done in La Creuse, she was similarly to 'locate suitable landing fields and parachute drop sites'. But finally, and most importantly for Virginia, came her official call to arms: 'Assist the Resistance and plan acts of sabotage.' Her guerrilla war was to begin – but where?

Marcel Leccia had previously briefed Virginia about his family's Resistance contacts in Cosne-sur-Loire in the Nièvre, five hours south-east of Paris at the heart of France. She had heard that the Maquis there had been suffering from poor leadership and factional in-fighting – a common and infuriating problem across France, particularly since the loss of the unifying presence of Jean Moulin. Volunteers had also been starved of supplies. Although one of the most dangerous areas in the country, it was neverthe less clear that Allied command would need a viable guerrilla force in the Nièvre to mount hit-and-run attacks on German forces heading north to reinforce the Channel defences and to sabotage their communication links before, during and after the Allied invasion. When Virginia chose it for her next location, SFHQ readily agreed but reminded her that it was 'very hot' with round after round of arrests, so 'please be careful'.[13]

Virginia and Mme Rabut travelled together to the home of Colonel Vessereau, a retired gendarmerie chief and one-time assistant to the former prime minister of France, Edouard Deladier. He had been forewarned by Leccia, the brother of his daughter-in-law Mimi, to expect an important visitor and was eagerly awaiting her. A divisive and overbearing Resistance leader had recently left the area – to the joy of many locals – and since then the colonel had worked flat out to recruit a hundred maquisards and the support of several serving gendarmes. Yet they had little more than pitchforks and broom handles to fight with, and were even short of food and clothes. Virginia's appearance at this point was thus cause for rejoicing, as Vessereau had felt that his area had hitherto been forgotten by the Allies. Through her transmitter, she had the ear of London – a place that by now had for many Frenchmen acquired an almost mythical status of hope and bounty. Finally he would be able to ask for arms, ammunition, money and more agents to train up the recruits.

Virginia set to work to transform his men into a makeshift but effective guerrilla force with Colonel Vessereau 'doing his best as my second'. Together they decided to form a Maquis split into four groups of twenty-five, to train, organise and ultimately arm them. It was a solution straight out of SOE's new *Partisan Leaders' Handbook*,* considered the bible on ungentlemanly warfare. Small groups were best for moving quickly and avoiding detection – indeed Virginia made clear to the men that their motto should be 'shoot, burn, destroy', followed by 'leave'. Operations were best conducted at night, wearing rubber-soled shoes and darkening their faces with mud. She directed them to begin small-scale sabotage or 'leech' missions – persistently attacking less protected spots – with such simple techniques as knocking a hole in the bottom of the petrol tanks of German vehicles and setting fire to the escaping fuel. Telephone wires could be downed by throwing a weighted rope over them or by felling a nearby tree, and railway points could be jammed by hammering in a wooden wedge. These would all be useful harassing tactics, but for the real fight ahead Virginia would have to bring in supplies from Britain. She arranged a parachute drop of twelve containers of explosives, guns and ammunition for the next full moon – in ten days' time, on 15 May – and in the meantime she would continue the training in the basics.

Virginia asked Mme Rabut to be her courier but to tell no one where she was, including *Aramis*, who was still in Paris.[14] Virginia knew that she must cut free from weak agents quickly and cleanly, whether or not they were technically her superiors.

---

* A detailed manual on all aspects of guerrilla warfare, emphasising the importance of surprise, planning, mobility and most of all ruthlessness.

At times she could seem almost brutal. She informed London that *Aramis* had 'made no progress with his mission' and simply cast him adrift without any means of communicating with London. 'I said to myself "what the hell",' she reported 'and started to get on with it in my part of the country.'[15] Fortunately, such insubordination was tolerated, even encouraged, by Bill Donovan, who liked to say 'I'd rather have a young lieutenant with guts enough to disobey an order than a colonel too regimented to think and act for himself.'[16] But it was an unusual move for a woman. That said, *Aramis* had failed to identify more than one hideout for incoming agents, when three were required. It was evident, as Virginia herself pointed out, that he was not suited to the demands of special operations in a lawless and violent country. He rather feebly blamed the frustrations of his 'undertakings', as he called his mission, on the fact that it was 'very hard for an outsider without references to break in'.[17] This was not a problem that seemed to afflict Virginia; his failure highlighted her success.

Marcel Leccia – now considered a sabotage ace by his new SOE bosses in London – was meanwhile still having difficulties of his own. The Gestapo was cutting swathes through the Resistance around Tours and he was struggling to find the supporters he needed for blowing up the railway hub. To his relief he was finally introduced to a medical student codenamed *Lilias* who offered to help. He would pick up Leccia and Allard from their safehouse in the Indre and drive them on to Paris to make useful contacts. Waving them goodbye was Leccia's new fiancée Odette Wilen, also on mission in France. The couple had fallen in love on the SOE training course in Britain and had got engaged a few days previously. Wilen and the instinctively more cautious Allard had not quite trusted *Lilias* – where did all his petrol come from, for instance? But the headstrong Leccia – SOE would later call him 'cocksure' and 'perhaps a trifle careless'[18] – thought he could handle him and that he might prove to be the breakthrough they urgently needed.

Off they went, Allard and Leccia bidding an emotional farewell to all the honourable French people who had hidden and helped them thus far. But Odette's fiancé and his closest friend never returned. *Lilias*, yet another double agent on the make, drove them straight to the Cherche-Midi, the former military prison in Paris that had once housed Captain Alfred Dreyfus.* Here they were kept in solitary confinement to await interrogation by the Gestapo. News of their fate emerged only because Leccia had persuaded a guard to smuggle out a message. Soon after, Leccia was taken to the Gestapo building on avenue Foch (unaffectionately known during the war as avenue Boche) just a short stroll from the Arc de Triomphe. For the next fifty-two days he was subjected to the most degrading and horrific treatment. Passers-by in the leafy side-street below were becoming accustomed to hearing the screams from the notorious fifth floor. Allard and Geelen were interrogated separately but all three were repeatedly tortured almost to the point of death, Geelen somehow managing to scratch his name and some dates onto one of the walls as a record.

Odette Wilen, codenamed *Sophie*, had followed her fiancé to the capital but now raced down in floods of tears to tell Virginia what had happened. War had already caused such heartache but this news, just two days after her arrival in Cosne, was truly devastating. Leccia was a real friend who had never deserted her on her mission to Lyon, narrowly avoiding capture countless times on her behalf. The nephews had shown courage in coming back, and because of her encouragement they had paid the price.

---

* The Dreyfus affair was a notorious late-nineteenth-century miscarriage of justice in which a Jewish artillery captain in the French army was wrongly convicted of treason and evidence pointing to the real culprit suppressed.

It was not only their lives on the line, however, but Virginia's: at least three imprisoned agents knew that she was in France, and two that she was in Cosne. It would not be long – thanks to the intelligence gleaned by Alesch in Germaine Guérin's Lyon kitchen – before the interrogators linked them all with their beloved 'auntie'.

Agents were trained to hold out for forty-eight hours before revealing anything important, allowing their circuit time to go into hiding. The first fifteen minutes were generally considered the worst and captives were advised to try to shut themselves down, mentally transporting themselves into another place if possible and coping with each minute at a time. They could let slip the odd grain of truth over the first two days so that they might be fed or given water as reward – but after that it was understood they might not be able to stay silent at all. Many agents were put under the most intolerable psychological pressure to work for the Germans. As with Léon Guth, threats to their families were particularly effective. However brave the nephews, there could no longer be any doubt that the Gestapo – and Klaus Barbie himself – knew that Virginia was back in France and that they would intensify their hunt for her. She had to shut down the risks one by one, no matter whose feelings she hurt.

Virginia first targeted *Sophie* as it was conceivable that she had allowed herself to be followed back to the Vessereaus' home. Stifling any trace of emotion, she banned her astonished messenger (who had already lost her first husband in an RAF flying accident) from doing anything to try to rescue the three agents. *Sophie* was 'greatly excited and dramatic and in favour of going and shaking the gates' of the prison, Virginia reported, and 'would get everybody else in trouble if she did not leave matters alone'. Virginia knew she was being cold but also knew the crisis required an effective plan rather than a panic reaction. Virginia ordered her to leave at once and stay away until she could be sent back to Britain. Her verdict was ruthless: '*Sophie* was too emotional and too noticeable to be useful to me as courier or in any other capacity.'[19]

The arrests forced Virginia to move even though her parachute drop had still to take place. She had already begun to transform the Cosne Resistance into a viable guerrilla unit so it was frustrating not to be able, once again, to stay long enough to command major operations. Only Colonel Vessereau and his wife knew where she had gone and Virginia asked them to tell 'no one at all' – although she kept in constant touch with both of them, via another courier, with instructions on training. She also arranged for a new agent to parachute in to Cosne to replace her and it was to her great satisfaction that the group she had formed proceeded to fight a bloody but ultimately victorious battle against their occupiers, helping to liberate the area in September.

Virginia had to make sense of a mission that had already placed her dearest friends in the greatest of danger. It was not her fault that Leccia had trusted *Lilias*, but the nephews' connection with their aunt would always have made them more vulnerable. And so now she had to prove to herself that pushing so hard to come back had been both wise and worth it. Perhaps that was why she next chose to move into an area particularly overrun with Germans, fifteen miles away at Sury-en-Vaux in the Cher, considered one of the hardest areas in central France to crack. She was testing herself to the extreme, but it would give her a valuable vantage point to observe enemy troop movements and take note of numbers, regiments and armaments. Virginia remained in her peasant woman disguise and offered to tend goats for another farmer. Some of the roadsides and fields had been mined to prevent Resistance ambushes, but she worked out where to stand with her flock and leant on a shepherd's staff while again listening in to German conversations. The weather during the spring of 1944 was filthy but she went out through the rain and wind almost every day, slipping in the mud in her wooden clogs. She took care not to talk. When she opened her radio case at night she had plenty of intelligence to report, opening her messages to London with the signal 'QRV?' meaning 'Are you ready?'

In the circumstances, she was lucky to find someone willing to risk certain death by helping her in an area riddled with Milice as well as Nazis. At least 10 per cent of the locals in this conservative heart of France were believed to be directly working for the Germans and many of the peasants were making a lucrative living from them. Too many took advantage of the offer of up to a hundred thousand francs – an enormous sum – for information on the location of Maquis camps, which the Germans would then attack with mortar and machine-gun fire. One agent calculated that only 'two per cent at most' of the Cher locals were 'willing to risk their lives to liberate France'.[20] But once again Virginia seems to have shown a remarkable insight into people and had an equally powerful sway over them. Her new landlady, the widowed Estelle Bertrand, then in her fifties and no stranger to hardship, no doubt knew the risks she ran in taking in *Madame Marcelle*. Maybe it was flattery or the lure of excitement or simply Virginia's obvious commitment to freeing France, but Estelle quickly became yet another devoted supporter prepared to put her life on the line for her guest and was in return taken into her confidence. A few days later, on 15 May, Estelle was at Virginia's side when she sneaked back under cover of darkness to receive the parachute drop of weapons she had arranged for the Cosne Maquis.

Estelle's eighty-four-year-old father Jules Juttry was, by contrast, more of a problem and wondered what the women were up to. Virginia found him suspicious of her and afraid that she herself might be German. She explained away her foreign accent by claiming to come from the extreme north of France and was able to assuage any further concerns with the gift of a *barrique* of wine. Now she was free to recruit and equip yet another band of partisans to harass the local Germans, informing London on 20 May that she needed urgent supplies of batteries, charges for explosives, tea, clothes, money, bandages and soap.[21]

The thought of her three nephews in the hands of the Gestapo never left her, however. As soon as she was settled in her new quarters, Virginia braved the Nazi controls again and dashed back to Paris in disguise to hatch an escape plan and smuggle a message to the boys. She received a message in return: 'We are eight not three.' Five others had also been arrested, including the two doctor cousins recruited by Leccia, and he would on no account leave them behind. Virginia knew with bitter dismay that it would be virtually impossible to pull off a mass break-out from one of France's highest-security jails. It was not in her nature to give up altogether, though, and she repeatedly put herself in mortal danger by returning to the capital every week to try desperately to work out a new plan. She needed to move fast. At the beginning of June, Allard was transferred to Fresnes prison, a move that suggested that deportation or execution was imminent. Leccia and Geelen would not be far behind. She could not bear the thought that the nephews would have to pay the ultimate price for the qualities that she so admired in them: their nobility and valour.

Time was running out on all fronts. Britain was in a state of alert for the D-Day landings. Camps in southern England holding Allied assault troops and the ports harbouring their ships were already in lockdown. The tension was palpable on both sides of the Channel now that it was clear that Operation Overlord was imminent. A week earlier London had signalled Virginia with 'Period of activity is commencing. Stop. Please communicate before next Friday [2 June] all information gathered since your arrival concerning large movements by train or road. Stop.' Since then she had been transmitting every detail she had observed on German convoys: their size, regiment, route and supply lines – high-quality intelligence lapped up by Allied command. There was virtually no time for sleep, and she had become more reliant on her Benzedrine tablets than ever. Every night she tuned in to the BBC French Service to listen out for pre-arranged messages that the invasion was about to take place. Night after night she heard only dummy messages and the nervous suspense continued. The priests in their pulpits picked up on the agony of waiting, and started urgently praying to God for deliverance.[22]

The Germans stepped up their brutal repression of the Resistance. Anyone even suspected of links to the Maquis was likely to be summarily executed, and the Milice in Virginia's area were offering rewards of two thousand francs for denunciations. Careless talk was more dangerous than ever, and with the influx of vast numbers of new recruits in the weeks leading up to D-Day came a similarly increased chance of infiltration by double agents. Some would-be warriors rejected as too unreliable sought their revenge and monetary gain by tipping off the Milice. In these cases, agents were expected to take the necessary action on the spot. 'If members were inclined to talk, they were dropped from the organisation,' Ben Cowburn explained, and 'if they knew too much, and were inclined to talk, they were shot.'[23] A salutary note was duly pinned on the body, explaining that he or she had been executed for being an informer.

Virginia sensed that she was in imminent danger. She heard that gossip was going round about why the lights were on late into the night in the Juttrys' attic. She had also spotted a number of German radio detector vans touring the lanes, obviously having picked up her signals. So to save her brave hosts Virginia swapped houses once again. Just before D-Day she installed herself in a farm at Sury-ès-Bois.

While Virginia was playing cat and mouse with the Germans in France, Mrs Hall was following progress of the war in the newspapers and agonising about her daughter now that it was clear that the battle for France would soon begin. She had heard nothing from Virginia for months, but knew her younger child well enough to suspect she was in danger somewhere. In April Mrs Hall had written to Captain Grell – whose name and address Virginia had given her before she left – for reassurance. On 2 June a Charlotte Norris in New York finally responded on his behalf. She apologised for being imprecise for reasons of security but added that 'your daughter is connected with First Experimental Detachment of the United States Army' without revealing that this was a front for the OSS. Virginia was 'doing important and time-consuming work' that had 'necessitated a transfer from London' and had reduced 'correspondence to a minimum'. She added: 'Please feel free to write to me when you like, Mrs Hall. We are in constant contact with your daughter and are immediately informed of any change in her status. I shall be happy to communicate whatever news I have of her.'[24]

Virginia was awaiting news of her own. There is some discrepancy over exactly where she was when she heard that D-Day was finally under way. One plausible version is that on the evening of 5 June she was with Estelle Bertrand and a few other supporters listening to the radio at her new farmhouse at Sury-ès-Bois. They were tuned in to the BBC's French broadcast which announced, as it did every evening, *'Ici Londres. Les français parlent aux français. Veuillez écouter quelques messages personnels.'* (This is London. The French speaking to the French. Please listen to a few personal messages.) The sitting room was stuffy and the radio reception poor, so the little group drew closer to the set as the announcer began: *'Blessent mon cœur d'une langueur monotone.'* (Wound my heart with a monotone languor.[25]) That message signalled the news that Virginia had waited for since her first days as an agent three years previously. All she had been through, all she had done, the pain, the grief and the fear she had endured had all been in preparation for this moment and the return, at last, of Allied armies to French soil. Here she was, waiting, courting danger, risking her life in a deadly part of France for one reason alone. Huge convoys of ships would now be moving through the darkness to their battle stations in the Channel. The first wave of 150,000 men under General Eisenhower's command would be preparing to step onto the long sandy beaches of the Normandy coast to face the steel and fury of the Wehrmacht. D-Day or Jour J was finally happening.

Over the course of the evening there followed no fewer than three hundred coded 'action messages', each one instructing a circuit to carry out pre-arranged attacks on railways, bridges and telephone lines. The call for action was sounded throughout virtually every town, city and village. Now it was up to the Resistance to do its best to make the largest seaborne invasion in history a success. The orders from Allied Command were clear: harass the enemy to the maximum and sabotage communication links by any possible means. 'A wave of elation spread' over France, an equally excited Maurice Buckmaster later recalled. 'Arms were brought down from lofts and dug up from beneath cellar flagstones. Uniforms were brought out and buttons polished. France was ready to help in her own liberation.'[26]

News of the landings three hundred miles to the north galvanised Virginia's entire region. Three years after she had struggled to recruit her first handful of helpers in Lyon, thousands of

volunteers now poured out of nowhere, far exceeding anyone's expectations. If her life had been hectic in the lead-up to
D-Day, now it was a whirlwind. She ordered the groups she
had so recently armed and organised to swing into action – to
paralyse enemy communications by cutting telephone wires,
packing explosives on roads and railways, blowing up bridges
and even removing signposts to confuse the Germans rushing
up to Normandy to help repel the invaders. New signs made by
a local carpenter were installed, directing them the wrong way
round bends and, where possible, 'preferably over a precipice'.[27]
Others laid SOE's explosive horse manure on the main roads,
taking pleasure in waiting for a German vehicle to approach and
then watching it being thrown into the air. Soon entire German
convoys screeched to a halt every time they saw dung – genuine
or not – until it had been investigated, causing hours of delays.
Across France, the sabotage efforts of the Resistance were more
successful than anyone had thought possible. The Germans could
no longer rely on controlling any part of France or any line of
communication. But the reprisals were to be barbaric and the
French fighters were let down again and again by lack of supplies.

For that reason, every Resistance chief in the region urgently
wanted Virginia's help to call in more guns and explosives.
Barely eating or sleeping she roamed over hundreds of miles of
countryside to inspect Resistance groups for their reliability and
needs and transmit her recommendations back to London. Cars
or trucks and petrol were rarely available so, incredibly, Virginia
made many of these trips by bicycle. She was well aware she made
a conspicuous figure and that these were perilous days particularly for a woman (old or young) on her own. Any semblance of
order was breaking down and whole areas were patrolled by ban-
dits, with robbery, rape and summary execution an ever-present
danger just for being in the wrong place at the wrong time. Now

that the Allies were on French soil the Nazis also felt themselves in mortal danger, taking out their anger through random but appalling violence on innocent civilians. And it was also still possible that D-Day would not succeed. Eisenhower's forces took six days simply to connect the five slender bridgeheads on the landing beaches, and efforts to penetrate the interior were meeting determined German resistance and getting bogged down in the hedgerows and ditches of the Norman *bocage*. Virginia knew not to expect the arrival of Allied troops for quite some time yet.

Every day more convoys of German reinforcements were also driving north under Hitler's orders to 'throw the Allies back into the sea'. In the northern Cher, *Colonel Colomb* – in normal times the Count Arnaud de Voguë but currently the local Resistance chief – could only look on in agony without the arms to attack the convoys passing through his area. His men were also suffering constant incursions from the Milice, who were capturing and torturing supporters to find out the location of their camps. It was almost impossible for them to protect themselves without weapons, ammunition or even food. In desperation, maquisards were turning on their own, raiding shops for bread, and banks or post offices for cash. They often left a bond signed in front of witnesses as security for the money they took, committing them to paying it back as soon as cash was parachuted in or liberation came. But in truth no one knew when that would be.

The only hope for *Colomb* was word of a legendary 'English' radio operator in the region called *Diane* who spoke atrocious French but who seemed to have the ear of the powers in London. Yet time and time again, due to her rigid security measures, he had failed to find a way to contact her. He did, however, hear that his old friend and SOE agent Philippe de Vomécourt – once codenamed *Gauthier* but now *Antoine* or *Major Saint-Paul* – was operating near by. After breaking out of prison, followed by a

stint of formal SOE training in London – experiences that seem
to have recast some of his views – *Antoine* had recently returned to
France. The two Frenchmen met for a council of war a few days
after the landings, when *Colomb* asked whether he knew how to
contact the elusive *Diane* as he was in urgent need of her help.
Antoine immediately guessed her true identity – how many other
women could possibly fit the bill? He found a way of sending her
a cryptic note: 'I salute you – from one of the three brothers –
which one?' The answer came straight back, confirming it was
Virginia by using her old Lyon field name and identifying which
of the three de Vomécourt brothers he must be, *Constantin* and
Sylvain both having been deported. 'I salute you also,' she replied,
'from *Marie* to *Gauthier*.'

Virginia agreed to a rendezvous with her old colleague and
Colomb deep into the twilight of a thick local wood. In Lyon,
Antoine had gone out of his way to make Virginia's life more difficult and she needed to reset their relationship and exude all the
authority she could muster. She shed her peasant disguise for the
occasion, to look and sound like the hard-bitten guerrilla leader
she had become. As she approached him through the trees he saw
that she was the 'same extraordinary woman who I had known,
hiding brilliantly her artificial leg with big strides'. Still alive,
still eager, still courageous to the last, even de Vomécourt now
appreciated that 'Virginia Hall was not to be measured by normal
standards'. She was an agent, he conceded, who had already done
'many things considered improbable, if not impossible'[28] and
was to do many more. It was high praise indeed from a fiercely
patriotic man who, like many of his compatriots, suspected *les
anglo-saxons* – particularly now that hundreds of thousands of
Allied troops were on French soil – of wanting to dominate his
country after the war. Particularly when he had also taken a low
view of women's achievements outside the home and was still

playing antagonistic games with most other American operatives whom he repeatedly dismissed as 'absolutely worthless'.[29] In turn Virginia was no doubt pleased to see her old colleague back in the field – and delighted to note the due respect he now showed her.

Yet she remained cautious. She would not agree to intervene on *Colomb*'s behalf until she satisfied herself as to his integrity. There were too many chancers and impostors. She questioned him in detail and inspected his men before finally deciding that his 'group was good' and signalling London to send him supplies. Virginia was now a power in the land; it was she who was effectively deciding whether Resistance groups would be backed by the Allies or left to wither without support. Her rigour and military manner left the grand but grateful Count de Voguë in a state of awe. After months of waiting in vain, Sten guns, ammunition, explosives and detonators poured in from the skies just five days later, and were expertly distributed by *Diane*. She also brought in 435,000 francs so that he could honour his debts and avoid incurring more. Shortly after the first drop came another, bringing a dedicated radio operator for *Colomb*'s group so he could contact London himself. *Colomb* could not have known that Virginia was secretly planning ahead or that he would never see her again. For the rest of his life, however, he remained struck by 'her courage, her authority, her decisive spirit . . . Those of us who had the chance of meeting her "in action" . . . could never forget this very remarkable figure of the Resistance army.'[30]

Given her constant travelling to inspect groups of guerrilla fighters, Virginia had not had the time to return to Paris to work on the escape plan. She had, however, been pressing her contacts for news and it was not long after her meeting in the wood that she heard that Geelen and Leccia had like Allard been sent on to Fresnes for deportation to Germany. Her hope was that with Eisenhower's armies gradually advancing towards Paris she

would be able to spring her nephews and their friends in the ensu-
ing chaos or, failing that, they would be liberated by the Allies.
In the meantime, the best she could do was to exfiltrate Odette
Wilen (the distraught *Sophie*) via the Vic line to Spain.

Right now, though, Virginia was over-stretched. She was
transmitting for several different groups of Maquis in at least
three *départements* in a vitally important part of France. Thanks
to her days spent by the sides of the roads she was providing what
would later be ranked as vital intelligence on troop movements,
notably on the progress northwards of the Germans' Seventh
Army (on which Nazi High Command was relying to shore up
its defences against the Allied invaders). She was also involved in
training, directing attacks and sabotage and ordering and receiving parachute drops. With the Maquis's success, however, came
the most appalling retribution. In response to her Cosne group's
ambushes on German convoys coming up from the south-west
to the fighting in Normandy, the Gestapo looted and torched
three local villages with flame-throwers. In one they massacred
twenty-seven residents including the local priest, whom they
reportedly hanged, partially clothed, in the belfry.

By the end of June London realised the situation was unten-
able, so during the full-moon night of 8 July OSS parachuted in
another organiser-cum-wireless operator, *Léon*, to take over from
her in Cosne. He was to be followed a month later by Lieutenant
René Défourneaux, who would serve as an instructor. All idea
of Virginia being someone else's assistant had mercifully been
dropped – she was now held up as an exemplary chief. In fact, it
was made clear to *Léon* before he left that he could utterly rely
on *Diane*'s favourable reports of the group he was to join as she
was an 'experienced organiser ... and we have the very greatest confidence in her judgment'. She was proved right. After
receiving several more deliveries the men pulled off 'a most

efficient demolition of the St Thibaud bridge across the Loire on the direct orders of [the American Third Army commander] General Patton' and cut sixteen railway lines, derailed eight trains, blew up four railway bridges, cut all telephone wires in the area and killed eighty Germans while suffering just twelve casualties themselves.[31] It was judged that Virginia's efforts had enabled the Cosne Maquis to become 'a most powerful factor in the harassing of enemy troops'.[32] Her other groups performed similarly effective attacks – including a spectacular one on the station in Saint-Sébastian that she had sized up on that first day of her mission.

The exclusively male OSS agents joining her in the field quickly became 'quite as astounded by her as were her French associates'. Arguing to his commanders that this 'outstanding' woman deserved 'high honor', one Lieutenant Martineau watched her direct many successful 'guerrilla activities with the assurance and good humor of a Sunday school teacher arranging a picnic'.[33] Yet as soon as she had formed an effective fighting unit and started to wage a campaign, to her frustration Virginia was inevitably called elsewhere and obliged to hand over to someone else without her experience in the field. She had brought in fifteen parachute drops supplying arms, ammunition, wireless operators, organisers, food, medicines and much else besides. She had formed eight hundred fighters into the nucleus of what rapidly became 'significant' forces of around twelve thousand men 'ready for combat'.[34] Yet still Virginia had not been given command of her own band of guerrillas for any length of time. That was about to change. She sent a final message to the still-struggling *Aramis* to tell him she was 'leaving for parts unknown following orders'. She said 'good-bye' and added nonchalantly that he would 'surely hear from somebody somehow' although he claimed he never did.[35] Then she vanished.

Chapter Ten

Madonna of the Mountains

High on the mountainside above the village of Saint-Clément in the Haute-Loire stood a solitary sentry with his eyes fixed nervously on the vast landscape below him. From up here the maquisard on patrol could observe the routes in and out of the Vivarais-Lignon plateau, from Le Puy to the north-west and the Ardèche region to the south. Normally, friendly local police would try to warn them of an impending raid, but the Milice had got wise to that and so planned their assaults from down in the valleys. The most deadly had been in April 1944 when the hated Miliciens had joined forces with the Germans from Le Puy to make a quick and deadly incursion, killing five maquisards and four villagers who had helped them. Many of the remaining Maquis had reacted by retreating higher and higher into the wooded uplands, some into makeshift camps with little more than branches and leaves to protect them from the weather – or indeed their attackers. What they possessed in devotion to the idea of armed resistance they lacked in weapons to defend themselves, let alone harass the enemy. Yet key German road and rail routes for supplies and reinforcements – and later on for retreat – ran through the region so cutting or blocking them was essential. Allied command believed the area was ripe for insurgency. It was also the keeper of one of the most extraordinary secrets of the war.

On 14 June, the day after her covert meeting in the wood with *Colonel Colomb* and *Antoine*, Virginia had made the two-hundred-mile journey south to Le Chambon-sur-Lignon, one of the bigger villages on the Vivarais plateau. She had received orders from London to inspect the local Maquis, described in a radio message as 'a little trustworthy group of disciplined men, ready to take military orders'[1] and report back on its quality, size and needs. As with so much else of France, the area was not entirely unknown to her. She had visited it during her first mission, when some of her many loyal contacts, such as the Joulians, had lived at Le Puy. This time it had taken a day fraught with danger to travel from Cosne to St-Etienne with Madame Boitier, her new landlady-cum-chaperone from the Cher, ending with a two-hour drive through the mountains.

As the road to Le Chambon wove its way up to the plateau the terracotta roofs and pots of geraniums of the rest of southern France gave way to solid, slightly forbidding-looking houses of grey basalt and granite. The tiny windows were essential to keep out the wind and cold – in winter, the mercury could fall to minus twenty-five degrees centigrade – as few had proper heating or even electricity. The sturdy stone roofs were capable of bearing the heavy winter snow, which would drift onto the roads and cut off the plateau for weeks at a time. Now it was June and the sun was hot, but a thousand metres above sea level there was a freshness to the air and it was not unknown for it to snow even in summer. The soil was poor and with no tractors everything was done by hand with hoes and scythes. Albert Camus, who came from Algeria in summer 1942 for the tuberculosis in his lungs, called it a 'handsome country' but also 'a little sombre'. He thought of the fir trees massing on the crests of the hills as 'an army of savages', waiting as it grew light to rush down into the valley – and the real world. For the plateau had the ambience of a land apart, a mysterious place suspended in the skies, a community sometimes likened to the Amish in America (with whom Virginia was familiar through her Pennsylvania Dutch relatives). It was unlike anywhere else in France.

Closed off geographically, the plateau was nevertheless unusually open in spirit. Its people had a proud tradition of sheltering the persecuted dating back four hundred years to when the Huguenots had flocked there to escape the Catholic *dragonnades*. Ever since, the locals, most of whom continued to follow a quiet and temperate form of the Protestant faith, had maintained a custom of hospitality to outsiders and resistance to oppression. During this new period of turmoil, local youths had chalked V-for-victory signs on walls across the plateau before such pro-Allied symbols were spotted in most of the rest of France. No wonder it had become a magnet for those fleeing from the Nazis, whether Jews avoiding the camps or young men dodging slave labour in Germany to join the Maquis. As Virginia was to discover, virtually every family in the area was risking their lives by sheltering at least one person on the run.

On their arrival, the women walked past two burned-out farmhouses up to a hamlet above Le Chambon and a three-storey children's home known as L'Abric. Virginia knocked on the door and when a tall, thin man with an earnest face answered, she asked 'Monsieur Bohny?' Virginia, dressed as her own age in a plain summer frock, introduced herself as a Belgian journalist reporting on conditions for children in France. She began to ask questions about his 'remarkable' work with orphans and the mal-nourished, and although somewhat mystified by this woman with her 'Anglo-Saxon' accent Bohny invited her inside. He had been warned of her possible arrival by a friend near Paris[2] but it was still rare to receive visitors up here when travel was so perilous.

A twenty-five-year-old schoolteacher from Switzerland who had come to Le Chambon to help care for child victims of the war, Auguste Bohny always had his answers carefully rehearsed.[3] As a member of the aid agency Secours Suisse, he was one of a tight network of doughty Protestant pastors, teachers, doctors and farmers on the plateau who had worked together since the begin-ning of the war, almost uniquely in France, to shelter thousands of young refugees. He knew all too well the threat to his young charges, many of whom were Jewish children in hiding with false papers, and had helped to protect them from attempted round-ups in the past.* Bohny was naturally wary of giving anything away.

After about an hour getting nowhere, Virginia confessed that she was 'English' and that in reality she was not interested in the children so much as looking for a way to contact the Maquis. Like many on the plateau, however, Bohny had taken a vow to oppose violence and had refused to support any form of armed struggle. He could not help her. It was a bitter blow. Clearly Virginia had been badly advised to approach him and now thought her gruel-ling journey had been pointless. Too late to leave Le Chambon immediately, the two dejected women booked in to one of the local hotels before returning to Cosne in the morning.

Immediately after they left L'Abric, Bohny had second thoughts

---

* The plateau was to save the lives of some three thousand Jews, and in 1988 Le Chambon became the only village in France to be honoured by the state of Israel as Righteous Among the Nations.

about Virginia's request. He told a tutor at the home (who had run away from the STO in Marseille to join the Maquis), who told his Maquis superior Maurice Lebrat (also a teacher), who decided later on that Virginia's visit was important enough to wake up one of the local chiefs, Pierre Fayol (a former army reserve officer in hiding with his wife Marianne in an isolated farmhouse). Shortly before midnight Fayol was drifting off to sleep, sub-machine gun and grenade by his pillow, when his comrades burst in with the news.

This unexplained emissary from London – Virginia had given no indication which organisation she represented – had come at a crucial time. Since the beginning of the month other members of the Haute-Loire Resistance – or Secret Army, as some preferred – had been battling thousands of German soldiers on the slopes of Mont Mouchet to the south-west of the plateau. They had succeeded in killing hundreds, and delaying the survivors' journey to Normandy, but had suffered a bloody counter-attack by hugely superior forces who had also then desecrated local villages in revenge. Three days before Virginia's arrival, partisans had had to retreat rapidly after losing dozens of men. They had scattered into the mountains, some finally regrouping at the Maquis camp near St-Clément. Now they feared worse was to come from the German garrisons at Le Puy and St-Etienne, the Luftwaffe having already machine-gunned the village of Saint-Agrève at the gateway to the plateau. They were all too aware of the slaughter at Glières and feared a repeat of the tragedy. Yet there had so far been virtually no Allied supplies of weapons or ammunition: the one drop, a year earlier, had been discovered by the Gestapo. A week after D-Day, as Allied forces were finally breaking out of their beach-head five hundred miles to the north, the two hundred or so men at Fayol's disposal were ready and willing but had virtually nothing left with which to fight. As Supreme Allied

Commander, Eisenhower had sought to rally his soldiers, sailors and airmen just before the landings with the words that 'the eyes of the world are upon you'. In the Haute-Loire, the feeling was that the world had forgotten their struggle completely.

'We didn't have the time to check out who she was. We needed to see her straight away,' Fayol concluded after they briefly talked it over. 'It was just possible she might be able to help us.'[4] The men crept through the curfew to arrive at her hotel at three in the morning and made their way up to her room. The thirty-nine-year-old Fayol was old school in his views. In every Resistance group, women had had to combat stereotypes of their presumed weaknesses, and if they were accepted at all it was to do 'womanly' chores such as cooking and mending. In many groups, there were men who had escaped from prison – in normal times they would probably have still been there. Instances of sexual assault were common. Most of the men, Fayol included, believed war was a man's affair.

He had, however, never before come across a woman like the tall, battle-hardened figure who answered the door in the heart of the night with such a commanding air. Madame Boitier sat in a dark corner of the small, dimly lit room without saying a word, but after cursory introductions Virginia got down to business. The men could hear the loud drone of a plane flying low above them to some other part of France as she fired questions one after another in a 'full-blooded accent': what is your rank? Where do you operate? Who gives you orders? Have you set up parachute drop zones? Can you summon forty good men? What do you need? And lastly, with considerable force she demanded: will you execute my orders without question?[5]

Astonished by this magisterial interrogation, Fayol replied that he had a reconnaissance team called Compagnie Yssingeaux Parachutages, which had drawn up a list of possible drop zones.

Finding forty men would not pose a problem, and there would be plenty more if only he had the supplies to sustain them.

'What kind of operations do you have in mind?' Fayol asked.

'Sabotage,' she replied. 'And what do you need?'

'Arms, explosives and money, especially for food,' came the answer.

Virginia instructed her visitors to come back with a car at eight, less than four hours away. 'We will go to look at the drop zones,' she told them.

Fayol had his work cut out. It was forbidden to drive without a special permit; vehicles of any sort were hard to find and petrol even more so. Yet a car was duly requisitioned and Fayol pulled up at the hotel at the appointed hour in exactly the sort of low-slung front-wheel-drive black Citroën favoured by the Gestapo for their elegance and handling, but with two superior features. It could go faster as it had a souped-up engine (adapted to run on a secret supply of benzene), and the windscreen could be folded back, allowing the occupants to fire out of the front. Most important, however, was that German patrols would assume its occupants were friendly and allow it to pass freely.

It was a quiet Thursday morning when Virginia, Fayol and two other maquisards set off on their tour of nine possible drop zones across the vast plateau. She had a system for each one. First she paced out the dimensions: the drop zone had to measure about half a mile across on flat, dry ground with no obstacles or dips. She tested the strength of the wind by holding up a handkerchief by the corner – if it failed to fly fully horizontally then it was less than fifteen miles an hour and would be good for parachuting. She noted the coordinates, chose a codename (after a fish) and a recognition letter to be transmitted by lamp in Morse code to the pilot of an approaching plane. Each zone also had a specific message attached to it. Virginia's favourite drop zone, on the highest part of the plateau, was codenamed *Bream*, had the recognition letter R and the BBC French service would announce '*cette obscure clarté tombait des étoiles*' or 'this dark light falling from the stars' a few hours ahead of a drop to allow a reception committee to prepare.

Virginia was impressed by the possibilities but could not contact London immediately – she had left her transmitter behind because of the danger of being caught up in a Nazi or Milice control. She told the men that she would have to report back before taking further action: 'I can't make the final decision alone but either I will come back or I will send you a mission to carry out.' Sitting above them on a large rock, she explained that they would have to compete with other deserving groups for limited resources – indeed areas such as Haute-Marne had been waiting five months for a drop. The Germans were using their roads and railways with impunity because the local Maquis had no arms at all.[6] 'Money, though, I can give you today, it is right here,' she said, patting her stomach.

That afternoon they reconvened in a smoke-filled room behind a haberdasher's shop belonging to the mother of Maurice Lebrat.[7] As soon as she loped in – the old-lady shuffling had been abandoned – Virginia opened the money-belt round her waist and handed Maurice a wad of thousand-franc notes. 'Here's 150,000 francs. Count them.' Maurice thumbed through the money before replying: 'There's 152,000 francs'. 'Count again. There's definitely 150,000.' Maurice recounted, but insisted she had given him two thousand extra. She smiled knowingly. He had passed her integrity test. She pushed her chair back from the table, signalling her departure. The last thing that Virginia gave them was a scrap of paper with a name, an address in rue de Donzy in Cosne and the password 'I have come on behalf of Jean-Jacques'. They could, if necessary, leave a message for her there.[8] Then she vanished, leaving behind a group of men almost speechless in awe – although one of the party had already begun to resent her authority, as she would soon find out.

Virginia made her way back north with Mme Boitier and returned to her frantic round of organising and equipping her groups in central France, and directing their full-scale sabotage campaign. No one there knew where she had been, let alone dared ask her. On 17 June she signalled London that the group at Chambon-sur-Lignon had at least two hundred 'excellent and well led' men, and was capable of increasing rapidly to five hundred. She recommended that two officers should be urgently sent in to take charge, along with a radio operator and adequate supplies of arms. Two days later, her OSS commander thanked her for her 'excellent' work and suggested she herself should become the radio operator for the Haute-Loire mission,[9] 'where it was felt that her unusual talent for organization would be better utilised'.[10] For the first time she was officially to be given command herself. OSS records of 18 June state: 'It is planned to put her in charge of this Maquis.' As usual, it was never going to be that simple.

Virginia was reluctant to leave at once. She wanted to see through a series of parachute drops, ordering in much-needed surgical supplies and even bicycle tyres along with the guns and ammunition. She also wanted to settle in the new radio operators she had called in to replace her in the Cher and Nièvre. In Le Chambon, though, Fayol was becoming impatient at the lack of news. The days passed and after a fortnight still there was no word from her. The money had been useful but by early July – a whole month after D-Day – the men remained without guns or explosives. The worst fighting in the region was away from the plateau, but its proximity was provoking panic, particularly after a battle at nearby Le Cheylard saw the deaths of hundreds of locals and fighters. The Germans were also now moving en masse towards Normandy from the south-west of France, shooting and burning everyone and everything in their path. Without arms, Fayol's men could neither help their comrades nor send down raiding parties to ambush the enemy in the valley below.

Finally, Fayol could stand it no more. He dispatched two emissaries to find *Diane* and bring her back at whatever cost. They were Jacqueline Decourdemanche, a teacher whose husband had been shot by the Germans, and Eric Barbezat, a bookseller in Le Chambon. Both agreed to undertake the perilous mission and cycled the forty miles down to St-Etienne, avoiding the German patrols as much as possible, and taking the night train to Cosne-sur-Loire, where they arrived on the morning of 6 July. They disembarked separately and Jacqueline went alone to the address in rue de Donzy. Miraculously she found Virginia passing through, even though she now stayed nowhere for more than a few hours. Virginia explained to her visitor that she had sent a message to Le Chambon warning of her imminent arrival, but that it must have been lost. In any case, she was ready to leave, and she grabbed the three suitcases standing in the hall. One contained her clothes, the other two her radio set and an assortment of firearms. Jacqueline marvelled at *Diane*'s serenity, knowing they would have to pass through several controls on their journey and that if caught at any one she would face certain death. Yet far from seeming cowed by the dangers she faced, Virginia looked her most radiant, as if she had found an almost spiritual peace in the midst of the deadliest turmoil. She reminded Jacqueline of a Renaissance statue of the Madonna – 'very beautiful' and suffused with a 'remarkable calm'[11] despite the 'contents of the cases she was carrying'.

It was not as if Virginia could rely any longer on her disguise. Having abandoned her peasant garb, Virginia's striking looks (her hair was now a glossy chestnut) meant she cut a conspicuous figure. When making their way through the station to meet Barbezat, a member of the railway staff immediately assumed she was foreign and sidled up to her to whisper warning of an imminent German control. He beckoned for the three of them to hide in the train depot, and they had little choice but to follow him, not knowing for sure for several nerve-racking minutes that they were not being lured into a trap. The Gestapo did indeed turn up for a snap inspection – they could hear the sound of heavy boots on the platform and German voices shouting – but mercifully they did not search the shed and left empty-handed before the train arrived. The three clambered aboard and stood in the hot, packed corridor, worrying about how they would deal with another control when there was nowhere to hide.

The train set off and the last sun rays were peeping over the hills when they heard the wail of an air-raid siren. The crowded carriages came to a screeching halt, sending passengers tumbling on top of each other and cases flying. The train guards led the charge to jump out and disperse into the fields for cover. Doors were flung open and men, women and children screamed as they pushed over each other to get as far away as possible from the sitting-duck train before the bombardment began. The planes were almost directly above them when Eric and Jacqueline finally managed to scramble towards the open doors, but Virginia grabbed their arms before they jumped. Speaking softly and calmly she advised her two companions to remain in the carriage. 'It's the English who are bombing,' she explained. 'I warned them. They know I'm on this train. We won't be touched.' The bombs were raining down all around them now, rattling the carriages and filling the air with acrid smoke. Eric looked in astonishment at the completely unruffled Virginia and could not believe that they would survive the rest of their journey if their route was now being targeted by the RAF. 'But what if the railway bridge at Nevers is bombed in the night?' he gasped. 'Oh, it will be demolished,' Virginia confirmed. 'But not until tomorrow, in the morning, after our train has passed through.'[12] She was right.

Virginia's constant communications with London meant she was fully briefed on RAF operations in the region and could equally warn her commanders of her whereabouts so that she was not put in unnecessary danger by her own side. The planes, having discharged their bombs on targets close – but not too close – to the train duly flew away into the distance. It had, however, been a long night by the time the three arrived at St-Etienne early in the morning, only to discover the car that should have been waiting to take Virginia to Le Chambon had not turned up.

They waited in vain at the station, knowing they were painfully easy to spot on the wide-open concourse. Finally, as Virginia would not be parted from her cases, Eric left the two women to chase up the missing driver from his home. On his way, a man he had never seen before made a point of bumping into him and asked for a light. As Eric struck a match the stranger leant in and whispered not to proceed to the house as the driver had been denounced and his home put under surveillance. He then disappeared into a side street and Eric never found out how he had known to warn him. It was clear, however, that Virginia would have to make her own way up to the plateau.

Eric had to think quickly. Virginia could hardly be left much longer as at any moment a patrol might decide to search her cases. St-Etienne was a garrison town for German troops and security was tight; the atmosphere was particularly edgy since a recent American air raid had killed a thousand people – French civilians as well as German soldiers. Americans were consequently not universally popular and the likelihood of a denunciation was high. And although Allied troops might now be on French soil, they were still stuck hundreds of miles away in Normandy and here the war was far from over. All Eric could come up with by way of a plan was to visit his old boss in the factory where he had worked back in 1939. The two men were on good terms, but Eric could not vouch for his former employer's current loyalties, particularly as so many local children had been killed in the bombing. To ask him for help was yet another gamble, but he had no choice. He ran to the factory and explained to the *patron* that two women friends were stuck at the station because someone had failed to turn up to meet them. Could he help? To Eric's relief, the response was 'spontaneous ... he would go to fetch them himself' and they could rest in a quiet room until four in the afternoon when a bus left for St-Genest-Malifaux, a quieter town on the route to Le Chambon. There they could book into a hotel and look for a taxi.

After taking refuge in the factory the party boarded the bus separately and Eric and Jacqueline put their bicycles on the roof. Virginia, as ever, was alert to any potentially useful information and overheard talk on the bus of a milk cart that was to take passengers from St-Genest all the way to Le Chambon. At St-Genest she instructed Eric to track down the milk cart urgently, as she had to reach Le Chambon within two hours to make a scheduled transmission to London. He went running around the streets but found they were too late. The cart was 'already rammed', he told her. No one else was allowed on. Now stuck, Virginia booked into a hotel and began her transmission just in time. It would be folly for her to stay there for more than a night at most, however, as in a small town her signals would be easy to track down and her foreign accent, reddish hair and pale skin were too obvious. Eric would have to dream up another plan, and quickly.

During the night there was an emergency at the hotel and around dawn an ambulance pulled up outside. Two medical staff dashed up the stairs and a few minutes later a figure wrapped head-to-toe in blankets was brought out on a stretcher and put in the ambulance, which began to edge slowly towards the local hospital. As it reached the turning to Le Chambon, however, it veered off and started pelting up the road to the plateau. Inside, emerging from the covers, Virginia was finally on her way with her precious cases at her side thanks to another of Eric's old friends doing him a favour.[13] The following day Eric learned that the Gestapo had stopped the milk cart, arrested the driver, fired shots at the luggage piled on top of the milk and carted off several passengers for interrogation. It had been another close call.

The ambulance dropped her off on the outskirts of Le Chambon with a pastor who had no idea who she was or what to do with her. None of this impressed Virginia at all. Particularly when German troops were often walking through the village streets – indeed some were staying at the Hôtel du Lignon, next to a guesthouse sheltering Jewish children. 'Nothing had been arranged about a place for me to live and work,' she complained, beginning to regret that she had come at all. She blamed Fayol for not having made arrangements for her as she was patently risking her life coming to help him. He and other Resistance chiefs had also quarrelled among themselves over the money she had left on her last visit. It was, she decided, 'a bad beginning', and a portent of things to come. There were clearly a lot of egos at stake, and not much in the way of effective leadership, although most of the rank and file she considered very good. Yet with nowhere else to go, Virginia had to insist she move in, at least temporarily, with Fayol and his wife in the farmhouse at Riou so that she could begin transmitting.

Her arrival made an instant impression. Marianne Fayol was yet another struck by *Diane*'s mesmerising charisma and 'very British' appearance, her authority and the 'physical impact that reinforced it'. As the local Resistance welfare officer, Marianne was accustomed to trying to deal with endless requests from the Maquis for more food, clothes, medicines or cigarettes. But *Diane* 'demanded no personal comforts and slept for days on strawstacks without complaining',[14] while she and her husband took the only bed.

Even though they were sharing a house, Marianne had no idea about Cuthbert until she suggested bathing together in the stream running by the house, the only running water. Virginia agreed, but pulled up her skirt to show her amputated leg and, clearly worried about Marianne's possible reaction, said 'If I don't frighten you.' It was a rare and fleeting glimpse of Virginia's insecurities. In the end, neither bathed.

Virginia's sole requirement at this point was somewhere to transmit. She spent hours every day sending and receiving radio messages, and coding and decoding them at the kitchen table. Encryption techniques had changed rapidly during the war, as each one was tried and often swiftly abandoned when broken by the Germans. Using the latest and more secure 'one-time pad' system, Virginia could be seen poring over a square of silk the size of a handkerchief printed with fifty columns and fifty lines of random numbers and letters (Home station held the only duplicate set). Each time she used a column for coding or decoding a transmission, she assiduously ripped it off the square and burned it.[15] She knew of far too many radio operators who had not taken care to destroy such evidence and who had paid with their lives.

Now that the Germans had highly sophisticated radio detection equipment, the job of radio transmitting was more dangerous than ever. She explained to Fayol that she had frequently to change her base because of low-flying German detector planes. Known as Storks[16] because in flight their wheels hung down on long struts, looking like birds' legs, these small aircraft regularly scanned the skies for signs of clandestine radio transmissions. (They were more effective in open countryside than the Funkabwehr vans because of the distances involved.) If he saw one or heard their unusual whirring engine noise, Fayol should throw himself face down on the ground and stay absolutely still, she said, and when it had passed over immediately sound the alert. If it had found a signal, it would be followed by other planes that would 'paste the place ... with bombs'. Even a three-second acknowledgement transmission could be traced to within half a mile, and a longer message could be pinpointed to within several yards.

In truth, both parties were eager for her to move on. After two days, and another in Camus's former boarding house, she installed herself in a barn owned by a hospitable baker in the village of Villelonge, nearer to the Maquis camps and best drop zone. Again she made do with no running (let alone hot) water and sleeping on wooden pallets, but at least she could use the barn as her headquarters and trust the baker to warn her of trouble. It was here that she was finally able to train up her own loyal group of partisans, with the help of twenty-four-year-old Lieutenant Bob – a wisecracking former sailor called Raoul le Boulicaut, whom Virginia immediately found far more obliging than Fayol. Bob and his men had lived and operated in the mountains as outlaws for over a year, through the harshest of winters, but Bob had managed to maintain discipline, rigidly excluding those he considered trigger happy or unruly. It had taken nearly everything for his men simply to survive, hide, eat and dress themselves, and they had relied on handouts from locals. Most of the troop, a third of whom were Jewish, all very young, were billeted in a derelict farmhouse and operated on the eastern slopes of the plateau with views of the roads from Lyon and St-Etienne. They saw Virginia's devotion to duty and willingness to endure the same hardships. Their admiration was mutual. 'I knew he was a bit of a comedian but he was so solid and so good and his men loved him so much,' Virginia related, so 'I took Bob and his particular Maquis of about thirty unto myself.'[17] Soon her men were exchanging tales of how she had lost her leg on a mission in the Far East – gossip she thought useful and did nothing to dispel.

Bob's men agreed to stand guard while she frantically transmitted her findings back to London, watching out for Storks, the Gestapo, the Milice or any other predators. Until now they had had to make do with a handful of weapons smuggled in overland but this mysterious newcomer, Bob told them, was a 'very important figure in the inter-Allied secret services' who would 'arrange extraordinary supplies of arms and sabotage materials'.[18] Word of such an apparently powerful figure soon spread and brought in more recruits – not least a local farmer, Victor Ruelle, who volunteered with 150 of his friends and relations. Virginia was all too delighted to accept and set about organising and training them, and identifying suitable targets for ambushes or bombings. When London also offered her the services of the under-employed *Aramis* – no one seriously thought of him as her commander any longer – unsurprisingly she promptly 'replied in the negative'.

Not everyone was as helpful or friendly to Virginia as Bob's men, however. In fact, some *résistants* were suspicious or even positively obstructive despite her offers of help. Resistance in France was by now more factional than ever, riven by personality clashes and political allegiances, particularly between the Gaullists and the communists, who resented de Gaulle's growing power and conservative views. Virginia made sure never to discuss politics and as a true agent she was willing to work with anyone who could help her defeat the Nazis, including the communist Francs-Tireurs et Partisans, because she thought them brave and efficient. She tried hard to bring the warring tribes together but often it was impossible – and both disliked the fact she worked with their rival factions. They were more accustomed to putting bounties on each other's heads, while others engaged themselves in vengeance killings and summary trials against suspected collaborators. Indeed, there was so much fighting between the French themselves that some historians refer to the *guerre franco-français* of this time, a French civil war playing out as a kind of subplot as the European war reached its climax.

War is always messy and confusing, but for some of these French fighters the question of who was going to run their country after liberation had become the single most important consideration. Almost everything they did was to advance their own post-war position. Fayol had thrown his loyalty behind the more Gaullist elements of the Resistance, some of whom, like *Antoine*, harboured deep suspicions of Anglo-American plans for his country, even fearing a sort of reverse Norman Conquest. Still feeling the humiliation of France's rapid defeat in 1940, they particularly disliked what they saw as the way that President Roosevelt excluded de Gaulle, the only plausible future French leader, from the Allied Big Three (Churchill, Roosevelt and Stalin). This may well have been behind Virginia's refusal to reveal that she was American, let alone the fact she worked for a United States secret service. This seething background also perhaps explains if not excuses Fayol's conduct.

Indeed, Fayol began to undermine the very woman who was trying to help him, by stoking up distrust of her. On whose authority was Virginia giving orders, he spluttered. How dare a woman, especially a foreign one, start throwing her weight around? Neither the French secret services nor the French military deployed women in the field, and there were very few in the fighting elements of the Resistance. Who seriously believed that the *sorcière rousse* (or ginger witch), as she was now called, could produce the guns and explosives she was promising? Virginia knew too well what was going on and believed that Fayol's commanding officer *Gévolde*, a former veterinary surgeon stationed down in the valley, was also involved. 'I disapprove [of them] as men,' she reported to London. Fortunately, Bob continued to do 'a swell job' and 'stood by' her 'through any amount of trouble'.

In the power struggle that ensued, Virginia came to view the Fayol group as poor leaders guilty of 'personal prestige greed'. They wanted to 'take everything and give nothing', she said, raging at the fact that they were eager for the supplies she was offering but refusing to guarantee they would use them to follow her orders as set by Allied Command. Simply by being 'more worldly' they had been able to seize control of the Haute-Loire Maquis but she thought them self-aggrandising, despised by their own men and reckless in their security arrangements. A number of volunteers had already drifted away but most had stayed on because they were on the run from the Nazis or the Milice and could not return to civilian life, and simply wanted to 'do something about the Germans'. She said she 'got along very well with the men' and in the circumstances did her 'best for them'.[19]

She wanted to bring in two specialist officers from London to provide badly needed training in the hit-and-run tactics of guerrilla warfare. But Fayol and *Gévolde* vehemently opposed the idea of British or American officers interfering in their patch – or perhaps showing up their inadequacies – and so she thought it better to cancel the plans. She later called for two sergeants instead, believing their lower rank to be a less confrontational option, but now her repeated requests for support were ignored. Without backup from SFHQ, however, Virginia was on her own with hundreds of untrained men and knew she was dangerously exposed. Fayol was meanwhile making inquiries about her authority – although fortunately word came back suggesting (incorrectly) that she was a lieutenant-colonel, four levels more senior than her actual rank. This helpful report sustained her for now, but unless she could conjure up her first parachute drop of supplies very soon she knew her life could become impossible.

War films may sometimes give the impression that success on D-Day marked the end of the worst of the fighting, but across many areas of France, including Virginia's, it created new challenges of its own. The remaining Germans – and their French collaborators – were edgy, afraid and more brutal than ever. Virginia had to keep moving around to stay ahead of the Storks while she pressed on with arranging her first drop. Next stop was a modest farmstead on a hill above Le Chambon belonging to Maurice Lebrat's cousin Léa.[20] Madame Lebrat's husband was a prisoner of war in Germany, and she had her hands full running her farm and bringing up two small children on her own. Yet this diminutive woman in a homely floral apron not only made *Diane* welcome – and fed her extremely well – but turned out to be another pillar of the Resistance, keeping open house for the Maquis but refusing to take payment. 'My mother was never afraid, just careful,' remembers her daughter, Georgette.[21] The penalties for being caught were all too clear. One recent weekend, the Germans and Milice had swooped on nearby farms they suspected of sheltering members of the Resistance, gunning down nine unarmed farmers and leaving their bodies on the ground. Eleven more were arrested and three farms set ablaze.[22]

Yet Léa took Virginia in 'without question – anything to help'. Léa put her foot down on only one thing: she would not hide guns. Keeping one eye out for anyone coming up the lane, Georgette remembers that her mother did allow Virginia to run her aerial through the window on the north side of the house where reception was good. In the absence of electricity, Virginia modified a loaned car battery to power her radio, which was recharged by the young Edmond Lebrat (yet another member of the clan) pedalling hard on an adapted bicycle. She would sit beside him, headphones on, tapping out her Morse code to the receiving stations in England who recognised her transmitting style at once.

Léa Lebrat was also sheltering a sweet-natured twenty-two-year-old teacher from Alsace, Dédé Zurbach, who was on the run from the Service du Travail Obligatoire and traumatised by the fact the Germans had taken his mother and sister as hostage in revenge. Dédé had been one of the Maquis who accompanied Virginia on her inspection tour of the drop zones back in June. He now became her 'Man Friday' – a combination of driver, assistant, courier and bodyguard – an exhausting role as Virginia herself admitted that she often behaved like a 'slave-driver'.[23] She got her 'boys' to work flat out at procuring batteries, dynamos and sometimes even perfumes for her own use, and taught her favourites how to keep the accounts and even decode signals. 'She was very active,' he recalled fondly, and 'demanded our presence at all times'.

Virginia bought bicycles for herself, Dédé, Edmond Lebrat and Bob and pedalled furiously up and down mountains, checking drop zones and training her team for the vital first delivery. Every evening she listened to the BBC, but while there were plenty of messages for other parts of France, none of them was for her. Until the men heard one of the pre-agreed phrases recited back to them, she had in truth no real proof of her authority in London. It was a nervous wait. Finally, one night the BBC announcer said 'Cette obscure clarté tombait des étoiles' three times, meaning three planes were now on their way.

The reception team rushed to the Bream zone, high on a vast open stretch of the plateau. There were no tarmac roads up here and only a handful of houses scattered round the edge of what felt truly like the top of the world. On the horizon, the volcanic

Massif Central mountains stood out against the fast-fading light, the curious tooth-shaped peaks of Mont Mézenc and Mont Lizieux standing guard at either end. As the sky darkened to an inky purple, Virginia herself made an appearance to a collective gasp from the thirty or so men on duty. The mysterious 'woman English officer' they all now referred to as *la Madone*[24] had discarded her summer dresses in favour of an army jacket and khaki trousers, her only adornment an orange silk square knotted at her neck (a handy way of hiding her transmitting codes). Several of the men exchanged appreciative glances at her military look – accompanied, whenever she could, by the hint of an expensive French scent. Their chatter came to a halt as she approached to check that bundles of sticks had been placed perfectly, 150 paces apart on the flattest area of grass in a giant Y shape. These would help the pilots to position themselves to drop their loads, by flying up the wider end of the Y, into the prevailing westerly wind. Several took their posts as sentries on the perimeter to deal with anyone who approached; others stood by for the signal to set light to the sticks or start flashing the zone-identity letter R in Morse code to the pilots. Gabriel, a young orphan for whom Virginia's Maquis was to become a surrogate family, had the job of straining his ears for the first suggestion of plane engines in the distance. Virginia ordered everyone to be completely quiet while he listened, keeping one eye on Fayol, who had just arrived to observe. It was clear that long, tense night that Virginia's credibility – and maybe even her life – was on the line if she did not deliver. The velvety sky was dressed in sparkling stars, the wind was gently brushing the grass, but long past one in the morning still there was silence. Would no one come after all? Were they still to be alone? Was *la Madone* a fake?

At last Gabriel thought he could hear a low, deep sound, and as it grew louder Virginia signalled to the men to light the fires.

Soon a throaty roar was cutting through the darkness and they could make out the unmistakable silhouette of three RAF Halifax bombers flying in formation. Trying to stifle their cheers the men ran to their positions. Taking their cue from the mountain outlines the pilots banked to their right, pulling back on the throttle now, losing height and flying straight towards the electrified crowd on the ground. Down and down the bombers came, to less than six hundred feet above their heads, and when each one reached the centre of the Y they opened their hatches. Instead of bombs came showers of silk parachutes carrying huge cylindrical containers that thudded onto the ground all around them. As the Halifaxes rose back up into the darkness, more than likely the pilots performed the customary dip of the wings in farewell, triggering a wave of emotion inside everyone on the ground. The long, lonely months of waiting were over; this distant part of France was no longer forgotten. *La Madone* had delivered.

Virginia snapped the men into action. She had drilled them to split into teams to stamp out the fires, cut the ropes from the twenty metal containers and ten packages now scattered across the plateau, and to fold the parachutes into bags. Each metal container, produced by the Southern Gas Board in Croydon, weighed about 145 kilograms, and a total of more than three tonnes of supplies had to be quickly and noiselessly loaded onto waiting ox-drawn carts and driven to a nearby safehouse before being distributed amongst the Maquis. Virginia gave them precisely fifteen minutes to finish the job and leave the scene. Gabriel remembered that 'this ... operation, like those that followed, had to leave no trace. Not to retrieve a cord or piece of parachute fabric ... or a container could lead to tragic consequences for one person or the group or even the local population as a whole: arrests, torture, death.'[25] The containers themselves were thrown into a raging waterfall at the near-end of the plateau at Gouffre de la Monette. The silk from each parachute, however, was fashioned by the women of the villages into twenty or so blouses and dresses.

In the safehouse, Virginia and her team made an inventory. That night they listed medicines, battle dress with the Croix de Lorraine on the breast pocket (so that the Maquis could abandon their rags); pairs of boots (most Maquis were making do with old clogs or no footwear at all); comforts (biscuits, cigarettes, and packets of her favourite tea from SOE marked '*pour Diane*'); but above all arms. There were Brens (the principal Maquis automatic weapon), Stens (the simple Maquis close-combat gun, much loved because it could fire captured German ammunition) grenades and explosives. Virginia's knowledge of the different weapons, their qualities and condition impressed them, and she expertly divided, repacked and hid them under straw. There was also an S-phone – a cutting-edge portable transmitter worn on a strap around the neck. Developed by SOE boffins, it would allow Virginia to talk directly to approaching pilots from the ground. It was a grand haul by any measure. There was also an exhilarating sense, according to one maquisard (a former teacher) that night, of recognition, renewed pride and of being brothers in arms with strangers many miles away: 'We were no longer terrorists, or dodgers of STO service, but part of a liberating army; and recognised as such.'[26]

Night after night came more planes and more parachutes – bringing weapons, but also chocolate, petrol cans, bandages, vitamins, medicines and more Benzedrine (and on one poignant occasion a letter from Virginia's mother revealing she had been unwell). In a sealed container marked '*pour Diane*' there was an envelope containing a million francs for her to distribute as she saw fit, and several pairs of the special socks for Cuthbert that had been personally packed by Vera Atkins. For her men – and the villagers who watched with awe from afar – it was as if wherever *La Madone* turned up the night skies came alive with the roar of Halifaxes. In all there were twenty-two drops, twenty on the *Bream* ground and two on neighbouring zones. The fires were swiftly replaced with more efficient battery lamps or head-lights; the ox-carts were supplemented by a gazogène lorry with Maréchal Pétain scrawled on the side; and Virginia now used the S-phone to direct the approaching pilots from the ground (such advanced technology for 1944 merely added to her allure). News of this 'Madonna of the Mountains' travelled quickly. Some said she had descended from the skies herself and that she could apparently summon guns and explosives at will.

The night-time balletics were undoubtedly Virginia's show and the first one had gone without a hitch. But the second saw an inexperienced pilot release his cargo on another zone by mis-take, at Devesset, fifteen miles away in the Ardèche. When he told Virginia what he had done via the S-phone, the poor young pilot soon regretted it. She responded with a furious torrent of Anglo-Saxon curses before dispatching Bob to Devesset with the lorry to retrieve the containers and hide them in a neighbouring farm. On other long watchful nights the planes never turned up at all; others came in too low so that the containers exploded on impact with the ground; or thick cloud obscured the Y-shaped navigation lights; or, worst of all, they were shot down on their way over. (The RAF SD or Special Duties squadrons had become the lifeblood of the Resistance but paid heavily in the number of crew lost.) One message was intercepted by the Germans, who turned up at one of the lesser-used drop zones – but fortunately that was a night when the Halifaxes did not come. The intruders were dealt with, and their bodies thrown in the Lignon river. But the strain of keeping everyone on side was taking its toll. Virginia found her time in the Haute-Loire to be 'different and difficult . . . spending the nights out waiting, for the most part in vain, for deliveries'.[27] Sometimes she went several nights at a time without sleep, delving into her supplies of Benzedrine to keep going, and sharing the tablets around her bleary-eyed team. Such was the pressure that the slightest failure triggered an explosion of temper, swearing and smoking, and spitting on the ground in frustration like the trooper she had become.

'*Diane* breathed energy, courage and charm. But she could also be imposing and imperious,'[28] said André Roux, one of Bob's men. 'From time to time we were treated to Homeric bollockings,' agreed Dédé. '*Diane* was not always easy to be with . . . but she left a huge mark on all those who lived by her side. I would not have missed knowing her for all the world.'[29] Virginia was well aware that she was demanding, not least because very unusually she was both organiser and radio operator (each a full-time job in itself and requiring very different skills). But she made sure, after her experiences in Lyon with difficult colleagues, that she was also appreciative. She would say that it was Dédé and the men of 'Bob's company' who 'made it possible for me to live and work in the Haute-Loire'. And she joined in the male camaraderie, not least the traditional Maquis farewell: '*A bientôt, mon cher. Merde!*' If she had once treated Leccia and Allard as nephews, the youngest members of the Maquis were her sons. Jean Nallet, a school-age orphan taken in by Bohny, once told her he dreamed of being a doctor. She responded by appointing him her medical assistant, giving him the bandages and medicines to look after and teaching him the first-aid skills she had learned as an ambulance driver back in 1940. By the last week of July, such was her fame and popularity that she was besieged by volunteers. From an initial thirty she was now in command of four hundred maquisards, whom she had organised into five companies. 'Unlimited recruitment' was possible, she signalled London, if they could guarantee her the delivery of more arms. On good nights Virginia would treat her closest followers to glasses of schnapps – liberated from the Germans of course. At times like these, Dédé later recalled, they found themselves sharing the most vivid 'moments of happiness.'[30]

With more supplies, though, came more problems. It was clear in Virginia's mind that the deal with Fayol was that she would finance his groups and give them weapons, and in return they should take orders from her as part of the wider Allied post D-Day strategy. He recognised no such obligation, and wanted to follow only orders from Commander *Gévolde* of the FFI, or French Forces of the Interior (now the formal name for the French-run elements of the Resistance and expected to conduct itself more like a regular army). She tried to work with Fayol and company as what she called *hommes de confiance*, or trusted insiders, but they were 'all take, no give'. Virginia was far from the only British or American agent to encounter such hostility – but she was determined that the power struggle would not impede the real battle against the Germans. Fortunately, they could at least agree on the principal targets for attack. 'As long as *Gévolde* and Fayol . . . were willing to do sabotage and guerrilla work I did not care about the fact that they would not cooperate with me in the matter of my own existence,' she later reported ruefully. In any case, Virginia could call on Bob's company and Victor Ruelle's large band of men for her own operations. In a remote barn she trained them up in sabotage as well as she could. One key point to remember was that plastic explosive could be safely secreted in a trouser pocket and body heat helped mould it to fit a target object, but equally detonators were temperamental and could not be carried in the hand as they might explode by themselves. Virginia now directed dozens of sabotage missions, although to her frustration she could not take part in the action. The price on her head was still too high for her to come out of the shadows, and Cuthbert would certainly impede her chances of escape, but she masterminded every detail until the last moment.

Fayol was still being unhelpful, even though she continued to keep him fully supplied. As she had learned to do when someone was being obstructive, Virginia decided to find another FFI officer who *would* help her break the stalemate. This time she would go with the money, as she knew that the FFI was desperately short of cash. She contacted the FFI treasurer-paymaster via a liaison agent, deliberately using the male codename *Nicolas* and allowing him to believe she was British (which she thought more conciliatory), to offer him financing. When he agreed to a meeting she paid a local English teacher with cigarettes to borrow her car and drove down to Le Puy to see him. Commandant Emile Thérond was no doubt astonished when a commanding woman walked into his hideout offering him cash. Immediately he took a more collaborative approach than Fayol or *Gévolde* and together they struck a deal. If the FFI cooperated with Allied objectives – including the choice of targets for attack and the techniques to be used – she would hand over a total of three million francs, payable only on results. Both parties were delighted. The money was enough to fund three battalions of fifteen hundred men as well as a sustained sabotage campaign and would put the local FFI on a sound financial footing at last. Virginia had got her way by the back door and earned Thérond's respect for her hard-bargaining style. He praised her 'firm resolution, energy and order and very great organising ability' and found working with such an 'accomplished leader' the 'greatest pleasure'. In fact, he aligned himself so closely with her that when she left the area he resigned from the FFI with immediate effect.

Allied Command now identified Le Puy, a medieval city surrounded by cone-shaped extinct volcanoes, as the primary target. Thanks to her network of observers, it was Virginia who had broken the vital news to London that the German General Staff was moving its headquarters there from Lyon (where it had been since the 1942 occupation of the Free Zone) because it was considered safer territory. The goal was to draft in the FFI, thanks to Commandant Thérond's cooperation, to help make the Nazis regret the move. Soon there was a major explosion almost every night as Virginia unleashed dozens of what she called 'bridge and tunnel wrecking' operations to delay German troop movements in and around the city and cut off their supplies. She sent teams down from their hiding places on the plateau to blow up roads and cut railways, to derail German freight trains and destroy several bridges.

One of the most spectacular missions – now finally with Fayol's collaboration – was on 2 August, on the major railway line between Le Puy and St-Etienne. It crossed the Loire on a high one-track bridge at Chamalières, just north of Le Puy – an ideal spot for sabotage. Under cover of darkness a small team of maquisards placed Virginia's explosives along the floor of the bridge as she had trained them to do, and at six in the morning blew out a huge hole. Other Maquis, meanwhile, stopped an approaching train ten miles away by felling trees across the tracks and setting off firecrackers. The Miliciens travelling in the carriages were taken prisoner and once the driver and fireman had climbed down from the cab the trees were hauled away and three partisans took over the controls. They then stoked up the fire and drove the train down the line at maximum speed towards the semi-collapsed bridge. Just one hundred metres short all three jumped out into the bushes at the side of the track while the hissing locomotive ploughed into the breach, putting the railway between St-Etienne and Le Puy completely out of service.[31] By 8 August Virginia reported Le Puy in a state of siege and all major approaches to the city cut. She then turned her attention to destroying electricity and phone lines, leaving the German occupiers without power and unable to communicate with other units for days at a time, except by wireless signals that were easy for the Allies to intercept.

Virginia kept her London controllers informed of progress at least once a day. While the huge Allied forces were still battling it out in Normandy – only taking the city of Caen on 21 July, after six weeks of battle – Virginia was reporting that partisans in the Haute-Loire were successfully harassing German troops and taking control of more and more of their *département*. In this new stage of warfare, and with hundreds of volunteers at her bidding, the ambush of German vehicles or even convoys was as important as sabotage. Both the Germans and Allied command were astonished by the numbers of French would-be warriors who now came out to fight in regions such as the Haute-Loire. The results across much of France in the weeks following D-Day surpassed expectations and also created serious military diversions that, together with massive Allied bombardment, prevented the Wehrmacht from reforming against the Allied forces further north and south.

Virginia's operations – meticulously researched by numerous reconnaissance trips – were certainly among the more successful. From his office at the new SFHQ, Maurice Buckmaster marvelled at how adeptly her groups 'violently engaged with the enemy',[32] using the rocky, forested terrain to their full advantage to maximise the element of surprise and to disappear without trace. One such attack came from the wooded banks of the Loire at Lavôute, just north of Le Puy. Eighteen of Virginia's men took well-camouflaged positions between the trees to launch a highly successful attack on a convoy of 135 German soldiers, killing fourteen and destroying several trucks without casualties on the French side.[33] On another occasion they destroyed a German truck full of troops with a well-hidden bazooka and surrounded and arrested nineteen Miliciens and seized their valuable documents, again without loss. More explosions came on railway lines, with tunnels a favourite target because the damage was more difficult to repair, keeping the track out of action for longer. On one occasion, they blew up a railway tunnel once and then blew it up again when a repair train was inside it. The earth would repeatedly shudder with the force of the explosions. 'This extremely courageous woman [is] doing fine work,'[34] senior OSS officers acknowledged on 14 August. She even received a modest promotion to first lieutenant – although that still hardly reflected the job she was doing and did not immediately lead to an increase in pay.

The tide of war was turning fast, but Virginia was still in constant danger from remaining elements of the Gestapo, who were now engaged in frenzies of killing. Over in Lyon, Klaus Barbie was murdering hundreds of his Resistance prisoners at Montluc prison, including a dashing young doctor, Roger Le Forestier, who had looked after Virginia's men on the plateau and who had been arrested on 4 August just outside Le Puy. Such was the carnage that there were reports of blood seeping through the prison ceilings, and yet the deadly round-ups and Barbie's obsession with closing in on Virginia and other leaders continued. She moved house once again to avoid the Storks, this time taking a handsome three-bedroom house abandoned by the Salvation Army at Roybet, halfway between Léa Lebrat's farm and the *Bream* drop zone. It was well-hidden from the road and she was thrilled to have her own place, for which she paid a generous thousand francs in rent. She tidied and cleaned it and made the spare bedrooms comfortable for 'incoming personnel' while hiding her radio in a disused water tunnel at the back. Somehow she even found time to pick mushrooms in the woods and pluck fish from the trout stream that gurgled past her gate. Mme Lebrat continued to cook for her, sending her young daughter down the two-mile path through the woods like Little Red Riding Hood, with delicious hot meals wrapped in paper.

Of course, Virginia was still thinking of her nephews – and despite all the other claims on her time continued to organise food parcels for them in prison. She could no longer leave her post so she radioed her old SOE champion Ben Cowburn, whom she thought most likely to be able to help. In early August Cowburn contacted a friendly prison orderly on her behalf, only to hear the dreaded news that Leccia, Allard, Geelen and the five others with them had already been transported to Germany and out of her reach for ever. The nephews had been sent to what Virginia called Weimar, once the classically handsome centre of the eighteenth-century European Enlightenment. What she meant was the death camp at Buchenwald, a wooded area on its outskirts. 'I do not know what happens to such prisoners after they arrive at Weimar,' she signalled in distress to London, but no doubt she had a good idea. They were paying the highest price for unshakeable loyalty.

Diane may have been an iron figure forged in the flames of war, but Virginia would not be able to come to terms with the fate dealt to so many of her bravest friends. If there was never a let-up in her fight against the Reich, there were moments now when her very being yearned for it all to end. Perhaps there were times too when she wondered whether it had all been worth it. Occasionally she let her guard down with Dédé and Edmond Lebrat over late-night cups of her beloved tea when they met to plan the next day. She talked of her homesickness[35] and yet she never hinted at where home was.

Every day in August she directed more attacks on the Germans, although not all went to plan. One small ambush unit unexpectedly stumbled across a large convoy of fifty-four Nazi vehicles and had to retreat rapidly, but not in time to save their operation leader, who was killed. But the continual assaults on personnel and communications took their toll on the SS, the pro-Nazi Russian volunteers and the Miliciens still holding out in the area. They had retreated into Le Puy, which being surrounded by hills was relatively easy to defend. The FFI and others now tightened the noose – with the idea of forcing the Germans out, as Virginia put it, by 'sheer bluff'. Under Virginia's direction, they cut the phone lines so that the Germans had no direct link with other units outside, reinforcing the impression of being under siege. They then intercepted German wireless signals so that every time the enemy ventured out of their garrison the partisans knew about it beforehand and were able to attack – giving the impression of omniscient guerrilla forces. The partisans also ambushed incoming supplies of food and fuel, so that the Germans started to panic about starving. Finally, on 18 August a German column of fifty lorries and eight hundred soldiers tried to make a dash for it. Forewarned, Virginia's guerrillas helped to encircle the convoy and by blowing up several bridges prevented them from escaping and reinforcements from joining them. The fighting was brutal and the hard-pushed partisans were fast running out of working guns and ammunition. Yet finally they were to triumph, having killed 150 Germans and taken five hundred troops and Miliciens prisoner. They then moved on to attack the town itself and over-ran the German garrison the following day, taking more than a thousand prisoners. On 22 August, the exhausted but valiant partisans trapped the ragged remnants of a final German convoy twenty miles north of Le Puy while Virginia desperately called in more weapons and ammunition. For five long days the fighting raged in the torrid late-summer heat as the enemy tried to push its way through and the FFI held their positions under intense fire. Five French were killed in this dogged last-ditch stand by the Nazi troops, but thirty-one Germans lost their lives. This was the decisive moment, marking the end of fighting in the region. To much jubilation the local commander, Major Schmähling, running out of supplies and hope, surrendered at Estivareilles along with six hundred men. The area was cleared of the enemy at last.

Thanks to Virginia, the French had saved themselves. Teachers, farmers, schoolboys and factory workers financed, organised, armed and often directed by her had liberated the Haute-Loire without professional military help. They had defeated the Germans two days before the Allied armies even reached Paris, let alone freed most of the rest of France, where the battle was still raging. It was an incredible achievement and she signalled London with the news – and asked for new orders. It was in officially recording her 'truly amazing performance' in the region that SOE files mention for the first time her prosthetic leg.[36]

News travelled quickly. In the Cher, Philippe de Vomécourt heard word of her exceptional guerrilla work, which even he hailed as on equal terms with any other in the field. It was also gratifying to hear that the regions of Central France she had armed and organised – notably the Creuse – were also among the first outside Normandy to be liberated. Charlotte Norris wrote to Barbara Hall on the day the Haute-Loire was freed to apologise for the fact that Virginia had not been in touch. 'I fully realise how upsetting Virginia's silence must have been. You must not worry, Mrs Hall . . . You have every reason to be proud of her. Virginia is doing a spectacular, man-sized job.'

What they could not have known at this point – and which was not to be revealed for another forty-four years – was that Virginia's work had also helped to pave the way for the Allied re-capture of Paris two days later. According to a 1988 report in

Army, the Association of the United States Army's magazine, her intelligence on the disposition and direction of the Germans' Seventh Army from her time as a milkmaid in central France and thereafter had been 'vital'. Her signals had been used to direct specific aerial reconnaissance and eventually, the magazine explained, helped the Americans to locate and trap the bulk of the opposing German forces in the so-called Falaise Pocket in the Calvados countryside west of Paris. The engagement cost the Nazis up to a hundred thousand men killed or captured and became the decisive Allied breakthrough in the Battle of Normandy more than two months after D-Day. Just three days later, on 24 August, Paris was cleared of the enemy and became a free city again for the first time in more than four years.[37] It was yet another moment when Virginia's efforts played an unsung role in the progress of the war. But Virginia being Virginia, she still had more to prove.

Chapter Eleven

From the Skies Above

The breeze smelt of autumn, the night of 4 September 1944, as Virginia waited on the top of the plateau for the plane bringing two American agents. Three other officers had turned up a few nights previously, one dropping down from an RAF plane apparently in a kilt[1] – an unfortunate choice of uniform considering he landed on top of a pine tree. But at least Captain Geoffrey Hallowes and his radio operator Sergeant Roger Leney had been on time and proved themselves useful. By contrast, these new OSS agents coming in with the US Air Force were nowhere to be seen. At one point she thought she could hear a plane in the distance but when she called the pilot on the S-phone he did not answer. 'Such a performance is inexcusable,' she reported crossly to London, 'but then I find American planes abominable, nonchalant and careless in their work.'[2] Just before dawn she called off the operation.

Lieutenants Henry Riley and Paul Goillot had in fact been dropped twenty miles away at the foot of Mont Gerbier-de-Joncs, close to the source of the Loire. Bad turbulence and strong winds had shaken up the plane and blown them off course, and another brutal landing onto trees had then forced the pair to spend several frantic minutes trying to disentangle themselves from the branches. Fearing the imminent arrival of the Gestapo they rushed around in the dark trying to locate the five packages dropped with them. They gave up after finding only three and set off on foot for Le Chambon, avoiding farmhouses they thought might be occupied by Germans. In the chaos of war no one had briefed them that the area had been liberated; they had no idea until they reached Le Chambon and gave the password to Madame Russier, a contact of *Diane*'s, who ran the village bicycle shop. She told them that the official French Army of General de Lattre de Tassigny, newly arrived in France from the Allied landings of 15 August on the Mediterranean coast, had even come through the village on a victory march a couple of days earlier. Dédé was summoned to look after them and explain that *Diane* could not be disturbed because she was transmitting. He would inform her of their arrival and she would meet them that evening.[3]

The two men were apprehensive. OSS had very few women behind the lines, let alone in positions of command, but Riley and Goillot had been briefed to act as *Diane*'s organiser and weapons instructor. They confessed to feeling uncomfortable about the thought of serving beside, let alone under, a woman in combat but it had been made quite clear to them that 'in view of her wide experience in the field you will place yourself under her orders'.[3] Virginia, on the other hand, recalled with some irritation that 'I finally received the two [back-up] officers I needed so badly when everything was over'.

Bob was his usual supportive presence when he joined them that night for supper in the kitchen at Roybet. No doubt a fire was lit to ward off the autumnal chill as even in war Virginia liked to create as stylish a setting as she could and had made the solid old house with its white shutters and pitched stone roof comfortable and welcoming. Those who were with her in those heady days after the liberation remember her as radiant and serene; the open air and cycling had given her a tan, and she looked at home in her army trousers and battle jacket. This was a happy interlude, Sergeant Leney recalled,[4] and she left an indelible impression – or as they still say of Virginia in Le Chambon, '*les étoiles dans les yeux*' ('stars in their eyes'). Many who were with her at that time recalled with wonder to the end of their lives the contrast between her eye-catching beauty and military savvy. No one could have guessed she was taking 'downers' to try to counteract all the weeks and months of surviving on Benzedrine, which had left her with chronic insomnia. Or that she was again suffering from a nasty, itchy rash across her back (later diagnosed as nervous dermatitis[5]) as a result of the perpetual strain and sleepless nights. Or just how lonely she must have felt.

While Gabriel and Edmond Lebrat counted the two million francs the new arrivals had brought with them, the three Americans got to know each other. Virginia studied her compatriots with a critical eye. Would they help or hinder her? Henry Riley was an all-American Princeton man; he was debonair, charming and a highly trained army officer with every gift except combat experience. It was, however, the more junior Paul Goillot, chain-smoking and chatting amiably in 'pure slang',[6] who caught Virginia's attention. Eight years younger than her and six inches shorter, he had been compared to a bantam[7] by his SOE trainers but his energy and personality were larger than life. Born in Paris to a humble background, he had emigrated to New York as a child after losing his mother but still spoke English with a beguiling trace of a French accent. Lean, fit, tanned, and with a ready smile, Paul had worked before the war as a cook, wine steward, handyman and mechanic. He appeared to be able to mend just about anything and also, after excelling on his sabotage course, blow it up.[8] Most of all, it turned out that he would do exactly as she asked while making her laugh; he was respectful but also a little flirty. Her father Ned might not have approved, but after five long years of war alone she was captivated.

Virginia told them about the realities on the ground – the parachute drops, the operations, the losses and the triumphs, and the feuding amongst the French themselves. She also explained that while she was pleased to see them now she had never received back-up when she had needed it, despite clamouring for it again and again. Fatigued though she was, she made a big impression. The two men marvelled at what she had achieved and, despite everything she had endured, her hunger to do more. Henry and Paul realised that they had arrived too late, but 'decided on the spot to continue to help *Diane* in whatever way possible'. That sense of loyalty to her grew still stronger the next day when they met *Gévolde*, who had now promoted himself to colonel at the FFI headquarters in Le Puy. They both came away 'rather disgusted' with all the political intriguing, and with *Gévolde* for giving himself military airs while knowing 'nothing of army tactics, not even the fundamental laws governing small unit fighting'.[9] It was a view shared by Geoffrey Hallowes after his visits to Le Puy – which Virginia had now taken to referring to as a 'seething salad'. He was also aghast at the 'cheaters' who had joined the Resistance a week after the Germans had been driven out and were now trying to cash in on the glory. 'Many of them had just recently put on uniforms, stuck majors' insignia on them and were out for all their false rank could get them,' he reported. 'Feelings ran high against these headquarters fakers.'

Virginia had asked Hallowes and his Anglo-French commando team, known as a Jedburgh unit or Jed (motto: Surprise, Kill,

Vanish), to work with *Gévolde* and Fayol. Although wearing Army uniforms, Jeds were three-man units specially trained in guerrilla tactics as well as leadership, with the object of coordinating Resistance activities with regular forces. Virginia instructed the team to find a way to shape the Haute-Loire FFI into a properly trained and cohesive fighting force that could help free other parts of France. Now that she had financed, armed and provided the French with their own uniforms she was determined that they should continue to align themselves fully with the Allied campaign. And although the Germans in the Haute-Loire had been liquidated many feared they would come back with a counter-attack. In her view, the FFI needed to retain a 'sharp watch'[10] on its home turf and mine the roads leading into Le Puy from the south and south-west. She instructed the Jeds to take tactical control to make all this happen, as now that their own area was liberated Fayol and Co. were once again proving difficult. As male military officers the Jeds might be able to enforce discipline in a way that had been impossible for her. She had forewarned them about the truculent personalities involved but was pleased to see them doing a 'very nice' job in the circumstances.

There was one exception, however. The unhelpful Gaullist instincts of the French Jed member, Captain Frontcroise, saw him joining forces with *Gévolde* in defiance of Virginia's wishes and the orders under which she was operating. The two men authorised a highly risky freelance expedition to the Belfort Gap, the mountain pass through which much of the Wehrmacht intended to make a last dash for home. The plan was to take a large and highly visible group of men who had been armed and financed by her without consulting the regional Allied commanding officer. Raising 'a howl', as she put it, Virginia insisted that they obtain permission for what she considered the 'stupid' idea of taking fifteen hundred half-trained men towards a major battle zone, where the Germans were viciously defending their positions. Fontcroise's response, however, was merely 'Who the hell are you to give me orders?' As if deliberately provoking her still further, he then blatantly authorised *Gévolde* to take one million francs provided by Virginia specifically for safeguarding the Haute-Loire to fund the whole adventure. Virginia's frustration boiled over, and she complained to headquarters: 'You send people out ostensibly to work with me and for me but you do not give me the necessary authority.'[11] Henry Riley, sympathising with Virginia's predicament, could also see that while most were honourable, certain FFI elements were 'getting out of hand'.

For a time Hallowes and Leney stuck with Fontcroise and the FFI and set off northwards, where they attacked a German convoy in the Allier *département*. In nearby Vichy, Hallowes came across Virginia's friend and OSS recruiter Captain Grell. He had arrived in France a few days earlier and was looking for her, and so Hallowes told the American where to find her. Soon after the FFI began to merge with the official French Army and it was made abundantly clear to the two foreign Jeds they were no longer required.[12] It was a rejection of foreign supporters that had been playing out across France since de Gaulle had seized power as provisional president on 10 September and established his government of 'national unity'. Although he had started virtually alone four years ago, now he rejected any challenge to his authority over millions. Even French partisans were to be denied his gratitude and glory, and he told them to go back to their regular jobs and stop being pretend soldiers. Only he, de Gaulle claimed, represented a free France and many French men and women were indeed ready to hail him as their political saviour and garlanded the streets through which he passed with flowers. On 12 July the Allies had finally recognised de Gaulle's legitimacy as French leader (although the official proclamation was not made until 23 October). Meanwhile, on 7 September, the Nazis escorted Pétain and his Vichy ministers out of the country to Sigmaringen, a Vichy enclave in Germany, as semi-prisoners.

Virginia yearned to break away from noxious politics and return to where she was happiest – the comparative certainties of battling with the enemy. Her next move was nothing if not audacious. She had been pestering headquarters for a new mission and London finally radioed back giving her the authority to move on to help liberate other parts of France. She gathered her most loyal men from the Villelonge Maquis and made them an offer. She was to command her own guerrilla force drawn from what London termed her 'rough men of the woods'[13] and harass Germans through carefully targeted ambush and sabotage raids. She had food, money, weapons, explosives, vehicles and a wireless. Were they with her?

Most of the men she had hoped for did indeed sign up, including of course her beloved Bob and Dédé. 'The rest of the Maquis and another Maquis in the neighbourhood were sent into [FFI headquarters at] Le Puy much against their will,' Virginia reported, although they had been 'wanting urgently to go with us'. There were in the end nineteen volunteers in all – an ideal size for mounting commando-style *coups de main* or hit-and-run missions – even if most of them were barely out of their teens. In addition, she was supported by Henry and Paul as the instructors she had so long been waiting for. And at last – perhaps most importantly – with their support she could, Cuthbert notwithstanding, join in the fighting herself. She was, after all, not afraid to fire a gun and she had shown over and over again her courage under pressure. She now had a clear command and as the fighting in France was entering its final stages she could finally emerge from the shadows and fight a more conventional war.

Indeed, Virginia seemed to cherish the prospect of full-frontal combat and the next few days passed in a whirl of preparations. The only delay was down to orders from London – 'much to our grievance'[14] – to wait until after 11 September so that they could receive another incoming French officer and further supplies. In the meantime, she asked Henry and Paul to give the boys their first formal drill in small-arms firing and guerrilla tactics. The woods outside Villelonge soon rang with the sound of gunfire. Paul, who had undergone intensive training in both America and Britain, rigged up targets for shooting practice and special pits in which to throw grenades. Henry thought the men's firing skills were 'deplorable' but as they were 'intelligent, willing and full of fight, they learned quickly and soon formed a well-knit group of fighting men'.

Virginia and Henry made an inventory of their arms and provisions, and concluded they had a 'completely mobile and self-contained unit'.[15] They mounted a Browning thirty-calibre machine gun on the cab of a seven-ton gazogène truck, with a Bren to protect the rear. Another Bren was mounted pointing through the windscreen of a reconnaissance car. They also loaded up a five-ton collection of Springfield rifles, Colt .45s, Stens, carbines and grenades, plus fifty pounds of explosives and a demolition kit. Most of the men would travel in the truck with Henry, while Virginia, Paul, Bob and a couple of other men would go in a total of three cars. The *Diane* Irregulars, as the group became known, were ready to go.

With the green light from Allied command, the convoy moved off the plateau at sunrise on the morning of 13 September dressed in a cobbled-together assortment of American military trousers and captured Italian leather jackets. Virginia's orders were to head north towards Montluçon via Clermont-Ferrand. While they remained in liberated territory Virginia travelled with Paul in the first of the two cars ahead of the truck, with the third car bringing up the rear of the convoy. It felt good to be on the road but it was also to be a journey of bitter discovery. Progress was slow and it took until nightfall to cover the 150 miles to Clermont-Ferrand because the roads were strewn with debris. The retreating Germans had abandoned farm carts, cars, bicycles and even wheelbarrows, which they had been using to carry their equipment. Locals told the Irregulars of how, on their way out, German convoys all over France were indulging in an orgy of bloodshed, taking pot shots at anyone they saw. 'They shot a man working on a hedge ... They shot a peasant in a vineyard a hundred yards from the road. They murdered seven woodcutters going home after a morning's work in the forest,'[16] reported one eyewitness of the time. In Clermont-Ferrand itself, Virginia found the locals unearthing the mangled and tortured bodies of their relatives, friends and neighbours cast into rubbish dumps, manure heaps and roadside ditches. The gruesome sight galvanised the Irregulars, and with Paul at her side Virginia went to see a regional Allied commander to seek advice on where they were most likely to be able to hunt down Germans and, in truth, take revenge. He advised against proceeding to Montluçon as other OSS personnel were already there, including Captain Grell's unit, who had discovered the blood-coated walls and floors of the former Gestapo headquarters where SOE agents had been among those tortured. The commander urged Virginia to take her men north-east to Bourg-en-Bresse, up near the Swiss border, to contact an outpost of the US Seventh Army on its way north from the Mediterranean coast. She agreed that they would set off in the morning, but liking to look after her boys, she arranged for them to spend the night in the comfort of a hotel with police protection for their vehicles while they slept.

As they progressed into enemy-held territory the next day, it became clear just what they were up against. One of Virginia's best shots moved to position himself on the running board of the reconnaissance car, finger on the trigger of his automatic weapon. At Noirétable villagers warned the Irregulars that a heavily armed band of pro-Nazi Miliciens was holding out in the rolling badlands to the north-east and attacking every vehicle on the road to Roanne, their destination for the night. Virginia ordered all the weapons to be loaded and devised a plan in case of attack. Now the reconnaissance car, armed with Brens and Stens, took the lead, half a mile ahead of the truck, with Virginia in one of the other two cars just behind. She ordered the truck at the rear of the convoy not to stop under any circumstances, unless forced to do so by a steel or stone road barricade.

The drive was tense, but in the end uneventful. 'Much to our regret,' Riley reported, the Irregulars 'pulled into Roanne without having met any enemy – and in time for dinner.'[17] Drawing on her experience of the sisters at La Mulatière in Lyon, Virginia asked the nuns in the town's convent to look after her men while she bought up Roanne's supply of fighting daggers (originally made for the occupiers) for the next stage of their journey. The Germans were accelerating their retreat but reports were coming in of them snatching British uniforms from prisoners of war and capturing British command cars or American jeeps to impersonate Allied troops. She wanted to be ready for hand-to-hand combat.

The Irregulars continued on to Allied command at Bourg-en-Bresse, where Virginia offered her platoon for ambushes in the Vosges, a mountainous area in north-eastern France near the German border where the retreating Wehrmacht had managed to establish a secure defensive line against Allied attack. Her plan – worked out in impressive detail – was for the Irregulars to attack isolated Nazi units at a blindspot she had identified. 'The reaction to this proposal was immediate and keen and we were told to return in a few days,' she reported.

While they waited for the response she commandeered a deserted château a few miles away at Roissiat. Owned by a wealthy lawyer who had disappeared, the pale stone mansion had large windows, enough bedrooms for a small hotel, a grand piano and even a wine cellar. Henry and Paul 'had the boys clean the place up and make it habitable,' Virginia reported. They threw open the shutters and as respectfully as possible pulled down the wall-hangings to use as mattresses. 'These two officers are extraordinarily efficient at getting things done – just the sort I might have wished for from the beginning.' Having seen almost unimaginable hardship and danger in their young lives, it was also gratifying for Virginia that her boys were prepared to take orders 'with a will' from these newcomer Americans straight out of training school.

They later congregated on a large balcony overlooking the grounds where, to their joy, they found a boating lake and even a boat. Even in such seductive surroundings, however, the wait to find out about their mission was trying their patience. There was a feeling that the war was rolling away from them and that they were wasting their time. Virginia tried to keep the boys occupied with further military training, 'a regular schedule of army life consisting of calisthenics, road marches, compass work and small unit warfare tactics' directed by Henry. But it was no doubt with some trepidation that she set off a couple of days later, on 19 September, to find out whether they were to be deployed in the Vosges as she had hoped.

It turned out that the regular armies were advancing faster than expected. The day of the Maquis as a fighting force of romance, endurance and in some cases exceptional courage was all but over. From nowhere when she had arrived back in 1941, the Resistance had risen to perform a role more towering and imaginative than anyone could have foreseen. Eisenhower himself would go on to say that its combined actions – sabotage, ambushes, harassment and constant sapping of Nazi morale – had shortened the war in Europe by at least nine months and kept eight German divisions permanently away from the D-Day battlefields. But now it was time for the professionals to finish the job. Her offer to help was rejected. It was all too late.

It was a humiliating end to what perhaps had always been an unlikely dream. Virginia, Paul and Henry returned to the château, where she gathered the boys and delivered the news that she was to disband the *Diane* Irregulars with immediate effect. Her words met an appalled silence. She tried to rally their spirits by raising the possibility of re-forming in Scotland to receive further training and parachuting back into France as commandos at a later date. No one took the idea seriously. The men wanted to fight the Germans now; their quarrel with them could not wait for some nebulous plan in the future. Virginia and her men had endured so much and this was the sudden and brutal end of the road. Sharing days and nights in a struggle for survival had created powerful feelings. But now she had to bid a fond farewell to Dédé, her Man Friday; Gabriel, whom she called her *chouchou*, or pet; and Jean, the orphan whom she had encouraged to follow his dreams of becoming a doctor. 'What will you do now?' she asked them all one by one. Some found it hard to hide their emotions. 'I held *Diane* in great esteem . . . and I deeply regretted that we had to part so abruptly,' Dédé recalled.[18] For him, the times in the Resistance with Virginia had taught 'tolerance, friendship without calculation and a true notion of service to one's country'. It was, he said, 'worth being born just for that experience'.[19]

Another devoted member, André Roux, a viticulteur, felt a deep sense of loss when they were to part from this 'impressive Englishwoman' who 'breathed energy and determination' but who remained a mystery to them all: 'We didn't know anything about her ... The group melted away and we never saw the woman we called the Madonna again.'[20] To capture the final hours together, they posed for a photograph on the balcony. As commander and the only woman, Virginia stands at the centre of the group, hair pinned up, in tie, khaki trousers and jacket. Gabriel is to the right of the picture; for once his infectious grin is missing and his face sombre. Yet once the initial shock had passed, candles were lit, Paul cooked up the last of the rations and the wine cellar was raided. After dinner one of the boys played the piano and Virginia joined in the singing of bawdy navy songs.

Later that last night Paul and Virginia walked down to the lake, clambered into the little boat and rowed together across the water under the stars.[21] They had become firm allies the first evening they met at Roybet and Paul had been by her side ever since. He had not challenged or crossed her like so many of the other men she had encountered but had constantly looked out for her; his respect for her as a commander was obvious but now there was more. Finally, the battle-hardened secret warrior, full of emotion for her boys, was to find love with a man.

For months, if not years, she had not dared to dream of a future. She had not felt able to show vulnerability or need – let alone faith. Trust could get you killed and so she had not given anything of herself in a brutal world where her life had been in constant danger. She had disguised herself, her disability, even her true nationality, and certainly her fear. She had always held back, putting war before self by day and long into the night. At the age of thirty-eight Virginia had finally found fulfilment as the real Resistance heroine *Marie* or *Diane*, and as the legend of the Madonna of the Mountains. She had helped to keep the flame of French resistance burning through the darkest days and had built the foundations of a secret army. When the time finally came, she had played a pivotal part in liberating huge swathes of France. For so long she had been rejected and belittled, but now she was the toast of the OSS and her ardent supporters in the Resistance. But it had all been at such a high price. That night on the lake at Roissiat with Paul was the first time for as long as she could remember when she had felt safe and put herself first. Exhausted and gaunt, she allowed her mask to slip. Thrilled but fearful of losing this delicious new feeling, Virginia wanted more than anything for Paul to remain with her from now on. If she were to go out on another mission, she informed headquarters soon afterwards, she wanted Paul and Henry 'and no one else to go with me'.

The three Americans had been recalled to Paris but the French men were free to go home or sign up with the regular French Army as they saw fit. Those opting to return to their families were to leave their weapons behind except their new fighting knives and a pistol and six bullets each as protection. Virginia gave each of them a farewell payment of three thousand francs 'as something to start on as most of them had been in the mountains for over a year'.[22] Always meticulous about the money entrusted to her – Dédé once described her as bordering on stingy[23] – she asked them for a signed receipt. She also gave them a letter releasing them from the group, so that no one would think them deserters or, worse still, collaborators. Old scores were being settled across France with thousands simply shot in the street by fired-up maquisards (or pretend ones). The *Diane* Irregulars then split up. Seven went straight into the Ninth Colonial Division of the French First Army and on to fight in Germany; another nine joined up after visits to their families.

After a brief pause Virginia, Paul, Henry and Bob (who wanted to re-establish links with the British) made their way to Paris, arriving at SFHQ at Hôtel Cécil near the Champs-Elysées on 22 September. After a month of freedom, Paris was a different place from when she had last passed through, six months earlier, in her disguise as a peasant woman. The atmosphere was jubilant, with people smiling on the streets and the *tricolore* draped over balconies and pouring out of windows. Virginia presented herself to Lieutenant-Colonel Paul van der Stricht, the OSS officer who had signed her initial contract of employment, to declare her mission over and to request to be sent back to London. When she turned up a little later than expected, she seemed embarrassed. She explained she had been dodging a Gestapo search party but if she had stolen an extra few hours in the château with Paul before coming up to Paris who would have blamed her? Yet she apologised profusely, apparently 'appalled by the inconvenience caused to those who were waiting for her,' according to one of the officers present.[24] Van der Stricht was merely pleased that his exceptional agent had come back at all. News of her safe return travelled quickly. A message was relayed to Mrs Hall the following day: 'Virginia continues to be in good health and good spirits, and her work is progressing very well. Reports on the war are full of hope . . . It's not unreasonable to suppose that Virginia will soon be coming home.'[25]

Paul was back in the city of his birth for the first time in nearly twenty years, and eagerly made his way to see his father and sister. It had been a decade since they had returned to France, leaving him to live alone in the United States when still in his teens. When he rang at her door on avenue Georges Lafenestre, his sister Jacqueline barely recognised the thirty-year-old American officer grinning in front of her. It would have been a magical reunion but she had to step back from his embrace to break the news that their father had passed away from cancer. Paul had missed seeing him by only a few months. Jacqueline introduced her brother to her husband and her two daughters, one of whom was just a few weeks old. Yet even with the excitement of these additions to the family, Paul took the shock of his father's death badly. He felt rootless, an orphan, and uncertain where to call home. His fledgling relationship with Virginia seemed more significant than ever.[26] Jacqueline invited Paul to bring his new girlfriend and friends Henry and Bob to dine at their apartment the following evening and laid on the finest food and wine they could muster. It was the first time that Paul and Virginia were treated as a couple, however unusual they might seem, with Virginia older, taller and more battle-hardened than her lover. War often intensified even unlikely relationships into a deep bond within weeks or sometimes days. It was still remarkable, though, for the woman so obviously to play the lead role and for the man to be apparently comfortable with her doing so.

Back in London on 25 September, Virginia wrote up her report on her six-month *Saint-Heckler* mission in France. Falling in love had not softened her views. After outlining some of the challenges in the field as well as her own and her helpers' achievements, she was generous in her praise of those who had contributed the most. But she had no truck with those who had hopes of glory through medals, believing that the respect of their peers, fulfilling their patriotic duty and restoring the freedom of France should be reward enough. She had observed too often in the field how those such as *Alain* in Lyon or *Gévolde* in Le Puy who actively sought preferment were so often less able or industrious. She responded to the question as to who should be recommended for an American honour with the curt: 'In my opinion, no one deserves one.' And there was, she stated, 'no reason' for her to be decorated either.[27]

Paul spent a few days with his sister before joining Virginia in London in early October 1944. Back in Britain, there was time for old friends, and he arranged to have dinner with one of them in the officers' club. Lieutenant René Défourneaux, an American comrade from Paul's training days, had just returned from Cosne, where he had been one of the three agents to take over the groups Virginia had set up in Nièvre after she left for the Haute-Loire. He had never met her, but of course knew her by reputation and was excited when Paul (no doubt proud to show off his exalted new lover) said Virginia would be joining them. Défourneaux was astonished as he pushed through the crowds of diners to see a figure apparently in her sixties, dressed in an elegant but severe look of black dress, wide-brimmed hat and pearl choker. Could the famous guerrilla leader *Diane* really be an ageing British aristocrat? 'She looked like an old lady with dark grey hair' and had with her an umbrella that doubled as a cane. But 'she exuded authority', he recalled, 'like a queen'.

Over dinner Défourneaux had the feeling that Virginia, for all her beguiling disguise, was 'so iron-willed that the Germans really [wouldn't] want to tangle with her'. There was also an exceptional alertness in the way she conducted herself, 'as if she were still watching for an ambush'.[28] Indeed, although she was careful not to reveal her hand, Virginia was trying out this new disguise for a future undercover mission. Far from preparing to go home, as OSS and her mother expected, she was already jockeying for a new job in the field. France was almost free from Nazi occupation but the fighting in Europe was far from over and Virginia wanted to be involved until the end. The conversation turned to their service in France and the two men began to speculate whether they and others would be decorated. She proceeded to address them both for half an hour on her pet theme, 'that we hadn't fulfilled our missions for medals, honours or official recognition',[29] but for more noble motives.

Given her views, there was some irony that, while Virginia was in London, over in Paris Lieutenant-Colonel van der Stricht at the OSS took a different stance. He considered Virginia eligible for America's second highest military honour, the Distinguished Service Cross, and had set in train the necessary enquiries. An officer was given the task of questioning her colleagues in the Haute-Loire such as Geoffrey Hallowes, Bob and Henry about the 'woman member of their team'. His initial conclusion was: 'She is a very courageous woman who showed a great deal of initiative.'[30] OSS wrote to her SOE comrades including Gerry Morel, whom she had rescued from his hospital bed and sent over the Pyrenees to safety, and who delivered a fulsome appraisal of her role. In December, OSS visited Pierre Fayol for his opinion.

Over the past few months of freedom, Fayol had found himself unable to stop thinking about *Diane* – although it came as news to him that she was American rather than British and that her real name was Virginia Hall. Perhaps it was because he no longer had reason to see Virginia as a threat to his status or pride that he was able to see her contribution more clearly. Perhaps in the glow of victory he was simply able to cast off his negative judgements of women's capabilities to acknowledge that Virginia had been outstanding and selfless in her actions. Whatever the reason, Fayol had undergone a dramatic conversion to become one of her greatest admirers. He told the American officers that he had realised that there was no doubt that the rapid and extraordinary success in defeating the Germans in the Haute-Loire was in large part because of her, whoever she was. On reflection, he had appreciated just how pivotal her role had been. '*Diane*'s intervention made the proper arming of our men possible,' he told the investigating officer Lieutenant George Schriever, 'and consequently the rapid liberation of the department . . . well in advance of the Allied columns . . . All of us . . . esteemed the complete devotion to duty and the exceptional courage which [*Diane*] showed.'

Remorse is a strong motivator. Perhaps regret for his

obstructive behaviour was the reason Fayol was to devote a decade of his later years to researching Virginia, writing hundreds of letters, travelling to Lyon, Paris, London and even America to try to find out more and commemorate her memory. He lobbied ministers to award her the much-coveted Légion d'honneur, but he was unsuccessful because by the time he had found out the true extent of her contribution she was already dead and the decoration cannot be made posthumously. What happened in the Haute-Loire seems to have long tugged at his conscience, until he wrote in 1990 that finally 'we know perfectly well just how much we owe her'. Virginia's 'spirit soared' above the plateau, he recorded in his book *Le Chambon-sur-Lignon sous l'Occupation*, and for those who knew her from those days she was for ever 'La Madone'.

In early 1945 the recommendation for her DSC began its tortuous way through numerous official procedures. As ever with Virginia, its path would not be smooth. Meanwhile, in France it seemed that her contribution to its freedom would simply be ignored. De Gaulle was famously antagonistic towards American or British agents working on his patch, misconceiving their role as mercenaries of little importance and even worthy of contempt. By now, for the most part, they were eager to hand over power to him as soon as practically possible. Nevertheless he, ungracious in the extreme, imprisoned one SOE operative and threatened others with incarceration unless they left liberated France immediately. And in a sign of what was to come, he was apparently particularly keen to remove all women from the front line and have their role largely expunged from the record.

Virginia was strongly recommended by SOE's Maurice Buckmaster for the Croix de Guerre; the citation referring to her heroism in the field as 'a most powerful factor in the harassing of enemy troops'. Despite her American accent, memorable face and wooden leg, he recorded how she had spent much of the war behind enemy lines without being caught. True, she did not submit easily to discipline and liked to make up her own mind, but she had rendered 'inestimable services to the Allied cause and is a very great friend of France'.[31] There is no record of any such honour having been awarded in her SOE or OSS files; there is no mention of it in subsequent personnel records and her niece is also unaware of it being conferred. Even the French president Jacques Chirac believed that his country was honouring her for the first time when he declared her in 2007 to be a 'true hero'. Yet on 16 March 1946 France had awarded Virginia the Croix de Guerre with palm, a high-ranking medal for heroism in combat. The honour was yet another secret she took with her to the grave, as records were destroyed in a fire at the French National Archives in 1973. There is no definitive list of Second World War recipients and her decoration has disappeared into the mists of history. What seems to be the sole official confirmation is buried in obscure departmental archives in Normandy, uncovered during the researches for this book.[32]

Virginia's many supporters in France, such as the eminent historian Henri Noguères, believed that her case for a greater honour had fallen victim to the petty nationalist reflexes of de Gaulle's supporters, who wanted to establish the myth that the French had freed themselves.[33] 'The services rendered to France, to the Allied cause, by Virginia Hall have not been recognised by France as they should,' Noguères wrote in the 1980s. Count de Vogüé, or *Colonel Colomb*, whom she had helped in the Cher, also thought she should have been bestowed with the highest French honour of all, the Croix de la Légion d'honneur.[34] Virginia, however, had not wanted any of it, telling one of her Resistance colleagues: 'I don't want people to talk about what I did. Everything I did, was for love of France, my second country.'[35] No doubt that was why she kept her Croix de Guerre to herself.

In autumn 1944 Virginia had never been so sought-after in her professional life. Although more than two years old, OSS was forever having to justify its rapacious spending and even its existence to a hostile military establishment in Washington. Virginia's successes in the field were seen as providing compelling answers to the inevitable questions about the service's achievements. OSS had long needed a hero; now they had one.

Virginia herself was eager to get back to work and Paul van der Stricht, who oversaw operations in Western Europe, was just as keen to have her. Any thoughts of returning to Baltimore were shelved when he summoned her back to Paris at the end of October under her old field name of *Marcelle Montagne*.[36] Hopes that the war would be over by the winter had been dashed by military reverses in Belgium and Holland. In September a British offensive to push over the Rhine from the Netherlands into Germany had ended in abject failure. Three months later, as late as Christmas 1944, the American armies sustained their worst casualties of the war in the Ardennes, when they were taken by surprise by the Germans' last major counter-offensive on the Western Front. After the triumphant liberation of France, the Allies were now faced with the bitter fact that the fighting against Hitler still had a long road to run.

'Wild Bill' Donovan was determined to mount a spectacular mission that would silence his critics once and for all. In this spirit Virginia had been handpicked from dozens of the most highly rated OSS agents to carry out an ultra-secret expedition that could play a major part in the final months of the conflict. It is testament to how she alone had successfully changed opinions about women in warfare that she was chosen in place of so many rugged men – and the files show that her disability was not even raised as an issue. Instead, Virginia's courage, her resourcefulness and 'perfectly carried out' operations in France, 'excellent personality', extensive contacts, German language skills and intimate knowledge of Austria from her time as a student in Vienna made her the obvious choice. She would, it was decided, make an 'admirable contribution' to the penetration of the heart of enemy territory.[37] Such was her stature now, that she responded by asking van der Stricht that Lieutenant Goillot be allowed to work with her on the mission and he agreed. Paul was also, at her request, granted the American citizenship he had long desired.

Codenamed Operation Crocus, the mission was still a hypothetical prospect as it would depend on how the Allied offensive developed. However, if it went ahead it would surely rank as one of the more daring clandestine operations of the war. Virginia's chances of survival were put at no more than one in three as she and Paul would be organising Resistance forces around Innsbruck in the Tyrol. The area possessed a special mystique for the most fanatical adherents of National Socialism and the fear was that the Wehrmacht would retrench into an invincible subterranean fortress in the Austrian Alps to hold out against the advancing Allied armies. Hitler had already installed underground arms factories, notably one making Messerschmitts at Kematen, where hundreds of foreign prisoners were working in unheated and unprotected caverns under continued Allied bombardment. Now there were rumours that mighty fortifications were under construction to create a Nazi redoubt with massive stocks of arms and two years' worth of provisions for a hundred thousand men, guarded by crack troops from the SS. No one knew whether it was a Wagnerian phantom threat, the ultimate deception plan by German agents, or a genuine stumbling block to Allied victory.[38] The British were more sceptical about its existence than the

Americans. But the OSS, which seems to have judged it a serious hypothesis, wanted to pre-empt what threatened to become the war's bloodiest battle by infiltrating small teams of agents to work with the local maquisards. Virginia (whose codename was slightly altered to *Diana*) and her team would have to find out whether the redoubt existed, and if it did, to plan an attack.

She and Paul immersed themselves in new security techniques for the next few weeks, and for a short while led an almost normal life. One lunchtime they were in a restaurant on the Boulevard St Germain when she noticed a familiar face. She rose from her table and walked across the room to Pierre Fayol and his wife Marianne, who both recognised her gait as well as the striking looks and powerful presence that had had such an impact on the plateau. She told them that she was waiting to go on a new mission in central Europe – without, of course, giving any details – and the foursome shared a farewell drink. Virginia probably had no idea as to her taunter's change of heart. But for the rest of his life Fayol remembered this moment with intense emotion. It was the last time he was to see Virginia, and he admitted his life was never as vivid or exciting again.[39]

In November 1944 the Paris police pulled in a woman in her thirties by the name of Irma Alesch for questioning about her brother Robert. A Reims shopkeeper called Pierre Decley, who had been one of those who had entrusted the priest with putting Germaine Guérin's personal treasures into safekeeping when she was arrested, had visited Lyon once it had been liberated in September, only to find her apartment ransacked. Thirteen million francs (some three million pounds in today's money) of cash and valuables had gone missing, along with Alesch himself. Decley had alerted the Paris police, who launched an investigation. The abbé had swiftly become the principal suspect.

Irma, who now lived alone in his splendid apartment, admitted that her brother had worked for the Germans, notably for some of the most dreaded agents of the Abwehr. She also confessed that after going to Lyon in January 1943 to help them with the arrests he had returned with several suitcases of furs and silverware.[40] The police searched Alesch's apartment and found at least some of the goods stolen from Germaine Guérin's home. The crime was proved but the suspect had long since fled.

The investigating judge issued an arrest warrant for Alesch, dispatching police to La Varenne-Saint-Hilaire, where the parishioners had already worked out it was their former priest who was responsible for luring many young *résistants* into the Gestapo net. One, for instance, had been arrested after providing Alesch with intelligence on the deathly V-1 flying bombs or doodlebugs that had been used to bombard the south-east of England after D-Day, thinking that it would be sent on to London. Alesch himself had not been seen since mid-August, when the Allies had reached the outskirts of Paris. Despite their efforts, the police had drawn a blank.

On Boxing Day 'Diana and friend', as Virginia and Paul were often now known, were dispatched to OSS Central European headquarters in a royal palace at Caserta, north of Naples (also Eisenhower's seat as Supreme Allied Commander), to receive intensive training. Here in the opulent Versailles-style rooms and two-mile long landscaped park Virginia was instructed in garroting, handling a dagger and how to bring death to a man silently with bare hands. A gun should be fired in a crouching stance, with a two-handed grip on the pistol held at waist level and using the double tap – two shots fired in quick succession. In another classroom, she was taught how to perfect her radio transmission. The weeks were racing by, however, and the Allied push through

Italy was locked in a bloody stalemate hundreds of miles away to the north. Virginia's patience with what she deemed unnecessary diversions started to wear thin.

Over in Washington, on 5 February 1945 the formal recommendation to grant Virginia the Distinguished Service Cross reached Wild Bill's mahogany desk at OSS headquarters on E Street. Virginia's derring-do in the face of the enemy strongly appealed to a man who revelled in the unorthodox and adventurous. From then on, she became one of his favourite subjects, his stories of her embellished a little more with each re-telling. One of his favourites was an apocryphal tale of her parachuting into battle zones with her false leg tucked under one arm. Such was the director's enthusiasm for spreading the word (fact or fiction) about his star agent that her commanders in the field were beginning to fret. Reports were appearing in titles such as *Reader's Digest* of an almost superhuman 'American girl' involved in high-risk secret operations. Colonel James Forgan, OSS Commander of European Theatre Operations, warned that announcement of the honour 'must be pushed back until the moment when it no longer puts in danger the security of the recipient, who is still engaged in similar activities'.[41]

Meanwhile, Virginia was with Paul but both were frustrated by *not* being currently engaged on a mission. In fact, it was not until March, when the Allied Armies were already crossing the Rhine into Germany, that the remit of Operation Fairmont, as Crocus was renamed, was finally drawn up. Even then it remained uncertain and subject to constant change. Incredibly, it was decided that the best way of infiltrating Virginia into Austria was for her to scale another high mountain pass, carrying her radio. 'Diana, who crossed the Pyrenees on foot at 10,000 feet, seems unafraid of walking,'[42] Gerry, an astonished senior OSS officer at Caserta, observed. Afraid, no, but livid at being let down. Paul had been banned from accompanying her because of his poor German, and had been informed he would not parachute in until later. They were, she insisted, an inseparable team and she tried to take control of the infiltration plans herself, even visiting some of her contacts in Geneva to find a way for them to enter Austria together. Her commanders interpreted her reaction as an unwelcome 'desire for independence' with one senior officer writing that '*Diana*'s attitude seen from here looks silly . . . [but] I still have hopes to make her see the light.'[43] Virginia was never easy to tame, and her fury reflects her determination to be with Paul, both as her lover and a trusted comrade-in-arms. She resented how her wishes had been countermanded by superiors without her experience in the field. Some who had not met her seemed unable even to countenance that she was a woman, at least one referring to her as 'he'.[44]

On 10 April, Virginia nevertheless backed down. She agreed to go into Austria without Paul and the final countdown to Operation Fairmont began. With a new codename of *Camille*, she was confirmed as team leader and was to recruit her own Austrian guerrillas tasked with launching ambushes of Nazi convoys – the attack codeword would be 'marry'. *Camille*'s main priority, however, was to find out about the redoubt that continued to haunt the minds of Allied command and divert their resources. Fear that such a Nazi bastion could prolong the European war by up to two years has been cited by a number of historians as one reason that the Americans held back from advancing on Berlin, a decision later blamed by some for effectively delivering the German capital to the Red Army. (Other analysts believe the transfer of troops to the Austrian Alps was the result, not the cause, of the decision to allow the Russians to enter Berlin first.) Either way Virginia once again found herself at the centre of the European war but she was ordered to operate only with a small band of men as it would be impossible, given the mountainous terrain, to deliver enough weapons for larger numbers: 'You must concentrate on <u>quality</u> of personnel rather than <u>quantity</u> so as to be quite sure that each weapon and each pound of explosive will be in the hands of a man who will kill Nazis, obey orders and <u>keep his mouth shut</u>.'[45]

Virginia and Paul travelled to Annemasse on the French-Swiss border for the final preparations. The weather was warming up nicely and she was set to travel to eastern Switzerland to cross into Austria on the night of 15 April, only for the unexpectedly rapid advance of Allied forces to delay her departure. Finally, her commanders began to acknowledge that her on-off situation was intolerable. 'Something should be done about this woman. If she is a good agent she deserves better treatment than she has been getting,' signalled one clearly embarrassed senior officer. The answer from Bern, a classic example of official buck-passing, came back: 'Agree with conclusions but not with being blamed for apparent neglect outstanding agent.'

Events were rapidly overtaking them. On 25 April Soviet troops met up with American forces for the first time on the banks of the Elbe. Five days later, at the Führerbunker in Berlin, Hitler took his own life. On the day marked for her departure came news that the American Seventh Army was now just thir-teen miles from the supposed redoubt area and had met none of the ferocious last-ditch resistance they had feared – in fact, in some towns the residents actually applauded the GIs as they marched through. The Nazi mountain fortress that had shaped the tactical thinking of the Allies in the closing weeks of the war turned out to be a chimera. It never really existed, except in the minds of a handful of die-hard German generals and the fevered imaginations of a few American commanders. Caserta aborted Virginia's mission with the words 'In view rapid developments military situation believed pointless to risk lives of *Diana*, [Paul] and Group. Cancel plans.'

On 7 May, in Reims, the Third Reich surrendered unconditionally. Fighting ceased just before midnight the following day, which became known as Victory in Europe (VE) Day. The sudden silence was strange at first. Virginia had not been expecting peace to come so soon. She was not alone among agents who had risked so much yet had somehow survived the war in feeling a sense of purposelessness at its end. Paul's presence was a soothing one, though, and they set off for Paris, their favourite city, to sit in cafés, drink wine, smoke American cigarettes and soak up the sun. It was joyful to share love and laughter, to be together. Perhaps it was also a shock to be alive. And the war still hung over them. There were food shortages and queues in the shops. Millions were homeless, the streets were drab and electricity only sporadic. Most haunting of all, though, were the questions about those who had been deported or simply gone missing. Would any of them come back? And what would they be like if they did?

This short interlude was interrupted by a telegram from OSS in Washington, where Harry Truman had been sworn in as president following the untimely death of Franklin Roosevelt. Now that the hostilities were over in Europe, Bill Donovan was eager to press on with Virginia's award for arming, training and organising three highly active FFI battalions, directing a successful large-scale sabotage campaign that led to the ambush of German troops and excelling in the highly perilous work of radio transmitting. In short, it was decreed that she had shown 'extraordinary heroism in connection with military operations against the enemy'.[46] Donovan was delighted that an OSS officer was to be the only civilian woman of the war to be decorated with the Distinguished Service Cross. OSS's future looked increasingly uncertain now that the war was drawing to an end and its original patron dead, so he was anxious to publicise the award to burnish the Agency's prestige. Donovan therefore took the unusual step of suggesting a ceremony at the White House. 'Inasmuch as an award of this kind has not been made previously,' he wrote to the new president, 'you may wish to make the presentation personally.'[47] Truman agreed.

Virginia, however, was embarrassed and alarmed. She was not only ambivalent about honours but also did not think it advisable for a secret agent – as that is what she wanted to continue to be – to be the focus of a public occasion.[48] For her, fighting the good fight had become a vocation, not just any job, and perhaps she was also wary of her disability once again becoming an issue under the glare of the media. On 13 June she asked her Paris commanders to reject the president's invitation to the Oval Office on her behalf: 'Miss Virginia Hall . . . feels very strongly that she should not receive any publicity or any announcement as to her award . . . She states she is still operational and most anxious to get busy. Any publicity would preclude her going on any operation.'[49] Later Virginia dropped into the OSS office in London to pick up her citation and a young female army officer remembered the occasion with amazement. 'I had read her reports and was anxious to meet her,' WAC Mary Donovan Corso recalled, having been 'so impressed by her great courage.' But instead she found her 'unnecessarily terse, as if she was not particularly impressed with being awarded the DSC'.[50] It seems that Virginia neither courted glory nor dealt with it graciously.

Virginia also knew her job was not yet done. She felt compelled to return to where it had all begun. The happiness in her personal life had not blinded her to the tragedy that had befallen her friends in Lyon and the other places where she had operated across a thousand miles of war-torn road. American troops were enraging many *résistants* by supplying their German prisoners of war with cigarette rations – when the French had for so long been deprived of anything to smoke and still had precious little. There was a widespread fear that never having witnessed the realities of life under the Nazi heel, Americans were 'obstinately incredulous'[51] of the depths of barbarity suffered in France and therefore too lenient with those responsible. Virginia was the rare American who had seen and shared it. She had not forgotten those everyday warriors who had risked their lives to help her fan the flames of resistance. She now found out just how heavy the toll had been.

Her return to Lyon, Paul at her side, was profoundly emotional. All the fine bridges spanning the rivers had been destroyed by the retreating Germans in September 1944. American bombardment in May 1944 had also caused devastating fires. Far worse than the damage visited on such a beautiful city, however, was the pain inflicted on its people. The glory of Lyon's defiance in 1941 and 1942 had been replaced – even as peace descended – by a pale despair at what had been lost. So many of Virginia's army of helpers had been deported to the hell of the German death camps. Too many – such as Alphonse Besson (who had been present at the party when the Newtons were arrested) and the society figure Vera Leigh – never came back. Even those who had been liberated by the Allies were like wraiths. They were ill, weak and hungry. They had lost everything to Nazi looters.

In rue Xavier Privat, Virginia found one of her couriers, Eugénie Catin, who had been arrested at the same time as Henry and Alfred Newton in April 1943. She had been deported to Germany and then a slave labour camp near Prague, and had returned to find her home stripped of furniture, clothes, crockery, even the light fittings and plumbing. More disturbing still was the sight of Germaine Guérin, just back from Ravensbrück, where many women had been held in wire cages and others deliberately injected with gangrene. Two-thirds of the inmates had died, but some miracle had saved Germaine from the gas chambers or succumbing to illness. Yet she was no longer the joyous force of nature of old. Her skin was sallow and her once-sleek dark curls flecked with grey. Her apartment, closets and bank accounts were bare and she was devastated by news of the death of her friend Eugène Jeunet.

There are no records of what happened to Germaine's *filles de joie* who had taken such risks to extract intelligence from their Vichy and German clients. Such was the angry state of confusion directly after the liberation that many prostitutes were subjected to brutal treatment for 'horizontal collaboration', whether they had actually been Nazi stooges or not. Doubly cruel was that often they had been forced into the trade to survive after losing their jobs or their husbands. Thousands were paraded naked on the streets to be spat at, shaved, tarred and feathered and even beaten as part of what was called *épuration sauvage*, or savage cleansing. Occasionally they would protest that they were patriots, at least one claiming to have personally put twenty-eight German soldiers *hors de combat* by targeted infection.[52] However, most people were interested only in clearly defined acts of heroism rather than these more complex displays of courage. Virginia, though, understood that valour came in many different forms.

When Dr Jean Rousset opened the door at her old *poste de commande*, Virginia was not sure for a moment whether this skeletal yet dignified figure could really be her old lieutenant. Rousset had just been repatriated after eighteen months in Buchenwald, where he had been interned alongside Virginia's other loyal agents, the Newton Twins. All three had survived and been liberated by American troops on 11 April, yet Rousset was never to return to his old jovial self. Suffering was written over his face. He told how he had been one of the *Nacht und Nebel* – night and fog – prisoners, considered a maximum danger to the Reich and therefore destined just to 'disappear' into the darkness, with their families never knowing what had happened to them.* Yet somehow his silver tongue had talked his way to survival. The camp guards had spared him from certain execution to serve as a doctor in the camp's sanatorium, caring for the sick without medicines, two patients to a bed. Now he relayed the horrific scenes of forced labour, the deadly epidemics, summary executions and the hideous pseudoscientific experiments conducted by the SS.[53] Perhaps he spared Virginia how the camp commandant's wife used the skin of prisoners for lampshades and book bindings.

Rousset could not cushion the blow of the worst news of all. He had seen glimpses of Marcel Leccia, bloodied and bruised, at Buchenwald. On the night of 10 September – when Virginia had been preparing to set off with Paul and the *Diane* Irregulars – he had watched the three nephews being marched out of their hut. He had dared to hope they were simply going for a walk but instead they had been taken to Blockhaus 17, where they were again severely beaten. At twenty to six that evening they were hanged on wires suspended from butchers' hooks. They died in excruciating slow motion, strangled in stages by their own weight. Once dead, their bodies had been casually thrown into the furnaces of the crematorium. (Virginia later found out that Leccia's cousins, whom he had refused to leave behind in Paris when she offered to spring him from jail, had been sent to a different camp. They had, with poignant irony, survived and were now free.)

Rousset could also not help but bring up the spectre of the

---

* *Nacht und Nebel* prisoners were typically Resistance leaders in occupied countries, and under Hitler's orders were imprisoned without rights to mail or Red Cross food parcels. Most were never seen again.

abbé Alesch. It was surely down to his treachery that so many of Virginia's helpers had been captured, even perhaps the nephews themselves. The doctor was agonised about having been taken in by him, when he should have known better. But surely Virginia should also take some of the blame for accepting him into the fold. The fact was that her decision to meet him, accept his intelligence and pay him handsomely – despite her discomfort – had been taken by many others, such as Germaine Guérin, as a signal that the priest was sound. This thought undoubtedly haunted Virginia for the rest of her days. In truth, Alesch's icy stare had never left her mind. But where was he now? On 11 June, following her harrowing meeting with *Pépin*, Virginia sent OSS headquarters a detailed report on everything she knew about Alesch's treachery and the suffering he had caused. For Rousset, Germaine, the Twins and most of all the nephews, she told them that it was vital he was caught. Her words were to have a dramatic effect.

Still reeling from what she had seen in Lyon, Virginia travelled on to the Haute-Loire to find out what had happened to her boys. On the way she visited the Joulians in Le Puy: Madame slowly recovering from her beatings from the Gestapo, and Monsieur still sick and weak after being repatriated from a camp in Germany. They and another of Virginia's friendly couples – the Labouriers, who had provided her with transport for parachute receptions – were also left with no money, no furniture, no livelihood, not even clothes to wear. Mme Labourier had fashioned her only skirt out of the cover of the mattress in her concentration camp. Many of these friends had declined payment for their work from SOE and were now, Virginia reported, being refused help by the French government on the grounds of having illegally worked for a foreign power.[54] Incensed, Virginia sent reports to London on the unsung heroics of these people, and demanding compensation for them. In Germaine Guérin's case at least, secret files opened for this book show that Virginia personally secured her friend eighty thousand francs as a bonus and a certificate of commendation for courage and devotion to duty[55] from the British government. There appears to be no such record of financial help for the others. The files also record the anxiety of the Twins, whom Germaine had so valiantly tried to save, as to whether she had survived the camp. Then in Le Chambon Virginia learned that two members of Bob's Maquis had been killed after joining up with the French Army. When would the bad news end?

Alesch was what kept Virginia awake at night. It would have been no comfort to know that back in autumn 1944 he had managed to inveigle himself into a congenial new position in the newly liberated city of Brussels. Ever the trickster, he had presented himself with a false letter from the archbishop of Paris recommending him as a 'good abbé' who had suffered greatly at the hands of the Germans.[56] The Belgians had taken pity and gave Alesch sanctuary, and then a living as chaplain for prisoners and deportees. He was so convincing that no one suspected his duplicity or bothered checking his past, but in May 1945 came word that the French police in the Germaine Guérin case were after him. Meanwhile, Virginia's report and another by MI6 (whose agents Alesch had also betrayed) had mobilised the American Army Counter-Intelligence Corps. Soon afterwards, Alesch's employers asked him to leave, warning that the American authorities wanted to question him too. The abbé fled to his home country of Luxembourg, but then with his usual venality calculated that he could perhaps turn even this situation to his advantage and avoid the vengeance of the French justice system. He returned to Belgium and on 2 July turned himself in to the Americans.

Wearing civilian clothes, he presented himself in the name of *René Martin*, an identity he had often used when visiting Virginia in Lyon. In a bravura performance, he painted himself as a victim of the Germans, forced to work for them to save his life after they had discovered his Resistance activities in his old parish. Surmising that the Americans were desperate for a good source on the Abwehr, he hinted that he would spill dozens of useful names in return for his freedom and financial support. In further interrogations with OSS counter-espionage in Paris on 6 August 1945, Alesch consistently made out he was on the Allies' side. He claimed that it was another double-agent who had infiltrated Virginia's network and passed on the names of its members to the Gestapo – and that by contrast he had tried to protect her. He insisted he had nothing at all to do with the arrests.

Fortunately, thanks to Virginia's detailed report on Alesch his interrogators knew the truth and were not taken in. That night they promptly handed him over to the Paris judiciary and within a week a long series of court hearings into his treachery began. At the same time as Marshal Pétain, who had now returned to France at his own request, was declared guilty and sentenced to death (later commuted to life imprisonment) for treason, Alesch was desperately trying every last trick to save his own skin. Surely, the abbé ventured, the French secret services would be interested in information on one of the most senior Abwehr officers in exchange for his life?

In Paris, Virginia was given her OSS appraisal before returning to the US. It could hardly have been more glowing. In the most testing of conditions, her motivation and practical intelligence, including speed and accuracy of judgement, had consistently proved 'superior'. The years behind enemy lines had shown her to be eminently stable, unemotional, fearless and able to lead and work with others. Her physical ability (including agility, stamina, ruggedness and daring) was judged 'very satisfactory'. The report stated that 'Miss Hall accomplished exceptionally fine results in all her assignments' and that she would continue to make an excellent agent. The enthusiastic comments added to the long list of plaudits that acknowledged Virginia as the most successful Allied female secret agent of the European conflict and one of the chief pioneers in the field of clandestine warfare. Her future was surely secure.

Virginia had once adored France and always wanted to live overseas, so why go home now? To rest – and surely to forget – but also to please Paul, who cherished the prospect of leaving behind the feuds of the Old World to lead a new life as an American. She set off across the Atlantic with the respect and admiration of her colleagues and superiors and the love of a good man. War had been her fulfilment. Would peace be the same?

Chapter Twelve

The CIA Years

Virginia returned to the United States in September 1945 as a stranger in her own country. She had lived in Europe for most of her adult life and the land she had left behind in 1931, in the throes of the Great Depression, had since become a victorious superpower. It had seen the defeat of fascism in Europe and the capitulation of Japan following the atomic bombs at Hiroshima and Nagasaki. Peace was now restored but her homecoming at nearly forty years of age was not as joyful as she might have hoped. There were few agents who had spent as long as she had in enemy territory and it took time to bounce back from the years of stress, endurance and semi-starvation. Her face finally bore witness to the realities of six years in war-torn Europe, now that the adrenalin of action had run dry, and she had extensive (unexplained) scarring on the left side of the back of her head. 'She looked dreadful, and so much older,' recalls her niece Lorna, who was sixteen at the time. 'We saw that the war had taken a lot out of her. She blamed all the pills she had taken to keep going – the downers as well as the uppers.' Sadly, reuniting with her mother after eight years apart was not quite the reviving tonic required. Virginia had not turned out the society daughter Barbara had wanted. She had not married, had no children, looked worn out and was evidently carrying on with Paul Goillot, a naturalised American of humble stock and mere high-school education whose ambition was to open a restaurant. Her wayward daughter might have done something important in the war but it was all a far cry from the fancy life of Halls of old.

Barbara was cold to Paul from their first meeting. Virginia tried to reason with her mother, arguing that he was a good man who was kind, clever and funny, and who made her happy – but Barbara resented what she saw as her daughter's bossiness. Paul took a different tack, trying to win over his putative mother-in-law by way of his Gallic charm, but all in vain. Barbara was not impressed and thoughts of marriage were put on ice. For all Virginia's rebelliousness, she did not go against her mother's wishes – although she refused to give up her lover altogether. The compromise was that she would live a lie by concealing her relationship with Paul.

It was Barbara alone who accompanied her, two weeks later, to the private ceremony in Bill Donovan's office in the undistinguished OSS buildings (next to an abandoned gasworks) in which Virginia was finally awarded her DSC. Paul was nowhere to be seen. Perhaps Virginia, who was dressed all in white with a white chiffon scarf across her hair, wanted to avoid any hint of tension, or maybe the secret nature of the event precluded her from taking more than one guest. Donovan greeted the women in his general's uniform, no doubt saddened by the fact that the low-key occasion was to be the last of its kind. The irrepressible general had cited Virginia's heroism to President Truman in a valiant battle to save his beloved OSS from closure, arguing that she represented exactly what the service could do in the future to keep the Kremlin in check. Not even her remarkable track record, however, had persuaded the president to continue with an agency run and created by Donovan. As a Democrat he instinctively distrusted the charismatic, Republican-leaning Wild Bill and anyone connected to him, a distaste reinforced by a vigorous media campaign (fed by rivals such as FBI director J. Edgar Hoover) comparing OSS to an American Gestapo. Foreseeing the end, Virginia had resigned from the service three days before she met Wild Bill, stating that her mission was completed. In hope rather than expectation she had written that she spoke six languages and hoped to serve her country again: 'I am deeply interested in the future of intelligence work and would like my application to be considered in the event that an intelligence agency is established'.[1] Her OSS file noted her down as an 'exceptional person' with a 'burning desire' to be useful.

The axe fell four days after the award ceremony, on 1 October, when the OSS was disbanded by presidential order. Thousands of staff, including Paul, were cast off, although Virginia was at least sent a cheque for $2067 in back pay. Incredibly she had only ever been granted a one-year contract with OSS, which was never renewed, but she was judged to be due thirty-three days' leave for the period between April 1944 and September 1945. In all that time she had taken just five days off.

Virginia was a war hero but finding work was anything but easy, especially for a disabled woman, now that so many servicemen were being demobbed and expecting their jobs back. Yet she plunged straight in, not so much for the income as she was still drawing healthy dividends from her inherited investments – and she always eked out her money cautiously – but her driving need to be needed. Like many other former secret agents, however, she discovered that not being able (or wanting) to explain exactly how she had served in the war was unpopular with potential employers in the private sector. Some suspected her reluctance to talk meant she must be hiding something seedy, reinforced by OSS's controversial public image. Many old colleagues were facing similar problems on both sides of the Atlantic. Denis Rake's courage with SOE (he had returned to France in 1944 and served in some of the fiercest fighting) had been celebrated with a chestful of honours including the Military Cross and the Légion d'honneur. Yet without employers' references he too was struggling to scrape a living. Bizarrely, his salvation came in the form of the Hollywood star Douglas Fairbanks Jr, who took him on as his butler-valet, describing him as a 'shortened, rounded and jovial incarnation of Jeeves'.[2]

Virginia considered signing up with the US Army but the thought of rigid order-taking was unappealing (although she did join the Reserves as a captain). The idea of returning to the State Department reminded her of all the nonsense about Cuthbert. She had made good friends in the press before and during the war but her curiosity was greater than her prose and journalism had always been more of a cover than a calling. Friends suggested she publish a book, but unlike other agents she felt obliged to remain silent and brushed aside such ideas with 'It was only six years of my life!'[3]

When her old friend Elbridge Durbrow, the former American vice-consul in Warsaw now running the Eastern Europe desk at the State Department, came to call at Boxhorn she quizzed him about her possible options. Durbrow reinforced her growing fears that the hard-fought peace was fragile and the West – and particularly America – could not afford to be blindsided as it had been at Pearl Harbor back in 1941. While Virginia was hardly an ideologue she agreed with Durbrow that in the defeat of Nazism came a new totalitarian threat from the East and that the seeds had already been sown for what would become the Cold War. In late 1945 came revelations that the Soviets had penetrated the heart of the US government and its atomic bomb programme, humiliating Washington and laying bare its espionage failures. Just weeks after abolishing OSS, Truman was forced to rethink, and in January 1946 he created the Central Intelligence Group. Virginia immediately started angling for a job. The Group initially neither had its own people nor its own budget, but Virginia doggedly worked on her contacts right through the period when Winston Churchill made his chilling Cold War speech in Fulton, Missouri, warning of fifth columnists across Europe spreading the tide of communism. Calling for the West to react with strength he pointed to the many countries already under the Soviet yoke and closed off from the free world. 'From Stettin in the Baltic to Trieste in the Adriatic,' he thundered, 'an iron curtain has descended across the continent.' The United States needed another tool to deal with this new threat, beyond the traditional alternatives of diplomacy or war.

In December, Virginia's lobbying finally paid off. She became one of the first women to join what would within nine months become the Central Intelligence Agency or CIA. She was entering an organisation at the centre of a geopolitical firestorm; American policymakers now saw the CIA as a key 'offensive weapon in an expanding Cold War'.[4] Indeed, the Agency's secret orders from the president included the specific command to execute 'covert psychological operations designed to counter Soviet and Soviet-inspired activities' across Europe and the world. Her fluent Italian saw Virginia being dispatched to Italy, which was considered particularly vulnerable to the so-called Red Menace (communists had been strongly represented in government since the fall of Mussolini's regime), raising fears in Washington of the seat of Western culture and home of the Holy See becoming a hostile totalitarian state. She found herself in Venice, working in the same consular offices near St Mark's Square as she had in the 1930s. Her brief as a GS-13 contract intelligence agent (equivalent to a captain) on a salary of four thousand dollars a year was to gather political and economic intelligence on Soviet infiltration. There was plenty of action to observe, with popular communist politicians calling for general strikes and food riots in the streets. Virginia diligently wrote reports on events in Italy, France, Greece and Yugoslavia but she yearned for a more active role. From her desk she watched male agents secretly intervene in the Italian elections of April 1948 by backing the conservative Christian Democrats, exchanging satchels stuffed with millions of lire at the stately Hassler Hotel at the top of the Spanish Steps in Rome (while elsewhere Russian agents were doing the same for the Communist Party with funds from Moscow). After a particularly lavish and well-targeted election campaign the CIA-backed party romped home with 48 per cent of the vote, keeping the Communists from power for decades. It was a pattern the Agency was to try to follow for the next twenty-five years.

James Angleton, a chain-smoking drinking buddy of Kim Philby (who had transferred from SOE to MI6, and was already passing secrets to the Soviets), played a key role in the operation, which was judged one of the Agency's first successful missions. Clubbable and ambitious, Angleton was to become a high-flier, although he and his unfortunate liaisons were eventually to prove a liability as head of CIA counter-intelligence. Virginia's role, by contrast, was restricted to mere desk-bound analysis, never her real forte, and she informed her superiors she found the work 'unsatisfactory'. In July she resigned. 'She did not specify exactly what she disliked,' the CIA noted in its files, but she made it clear in time that she 'preferred paramilitary work to foreign intelligence collection'.[5] Another reason was, most likely, that Paul had been unwilling to join her permanently in Italy,[6] and perhaps there was still one more factor. Border stamps in her passport show that around this time she was in France, where the investigations into Alesch were finally drawing to a close. Fortunately, Virginia's report on the abbé's manipulative cunning had been circulated to the French secret service. They therefore rejected his offer of intelligence on Abwehr officers in return for clemency. Indeed, most unusually, former Abwehr members in Paris, including Sergeant Hugo Bleicher, who had at times supervised Alesch's work, actively testified against him. Those few *résistants* who had survived his betrayal were giving evidence in Paris, including Germaine Guérin and Dr Rousset. Virginia was barred from appearing herself because of her status as a CIA operative but there was no need. The case against Alesch was so damning that his lawyer felt obliged to plead insanity, although an expert witness swiftly dismissed the priest's condition as depravity rather than delusion.

Alesch had by now become a *cause célèbre*, an embodiment of betrayal and Nazi evil. When he was summoned to the Paris court on 25 May 1948 to stand trial on charges of '*intelligences avec l'ennemi*' crowds flocked to see him in the dock. It is unlikely that Virginia was among them – although we cannot rule out the idea that she may have attended in one of her disguises or possibly as a reporter. If she had, she would have seen her nemesis, now forty-two years of age, still mocking and defiant, and flanked by two of his mistresses, Geneviève Cahen and Renée Andry. Reporters referred to him as the 'Rasputin of the Abwehr' and the newspaper *Le Monde* neatly captured his appearance in the dock: 'Robert Alesch, the traitor priest, grey jacket, face clean-shaven, yellowed, polished as if oiled with clever and hard falseness, with narrow lips and wary German blue eyes'.[7]

He continued to proclaim his innocence to the last but the jury were in no mood to believe him. After three days of evidence they returned a guilty verdict and a sentence of death. (They were more lenient with his lovers – Renée was discharged and Geneviève sentenced to ten months in prison.) Virginia could now finally be confident that there was no way that Alesch would ever be freed. It was a file she personally could close. Six months after she had returned to the United States to be with Paul, on 25 February 1949 Alesch took communion for the last time, with the chaplain at Fresnes prison, where so many of his victims had suffered. At dawn he was taken out of his cell and driven by van to a nearby fort. There he was ordered to stand in front of the firing squad and at five minutes to nine he was shot.

Virginia briefly visited some of her old haunts before she left Europe. It is thought she dropped in to see the Joulians in Le Puy, and perhaps the Juttrys in the Cher, but she was gone again before most knew she had even arrived. She remained as elusive as ever and when she arrived back in the United States in July 1948 she expected to slot back into another job at the CIA. America – and its intelligence agency – had changed in her absence, however. Three years after VE Day, war exploits were no longer understood or respected in the way they had been. Brilliant male brains and well-connected college kids had taken charge in the old OSS buildings in downtown Washington. Even among those who had served during the conflict few, crucially, had experience in occupied territory pitted against a cunning and implacable foe. The desk men from Yale and Princeton schmoozed over highballs and shared a narrow idea of an intelligence agent as someone in their own image. She applied for another position and was judged by a senior officer to be 'the most qualified person . . . that I have ever interviewed'.[8] Yet although Virginia was given a few short missions abroad, there was nothing substantial for her. In peacetime, the CIA bureaucracy apparently felt it could afford to waste such an unorthodox talent. Virginia was on the outside once again.

Early in 1950, around her forty-fourth birthday, she moved to New York to live full-time with Paul in an apartment on 54th Street, near Manhattan's theatre district. This was their first formal home together, and in the Big Apple they were tucked away from Barbara's disapproving looks. But Virginia's brother John was hardly less judgemental. 'When my father was asked if they were married, he replied "they oughta be",' Lorna recalls. 'Daddy was pernickety about that but Dindy was very liberated and up-to-date.'

The couple had a large circle of friends, including a couple of ambassadors and a number of spies – who were unbothered by the couple's unconventional status – and they all liked to party. Part of OSS's legacy was its legendary boozing, or as one historian has put it, 'all hands . . . sailed out of the Second World War on a tide of alcohol'.[9] Virginia and Paul were no exception, and Lorna was forbidden by her parents to go to stay with her aunt in New York 'because they worried about Dindy drinking and driving'.[10] The couple bought wine 'by the gallon' and an invitation to one of their gatherings was considered a hot ticket. Virginia's health was improved and she had invested in a new wardrobe from Peck & Peck on Fifth Avenue. Paul's OSS comrade, René Défourneaux, who had only previously met her when in her elderly aristocrat disguise in London, could not believe the transformation: 'She was wearing a gay floral dress, her face was bright and cheerful, her hair was soft brown. She seemed like a *jeune fille*.'[11] Virginia was an elegant hostess with an enigmatic air and a voguish home in the European style. Paul poured the drinks and cracked jokes.

Eventually the CIA came back with an offer: a lowly desk job that was not even on the staff. After eighteen months of waiting, in March 1950 Virginia started work as an administrative assistant at the National Committee for Free Europe, a CIA front organisation. From the third floor of the Empire State Building she helped prepare broadcasts for Radio Free Europe, a propaganda station aiming to support fledgling resistance movements in communist-controlled countries – an irony not lost on Virginia, who had been happy to work with the Reds in France during the war. She also questioned Eastern European exiles disembarking in New York for useful intelligence, and advised refugee groups on how, as she put it in a secret report, to 'keep alive the spirit of freedom and resistance' back home and to bring 'about the liberation of all Iron Curtain countries'.[12] Throughout the 1940s, one country after another fell under communist rule, including Czechoslovakia and Hungary in 1948 and then China the following year. Despite the seismic world events, it was repetitive work and not the paramilitary position she had requested after Italy. So in 1951 she submitted yet another application for a job at the heart of the CIA, where by rights she belonged. Six years after the war, Virginia was plagued by the same professional frustrations she had suffered in the 1930s. It was as if she had never proved her worth as a field agent at all.

Nor did Virginia's provenance absolve her from a painfully long security process. The CIA – like every other arm of the American state at that time – was fixated on the threat of Soviet infiltration. Moscow had already tested its first atomic bomb; Ethel and Julius Rosenberg were on trial for handing American nuclear secrets to the Russians; and Senator Joseph McCarthy had begun his reckless and obsessive campaign to accuse political opponents of 'unAmerican' activities. In this febrile environment, one tiny suspicion could destroy an entire career. Virginia was frustrated at the time taken up by answering fourteen pages of questions about her parents and brother, her education and the countries she had visited. Did she know her neighbours in

Manhattan? Was she dependent on her salary? Could she give the names of five people who knew her intimately? She put forward the names of Elbridge Durbrow, the journalist Charles Foltz and three girlfriends. She was surprised that the exercise was such 'a major operation' and apologised for taking so long to complete her questionnaire. Finally, after several more months of vetting she was subjected to a polygraph, or lie-detector test. On 3 December 1951 she became one of the first women officers to be admitted to CIA headquarters, now hugely expanded following the outbreak of the Korean War, a hot outburst of Cold War tensions. She took the oath of office that she would 'defend the constitution of the United States against all enemies, foreign or domestic' at a time when most still thought of the CIA as primarily a collector of intelligence. Virginia, though, had been appointed to its less well-known covert operations section. Her pay more than doubled overnight.

Virginia and Paul packed up the Manhattan apartment and moved down to Washington, where they avoided another scene with Barbara by officially living separately. The upside was that they saw more of Lorna and her brother, whom they took on idyllic weekend trips sailing, fishing and riding at Solomons Island, a picturesque collection of clapboard houses two hours' drive out of Baltimore. They rented a boat and Paul would catch eels and cook them in butter on an open fire in a special frying-pan with legs. He picked bunches of wild flowers for Virginia and they basked in the sun. Virginia remained a self-controlled figure and never the cuddly sort. But she doted on her niece – even attempting to teach her to drive (with gear shifts in the European style) – and there was always Paul to make it fun. 'Oh, mad Paul!' Virginia would shriek in delight at his latest prank designed to amuse the youngsters. On the verge of adulthood, Lorna observed how her aunt was unusually poised, sure of herself and often surrounded by admirers: 'She was a powerful person and ruled the roost but Paul was good for her. He was a little crazy, a tease, always into mischief. They worked together brilliantly and he lightened her life.'

There appears to have been a yearning on both their parts for children of their own, though Virginia was now forty-five and her mother's opposition to her marrying Paul may have put them off trying when they had first returned from the war. Some female agents found that they were in any case unable to conceive because of the devastating effects on their bodies of the stress and malnutrition – and pill-taking – that came with operating behind enemy lines. In her new job Virginia made friends with an unmarried secretary who was pregnant – a scandalous situation in the early 1950s – and was not sure how she would cope. With Paul's blessing Virginia made an offer to adopt the child, and the three entered into serious discussions about the idea. In the end, it did not happen, and although the reasons are not clear there was evidently disappointment. Paul and Virginia soon after began to collect poodles. She was never to have a family of her own.

Despite the emotional upset, Virginia was finally finding satisfaction in her work heading up ultra-secret paramilitary operations in France. The American, British and French governments jointly believed that the French Resistance was a useful model for setting up networks in several European countries known as 'stay behinds' that were designed to support NATO forces in the event of a Soviet attack. She was responsible for overseeing recruitment and training of potential guerrilla units as well as directing secret operations and organising escape lines. Her exceptional experience was finally being put to good use by her superior, Frank Wisner, an ex-OSS officer who had spent much of the war in neutral Turkey. Within a year she became the first woman operations officer within the entire covert action arm of the CIA, part of the euphemistically named Deputy Directorate of Plans. Her background was legendary amongst her colleagues and she had become a 'sacred presence' in a predominantly masculine world – but also a relic of what was already seen as a bygone age. She was described by one young male colleague as the 'gung-ho lady left over from OSS days overseas'. Young secretaries 'in sweater sets and pearls listened raptly to Virginia Hall gas with muscular paramilitary officers who would stop by her desk to tell war stories,' he recalled, remembering the way she coiled her dark brown hair on the top of her head with a yellow pencil to secure the bun. 'She was always jolly when she was around the old boys.'[13] And she had still not forgotten her old comrades in France, sending a few of them Christmas cards for several years – although it seems without a return address. On one occasion, one of the Irregulars doggedly tracked her down and, no doubt impressed with his initiative, she agreed to put up his children when they visited the United States. She refused, however, an invitation to a reunion on the grounds that she did not want anyone to talk about her deeds during the war. She would open up only so far.

By autumn 1952 Virginia was working on the Southern Europe desk, busy making hot and cold war plans, including overseeing the installation of a secret radio in Athens to broadcast propaganda to communist countries such as Romania and Bulgaria. Her work continued apace despite the death of Stalin in March 1953, and the slight if temporary thawing of relations with the West. Appreciating the value of her five years as a clandestine agent in the field, Virginia's male supervisors rated her as 'excellent' in her appraisal that year and noted that she had 'an unusually clear understanding of agent operations and problems'. Indeed, they would have liked her to be more forthcoming to others, instructing the less experienced in techniques that 'may be self-evident to her but which may be unknown or unapparent'[14] to her fellow officers. They judged her to be especially suited for detailed operational planning and thought 'her overall potential would be enhanced if she were given an opportunity to handle a project in the field'.[15] They thought she might be particularly skilful at the hard task of penetrating communist countries where the CIA was struggling to gather reliable intelligence – known as 'denied areas'.

What is strange, therefore, is that Virginia was not dispatched overseas to direct a major mission as suggested – normally it would have been in her character to jump at the chance. Instead she informed her employers she was 'not interested at present'[16] in a foreign posting – perhaps because she wanted to stay with Paul in the United States, where he had eschewed further military or clandestine work in favour of his real love, the restaurant trade. Recurring health problems – which Virginia privately attributed to her pill-taking during the war[17] – may also provide part of the answer. Photographs of the time show a hardening of her facial features and she was putting on weight as exercising with Cuthbert became increasingly difficult. There are suggestions that her heart may have been causing concern, a common side-effect from long-term use of Benzedrine. In September 1954 she signed a waiver of the normal CIA life insurance cover, perhaps because she had been denied cover due to an uninsurable pre-existing condition. It was clear that the strain of her exceptionally gruelling missions in the war were to affect her for the rest of her life.

She would, however, pay dearly for opting at this critical point in her career to remain at her desk in Washington. Intelligence officers can be divided to this day between headquarters operators and field agents – in Virginia's case her strongest suit was clearly as the latter but now she was stuck on the wrong side of the line. As the former CIA officer Craig Gralley puts it: 'The qualities – namely her age, disability and gender – that made her so good overseas by rendering her invisible, would make life difficult for her in an office environment.' Promotions, status and the 'right to be listened to' on the covert operations side of the CIA relied largely on recent experience in the field and now she had none to offer. She occasionally ventured abroad for the Agency, but only on so-called TDYs (temporary duty assignments) and these were deemed insufficient to refresh her operational skills. The most damaging part of her appraisal for the year 1953 was the observation that she was a woman – albeit one who was deemed 'pleasant', 'conscientious' and 'coopera-tive' – who dared to have views. In contrast to the celebration of a strong-willed woman under Wild Bill Donovan's wartime regime, the 'Father Knows Best' era of the mid-1950s expected a model female to be an obedient blonde at home with the kids. To be childless and characterised as 'frank and outspoken' was a danger sign. For Virginia, peacetime was slowly but surely imprisoning her.

In late 1954, she moved to the paramilitary desk for Western Europe to conduct a country-by-country review of 'uncon-ventional warfare requirements'. The operations were top secret – America could not be seen to be running or even sup-porting 'stay behinds' as some were linked to criminals or the far right. Virginia was now working at the centre of some of the least respectable aspects of the CIA's work in the Cold War. Colleagues valued her input, versatility and experience but there is also a suggestion that she was seen as difficult, possibly because of raising concerns about some of the operations in which she was involved. Her appraisal that year described her as 'an unusually strong person in terms of the requirements of the Agency' but there were also hints (without any apparent evidence) that she might not be able to contain her emotions or remain calm in an emergency. It was a subtle if classic undermining of a female officer who had coolly avoided capture by the Gestapo for three long years, was serving as a captain in the military reserve and had proved that even a devastating accident could not impede her performance. A further insinuation came in the remark that she had 'unrealistic' ideas about her value to the Agency and that her 'independence' was her most significant feature.[18] Virginia's card was now marked.

Her treatment may have been more extreme than most. But such attitudes were so widespread – and inflammatory – that when Allen Dulles, who had been OSS chief in Switzerland, became director in 1953 he had set up a taskforce of CIA career women to investigate. The so-called Petticoat Panel discovered that the notion that women were 'more emotional and less objective' than men and 'not sufficiently aggressive'[19] was indeed the accepted norm, whatever the evidence to the contrary. The recommendation that supervisors should be trained to be fairer to both sexes was accepted by the Agency's board, but seems to have had virtually no impact. The sole visible difference was that women were now admitted to the CIA gym once a week – but it was small beer when female employees were still expected to report for work in spotless white gloves. Morale generally at the CIA was low, with one in five officers leaving in 1953 alone. Many believed their bosses did not know what they were doing and wasted a 'shocking amount of money' on failed missions overseas, which were falsely claimed as successes. To the outside world, the CIA represented the highest form of public service and an omniscient muscular force intent on subverting and sabotaging communism. But insiders claimed that 'incompetent people were given great power and capable recruits were stacked like cordwood in the corridors'.[20]

Virginia now entered what the CIA has recently acknowledged

as the 'unhappiest period' of her career, defined by a 'serious dispute about the level of her performance'.[21] In May 1955, she transferred back to the Balkans desk in the paramilitary division. She was given the exciting prospect of planning and implementing an undisclosed 'major political action project' as the case officer and principal agent. From her passports it seems that she travelled through France, Switzerland, Germany and Britain, before flying back to Washington to file a highly sensitive comprehensive report in which she laid out her conclusions and recommendations. The dossier – which remains classified – was judged 'outstanding' and 'highly competent'[22] by her superior officer. Indeed, such was her success on this mission that on her return to Washington she was handpicked to become one of the first women ever to be accepted onto the Career Staff of the CIA (the most valued and permanent officers). The distinction marked her out for possible promotion – a preferment that did not go unnoticed in the seething macho environment of the Agency's headquarters. Unfortunately, her admiring superior officer was then immediately transferred to another job and it was at that point that her real problems began.

Without the backing of her sponsor her dossier, despite all the initial praise, was sidelined and there was murmuring about her being too cautious. Since President Eisenhower had entered the White House in 1953 the CIA had mounted ever more daring missions to wage what became almost a holy war against communism. Virginia's style of careful preparation was subsumed in a frantic drive for covert action that would eventually send the Agency, according to the critical historian Tim Weiner, lurching from 'international crisis to internal calamities'.[23] Virginia's ultimate boss, Frank Wisner, was working 'himself into a controlled frenzy, twelve hours or more a day, six days a week, and he demanded the same of his officers'. Eventually he was to take his own life but his critics claimed he avoided scrutiny of the wisdom of some of his actions by rarely telling the Agency's director what he was doing.[24]

The CIA's anti-Communist zeal had already led to Operation Paperclip, the codename for the wholesale recruitment of former senior Nazis on the grounds that however barbaric their conduct in the war, they also ranked as the ultimate anti-Soviets. The US Army's intelligence operation had taken on the Butcher of Lyon himself, Klaus Barbie. How must it have felt to know that men who had been responsible for the torture and deaths of so many of her friends were now being spirited away from their war crimes tribunals to safety by her own country? And that they were being paid handsomely by the American state including by her own employers at the CIA? Could it even be possible that she was forced to work with some of them when on her missions to Germany or elsewhere? Because of her refusal to talk about her work, what she thought of the policy or the impact on her can only be imagined. But her old comrade from Lyon, André Courvoisier, believed she would have been at least 'very disappointed' that her 'old enemies'[25] should be rewarded in this way. It puts the then prevailing CIA view that women were, as one station chief put it, 'just not as stable as men in critical positions'[26] into perspective.

When her report was in effect shelved, Virginia repeatedly asked for clarification of her duties which she described as 'nebulous' but was ordered to be 'patient' and left alone to work in what she called a 'total vacuum'. Further suggestions for useful assignments were seized on as 'fine ideas' and then handed to other (male) officers to execute. Finally, she was ordered to work on a task that, insultingly, entailed her reporting to a male officer two ranks her junior. For a war hero who had once been chosen in place of dozens of able-bodied men to conduct one of the Second World War's most dangerous secret missions it was scarcely credible that within a decade she was being humiliated in this way.

An unnamed senior officer blocked any hopes of promotion with a scathing end-of-year appraisal for 1956, despite admitting that he had never actually overseen her work. He denounced her results as 'negligible' and claimed that she lacked 'initiative, industry and creative thought'.[27] He posted the damning report before immediately going on leave, denying her the chance to discuss it. It can come as no surprise that Virginia was furious. In high dudgeon, she wrote an excoriating rebuttal of the points made in her appraisal, which she described as 'almost incredible' and 'unjustified'. The way in which she had been humiliated and ordered to report to a lower rank had been 'improper' and to question her capability in paramilitary work when she had excelled at it during the war was absurd. 'Certainly the rating given is based on nothing,' she stormed. Her former supervisor also insisted that there were no grounds for criticising her. 'Were I to seek an officer for the same or a similar task,' he stated, 'I should choose [Virginia Hall] to do it.'[28]

Once again, powerful forces had stepped in on her behalf, but the row spoke volumes about how the ranks were closing against a woman whom less able or experienced men saw as opinionated and a direct threat. Even the CIA later recognised that she had more combat experience than most male officers, including five consecutive directors, and had been highly decorated for it too. Indeed, Virginia's shoddy treatment was later cited within the CIA itself as a textbook case of discrimination.[29] 'She was head and shoulders above a lot of the men who rose much further up the organisation than she did,' notes Craig Gralley. Perhaps she could just never be forgiven for her glorious past.

*

Virginia and Paul were still living apart for Barbara's sake and she was now drinking heavily. Lorna believes that Virginia increasingly needed help to 'soften' memories of war, no doubt including the devastation to her own people caused by the traitor Alesch. The atmosphere at work – and the lack of respect shown to someone whose heroism had come to the personal attention of a king and a president – certainly did not help. Perhaps the fact that Paul was now co-owner of a French restaurant, where he was head chef, was also a temptation. Fortunately, in January 1957 her morale improved when she moved to another CIA division, this time the Western Hemisphere desk. She was now an area operations officer, helping to run political and psychological warfare against communism in South America from Cuba down to Argentina. 'She seemed to be back in her element,' notes the CIA in a secret report. 'Her supervisors regarded her as a distinct asset . . . It was her versatility, intelligence and competence that stood out. She had, they agreed, "no outstanding weaknesses".'[30]

Restored to some stability at work, Virginia decided that the time had now come to formalise her status at home. Barbara was clinging to her old views, but finally Dindy cast her concern aside.[31] On 15 April 1957 Virginia and Paul gathered a few friends, drove out of town and in a quiet, unfussy ceremony got married. They did not inform the family until a couple of weeks later. She changed her name at work and Mrs Goillot formally moved into Paul's villa at Chevy Chase in the suburbs of Washington. It was a relief to go public at last and a comfort to Paul, whose restaurant had gone under after being cheated by his business partner. At least now Paul was always around, becoming Virginia's 'house-husband'.

Virginia was now fifty-one and married. Neither acted in her favour at the CIA, where women with husbands were thought less reliable.[32] One of her colleagues, E. Howard Hunt (who later went to prison for his role in the Watergate scandal), was saddened by her 'reduced status'. 'No one knew what to do with her . . . She was a sort of embarrassment to the noncombat CIA types, by which I mean bureaucrats.'[33]

In 1959 the Marxist firebrand Fidel Castro came to power in Cuba, just ninety miles from the Florida coastline. Yet despite such a critical event taking place on her patch, Virginia's appraisal that year likened her to a glorified agony aunt, observing that she was 'confidant to many of the junior secretaries' and helped them solve their 'social' problems. True, it was recognised that she capably stood in for her boss when he was away – just as she had done all those years before in the Venice consulate. Neither was she wholly without supporters in the upper reaches of the CIA. Later that year she was belatedly moved up to GS-14, the equivalent of a lieutenant-colonel, the highest grade open to women at that time (only five female officers in the covert side of the CIA made it to GS-14 at all[34]). Her pay rose to a comfortable $14,120 per annum but it was the sole promotion in her fourteen-year career and not the solution Virginia might have hoped for. Her superiors continued to give her assignments below her abilities or rank. When she and Paul moved further away, to an elegant country house at Barnesville in Maryland, one boss even questioned her continued commitment. Yet there is every reason to believe that the new building at Langley, with its modern white-marble corridors and wooded grounds grazed by deer, was particularly attractive to her.

Virginia continued to divide opinion into her final years at the Agency. Her lack of recent field experience consistently counted against her but even her critics noted that she was unusually adept at 'picking out the flaws and pitfalls' of proposed operations – seemingly an all too rare talent at that time. In 1961, the

CIA had brought humiliation on itself and its James Bond-loving president John F. Kennedy in a cack-handed attempt to topple Castro in Cuba. As if nothing had been learned from the botched Dieppe raid in August 1942 about the need for meticulous planning, the CIA landed a force of Cuban rebels in the Bay of Pigs with the idea of storming the interior to seize control from the communists. Many either died or were captured yards from the sea, having got stuck in an impossibly tangled mangrove swamp. No one in Washington seems to have known about the conditions as they had relied on crude nineteenth-century survey maps to guide them. The bloody fiasco led to national humiliation and eventually the departure of Allen Dulles. Lorna remembers Virginia – whose patch included Cuba – making a rare comment about her work. Normally the family knew never to ask questions about the CIA, but on this occasion she revealed she was 'glad' the operation 'wasn't one of mine'.

In 1966 her salary was substantially boosted to more than seventeen thousand dollars. Shortly afterwards, on her sixtieth birthday, she drove away from her parking space at Langley for the last time. Sixty was the mandatory retirement age, but most officers of her calibre and experience would normally expect to continue as training consultants. No such offer seems to have been made to Virginia, or maybe she had just had enough of the whole fractious CIA scene. It seems that her heart was also continuing to cause concern, but it was by any measure an unsatisfactory end to her career. Her many fans at the Agency were aghast as they watched her pack up her desk and bid goodbye, and some determined that day to see her right eventually. In its own secret report on her career, the CIA admitted that her fellow officers 'felt she had been sidelined – shunted into backwater accounts – because she had so much experience that she overshadowed her male colleagues, who felt threatened by her'. One of them angrily observed that 'her experience and abilities were never properly utilized'. Returning to such a humdrum world of rejection after her triumphs in the war had indeed been hard to bear – for Virginia more than most. But then, as the historian Joseph Trento has pointed out, 'many World War II heroes went on to CIA careers that produced no real victories and many tragedies'.[35] Valour rarely reaps the dividends it should.

Virginia and Paul had each other and they had grand schemes for their pretty French-style house at Barnesville. She now had time to decorate, inspired by the châteaux and Venetian palazzi she had seen on her travels. Guests, including her old supporters from the CIA, were entertained in the light-flooded sitting room with its glazed area at one end. Virginia had such a knack of keeping her closest friends throughout her life and now at last she could spend some real time with them. She finally went easy on herself, moving into a ground-floor bedroom so that she would no longer have to face the pain of negotiating stairs. That one concession did not – at least at first – prevent her from a vigorous campaign of gardening in the thirty acres of grounds surrounding the house. She built a new greenhouse, grew vegetables (especially her beloved Jerusalem artichokes) and planted thousands of daffodils for a display of spring cheer. Paul would put on a leather apron and search for mushrooms on his hands and knees. They also kept particularly vicious geese, pushing them away from the house when needed with a broom and ultimately making them – or at least their livers – into foie gras. The couple even tried to replicate French cheese with milk from their herd of goats, although one batch went wrong and began to stink to high heaven on the porch. Cooking together was a favourite occupation, and afterwards Virginia would weave on an old-fashioned hand loom.

It was a companionable existence, a rare feat for many ex-agents from the Second World War, whose relationships often crumbled under the burden of what they had been through. William Simpson's marriage had broken down almost immediately on returning to Britain, his wife finding his experiences and disabilities an uncrossable barrier. Writing about *Waiting for Godot*, the theatre critic Robert Scanlan once observed that while the play is not a literal representation of Samuel Beckett's experiences in the Resistance, its imagery – and clearly the states of mind it represents – derive clearly from that time: 'All those who endured the war in Europe emerged transformed, and they had great difficulty expressing the magnitude of their inner tumult.'[36]

At least Paul had some understanding of what his wife had been through from his own service in France. From time to time, however, she would venture alone to find some inner peace in her old stamping ground in New York, on one drive up there showing some of the Virginia resourcefulness of old. She was already at the toll booth when she realised she had forgotten her wallet. Unwilling to make herself late by returning home to fetch it, she persuaded the operator to accept her Tissot watch (a gift from her time in the CIA) as security until she came back and settled her debt.

Even Virginia could not halt the slide in her health, however. Gradually she lost the strength and the willpower to use her false leg, and Cuthbert was abandoned in favour of crutches. She spent most of her days in a chair watching the birds through the window and feeding her five French poodles, arranged in a semi-circle around her, from a silver ladle. Her active brain devoured crossword puzzles and stacks of history and travel books, but especially spy stories. She still refused – despite encouragement from many different parties – to write her own. Lorna, who continued to visit her aunt regularly, often asked for tales of the war but Virginia dismissed her pleas with the fact that she 'had seen too many corpses of colleagues who had talked'. No doubt she kept track of the books written by and about her comrades at SOE, and noted how so many of them had never recovered from their wartime service and died often lonely deaths comparatively young. The Newton Twins were, for instance, immortalised in the book *No Banners* but crippled by the effects of their time in captivity, Alfred dying at sixty-five in 1979 and Henry at just sixty-one in 1980.

Paul was also in his sixties when he suffered a severe stroke that changed his sunny personality into something dark and gloomy. Both he and Virginia were now in pain and cantankerous, with only memories of happiness and facing a daily struggle to cope. Virginia was also in and out of hospital for medical treatment for a complicated range of conditions. After sixteen years of retirement and thirty-eight years with Paul, Virginia died on 8 July 1982 at the Shady Grove Adventist Hospital in Rockville, Maryland. She was seventy six.

As so often happens, death triggered a new curiosity. Newspapers such as the *Washington Post* carried admiring obituaries, describing Virginia as a 'Baltimore schoolgirl who became a hero of the French Resistance'.[37] The *New York Times* called her 'one of the most effective and reliable agents'[38] of the Second World War. What they did not say – and could not have known – was just how a woman of no hope, no prospects and apparently of no importance had risen to such heights. How in concealing her identity she had at last found what she really was and what she really could do. And how in fighting for the liberty of another nation she had found freedom for herself. Or, indeed, how her own country had not always served her well or, despite her Distinguished Service Cross, truly recognised her greatness.

Four thousand miles away, the old boys from the Haute-Loire Resistance wrote to each other to share the devastating news. They had enjoyed nearly forty years of freedom since spending a mere couple of months in Virginia's presence in 1944. But the warrior they called *La Madone* had shown them hope, comradeship and courage and they had never forgotten. In the midst of hardship and fear, she had shared with them a fleeting but glorious state of happiness and the most vivid moment of their lives. The last of those famous *Diane* Irregulars – the ever-boyish Gabriel Eyraud, her *chouchou* – passed away in 2017 while I was researching Virginia's story. Until the end of his days, he, like the others who had known Virginia on the plateau, liked to pause now and then to think of the woman in khaki who never ever gave up on freedom. When they talked with awe and affection of her incredible exploits, they smiled and looked up at the wide, open skies with '*les étoiles dans les yeux*'.

Epilogue

Virginia never received the recognition she deserved during her CIA career but gradually there were signs that her legacy was becoming better understood. Eloise Randolph Page, who became the first woman station chief of the CIA in the 1970s, talked of how the women of the OSS prepared the groundwork for 'their sisters who came after them'.

In 2018 Gina Haspel became the first female director of the CIA and talked of how she too stood 'on the shoulders of heroines who never sought public acclaim' who had served in the OSS and in the Agency itself. She was 'deeply indebted' to these women who 'challenged stereotypes' and 'broke down barriers' to make her appointment possible.

Today Virginia is officially recognised by the CIA as an unqualified heroine of the war, whose career at the agency was held back by 'frustrations with her superiors who did not use her talents well'.[1]

In June 1988 Virginia's name was posthumously added to the Military Intelligence Corps Hall of Fame. She was one of the first people to be honoured in this way.

After persistent lobbying by her supporters in France and

elsewhere, in December 2006 France and Britain celebrated Virginia's life in a ceremony at the French ambassador's residence in Washington. The ambassador read a letter of homage from the then president, Jacques Chirac, honouring her as this 'American friend' of France. It was the first time that the country publicly acknowledged her as a 'true hero of the French Resistance'. No one seemed aware of, or mentioned, her Croix de Guerre. The certificate for Virginia's MBE, which had remained in a desk in London for sixty years, was presented to her niece Lorna Catling by the British ambassador.

A painting by the artist Jeff Bass was unveiled at the same event. It showed Virginia transmitting a radio message next to the young Resistance fighter Edmond Lebrat at Léa Lebrat's farm in the Haute-Loire in the summer of 1944. The original hangs at the CIA's headquarters at Langley, just around the corner from a life-size statue of her one-time OSS boss and greatest admirer 'Wild Bill' Donovan. Copies of the painting have been put up all round the world, including in the Special Forces Club in London.

In the current official catalogue for the CIA Museum, there are only five OSS operatives deemed deserving of their own section. Four were men who became directors of the CIA; the other is Virginia, the only woman and only one to struggle in her postwar career.

In December 2016 the CIA named a building after her. New recruits are put through their paces, and taught why she was an all-time great, in the Virginia Hall Expeditionary Center.

There are six facets to today's CIA ethos: Service, Excellence, Integrity, Courage, Teamwork, Stewardship. Virginia has been chosen to represent Service. But she is not ranked as a Trailblazer, a special class of officer deemed to have shaped the Agency's history.

Yet SOE and OSS – and notably Virginia's pioneering work setting up networks in France – inspires much that goes on even in today's special forces. The CIA acknowledges that Operation Jawbreaker in Afghanistan before and after 9/11 was a direct descendant of Virginia's secret operations with the French Resistance in the Second World War. CIA officers were infiltrated into northern Afghanistan to collect intelligence and later to recruit, arm and equip local groups to assist in the forthcoming American offensive against the Taliban and Al-Qaeda.

When Klaus Barbie became too much of an embarrassment for his American handlers, they arranged in 1951 for him to flee via the so-called rat lines for escaping ex-Nazis, in his case to Bolivia. But in 1987, five years after Virginia's death, he was forced to return to Lyon to stand trial for crimes against humanity. He was found guilty and sentenced to life in prison, where he died in 1991.

Hugo Bleicher was captured in the Netherlands in June 1945, and taken to London to be interrogated by SOE. He was not charged, and sent to Paris where he was jailed as a suspected war criminal, but as a result of favourable testimony by his former enemies was released in late 1946 and repatriated to Germany. He returned twice to France after the war, once as a witness against Alesch. Incredibly, the second time he came as a guest of Peter Churchill and his wife, fellow SOE agent Odette Sansom, whom he had captured in 1943.[2]

Alain – or Georges Duboudin – showed the courageous side of his character when he returned to the region around Grenoble in south-east France in March 1943 but disappeared almost immediately. He was later found to have died from starvation and pleurisy in Elbrich concentration camp in March 1945, just weeks before the end of the war.

William Simpson married his nurse, had two children and found a way to live with his injuries after pioneering plastic surgery.

The nephews' sacrifice is recorded for history on a memorial at Valençay in the Indre, near where they landed in France for their last mission.

La Chatte was deported back to France as an undesirable alien at the end of the war, and met by French police. She was tried, sentenced to death, reprieved and ultimately released.

Denis Rake took part in a famous French documentary on the Resistance called *The Sorrow and the Pity*, in which he hailed Virginia as the 'greatest woman agent of the war'.

To his dismay, for years no one wanted to publish Pierre Fayol's extraordinary tribute to Virginia, despite all the effort he had put into it. She had long been forgotten by the French and by the time it was finally released she was dead and never saw it. His devotion to Virginia's memory led him to bring the *Diane* Irregulars together on several occasions, before they all became too old, to talk of the war and above all *La Madone*.

Gabriel stayed on the plateau and married happily. His widow keeps a room in their house in Le Chambon dedicated to souvenirs of the Irregulars. Dédé returned to Alsace, where he had come from, and worked as a schoolteacher. Neither ever saw Virginia again.

Paul never fully recovered from his stroke but survived Virginia by five years.

Such was SOE's enduring popularity in France that even twenty years after the end of the war there were still forty-six thriving F Section fan clubs called Amicales Buckmaster.

Virginia Hall is a legend on the Haute-Loire plateau to this day. *'Les étoiles dans les yeux.'*

Agent Names

Code names and field names appear in italics throughout the book. Agents often had multiple code or field names but for the sake of clarity I have used only the most relevant.

Alain	Georges Duboudin
Antoine	Philippe de Vomécourt (also *Gauthier, Major Saint-Paul*)
Aramis	Peter Harratt (also *Henri Lassot*)
Artus and *Auguste*	Henry and Alfred Newton
Bishop	Abbé Robert Alesch (also *René Martin*)
Bob	Raoul le Boulicaut
Carte	André Girard
Célestin	Brian Stonehouse
Christophe	Gilbert Turck
Constantin	Jean de Vomécourt
Fontcroise	Captain Henri Charles Giese
Georges	Georges Bégué
Gévolde	Serge Kapalski
Gloria	Gabrielle Picabia
Lucas	Pierre de Vomécourt (also *Sylvain*)

Marie	Virginia Hall (also *Germaine, Philomène, Nicolas, Diane, Diana, Marcelle, Brigitte, Camille*)
Nicolas	Robert Boiteux (also known as Robert Burdett)
Olive	Francis Basin
Pépin	Dr Jean Rousset
René	Victor Gerson (also *Vic*)
Sophie	Odette Wilen
Victoire	Mathilde Carré (or La Chatte)

Selected Bibliography

Alcorn, Robert Hayden, *Spies of the OSS*, Robert Hale, 1973

Binney, Marcus, *The Women Who Lived for Danger: The Women Agents of SOE in the Second World War*, Hodder & Stoughton, 2002

——, *Secret War Heroes*, Hodder & Stoughton, 2005

Bleicher, Hugo (ed. Ian Colvin), *Colonel Henri's Story: The War Memoirs of Hugo Bleicher, Former German Secret Agent*, William Kimber, 1968

Bollon, Gérard, *Aperçus sur la Résistance armée en Yssingelais (1940/1945)*, Cahiers de la Haute-Loire, 1997

Buckmaster, Maurice, *They Fought Alone: The Story of British Agents in France*, Odhams Press, 1958

Burrin, Philippe, *La France à l'heure allemande, 1940–1944*, Seuil, 1995

Casey, William, *The Secret War Against Hitler*, Simon & Schuster, 1989

Churchill, Peter, *Of Their Own Choice*, Hodder & Stoughton, 1952

——, *The Spirit in the Cage*, Hodder & Stoughton, 1954

——, *Duel of Wits*, Transworld, 1955

Combes, Gustave, *Lève-toi et marche: Les conditions du relevement Français*, Privat, 1941

Cookridge, E. H., *They Came from the Sky: The Stories of Lieutenant-Colonel Francis Cammaerts, Major Roger Landes, and Captain Henry Rée*, Heinemann, 1965

——, *Inside SOE: The Story of Special Operations in Western Europe, 1940–45*, Arthur Baker, 1966

Courvoisier, André, *Le Réseau Heckler: De Lyon à Londres*, France-Empire, 1984

Cowburn, Benjamin, *No Cloak, No Dagger*, Jarrolds, 1960

Dalton, Hugh, *The Fateful Years: Memoirs, 1931–1945*, Muller, 1957

Dear, Ian, *Sabotage and Subversion: Stories from the Files of the SOE and OSS*, Arms and Armour Press, 1996

Défourneaux, René J., *The Winking Fox: Twenty-two Years in Military Intelligence*, Indiana Creative Arts, 1998

Dormer, Hugh, *Hugh Dormer's Diaries*, J. Cape, 1947

Fayol, Pierre, *Le Chambon-sur-Lignon sous l'occupation: Les résistances locales, l'aide interalliée, l'action de Virginia Hall (O.S.S.)*, L'Harmattan, 1990

Fenby, Jonathan, *The History of Modern France: From the Revolution to the Present Day*, Simon & Schuster, 2015

Foot, M.R.D, *SOE in France: An Account of the Work of the British Special Operations Executive in France 1940–1944*, HMSO, 1966

Grose, Peter, *A Good Place to Hide: How One Community Saved Thousands of Lives from the Nazis in World War II*, Nicholas Brealey, 2016

Hastings, Max, *The Secret War: Spies, Codes and Guerrillas, 1939–1945*, William Collins, 2015

Helm, Sarah, *If This is a Woman: Inside Ravensbrück: Hitler's Concentration Camp for Women*, Little, Brown, 2015

Heslop, Richard, *Xavier: A British Secret Agent with the French Resistance*, Biteback, 2014

Howarth, Patrick, *Undercover: The Men and Women of the Special Operations Executive*, Routledge & Kegan Paul, 1980

Jenkins, Cecil, *A Brief History of France: People, History and Culture*, Robinson, 2011

Jones, Benjamin F., *Eisenhower's Guerrillas: The Jedburghs, the Maquis, and the Liberation of France*, Oxford University Press, 2016

Langelaan, George, *Knights of the Floating Silk*, Hutchinson, 1959

Leahy, William D., *I Was There: The Personal Story of the Chief of Staff to Presidents Roosevelt and Truman, Based on His Notes and Diaries Made at the Time*, Victor Gollancz, 1950

Leary, William M. (ed.), *The Central Intelligence Agency: History and Documents*, University of Alabama Press, 1984

Le Chêne, Evelyn, *Watch For Me By Moonlight: A British Agent with the French Resistance*, Eyre Methuen, 1973

Lottman, Herbert R., *Pétain: Hero or Traitor: The Untold Story*, William Morrow, 1985

Lytton, Neville, *Life in Unoccupied France*, Macmillan & Co., 1942

MacDonald, Elizabeth P., *Women in Intelligence*, privately published

Mackenzie, W. J. M, *The Secret History of SOE: The Special Operations Executive 1940–1945*, St Ermin's Press, 2002

Marks, Leo, *Between Silk and Cyanide: A Codemaker's Story 1941–1945*, HarperCollins, 1999

Marshall, Bruce, *The White Rabbit*, Evans Brothers, 1952

McCarthy, Linda, *Spies, Pop Flies, and French Fries: Stories I Told My Favorite Visitors to the CIA Exhibit Center*, History is a Hoot, 1999

McIntosh, Elizabeth P., *Sisterhood of Spies: The Women of the OSS*, Naval Institute Press, 1998

Moorehead, Caroline, *Village of Secrets: Defying the Nazis in Vichy France*, Vintage, 2015

Morgan, Ted, *An Uncertain Hour: The French, the Germans, the Jews, the Barbie Trial, and the City of Lyon, 1940–1945*, Bodley Head, 1990

Moss, W. Stanley, *Ill Met by Moonlight*, Harrap, 1950

Nouzille, Vincent, *L'espionne: Virginia Hall, une Américaine dans la guerre*, Arthème Fayard, 2007

Olson, Lynne, *Last Hope Island: Britain, Occupied Europe, and the Brotherhood that Helped Turn the Tide of War*, Random House, 2017

Paine, Lauran, *Mathilde Carré, Double Agent*, Hale, 1976

Paxton, Robert O., *Vichy France: Old Guard and New Order 1940–1944*, Barrie & Jenkins, 1972

Pearson, Judith L., *The Wolves at the Door: The True Story of America's Greatest Female Spy*, Lyons Press, 2005

Rake, Denis, *Rake's Progress*, Frewin, 1968

Ranelagh, John, *CIA: A History*, BBC Books, 1992

Rossiter, Margaret L., *Women in the Resistance*, Praeger, 1986

Ruby, Marcel, *La Résistance à Lyon: 19 Juin 1940–3 Septembre 1944*, L'Hermès, 1979

——, *F Section, SOE: The Story of the Buckmaster Network*, Leo Cooper, 1988

Simpson, William, *I Burned My Fingers*, Putnam, 1955

Smith, Richard Harris, *OSS: The Secret History of America's First Central Intelligence Agency*, University of California Press, 1972

Stourton, Edward, *Cruel Crossing: Escaping Hitler Across the Pyrenees*, Doubleday, 2013

Sweet-Escott, Bickham, *Baker Street Irregular*, Methuen, 1965

Thomas, Jack, *No Banners: The Story of Alfred and Henry Newton*, W. H. Allen, 1955

Vargo, Marc E., *Women of the Resistance: Eight Who Defied the Third Reich*, McFarland, 2012

Vomécourt, Philippe de, *Who Lived to See the Day: France in Arms, 1940–1945*, Hutchinson, 1961

Waller, Douglas, *Wild Bill Donovan: The Spymaster Who Created the OSS and Modern American Espionage*, Simon & Schuster, 2011

Weiner, Tim, *Legacy of Ashes: The History of the CIA*, Doubleday, 2007

Weitz, Margaret Collins, *Sisters in the Resistance: How Women Fought to Free France, 1940–1945*, John Wiley & Sons, 1995

Notes

Abbreviations

CHRD	Centre d'Histoire de la Résistance et de la Déportation, Lyon
HS	Records of the Special Operations Executive held at The National Archives, Kew
NARA	National Archives and Records Administration, College Park, Maryland
PF	Personnel File
RG	Record Group
Tr.	Translated from the original French

Prologue

1 Nick Hopkins, 'What you really need to join MI6: emotional intelligence and a high IQ', *Guardian*, 2 March 2017.

Chapter 1: The Dream

1 *Quid Nunc* magazine, Roland Country Park School.
2 Ibid.
3 Rossiter, *Women in the Resistance*, p. 190. Based on a telephone interview with Elbridge Durbrow before his death in 1984.
4 Telegram from the consulate in Izmir to the State Department in Washington, 25 December 1933, RG 59, NARA.
5 Lorna Catling, interview with author at her Baltimore home, 27 October 2017.
6 Consul W. Perry George, 16 May 1934, RG 59, NARA.
7 I am indebted throughout the book to Stewart Emmens, curator of

Community Health at the Science Museum in London, for his expert knowledge of historic prosthetics.

8 Foot, *SOE in France*, p. 156.
9 Virginia wrote these words on the back of a photograph of herself and Angelo on a gondola. Lorna Catling personal collection.
10 Virginia Hall, 123 File, RG 59, NARA.
11 From an interview with Barbara Hall in the *Baltimore Sun*, 12 June 1940.
12 *Baltimore Sun*, 12 June 1940
13 Vomécourt, *Who Lived to See the Day*, p. 22.

Chapter 2: Cometh the Hour

1 Taken from her testimony to the US embassy in London on her arrival in 1940, RG 226, NARA, and Fayol, *Le Chambon-sur-Lignon*, p. 93ff.
2 Baker Street was made famous as the home of the fictional detective Sherlock Holmes. In Sir Arthur Conan Doyle's stories, Holmes ran a motley group of street boys to gather intelligence, known as the Baker Street Irregulars, a name gleefully adopted by SOE staffers.
3 HS 9/647/4, Virginia Hall PF, 15 January 1941.
4 Foot, *SOE in France*, p. 9, ref Dalton, *The Fateful Years*, p. 368.
5 Hastings, *The Secret War*, p. 261, ref. *The War Diaries of Hugh Dalton*, Jonathan Cape, 1986, p. 52.
6 Olson, *Last Hope Island*, p. 166, ref. Christopher Andrew, *Her Majesty's Secret Service: The Making of the British Intelligence Community*, Viking, 1986, p. 476.
7 HS 9/647/4, 31 March 1941.
8 HS 9/647/4, 17 May 1941.
9 HS 9/647/4, several notes dating from 1 April 1941 onwards.
10 HS 9/647/4, 21 May 1941.
11 HS 7/121, F Section History and Agents.
12 HS 9/647/4, Lt-Col Edward Calthorpe, 5 April 1941.
13 Foot, *SOE in France*, p. 16.
14 Ibid., p. 55.
15 Ruby, *F Section, SOE*, p. 19. Some details of her training also come from an article by the CIA Historian Gerald K. Haines, 'Virginia Hall Goillot: Career Intelligence Officer', *Prologue* (Winter 1944), 249–50. Others came from the accounts of fellow agents, as well as her own SOE Personnel File.
16 Vomécourt, *Who Lived to See the Day*, p. 82.
17 *New York Post*, 4 September 1941.
18 Dear, *Sabotage and Subversion*, p. 141.
19 HS 9/647/4, article dated 22 January 1942.
20 Grose, *A Good Place to Hide*, p. 63.
21 Quoted in Smith, *OSS*, p. 38.
22 Suzanne Bertillon, 'Review of Chain – 1942 (HIHI)', <https://www.cia.gov/library/readingroom/docs/REVIEW%20OF%20OSS%20CHAIN%201942_0001.pdf>.

23 Much remains classified about Johnny Nicolas's intelligence activities but his presence was confirmed in correspondence with William J. Casey, then Director of the CIA, in May 1985, and released under the Freedom of Information Act.

24 Vomécourt, *Who Lived to See the Day*, p. 82.

25 Leahy, *I Was There*, p. 49.

26 Morgan, *An Uncertain Hour*, p. 89.

27 Ibid., p. 200.

28 OSS Aid to the French Resistance, RG 226, NARA.

29 HS 9/647/4, October 1941.

30 Churchill, *Of Their Own Choice*, p. 116.

31 Simpson, *I Burned My Fingers*, p. 36.

32 Corinna von List, 'Trois piliers de la Résistance sous couvert de féminité. Les services de liaison, les secretariats et l'hébergement', *Francia*, p. 37 (2010).

33 Weitz, *Sisters in the Resistance*, pp. 54–5.

34 HS 9/647/4, 2 April 1942.

35 HS 9/815/4, Clement Jumeau PF.

36 HS 9/681/1, JB Hayes PF.

37 Buckmaster, *They Fought Alone*, p. 85.

38 HS 8/1002, report on British circuits in France by Major Bourne-Paterson, 1946.

39 HS 7/121.

40 The same method was adopted by the BBC after the war to track down non-payers of its licence fee.

41 Foot, *SOE in France*, p. 155.

42 Courvoisier, *Le Réseau Heckler*, p. 149.

43 George Begue's testimony in HS 9/1491/2, Gilbert Turck PF.

44 Philippe de Vomécourt reveals in an interrogation in his Personnel File (HS 9/1539/5) that he was just one of those who believed *Christophe* was a traitor, although SOE interrogators cleared him of wrongdoing at the end of the war. Philippe was also invited to the Villa des Bois but suspected a ruse and although he travelled to Marseille, took flight and did not come to the house. *Christophe* continued to try to lure him to a café.

45 Foot, *SOE in France*, p. 157.

46 HS 7/121.

Chapter 3: My Tart Friends

1 Olson, *Last Hope Island*, p. 268.

2 Buckmaster, *They Fought Alone*, p. 35.

3 HS 9/647/4, Virginia Hall PF, 5 May 1942.

4 HS 9/647/4, report 22 January 1942

5 HS 9/647/4, undated, but late autumn 1941.

6 Simpson, *I Burned My Fingers*, p. 36.

7 Ibid., p. 35.

8　Ibid., p. 37.

9　Ibid., p. 35.

10　Colonel Gubbins in Germaine Guérin's Personnel File, HS 9/631/2 (originally closed until 2031, but opened for this book).

11　HS 7/121, F Section History and Agents.

12　HS 9/647/4, report 4 December 1941.

13　Vomécourt, *Who Lived to See the Day*, p. 82.

14　Simpson, *I Burned My Fingers*, p. 38.

15　HS 9/647/4, undated dispatch.

16　Combes, *Lève-toi et marche*, p. 62, quoted in Weitz, *Sisters in the Resistance*, p. 50.

17　HS 9/647/4.

18　Cowburn, *No Cloak, No Dagger*, p. 31.

19　KV 3/153, Enemy Secret Services in France, SIS report 1944, The National Archives.

20　HS 6/568 France: circuit and mission reports and interrogations. Cammaerts to Cruzel; HS 9/1651 Benjamin Cowburn PF.

21　HS 9/647/4, 8 October 1941.

22　HS 9/647/4, 8 October 1941.

23　Churchill, *Of Their Own Choice*, p. 131.

24　HS 9/647/4, 3 March 1942

25　Ronald C. Rosbottom, *When Paris Went Dark: The City of Light Under German Occupation, 1940–1944*, Little, Brown, 2014, p. 299.

26　Vomécourt, *Who Lived to See the Day*, p. 32.

27　HS 8/1002, report on British circuits in France by Major Bourne-Paterson, 1946.

28　HS 9/452/3, Georges Duboudin PF.

29　Oluf Reed-Olsen in Hastings, *The Secret War*, p. 273.

30　HS 9/631/2.

31　HS 9/647/4, 21 November 1944.

32　HS 9/647/4.

33　Churchill, *Duel of Wits*, p. 180.

34　HS 9/314, Peter Churchill PF vol. 1.

35　Churchill, *Duel of Wits*, p. 118.

36　HS 9/314.

37　HS 9/314.

38　Churchill, *Of Their Own Choice*, p. 136.

39　HS 8/1002.

40　Churchill, *Duel of Wits*, p. 154.

41　Ibid., p. 153.

Chapter 4: Goodbye to Dindy

1　13–15 December 1941, mentioned later in HS 7/244, F Section War Diary, July–September 1942.

2   HS 7/142 SOE France Basic Handbook Parts III & IV
3   HS 7/142.
4   HS 9/647/4, Virginia Hall PF, 5 January 1942.
5   Foot, *SOE in France*, p. 56.
6   Ruby, *F Section, SOE*, p. 166.
7   This extraordinary episode is outlined in many (sometimes contradictory) reports. I have used as near a consensus as to what really happened as possible. The sources include: Cowburn's Personnel File (HS 9/1651); his book, *No Cloak, No Dagger*, chapter seven; Pierre de Vomécourt's Personnel File (HS 9/1539/6); KV 3/75, the SIS file on German penetration of SOE, SIS and Allied organisations at The National Archives; Foot, *SOE in France*, pp. 171–5; Vomécourt, *Who Lived to See the Day*, pp. 98–103; and several references Paine, *Mathilde Carré*.
8   Cookridge, *Inside SOE*, p. 602, referring to sworn documents signed by Germans on trial after the war.
9   Foot, *SOE in France*, pp. 154–5.
10 HS 8/1002, report on British circuits in France by Major Bourne-Paterson, 1946.
11 HS 9/647/4, 3 March 1942.
12 HS 9/1651.
13 HS 9/1651, 28 October 1942.
14 Cowburn, *No Cloak, No Dagger*, p. 112.
15 HS 9/1059/1, Gerry Morel PF.
16 HS 9/1059/1.
17 HS 9/902/3, Marcel Leccia PF.
18 HS 9/647/4, undated but probably October 1943.
19 HS 8/1002.
20 OSS Archives, Second Draft Report on Virginia Hall's honour from Lt de Roussy de Sales to Lt-Col van der Stricht, 13 December 1944, RG 226, NARA.
21 HS 8/1002.
22 HS 9/647/4, March 1942.
23 HS 9/647/4, 22 April 1942.
24 Foot, *SOE in France*, p. 190.
25 HS 9/647/4, 3 March 1942.
26 Foot, *SOE in France*, p. 190.
27 HS 9/647/4, report 18 January 1943.
28 HS 9/452/3, Georges Douboudin PF, 17 May 1942.
29 HS 7/244.
30 HS 7/244.
31 HS 9/681/3, Charles Hayes PF.
32 HS 9/1651, 20 December 1944. See also Churchill, *Duel of Wits*.
33 Courvoisier, *Le Réseau Heckler*, p. 134.
34 Rake, *Rake's Progress*, p. 55.
35 Interview in Marcel Ophüls's television documentary *Le Chagrin et la Pitié*

(1971). It was not screened in France until 1981 because of its incendiary content on wartime collaboration.

36   Rake, *Rake's Progress*, p. 85.
37   Ibid., p. 104.
38   Ibid., p. 106.
39   Ibid., p. 123.
40   Millar, *Horned Pigeon*, p. 290.
41   HS 7/244.
42   HS 9/647/4, 19 June 1945.
43   HS 7/244.
44   HS 7/244.

Chapter 5: Twelve Minutes, Twelve Men

1   HS 9/815/4, Clement Jumeau PF.
2   HS 9/115/2 Georges Bégué PF.
3   HS 9/647/4, Virginia Hall PF.
4   HS 6/647/4.
5   HS 9/1346/5, Jose Sevilla PF.
6   HS 9/166/1, Jean and Gaby Pierre-Bloch PF.
7   HS 9/166/1.
8   Langelaan, *Knights of the Floating Silk*, pp. 161–2.
9   Ibid., p. 165.
10   Ibid., p. 164.
11   Ruby, *F Section, SOE*, p. 186. Jean Pierre-Bloch talks extensively in this book about Mauzac.
12   Ibid.
13   Ibid.
14   HS 8/171, Vic circuit: signals.
15   Foot, *SOE in France*, p. 183.
16   See Courvoisier's tribute to Virginia Hall and Mme Bloch in Archives Départementales, Lyon 31J/1F/24. In trying to establish exactly what happened from often confused and conflicting accounts, I have also been aided by further details of this astonishing story in (amongst others) Jean Pierre-Bloch's *Le Temps d'y Penser Encore*, Jean-Claude Simoën, 1977; Binney, *Secret War Heroes*; HS 8/174, Vic circuit: operational orders, interrogations, agents, helpers; HS 8/171, Vic circuit: signals; HS 7/244, F Section War Diary, July–September 1942; HS 9/115/2, Georges Bégué PF; M. R. D. Foot, *Six Faces of Courage*, Eyre Methuen, 1978; HS 9/923/4 Phillip Liewer PF.
17   Foot, *SOE in France*, p. ix.
18   OSS Archives, Testimony to OSS, Second Draft of Narrative for Granting of Award to Miss Virginia Hall, 13 December 1944, RG 226, NARA.
19   HS 9/647/4, 19 October 1942.
20   HS 9/647/4.

Chapter 6: Honeycomb of Spies

1   HS 7/244, F Section War Diary, July–September 1942, 28 September 1942.
2   Thomas, *No Banners*, p. 163.
3   HS 9/314, Peter Churchill PF vol. 1.
4   Ruby, *F Section, SOE*, p. 182.
5   HS 7/142 SOE France Basic Handbook Parts III & IV
6   HS 7/121, F Section History and Agents.
7   Corinna von List, 'Trois piliers de la Résistance sous couvert de féminité. Les services de liaison, les secretariats et l'hébergement', *Francia*, 37 (2010).
8   Interview with Lorna Catling, Baltimore, October 2017.
9   Foot, *SOE in France*, p. 178.
10 Ibid., p. 179.
11 HS 7/244.
12 HS 7/244.
13 Churchill in his report of 24 September 1942 in *Duel of Wits*, p. 121.
14 Alcorn, *Spies of the OSS*, p. 58.
15 HS 7/121.
16 Rake, *Rake's Progress*, p. 151.
17 Cowburn, *No Cloak, No Dagger*, p. 116.
18 HS 9/1648, Denis Rake PF, report 30 September 1942.
19 HS 7/244.
20 HS 9/647/4, report 30 September 1942.
21 Heslop, *Xavier*, p. 68.
22 HS 9/647/4, report 30 September 1942.
23 HS 7/244.
24 Cookridge, *Inside SOE*, p. 91.
25 HS 9/647/4, report 30 September 1942.
26 HS 9/314.
27 HS 7/244.
28 HS 9/647/4, report 30 September 1942.
29 HS 9/452/3, Georges Duboudin PF, comments by Maurice Buckmaster.
30 Le Chêne, *Watch For Me By Moonlight*, p. 57.
31 Quote from *Gauthier's* deputy *Joe*. From Thomas, *No Banners*, p. 136.
32 HS 9/1242/8, Jean Regnier PF.
33 HS 9/647/4, report 6 September 1942.
34 HS 7/244.
35 HS 9/647/4, Maurice Buckmaster's comments on debrief, 23 March 1943.
36 HS 9/647/4, report 6 September 1942.
37 Germaine Guérin's testimony in the Robert Alesch dossier, ANZ6-597-5024-01051946, Archives Nationales, Paris.
38 Bardet-Keiffer dossier, ANZ6-682-5790, Archives Nationales, Paris.
39 OSS Archives, Alesch interrogation reports of 6 and 8 August 1945, RG 226, NARA.

Chapter 7: Cruel Mountain

1   Churchill's third report 18 September 1942 in *Duel of Wits*, p. 117.
2   Churchill, *Duel of Wits*, p. 119.
3   HS 9/647/4, Virginia Hall PF, report 30 September 1942.
4   HS 9/647/4, report 30 September 1942.
5   Dossier 72 AJ 627, Archives Nationales, Paris.
6   I have conducted a number of interviews with British and American former agents.
7   Thomas, *No Banners*, p. 163.
8   Ibid., p. 164.
9   HS 9/1091/1, Henry Newton PF.
10 Leahy, *I Was There*, p. 80.
11 HS 9/1096/8, Alfred Newton PF.
12 HS 9/647/4, report 18 January 1943.
13 HS 8/1002, report on British circuits in France by Major Bourne-Paterson, 1946.
14 Thomas, *No Banners*, p. 168.
15 HS 9/1096/8.
16 Nouzille, *L'espionne*, p. 224.
17 HS 9/647/4, report 4 December 1942.
18 Stourton, *Cruel Crossing*, p. 250.
19 HS 8/1002.
20 US Department of State Central Files, memorandum 2 March 1943, RG 59, NARA.
21 This account comes from a number of sources including descriptions from Lorna Catling, Virginia's niece; Craig Gralley, an ex-CIA officer who retraced her steps in 'A Climb to Freedom: A Personal Journey in Virginia Hall's Steps', *Studies in Intelligence*, 61:1 (March 2017); Vincent Nouzille's *L'espionne*; accounts in Virginia's Personnel File and numerous other SOE documents; as well as extensive personal research on the conditions and topography.

Chapter 8: Agent Most Wanted

1   HS 7/245, F Section War Diary, October–December 1942.
2   Testimony from Dr Rousset, Robert Alesch dossier, ANZ6-597-5024-01051946, Archives Nationales, Paris.
3   HS 7/245, 21 December 1942.
4   Millar, *Horned Pigeon*, p. 283.
5   Thomas, *No Banners*, p. 206.
6   US State Department Central Papers, cable from Bern to Department of State, Washington, 20 February 1943, RG 59, NARA.
7   HS 8/1002, report on British circuits in France by Major Bourne-Paterson, 1946.

8   Simpson, *I Burned My Fingers*, p. 35.

9   Thomas, *No Banners*, pp. 197–8.

10 Germaine Guérin's testimony in Robert Alesch dossier.

11 Germaine Guérin, Dossier GR16P2474858, Service Historique de la Défense, Paris; Note on her, B 162/9816, Bundesarchiv, Koblenz. Thanks too to Monika Schnell at the Ravensbrück archives for further details.

12 KV 3/75, German Penetration of SOE, SIS and Allied organisations, The National Archives, 28 April 1943.

13 HS 9/647/4, Virginia Hall PF, 25 November 1942.

14 Ibid.

15 HS 9/647/4, 4 December 1942.

16 Churchill, *Duel of Wits*, p. 211.

17 Simpson, *I Burned My Fingers*, p. 160.

18 Hastings, *The Secret War*, pp. 260–1.

19 Burrin, *La France à l'heure allemande*, p. 438.

20 W. D. Halls, *The Youth of Vichy France*, Oxford University Press, 1981, p. 53.

21 Olson, *Last Hope Island*, p. 275.

22 HS 7/121, F Section History and Agents.

23 Foot, *SOE in France*, p. 209.

24 Ibid., p. 210.

25 Ibid., p. 88.

26 Rake, *Rake's Progress*, p. 196.

27 HS 9/647/4, 8 July 1943.

28 HS 9/647/4, 7 July 1943.

29 HS 9/902/3, Marcel Leccia PF.

30 HS 9/647/4, September 1943.

31 HS 9/315 Peter Churchill PF vol. 2.

32 Note in Foot, *SOE in France*, p. 499.

33 Vomécourt, *Who Lived to See the Day*, p. 213.

34 HS 9/647/4, 13 January 1944.

35 Weiner, *Legacy of Ashes*, p. 4.

36 Smith, *OSS*, p. 35.

37 Ibid., p. 149.

38 Casey, *The Secret War Against Hitler*, p. 11.

39 OSS Archives, OSS Aid to the French Resistance in World War II: Missions, F Section, Chronological Summery, RG 226, NARA.

40 David Bruce, quoted in Weiner, *Legacy of Ashes*, p. 4.

41 Hugh Trevor-Roper (ed. Richard Davenport-Hines), *The Wartime Journals*, January 1943, p. 128.

42 Ibid.

43 HS 9/647/4, 28 January 1944.

Chapter 9: Scores to Settle

1   OSS Archives, F Section Rolls 6 & 7, RG 226, NARA.

2 Sweet-Escott, *Baker Street Irregular*, p. 155.

3 Memorandum of 10 October 1945 for war crimes trial, quoted in Foot, *SOE in France*, p. 314.

4 OSS Archives, 18 March 1944, RG 226, NARA.

5 Interview with Lorna Catling, Baltimore, 17 October 2017.

6 McCarthy, *Spies, Pop Flies, and French Fries*, p. 46.

7 OSS Archives, Virginia Hall Activity Report, 30 September 1944, RG 226, NARA.

8 Ibid.

9 Ibid.

10 Interview with Lorna Catling; Pearson, *The Wolves at the Door*, pp. 187–8.

11 OSS Archives, OSS Signals, 18 April 1944, RG 226, NARA.

12 OSS Archives, F Section Rolls 6 & 7, RG 226, NARA.

13 OSS Archives, OSS Aid to the French Resistance and OSS F Section, RG 226, NARA.

14 OSS Archives, F Section Rolls 6 & 7, RG 226, NARA.

15 OSS Archives, Virginia Hall Activities in the Field Report, Saint-Heckler Circuit, F Section Rolls 6 & 7, RG 226, NARA.

16 Smith, *OSS*, p. 6, ref. Robert Hayden Alcorn, *No Banners, No Bands: More Tales from the OSS*, D. Mackay, 1965, p. 182.

17 OSS Archives, Aramis Activities in the Field Report, Saint-Heckler Circuit, F Section Rolls 6 & 7, RG 226, NARA.

18 HS 9/902/3, Marcel Leccia PF.

19 OSS Archives, Saint-Heckler Circuit, F Section Rolls 6 & 7, RG 226, NARA.

20 OSS Archives, Aid to the French Resistance; F Section, Activity Report of 2nd Lieut Roger B. Henquet (Aus), RG 226, NARA.

21 OSS Archives, Signal Report, 20 May 1944, RG 226, NARA.

22 HS 6/597, Maquis 1944.

23 HS 6/568 France: circuit and mission reports and interrogations. Cammaerts to Cruzel; HS 9/1651 Benjamin Cowburn PF.

24 OSS Archives, 2 June 1944, RG 226, NARA.

25 Vomécourt, *Who Lived to See the Day*, p. 218.

26 Buckmaster, *They Fought Alone*, p. 220.

27 Vomécourt, *Who Lived to See the Day*, p. 224.

28 Ibid., p. 212.

29 OSS Archives, F Section Rolls 6 & 7, RG 226, NARA.

30 Tr M. Le Comte Arnaud de Voguë letter to Pierre Fayol, 7 February 1987, Fonds Fayol, CHRD.

31 HS 8/1002, report on British circuits in France by Major Bourne-Paterson, 1946.

32 HS 9/647/4, Virginia Hall PF.

33 OSS Archives, Lieutenant Paul Martineau Activity Report, Ventriloquist Circuit, F Section Rolls 6 & 7, RG 226, NARA.

34 CAB 106/989, Basic notes for the report of the Supreme Commander by

Major F. D. Price, Part 13: French Forces of the Interior, The National Archives.

35 OSS Archives, Aramis Activities in the Field Report, Saint-Heckler Circuit, F Section Rolls 6 & 7, RG 226, NARA.

Chapter 10: Madonna of the Mountains

1 OSS Archives, Virginia Hall Activity Report, Saint-Heckler Circuit, F Section Rolls 6 & 7, RG 226, NARA.

2 Tr. letter Auguste Bohny to Pierre Fayol, 9 June 1984, Fonds Fayol, CHRD.

3 Tr. Nouzille, *L'espionne*, p. 280, from an interview with Auguste Bohny, 22 May 2007.

4 Fayol, *Le Chambon-sur-Lignon*, p. 137.

5 Ibid., p. 138.

6 HS 9/171/1, Nicolas Bodington PF.

7 OSS Archives, Virginia Hall Activity Report, 30 September 1944, and her financial report, RG 226, NARA.

8 Tr. account given to Gérard Bollon, Le Chambon's historian, by Samuel Lebrat.

9 OSS Archives, Saint-Heckler Circuit, F Section Rolls 6 & 7, RG 226, NARA.

10 OSS Archives, James Forgan recommendation for Virginia Hall's DSC, 5 February 1944, RG 226, NARA.

11 Tr. Fayol, *Le Chambon-sur-Lignon*, p. 146.

12 Tr. undated testimony from Eric Barbezat, Fonds Fayol, CHRD.

13 Ibid.

14 OSS Archives, Marianne Fayol's testimony reported by Lieutenant George Schriver, in charge of enquiring as to whether Virginia should be decorated, 6 December 1944, RG 226, NARA.

15 Tr. letter Desire (Dédé) Zurbach to Pierre Fayol, 31 August 1986, Fonds Fayol, CHRD.

16 The real name of this type of plane was a Fieseler Fi 156 Storch.

17 OSS Archives, Virginia Hall Activity Report, 30 September 1944, RG 26, NARA.

18 Tr. testimony from Georges Coutarel in Bollon, *Aperçus sur la Résistance armée en Yssingelais*, p. 54.

19 OSS Archives, Virginia Hall's Activity in the Field Report, Saint-Heckler Circuit, F Section Rolls 6 & 7, RG 226, NARA.

20 There are many branches of a few families on the plateau, such as the Lebrats and the Eyrauds.

21 Tr. from an interview with the author, Le Chambon, 3 August 2017.

22 Grose, *A Good Place to Hide*, p. 214.

23 Tr. letter Dédé to Fayol, 20 October 1986, Fonds Fayol, CHRD.

24 Tr. Coutarel testimony in Bollon, *Aperçus sur la Résistance armée en Yssingelais*, p. 54.

25 Tr. letter Dédé to Fayol, 3 May 1985, Fonds Fayol, CHRD.
26 Moorehead, *Village of Secrets*, p. 290.
27 OSS Archives, Virginia Hall Activity Report, 30 September 1944, RG 226, NARA.
28 Tr. Nouzille, *L'espionne*, p. 290.
29 Tr. letter Dédé to Fayol, 27 August 1985, Fonds Fayol, CHRD.
30 Tr. letter Dédé to Fayol, 24 January 1991, Fonds Fayol, CHRD.
31 OSS Archives, Saint-Heckler report, F Section Rolls 6 & 7, RG 226, NARA.
32 HS 9/647/4, Virginia Hall PF.
33 Several sources including OSS Archives, Saint-Heckler report, F Section Rolls 6 & 7, RG 226, NARA; Fayol, *Le Chambon-sur-Lignon*, p. 176.
34 OSS Archives, Saint-Heckler report, F Section Rolls 6 & 7, RG 226, NARA.
35 Tr. letter Dédé to Fayol, 24 January 1991, Fonds Fayol, CHRD.
36 HS 9/647/4, 21 November 1944.
37 Lawrence J. Cerri, 'America's Incredible "Limping Lady"', *Army*, 38:2 (February 1988), p. 65.

Chapter 11: From the Skies Above

1   Tr. letter Desire (Dédé) Zurbach to Pierre Fayol, 7 October 1986, Fonds Fayol, CHRD.
2   OSS Archives, Virginia Hall Activity Report, 30 September 1944, RG 226, NARA.
3   FO's SOE Adviser CM Woods of Room E 203 on 26 September 1985 in a letter to Fayol, Fonds Fayol, CHRD.
4   Roger Leney testimony from Gérard Bollon interview in *Aperçus sur la Résistance armée en Yssingelais*.
5   OSS Archives, Virginia Hall Health Check, undated (probably early 1945), RG 226, NARA.
6   Tr. letter Dédé to Fayol, 20 October 1986, Fonds Fayol, CHRD.
7   HS 9/596/3, Paul Goillot PF.
8   Heckler report in War Diary and the same from 2nd Lieutenant Paul Golliot 3 October, OSS archives, RG226, NARA.
9   OSS Archives, Henry Riley Activity Report, RG 226, NARA.
10 OSS Archives, Saint-Heckler Circuit, Geoffrey Hallowes Activity Report, RG 226, NARA.
11 OSS Archives, Virginia Hall Activity Report, 30 September 1944, RG 226, NARA.
12 Testimony from Roger Leney from Gérard Bollon interview.
13 HS 7/134, Judex mission report (1944–45).
14 OSS Archives, Henry Riley Activity Report, RG 226, NARA.
15 OSS Archives, Henry Riley Activity Report, RG 226, NARA
16 Vomécourt, *Who Lived to See the Day*, p. 19.
17 OSS Archives, Henry Riley Activity Report.
18 Tr. letter Dédé to Fayol, 24 January 1991, Fonds Fayol, CHRD.

19 Tr. letter Dédé to Fayol, 3 May 1985, Fonds Fayol, CHRD.

20 Nouzille, *L'espionne*, p. 22.

21 Interview with Lorna Catling, Baltimore, October 2017.

22 OSS Archives, Virginia Hall undated financial report, RG 226, NARA.

23 Tr. letter Dédé to Fayol, 20 October 1986, Fonds Fayol, CHRD.

24 Will Irwin, *The Jedburghs: The Secret History of the Allied Special Forces, France 1944*, PublicAffairs, 2006, p. 154.

25 OSS Archives, Charlotte Norris to Barbara Hall, 21 September 1944, RG 226, NARA.

26 Tr. letter Jacqueline Leguevel to Fayol, 3 August 1987, Fonds Fayol, CHRD. And from Jackie Drury, one of her daughters, in interview cited by Vincent Nouzille in *L'espionne*.

27 OSS Archives, Virginia Hall Activity Report, 30 September 1944, RG 226, NARA.

28 Rossiter, *Women in the Resistance*, p. 124. Interview Défourneaux, *The Winking Fox*, p. 70.

29 Défourneaux, *The Winking Fox*, p. 71.

30 OSS Archives, Draft of Narrative for Granting of Award to Miss Virginia Hall, from Lt de Roussy de Sales to Lt-Col van der Stricht, 27 October 1944, RG 226, NARA.

31 HS 9/647/4, Virginia Hall PF, 19 June 1945.

32 Pierre Fayol, who had extensive military contacts and started researching Virginia before the National Archives fire, also buries mention of it in an appendix to his French-language book, *Le Chambon-sur-Lignon*, on p. 217. He refers to it as Decision Number 105, 16 March 1946.

33 Nouzille, *L'espionne*, p. 15

34 Tr. letter M. Le Comte Arnaud de Voguë to Fayol, 14 March 1987, Fonds Fayol, CHRD.

35 Tr. testimony of Hubert Petiet, in Nouzille, *L'espionne*, p. 14.

36 OSS Archives, Memorandum from Captain Millett to Captain Calimand, 26 October 1944 (copy found in Fonds Fayol, CHRD).

37 OSS Archives, Stewart W. Kerman, Jr to Allen W. Dulles, 'Personnel Survey of Possible Candidates for Staff on Austrian Operations', 13 October 1944 (copy found in Fonds Fayol, CHRD).

38 For more on the redoubt, see Rodney Kennedy-Minott, *The Fortress that Never Was: The Myth of Hitler's Bavarian Stronghold*, Holt, Rinehart and Winston, 1964; Peter Grose, *Gentleman Spy: The Life of Allen Dulles*, Houghton Mifflin, 1994; William Casey, *The Secret War against Hitler*.

39 Fayol, *Le Chambon-sur-Lignon*, p. 18.

40 Tr. testimony of Irma Alesch, 24 November 1944, and others in Robert Alesch dossier, ANZ6-597-5024-01051946, Archives Nationales, Paris.

41 OSS Archives, Recommendation for Award of DSC, signed by Colonel Forgan, 5 February 1945, with the addition dated 26 February 1945, RG 226, NARA.

42 OSS Archives, Gerry (Caserta) to Chapin (Caserta), Sasac (Paris) for Brinckerhoff, 25 March 1945, RG 226, NARA.

43   OSS Archives, Gerry to Baker (Annemasse) and Brinckerhoff (Paris), 1
      April 1945, message from Gerry to Brinckerhoff, 4 April 1945, RG 226,
      NARA.
44   OSS Archives, 30 March 1945, RG 226, NARA.
45   OSS Archives, Operations General Directive for Camille, 7 April 1945, RG
      226, NARA.
46   OSS Archives, Washington Director's Office Administrative Files, 1944–
      1945, RG 226, NARA.
47   OSS Archives, Memorandum for the President, 12 May 1945, RG 226,
      NARA.
48   OSS Archives, telegram from OSS to Glavin (Caserta), 10 May 1945, RG
      226, NARA.
49   OSS Archives, telegram from Gamble (Paris) to the office of the OSS
      Director (Washington), 13 June 1945, RG 226, NARA.
50   Rossiter, *Women in the Resistance*, p. 125.
51   HS 7/134, Judex mission report (1944–45), 16 November 1944.
52   Morgan, *An Uncertain Hour*, p. 112.
53   Jean Rousset file, GR16P524616, Service Historique de la Défense, Paris.
54   OSS Archives, Lt Goillot and Hall to Chief SO Branch, Forward, 11 June
      1945, RG 226, NARA.
55   HS 9/631/2, Germaine Guérin PF.
56   Interrogation report of Robert Alesch, agent of Abwehr III Paris, by OSS,
      branch X-2 (counter espionage), 6 August 1945, document 8 August 1945,
      copy translated in French, judicial dossier Alesch, Archives Nationales,
      Paris.

Chapter 12: The CIA Years

1   OSS Archives, resignation letter from Virginia Hall, 24 September 1945,
     RG 226, NARA.
2   Rake, *Rake's Progress*, p. 11.
3   Lorna Catling, interview with author, Baltimore, 27 October 2017.
4   Leary (ed), *The Central Intelligence Agency*, p. 5.
5   Virginia Hall Official Personnel Folder, CIA.
6   Virginia Hall Official Personnel Folder.
7   Tr. *Le Monde*, 25 May 1948.
8   *The Petticoat Panel: A 1953 Study of the Role of Women in the CIA Career Service:
     An Intelligence Monograph*, CIA, Center for the Study of Intelligence, CIA,
     March 2003, Appendix B, <https://www.cia.gov/library/readingroom/
     docs/2003-03-01.pdf>.
9   Weiner, *Legacy of Ashes*, p. 20.
10   Lorna Catling, interview with the author, 27 October 2017.
11   Rossiter, *Women in the Resistance*, p. 124.
12   Virginia Hall Official Personnel Folder.
13   Recounted by Angus Thuermer in McIntosh, *Sisterhood of Spies*, p. 126.

14   Personnel Evaluation Report, 26 January 1954, CIA.

15   Virginia Hall Official Personnel Folder.

16   Secret Personnel Qualification Questionnaire, January 1953, CIA.

17   Interview with Lorna Catling, 27 October 2017.

18   Virginia Hall Fitness Report, 3 December 1954, CIA.

19   *The Petticoat Panel.*

20   Junior Officers' Committee Final Report on Reasons for Low Morale Among Junior Officers and Recommended Courses of Action, 9 November 1953, CIA/CREST. Weiner, *Legacy of Ashes*, p. 79.

21   Virginia Hall Official Personnel Folder.

22   Virginia Hall Official Personnel Folder, 3 July 1956.

23   Weiner, *Legacy of Ashes*, p. 77.

24   Ibid., p. 32.

25   Tr. letter André Courvoisier to Pierre Fayol, 6 August 1985, Fonds Fayol, CHRD.

26   Rossiter, *Women in the Resistance*, p. 242.

27   Virginia Hall Fitness Report, 28 December 1956, CIA.

28   Lyman Kirkpatrick Diary, Vol III, January 1956–December 1958, CIA; Virginia Hall Official Personnel Folder; Memorandum for the Record by [Name redacted] PP Staff, CIA; Hall Memorandum for the Record, CIA.

29   *The Petticoat Panel*, Appendix B.

30   Virginia Hall Official Personnel Folder.

31   Lorna Catling, interview with the author, 27 October 2017.

32   *The Petticoat Panel.*

33   McIntosh, *Sisterhood of Spies*, p. 127.

34   *The Petticoat Panel.*

35   Joseph J. Trento, *The Secret History of the CIA*, Prima, 2001, p. xi.

36   Weitz, *Sisters in the Resistance* p. ix, ref. Robert Scanlan, 'Another Go at Godot', ARTnews, xvi:2 (January 1995), 10.

37   *Washington Post*, 14 July 1982.

38   *New York Times*, 15 July 1982.

Epilogue

1   *OSS Exhibition Catalogue*, <https://www.cia.gov/library/publications/ intelligence-history/oss-catalogue/OSS%20catalogue.pdf>.

2   Paine, *Mathilde Carré*, p. 62.

Acknowledgements

There were many highlights when researching this book, but spending memorable time with Virginia's gracious niece Lorna Catling at her home in Baltimore must top the list. I am indebted to her for all the insights she gave me then and during the course of several phone calls, as well as the fine lunch we ate together in her kitchen while continuing to chat about her formidable aunt. She has been generous with her time, thoughts and memories, and opened her family photo album for me. I treasure every moment I have spent in her company. The hospitality extended by the kind and welcoming people of Le Chambon in the Haute-Loire will also stay with me for ever. My time researching on the plateau was made productive and highly enjoyable by many who went out of their way to help and welcome me. Special thanks must go to Mme Denise Vallat, deputy mayor, the historian Gérard Bollon (who kindly read over the Haute-Loire chapters), the staff of Le Lieu de Mémoire, Gabriel's widow, and Mme Lebrat's daughter Georgette, Michel Viallon and Jean-Michel, who took time out to drive me around the plateau. I urge anyone inspired by Virginia's story to visit this often overlooked but beguiling area of France, especially the *Bream* drop zone.

While in the Haute-Loire I was also lucky to meet Vincent Nouzille, who over a decade ago penned the French-language *L'espionne*. He was an early champion of Virginia's. In Britain I have been fortunate to be guided by Stephen Kippax. His knowledge of and passion for SOE knows no bounds and he has helped me unlock old secrets and to find my way through the world of intelligence. David Harrison has also been a wise and patient counsel and incredible fount of knowledge, and I thank him too for his huge contribution to my understanding of SOE. He also supplied some of the images. My thanks too to Paul McCue, who runs an admirable website at www.paulmccuebooks.com, and who provided several useful pointers. I must also mention the superb resources and staff at the National Archives in Kew, which are a true national treasure.

Pierre Tiller has been an invaluable consort through the maze of French archives of various sorts and I am deeply indebted to his patience and skills. Régis Le Mer of the Centre d'Histoire de la Résistance et de la Déportation (CHRD) in Lyon made the Pierre Fayol papers (Fonds Fayol) available to me even through his lunch hour. I spent many days scouring this extraordinarily rich but largely ignored resource, which to my delight filled in so many gaps in Virginia's story and answered many of my questions. The CHRD book, film and other document libraries are also compelling.

The National Archives and Records Administration in the US is a wonderful resource, if sometimes a frustrating one. The staff at the Spy Museum in Washington, DC were wonderfully welcoming and kind (including the director Peter Earnest).

I am grateful to Tony Duboudin, *Alain*'s son, for talking frankly about (and providing photographs of) his father who, despite his flaws, was undoubtedly a courageous man. Craig Gralley, a former CIA officer, has been a true support in my research, particularly regarding Virginia's CIA years but also her cross-ing over the Pyrenees. I wish him well with his novel *Hall of Mirrors*. Two serving officers of the CIA were very encouraging and I enjoyed my time with them at Langley. The CIA's Chief Historian, David Robarge, cast his eye over Chapter 12 and made many helpful comments. Douglas Waller was kind enough to read early drafts of the second half of the book pertaining to OSS, and I was also honoured to receive wise thoughts from the inimitable Lynne Olson. Alexander Noble read through the text, making further improvements. I am so grateful to them all. I thank Jeff Bass, the artist whose depiction of Virginia hangs at Langley, for allowing us to reproduce his fine painting in these pages and sharing notes with me. Stewart Emmens, curator of community health at the Science Museum in London, was of great help with his expert knowledge of historic prosthetics.

Tom White did a splendid job helping me with checking the early chapters, and I wish him all the luck with his future career. My son Laurie stepped in later, and showed me just what a remarkable historian he already is. His younger brother Joe also contributed to the research – and egged me on to finish!

My thanks must also go to the following for helping me in many different ways: Andrew Smith, Will Harris, Adam Fresco, Dr Vicky Johnson, Paul Marston, Sarah Helm, Martyn Cox, Gina Lynn and particularly Sarah Morgenthau. Thanks too to Justin and Biz, Hilary Sunman and Peter Prynn, Paul Prynn, Gordon and Babette, Tom and Anthony for their practical support in providing writing boltholes and emergency Wi-Fi – and everyone who has made me countless cups of coffee and mint tea.

Cheers to Jane, Ali, Tanya and Emma for keeping me enter-tained, and much else besides. Emma M, a fabulous host, generously put me up in the south of France on one of my research trips. Ali Walsh has been an absolute stalwart, dishing out encouragement and good cheer when needed most. I hope Sam Harrison knows just how much I value his sage counsel, and that I have not forgotten I owe him a very good lunch.

My wonderful agent Grainne Fox has believed in Virginia from the start, and the existence of this book has a lot to do with her sheer energy and wisdom. My UK editor Sarah Savitt has been a great cheerleader for Virginia and Andrea Schulz and Emily Wunderlich have kindly taken on that mantle from Joy de Menil in the US. Thanks for all the words of encouragement! Thanks also to the wonderful and dedicated Zoe Gullen, project editor in the UK, and to Jane Cavolina, copy-editor in the US. Thanks too to my publicists Grace Vincent and Rebecca Marsh for helping me get out there and tell the world about this exceptional woman. Thanks to Bad Robot and Paramount for recognising the epic (and filmic) nature of Virginia's life.

Last but not least, I am grateful beyond words to my extended family for backing me on this book and putting up with me writing it. It means a great deal that my big sister Sue was so thrilled about it before she left us. It means a great deal too that my husband Jon has helped and loved me more than I could ever deserve.

Index

Abwehr (German military intelligence) 62, 95, 211; *Funkspiel* or 'radio game' 95–9, 102, 143, 170; breaking of SOE codes 96, 143; focuses on VH 101, 104, 143; focuses on Lyon 143; penetration of VH's network 162–71, 173, 321, 323; intelligence on Dieppe raid 169–70; *see also* Alesch, Abbé Robert (Agent *Axel* of the Abwehr)

aerial reconnaissance 29, 102, 288

Afghanistan 353

Alain (Georges Duboudin) 53–4, 61, 145; exaggerated claims to Baker Street 78, 83, 111, 112, 113; as bad agent 78–9, 82, 111, 112, 113, 114–15, 158, 205, 304; irresponsible conduct 78–9, 82, 83, 111, 113, 114–15, 157–8; recalled to London 158; death of in Elbrich concentration camp 353

Alberte, Mme 71, 79

Alesch, Abbé Robert (Agent *Axel* of the Abwehr) 162–9, 170–1, 185, 320–1, 344, 353; La Varenne-Saint-Hilaire parish 163, 168, 312; gives

Gestapo description of VH 180; exposes VH's remaining network in Lyon 191–3, 194–7, 198–202, 205–6, 241; hunted by Paris police 311–12, 322; VH sends report to OSS (June 1945) 321, 322, 323, 331; surrenders to Americans 322–3; trial and execution of 331–2

Alesch, Irma 311–12

Alibert, Jean 183, 186–9, 204

Allard, Elisée 73, 106, 214–15, 232–3, 235; capture of in Paris 239–42, 244, 251–2; transported to Germany 285; murder of in Buchenwald 320; memorial at Valençay 354

amphetamine tablets 42, 75, 115, 245, 277, 279, 291, 338

Andry, Renée 331–2

Angleton, James 330

Anglo-Irish war (1919–21) 34–5

Antibes 58, 73, 81, 117–18

Aramis (Henri Lassot) 222–3, 224, 225, 229, 230–2, 238–9, 253, 270

Armée Secrète 208

Army magazine 288

Aron, J. M. 175

Atkins, Vera 204, 217, 277–8
Auxiliary Territorial Service 24–5
Avignon 73
SS *Avoceta* 177

Backer, George 38, 90, 91–2, 123
Baker, Josephine 11
Baltimore 7–9, 13–14
Barbezat, Eric 263, 264–7
Barbie, Klaus 143–4, 182–3, 241;
    brutality of 146, 197, 201, 208,
    284; at arrest of the Twins 201;
    frenzies of killing in last months
    of war 284; paid by CIA 342;
    imprisoned for crimes against
    humanity (1987) 353
Barnard College, Manhattan 10, 21
Basin, Francis (*Olive*) *see* Olive
    (Francis Basin)
Bass, Jeff 352
Beckett, Samuel 164; *Waiting for
    Godot* 348
Bégué, Georges: as first SOE
    wireless operator 38, 53; danger
    to from radio detection cars 56–7;
    and Villa des Bois 57, 58, 109;
    Georges codenames in honour of
    108; and Périgueux prison escape
    126, 129, 131, 132–3, 134, 135, 136,
    137, 139
Belfort Gap 293–4
Belgium 26
Bellows, George 29–31
Benoist, Robert 150–1
Benzedrine 42, 75, 115, 245, 277, 279,
    291, 338
Bertillon, Suzanne 46
Bertrand, Estelle 243–4, 245, 246–7
Besson, Alphonse and Marie-
    Fortunée 200, 318
Blanchet (MI6 traitor) 165–6
Bleicher, Hugo 95–9, 100–1, 102,
    104, 143, 166, 216, 331, 353

Bloch, André 59
Bodington, Nicolas 31, 32–4, 92–3,
    97, 111, 144–5, 176, 204
Bohny, Auguste 256–8, 279
Boitier, Madame 255–8, 259, 262
Bond, James (fictional spy) 5
Borrel, Andrée 148
Bourg-en-Bresse 297, 298
Bousquet, René 110
Boxhorn Farm, Maryland 8, 13, 14,
    19, 228
British intelligence: loss of
    contact with French 29; rivalry
    between MI6 and SOE 35, 165;
    traditional gene pool of posh
    boys 35; policy only to recruit
    British citizens 38–9; *see also*
    MI6; Special Operations
    Executive (SOE)
Buchenwald death camp 153, 197,
    285, 319–21
Buckmaster, Maurice 60–1, 101,
    103–4, 117, 120, 123, 124, 204,
    215–16; on women agents 146–7;
    accusations of lethal carelessness
    209–10; on D-Day 247; on
    VH's sabotage missions 283;
    recommends VH for Croix de
    Guerre 307–8

Cahen, Geneviève 331–2
Cammaerts, Francis 41, 226
Camus, Albert 256, 269
Carré, Mathilde (La Chatte)
    (*Victoire*) 95, 96–8, 99, 100, 108,
    143, 354
Carte (French SOE contact) 85–6,
    205
Castres fortress 153, 154, 176–8,
    184–5
Castro, Fidel 345, 346
Catholic Church 162, 165, 256
Catin, Eugénie 318

Catling, Lorna (niece of VH) 325–6, 333, 335–6, 344, 346, 348–9, 352
Cavell, Edith 117
Central Intelligence Agency (CIA): creation of (1946) 329; headquarters at Langley 3, 345, 346, 352; VH as agent in Venice 329–31; intervention in 1948 Italian election 330; lack of substantial role for VH 332–4; VH's lowly desk job in New York 333–4; National Committee for Free Europe 334; Cold War security process 334–5; covert operations section 335, 336–46; Deputy Directorate of Plans 336–7; Southern Europe desk 337–8; VH opts for headquarters desk job 338–40; VH at paramilitary desk for Western Europe 339–41; Petticoat Panel 340; shoddy treatment of VH 340–4, 346–7; Balkans desk 341; anti-Communist zeal 341–2; recruitment of former senior Nazis 342; Bay of Pigs fiasco (1961) 345–6; posthumous recognition of VH 351–3; Operation Jawbreaker in Afghanistan 353
Chamberlain, Neville 24
Chambrillard, Monsieur 72
Châteauroux 53, 56–7, 58, 109
the Cher, central France 242–6, 249, 262, 287, 308
Chicago Times 211, 212
China 334
Chirac, Jacques 308, 352
Churchill, Peter 80–9, 111, 149, 157, 172, 173, 216, 353
Churchill, Winston: creation of SOE (19 July 1940) 31; high hopes for SOE 36; and Dunkirk 62;

'end of the beginning' speech 182; Casablanca conference 205; on Nazi savagery 206; supplies dropped to French (early 1944) 225; Cold War speech in Fulton, Missouri 329
Ciano, Count 102
Clermont-Ferrand 296, 297
Clipper (long-range flying boat) 172, 176, 204
Cold War: start of 328–9; 'Red Menace' in Italy 329–30; Radio Free Europe 334; CIA backed 'stay behinds' 336, 339; VH's work in CIA 336–46; CIA's anti-Communist zeal 341–2
Colomb, Colonel (Count Arnaud de Vogüé) 249–50, 251, 308
communists, French 50, 72, 270
Constantin (Jean de Vomécourt) 111, 161, 172
Cookridge, E. H. 140
Corso, Mary Donovan 317
Cosne-sur-Loire, the Nièvre 237–9, 240–2, 252–3, 261–2, 263–4, 305
Courvoisier, André, 131, 140, 197, 342
Cowburn, Ben 53, 104–5, 114, 120, 123, 151, 245, 285; VH's high rating of 74; warns VH over La Chatte saga 94–100, 149; sabotage operations by 103, 149, 155; short missions of 103, 111; supports VH over recall order 124; as special to VH 149–50
Cuba 345; Bay of Pigs fiasco (1961) 345–6
cyanide tablets 42
Czechoslovakia 334

Dachau death camp 153, 210
Dalton, Hugh 35–6, 210*
Darlan, François 102

D-Day: preparations for 229, 233; SFHQ objectives for 229; arms drops in lead up to 238, 243; last days before 244–5; coded message on BBC's French broadcast 246–7; coded 'action messages' to agents 247; new Resistance volunteers due to 247–8

Decley, Pierre 311

Decourdemanche, Jacqueline 263–5

Défourneaux, René, 252, 305, 333

Dieppe raid (August 1942) 169–70, 346

Donovan, William 'Wild Bill' 219, 220, 239, 309, 313, 316–17, 326–7, 339, 352

Dreyfus, Alfred 240

Dubois, Monsieur 198

Duboudin, Georges (Alain) see Alain (Georges Duboudin)

Dulles, Allen 340, 346

Dunkirk evacuation (May–June 1940) 26, 29, 62

Dunton, Donald (Georges 35) 108–9

Durbrow, Elbridge 13, 14, 204, 328, 335

École Libre des Sciences Politiques, Paris 11

Eisenhower, Dwight 178, 249, 259, 299–300, 312, 341

encryption techniques 268

escapees from occupied Europe 56, 66, 71–2; over the Pyrenees 67, 70, 73, 107–8, 131, 180–2, 183–4, 185, 186–9, 205, 213–14; via Marseille 70; by boat from Côte d'Azur 73

Estonia 23–4

Eyraud, Gabriel 275–6, 291, 300, 301, 350, 354

Fairbanks Jr, Douglas 328

Falaise Pocket 288

fascism: rise of in Europe 12–13, 20–1; nationalist fever in Estonia 24; see also Nazi Germany

Fayol, Marianne 258, 267–8, 311

Fayol, Pierre 258–60, 262–3, 275, 282, 293; old school views of 259, 271, 306; VH stays with at Riou 267–9; undermining of VH 271–3, 280, 281, 306–7; becomes great admirer of VH 306–7, 354; sees VH in Paris 311; Le Chambon-sur-Lignon sous l'occupation 307, 354

Fellot, the Mademoiselles 71, 178

Figueres prison, Spain 189, 202–3

Fitzgerald, F. Scott 11

Fleming, Ian 219

Fleuret, Père 133, 135–6

Floege, E. F. 212

Foltz, Charles 335

Foot, M. R. D. 101, 139–40

Forgan, James 313

France: collapse of (May–June 1940) 1–3, 26–7; population's attempts to escape blitzkrieg 1–3; VH's abiding love of 12; armistice signed at Compiègne (22 June 1940) 27; distrust of Britain in 62–3; wartime privation and hunger 63–4; full German occupation 142–3, 155, 178, 179, 182–5, 206; fleet scuttled in Toulon 184; Nazi 'reign of terror' (early months of 1944) 226; random and appalling Nazi violence after D-Day 248–9, 252, 273; noxious politics of last months of war 271–2, 293–5; atrocities by retreating Germans 297; German defensive line in the Vosges 298, 299–300; settling of scores after German departure 302; US troops seen as too lenient 317–18; brutal treatment of prostitutes at end of war 319; *see also* Vichy France

Franco, General Francisco 29, 202, 211

Francs-Tireurs et Partisans 270

Free French in London 91, 130; Resistance takes orders from 225–6; *see also* Gaulle, Charles de

French Army 25, 26, 49, 294, 302

French language 236, 329

French National Archives 4, 308

French Resistance: early difficulties in recruitment 37; no blueprint for 41, 50; anti-Nazi tracts in Lyon 49, 78, 112; Lyon as birthplace/crucible of 49–50, 103–4, 122; Nantes shootings 54, 55; waiting game in early war 55–6; lack of guidance or support 57; and careless behaviour 61–2, 78–9, 114–16, 120, 123, 148, 161, 209; need for disciplined secret armies 72, 79; factional struggles within 72–3, 102, 158, 237, 270–1; solitude as eternal strain 77; Pétain's mass executions 90; high death rates 147; and Service du Travail Obligatoire (STO) 207–8, 274; 'taking to the maquis' phrase 207–8; beginning of guerrilla warfare 210–11, 225, 236–7; supplies dropped to 225, 238, 243, 251, 253, 262, 274–9; as serious threat to German military 225–6, 283; brutal crackdown of early 1944, 226; ambush of German vehicles/convoys 229, 252, 283–4, 286, 294, 300; La Creuse area 230–6, 287; in the Nièvre 237–9, 240–2, 252–3, 262, 305; brutal repression of in lead up to D-Day 245; summary execution of informers 245; and D-Day

247–8; new volunteers on D-Day 247–8; lack of supplies in D-Day period 248, 249–51, 255, 258–61, 262–3; appalling Nazi retribution after D-Day 248–9, 252, 273; Haute-Loire 254–63, 267–87, 290–4, 306–7, 352, 354; battle at Mont Mouchet 258; battle at Le Cheylard 262–3; French Forces of the Interior (FFI) 280, 281, 282, 286–7, 292–5; 'cheaters' (joiners after victory) 292; FFI merges with French Army 294; *Diane* Irregulars 295–302, 350, 354; towering achievements of 299–300; *The Sorrow and the Pity* (documentary) 354

Fresnes fortress-prison 191, 196–7, 244, 251–2, 332

Frontcroise, Captain 293–4

Gabriel (young orphan, Gabriel Eyraud) 275–6, 291, 300, 301, 350, 354

Gaulle, Charles de 72–3, 90–1; exile in London 48, 130; as divisive figure 91, 270, 271; as provisional president (from September 1944) 294; Allies recognise legitimacy of 294–5; disdain for British and US agents 307, 308

Gauthier (later *Antoine*) (Philippe de Vomécourt) 61, 111–12, 114, 124, 148, 160–1, 175, 249–51, 271, 287

Geelen, Pierre 233, 235–6, 240, 244, 251–2, 285, 320, 354

George, Perry 17, 18

George Washington University, Washington, DC 13

Georgette (daughter of Léa Lebrat) 273

Gerson, Victor (*Vic*) 53, 107–8, 131, 139, 178

Gestapo: presence in Vichy 47, 56, 59, 62; in Lyon 49, 81, 116, 142–4, 158–62, 184, 190–6, 197–8, 200–2, 208–9, 284; on trains 75, 107; in Marseille 84; round up of *Sylvain's* entire circuit 100–1; hunt for VH 104, 143–4, 175, 180, 190–1, 197, 201; black Citroëns of 122, 158, 159, 161, 174, 184, 260; targets cities of the south 142–3; brutal treatment of women 145–6; in Paris 150, 164, 165, 169, 170, 216, 226–7, 240; threats to Guth 153–4, 241; black leather jackets and felt hats 161; stooges working for 161–2, 198–9; liquidates *WOL* circuit 169, 170; mass arrests of agents in Free Zone 174–6; Alesch works for 180, 312; mass arrests of agents in northern and central France 209; VH as continuing target for 224, 241, 284; brutal crackdown of early 1944, 226; arrest of 'nephews' 235–6, 239–42, 244, 251–2; brutal reprisals in mid-1944, 252; frenzies of killing in last months of war 284; Montluçon headquarters 297

Gévolde (Resistance commander) 272, 280, 281, 292, 293, 294, 304

Gilbert (agent in Perpignan) 180–2

Glières tragedy (March 1944) 226

Goillot, Paul 289–92, 295, 296–7, 299, 300, 301–2, 303–4, 315; joins VH in London 304–5; and Operation Crocus/Fairmont 310, 311, 312, 313–14; in Paris with VH at end of war 316; with VH in Lyon after war 318; joins VH in USA 324, 326; and closure of OSS 327; unwilling to move to Italy 330–1; lives in New York with VH 333–4; lives apart from VH

for Barbara's sake 335–6, 344; in restaurant trade 338, 344; marries VH (15 April 1957) 344; house at Barnesville, Maryland 345, 347–8; suffers severe stroke 349, 354

Göring, Hermann 102

Gralley, Craig 338–9, 343

Great Depression 13

Grégoire (wireless operator) 159–60, 193

Grell, William 227, 246, 294, 297

Grover-Williams, William 151

Gubbins, Brigadier Colin 209

Guérin, Germaine 65–8, 71, 103, 120, 131, 139, 144, 173–4; and Alesch's treachery 192, 193, 194–6, 197, 241, 311–12, 321; arrest of 195–6, 198, 311; sent to Ravensbrück 197, 318–19; physical toll of war years 318–19; VH secures compensation for 322; gives evidence against Alesch 331

Guth, Léon 73, 105–7, 152, 153–4, 177, 241

Guttman, Leon 183, 186–9, 204

Halifax, Lord 36

Hall, Barbara: raising of VH 7; seeks rich husband for VH 7, 9, 10; social status of 7–8; and VH's leg amputation 17; in Venice with VH 20; and VH's ambulance driving 25–6; and VH in London 32; homemade fruitcake 92; and VH's move to OSS 228; enquires after VH in mid-1944, 246; Charlotte Norris reassures 287; news of VH's safe return to Paris 303; dislike of Paul Goillot 326; VH reunited with (September 1945) 326

Hall, Edwin Lee (Ned) 7–8, 9, 10, 12, 13–14

Hall, John 9, 13, 14, 333

Hall, John W. 7, 8

Hall, Virginia (VH): prosthetic leg (Cuthbert) 2, 19, 23, 37, 83, 84, 205, 214, 268, 277–8, 287; drives French Army ambulance 2–3, 25–6, 27; loses leg in shooting accident 3, 15–16; motivations of 5–6, 34, 228, 304, 305, 308–9; licence to kill 6, 42, 157, 158, 166; family background 7–8; hunting and shooting 8, 13, 15–16, 23–4, 83; physical appearance 8, 11–12, 263–4, 291, 325–6, 333, 338; rebellious streak 8, 9, 124, 308; at Roland Park Country school 8–9, 76; trips to Europe as a child 10; at five prestigious universities 10–12; in Europe (1926–9) 11–13; breaks with Emil in Vienna 12; foreign languages 12, 13, 211, 236; graduate studies at George Washington 13; rejections from State Department 13, 14–15, 22; works at US embassy in Warsaw 14; gravely ill in Smyrna 16–18; returns to USA (1934) 18–19; works in Venice for State Department 19–21; sent to Tallinn 23–4; resigns from State Department (March 1939) 24; rejected by Auxiliary Territorial Service 24–5; in London (1940–1) 28, 32–4; meets Bellows in Spain 30–1; recruited by SOE 33–4, 36; journalistic cover 34, 38, 43–6, 51–2, 63–4, 75, 90, 91–2, 110, 123, 144, 172–3; not given military rank by SOE 39, 114; SOE 'special' training 39–42; arrives in Vichy (3 September 1941) 43; as conspicuous due to gait 43, 77; Leahy's suspicions of 45–6;

formidable obstacles in Vichy 46–7; arrives in Lyon 48–54; changes in appearance 51–2, 104, 180, 223–4, 226–7, 233, 305; messages smuggled via Berne 52–3, 93–4; *Heckler* network 55, 56, 62–3, 64–74, 79, 175; isolation and self-reliance as vital 57, 77, 79, 93; left alone in the field 59, 61; informal police protection 67, 75, 80, 105–7, 116, 122, 124; command post at Rousset's surgery 69; and factions within resistance 72–3, 102, 158, 270–1; unsolicited approaches from French locals 74, 111; exhausted by constant travel 74–5, 77; freezing winter (1941–2) 76, 92–3; and *Alain's* irresponsible conduct 78–9, 82, 83, 111, 113, 115, 157–8; and Peter Churchill 81–9; burgeoning ruthlessness 83, 93, 158, 238–9, 242; caught in slave labour round-up 86–9, 207; Cowburn's warnings over La Chatte saga 94–100, 149; Bleicher focuses on 101, 104, 143; effectively runs entire Free Zone 101–4, 111–12; and mounting dangers 103–5, 121, 123–4, 144, 150, 158–71, 172–3; and escape of Gerry Morel 105–8, 126, 140, 153, 306; saves SOE from 'premature extinction' 108; imperious/ brusque behaviour 113, 279, 317; pressure takes its toll on 113–14; ordered to return to London 123–4, 131; plots escape of *Camerons* 127–41, 142; turned down for CBE 140–1; request for permanent envoy 148–9; Abwehr's penetration of network 162–71, 173, 321, 323; doubts over Alesch 165, 166–7, 171; decides

Hall, Virginia (VH) – *continued*
to leave France 172–3; delays
departure from Lyon 173–4;
Castres escape plan 176–8, 184–5;
settles affairs in Lyon 178; flees
from Lyon 179–81, 184–5; escape
across Pyrenees 180–2, 183–4,
185, 186–9, 205; Cuthbert and
Pyrenees crossing 182, 186–8,
203, 205; Barbie's wanted posters
183; 'Cuthbert is being tiresome'
message 187; arrested in San Juan
189, 202; in Figueres prison 202–3;
nervous dermatitis 202–3, 291;
at Barcelona consulate 203–4;
lies low in Lisbon 204; return to
England 204–6; guilt over Alesch
205–6, 321, 322; warnings about
choice of agents finally heeded
210; journalistic cover (*Chicago
Times*) 211, 212; role in Spain
(from May 1943) 211–15, 217;
awarded MBE 213, 352; desire
to be radio operator 213, 215,
217–18; desire to return to France
213, 214–16; German knowledge
of by 1943, 216–17, 241; back
in London 217–18; returns to
France as OSS agent 222–7,
229–31; refuses surgery to alter
appearance 223–4; as wireless
operator 224, 226–7, 231, 234–5,
245–6, 268–9, 273–4; in La Creuse
area 230–6; cover as a milkmaid
231, 232, 233–5, 288; provides
vital Overlord intelligence 233–4,
242–3, 245, 252, 288; roving
brief before D-Day 236–9; in the
Nièvre 237–9, 240–2, 262, 263–4,
305; tends goats as disguise
242–3; in the Cher 242–6, 262,
308; escape plan for nephews
244, 251–2; and D-Day 246–8;

in central France after D-Day
249–53, 262; rendezvous with
Gauthier and *Colomb* 250–1; and
post-D-Day parachute drops
251, 253, 262, 274–9; at Vivarais
plateau 255–62, 267–87, 289–94,
306–7, 352, 354; examines drop
zones on the plateau 260–1;
given command of Haute-Loire
mission 262; journey from
Cosne to Le Chambon 263–7; as
fully briefed on RAF operations
264–5; command in Haute-
Loire 269–87, 289–95, 306–7;
Fayol's undermining of 271–3,
280, 281, 306–7; provides vital
intelligence on Le Puy 281–2;
promotion to first lieutenant
284; in house at Roybet 284–5,
290–2; *Diane* Irregulars 295–302,
350, 354; love for Paul Goillot
301–2, 304, 314, 316, 326, 335–6;
vital achievements in France
301–2; report on *Saint-Heckler*
mission 304; in London (autumn
1944) 304–5, 309; awarded
Distinguished Service Cross 306,
307–8, 313, 316–17, 326–7, 349;
awarded Croix de Guerre 308–9,
352; Operation Crocus/Fairmont
309–11, 312, 313–16; intensive
training for Crocus 312; return
to Lyon at end of war 317–21;
demands compensation for
unsung heroes 321–2; returns to
USA (September 1945) 324, 325–6;
physical toll of war years 325–6;
seeks employment after OSS
327–8; joins CIA 329; in Venice
as CIA agent 329–31; spells of
heavy drinking 333, 344; lives in
New York with Paul 333–4; lowly
desk job at CIA in New York

333–4; and CIA security process 334–5; in CIA covert operations section 335, 336–46; lives apart from Paul for Barbara's sake 335–6, 344; CIA Southern Europe desk 337–8; post-war health problems 338, 346, 348, 349; opts for headquarters desk job 338–9; CIA paramilitary desk for Western Europe 339–41; shoddy treatment of by CIA 340–4, 346–7; 'unhappiest period' of her career 340–4; moves back to CIA Balkans desk 341; marries Paul (15 April 1957) 344; CIA Western Hemisphere desk 344–6; Western Hemisphere desk 344–6; GS-14 grade in CIA 345; house at Barnesville, Maryland 345, 347–8; retirement of (1966) 346; refuses to write memoirs 348–9; obituaries 349; death of (8 July 1982) 349–50; posthumous recognition of 351–3; *see also under* Lyon; Office of Strategic Services (OSS); Paris; Special Operations Executive (SOE)
Hallowes, Geoffrey 289, 292, 294, 306
Hambro, Sir Charles 209
Haspel, Gina 351
Haute-Loire 72, 254–63, 267–86, 289–94, 306–7, 350, 352, 354; final defeat of Germans in 286–7
Hayes, Charles 115, 116
Hayes, JB 137, 139
Hemingway, Ernest 11
heroin 68
Heslop, Richard 151–2, 153–4, 185–6
Himmler, Heinrich 159
Hitler, Adolf: rise of Nazi Party 12, 21; becomes Chancellor 21; and Munich agreement 24; Reichstag

speech (19 July 1940) 31; brutal crackdowns in France 142, 226; suicide of 315
Hoare, Sir Samuel 211
Hoover, J. Edgar 327
House, Colonel E. M. 22
Hull, Cordell 22
Hungary 334
Hunt, E. Howard 345
Hurlevent château, Feyzin 174

Ingersoll, Ralph 38
Innsbruck 310–11, 314–15
Italy: Mussolini's police state 12–13, 20–1; VH works in Venice for State Department 19–21; Allied landings in Sicily 208; Allied push through 312–13; 'Red Menace' in late 1940s 329–30; CIA intervention in 1948 election 330

Jedburgh units 292–4
Jeunet, Eugène 67, 192, 196–7, 319
Jews: in Warsaw 14; Vichy repression of 45, 59, 67, 75, 110, 126; SOE's Jewish agents 53, 58, 59, 107–8, 110, 130; fleeing the Occupied Zone 67; deportations from Vichy France 110, 206–7; in Paris 150; hidden in Vivarais plateau 256, 257, 267, 269
Joulian, Jean and Marie-Louise 71–2, 192, 201–2, 255, 321, 332
Jouve, Germaine 114–15, 157–8
Jumeau, Lieutenant Marc 57–8, 125, 130, 137
Juttry, Jules 243–4, 245–6, 332

Katyn forest massacre 12
Kennedy, John F. 346
Khan, Noor Inayat 209–10
Konsular Akademie, Vienna 11–12
Korean War 335

La Creuse 230–6, 287
Labourier, Eugène and Mme 73, 321
Langelaan, George 53, 58, 133–4, 137, 223–4
Lattre de Tassigny, General de 290
Laval, Pierre 109–10
le Boulicaut, Raoul (Lieutenant Bob) 269–70, 272, 274, 278, 280, 290–1, 295, 302, 304, 306
Le Chambon-sur-Lignon 255–63, 267–9, 273, 290, 291, 322, 354
Le Forestier, Roger 284
Le Harivel, Jean-Philippe 54, 57, 58, 137
Le Puy 72, 73, 177, 192, 201–2, 254, 258, 321; German General Staff moves to 281–4; final defeat of Germans in 286–7; FFI headquarters in 292, 295
Leahy, William 45–6, 47, 127–8, 179, 220
Lebrat, Edmond 274, 285, 291, 352
Lebrat, Léa 273–4, 284–5, 352
Lebrat, Maurice 258, 261, 273
Leccia, Laurent and Joseph 235, 244
Leccia, Marcel 73, 106, 153–4, 177, 192, 214–15, 233, 235, 237; capture of in Paris 239–42, 244, 251–2; transported to Germany 285; murder of in Buchenwald 320; memorial at Valençay 354
Legge, Colonel Barnwell 53
Legrand, Jacques 163–4, 165, 166, 168, 169, 170
Leigh, Vera 150, 318
Leney, Roger 289, 291, 294
Léon (OSS operative in Cosne) 252
Leprevost, Robert 70, 73
Lilias (double agent) 239–40, 242
Limoges 73, 105, 106, 107, 151–4, 177–8, 214
London Blitz 32
London Transport Rifle Club 40

Long, Madame 230, 236
Lopinat, Eugène 231
Lucas (later Sylvain) (Pierre de Vomécourt) 38, 53, 61, 94, 95, 96–8, 100–1, 108–9, 111, 161, 164
Lyon: seditious past of 48; geography and topography of 48–9; VH arrives in 48–54; Croix Rousse hill 49, 121–2; Gestapo in 49, 81, 116, 142–4, 158–62, 184, 190–6, 197–8, 200–2, 208–9, 284; Le Coq Enchainé, 49, 78, 112, 158; as birthplace/crucible of Resistance 49–50, 103–4, 122; stirrings of dissent in 49–50, 102–3; Sainte Elisabeth convent, La Mulatière 50–1, 66, 178, 298; Grand Nouvel Hôtel 51, 54, 80, 81, 126, 132, 139; American consulate 51–3, 64, 70–1, 80, 93, 143; and Alain 53–4, 61, 78–9, 82, 83, 110–11, 112–15, 144–5, 157–8; VH's Heckler network 55, 56, 62–3, 64–74, 79, 175; VH's early days in 55–6, 57; Germaine Guérin's brothel 65–6, 67–8, 139, 144, 192, 319; Rousset's surgery 69, 162, 163, 165, 190, 191–2; Passage de l'Hôtel-Dieu 72; freezing winter (1941–2) 76, 92–3; VH's apartment at 3 Place Ollier 104–5, 119–20, 122–3, 149–50, 151, 163, 173–4; deportations of Jews from 110; poor sanitation in 121–2; Fort St Irénée 122; as primary Operation Donar target 143–4; Hôtel Terminus 144, 182–3, 197, 201; Montluc prison 157, 173, 178, 186, 284; VH's apartment at rue Garibaldi 173–4, 179, 184–5; mass arrests of agents in 174–6; VH flees from 179–81, 184–5; full Nazi takeover of 183–5; Alesch

exposes VH's remaining network 191–3, 194–7, 198–202, 205–6, 241; pays highest price for its defiance 193–201, 208, 284, 317–21; liberation of (September 1944) 311; VH returns to at end of war 317–21; devastation of war 318–19
Lyon, Robert 137, 139
Lysander (three-seater plane) 105, 106

Madrid 211–13, 214, 217
Maginot Line 25, 26
Maquis *see* French Resistance
Marchand, Joseph 71, 159–60
Marion, Paul 91
Marseille 73, 156–7, 174; Villa des Bois safehouse 54, 57–8, 60–1, 73, 79, 83–6, 93, 125; VH and Peter Churchill in 83–5, 86–9
Martineau, Lieutenant 253
Maryland Jockey Club 7
Mauthausen death camp 170, 194
Mauzac internment camp 128–41, 142
McCarthy, Joseph 334
Menier, Mademoiselle 157, 186
MI6, 5, 35, 123, 216–17, 219; WOL circuit in Paris 162–5, 167, 168–70; agent *Blanchet* 165–6; report on Alesch 322
Milice (Vichy version of Gestapo) 206–7, 243, 245, 249, 254, 286, 298
Military Intelligence Corps Hall of Fame 351
Millar, George 193
Miranda de Ebro concentration camp 189, 204
Moley, Professor Raymond 21
Montluçon 296, 297
Morel, Gerry 105–8, 126, 140, 153, 306
Moulin, Jean 48, 91, 208, 237

Muggeridge, Malcolm 219
Munich agreement (September 1938) 24
Mussolini, Benito 12–13, 21, 208

Nallet, Jean 279, 300
Nantes shootings 54, 55
National Archives and Records Administration (NARA), Washington, DC 4
Nazi Germany: rise of Nazi Party 12, 21; invasion of Poland (1 September 1939) 24; invasion of France and Low Countries (May 1940) 26–7; invasion of Soviet Union (June 1941) 50; full occupation of France 142–3, 155, 178, 179, 182–5, 206; Operation Donar 142–3, 174–5; Nazi death camps 153, 170, 194, 197, 210, 285, 318–21; *Nacht und Nebel* prisoners 319–20
Nelson, Frank 60
New York Post 38, 43–4, 51–2, 63–4, 75, 90, 91–2, 110, 123, 144, 172–3, 203
New York Times 349
Newton, Henry and Alfred (the Twins) 176, 177–8, 179, 184–5, 194–6, 197–201, 318, 319; post-war health problems 349; *No Banners* (Jack Thomas book on) 349
Nicholas, Johnny 46
Nicolas (agent in Lyon) 173, 178, 179, 192–3
the Nièvre, central France 237–9, 240–2, 252–3, 262, 263–4, 305
Noguères, Henri 308
Norris, Charlotte 246, 287

Office of Strategic Services (OSS): founding of (June 1942) 154, 218–19; first agent parachuted

Office of Strategic Services (OSS) – continued
into France 213; enquiry about VH (January 1944) 218, 220–1; early innocence and naivety 219–20; VH's transfer to 222–4, 227–9; VH's returns to France as agent of 222–7, 229–31; *Saint* (VH's circuit) 224, 304; close cooperation with SOE 228; grants VH military rank 228–9; and D-Day 229; beginning of guerrilla warfare 236–7; VH's roving brief before D-Day 236 9; VH given command of Haute-Loire mission 262; VH as hero of 309, 313, 326–7; Operation Crocus/Fairmont 309–11, 312, 313–16; Central European headquarters at Caserta 312–14; uncertain future at end of war 316–17; glowing appraisal of VH 323–4; Truman closes down 326–7; legendary boozing 333

Olive (Francis Basin) 54, 61, 73, 85, 101, 111, 125; saves VH from police *rafle* 86–8, 156, 207; capture and imprisonment of 156–7, 172, 173; Mlle Menier as mistress of 157, 186; VH secures release of 178, 186

Page, Eloise Randolph 351
Paris: Années Folles in 1920s 11; VH visits (1938) 23; Germans enter (14 June 1940) 27; VH at avenue de Breteuil 27–8; VH's network in 67, 150–1, 162–4; Gestapo in 150, 164, 165, 169, 170, 216, 226–7, 240; *WOL* circuit in 162–5, 167, 168–70; Abwehr headquarters 170; VH returns to (March 1944) 226, 229–30; VH flees to (May

1944) 236; capture of Leccia and Allard 239–42, 244, 251–2; VH escape plan for nephews 244, 251–2; Allied re-capture of (24 August 1944) 287–8; VH arrives in (22 September 1944) 302–3; VH returns to (October 1944) 309, 311; VH and Paul in at end of war 316

Park, Arthur 42, 204
Partisan Leaders' Handbook (SOE manual) 238
Patton, General 253
Pejot, France 71
Périgueux prison 85, 93, 105, 106–7, 111, 125–8
Perpignan 73, 107, 180–2, 183
Pétain, Marshal Philippe 30; armistice with Hitler 27; repression of Jews 45, 59, 67, 75, 110, 126; cult of personality 47; handshake with Hitler 47; senility of 47; denounces Third Republic 49–50; Dunkirk spun as British desertion by 62; crackdowns on Resistance 90; meetings with Göring 102; and return of Laval 109–10; and Operation Torch 178–9; Nazis move to Germany 295; death sentence commuted 323
Philby, Kim 78, 330
Picabia, Gabrielle 164, 166, 167
Pierre-Bloch, Jean and Gaby 54, 58, 126–7, 128, 129–31, 134, 135, 137, 138, 140
PM magazine 38
Poinso-Chapuis, Germaine 85
Poland 12, 14; German invasion of (1 September 1939) 24
Pyrenees 67, 70, 73, 107–8, 131, 180–1, 213–14; *passeurs* (mountain guides) 181–2, 183, 185, 186, 188,

194; extreme winter conditions
186–9, 205

Queen Mary's Hospital,
Roehampton 205

Rabut, Madame 231, 232, 236, 237,
238–9
Radcliffe College, Cambridge 10
Radio Free Europe 334
radio operators *see* wireless
operators
radio signal detection: radio
detection cars/vans 57, 73, 122,
133, 159, 174–5, 197–8, 202,
245–6, 269; *Funkspiel* or 'radio
game' 95–9, 102, 143, 170; and
workload of operators 118,
119; Funkabwehr 122; German
detector planes (Storks) 268–9,
270, 273
railways, French: grim conditions
on trains 74–5, 77; trains as
dangerous for agents 75–6, 84, 99,
104, 107, 151, 180, 264; sabotage
of 103, 142, 155, 156, 210, 225, 233,
238, 239, 247–8, 253, 282, 284;
RAF bombardment of 264–5
Rake, Denis 117–18, 119–21, 151–4,
172, 185–6, 328, 354
Ravensbrück concentration camp
197, 318–19
Regnier, Jean-Marie 217
Reile, Colonel 170–1, 193
Remarque, Erich Maria, *All Quiet on
the Western Front* 207
Rigoulet, Albert 137, 138
Riley, Henry 289–92, 294, 295, 296,
298, 299, 300, 302, 304, 306
Roland Park Country school 8–9,
76
Rommel, Erwin 91, 154
Roosevelt, Franklin Delano 21, 22,

45, 90, 205, 271; and OSS 218, 220,
316
Rosenberg, Ethel and Julius 334
Rousset, Dr Jean 68–70, 71, 103,
116, 153, 161, 162–3, 165, 167,
205; arrest and torture of 190–1;
survives in Buchenwald 319–21;
gives evidence against Alesch 331
Roux, André, 279, 300–1
Royal Air Force (RAF): escape of
pilots downed in France 70–1;
bombardments of infrastructure
in France 103, 133, 264–5;
weapons and supplies drops 225,
238, 243, 251, 253, 262, 274–9; SD
or Special Duties squadrons 278
Rudellat, Yvonne 147–8
Ruelle, Victor 270, 280
Rundstedt, Gerd von 225
Russier, Madame 290

sabotage operations: on food bound
for Germany 63; on railway
infrastructure 103, 142, 155, 156,
210, 225, 233, 238, 239, 247–8, 253,
282, 284; ingenious explosive
devices 155–6, 248; 'A'-class or
military targets 156; cells along
the Côte d'Azur 156; blowing
up of radio detector vans 197–8;
beginning of guerrilla warfare
210–11, 225, 236–7; in lead up to
D-Day 233; coded D-Day 'action
messages' to agents 247; actions
on and after D-Day 248, 252–3;
VH directs in Haute-Loire 280–1,
282–4, 285–6; Chamalières bridge
attack 282; operations in Le Puy
282–4; *Diane* Irregulars 295–302,
350, 354
Sansom, Odette 353
Scanlan, Robert 348
Schaeffer, Karl 170–1

Schmahling, Max 287
Schow, Robert 46
Schriever, George 306
Second World War: fall of France
    1–3, 26–7; German invasion of
    Poland 24; Phoney War 25–6;
    Dunkirk evacuation (May-June
    1940) 26, 29, 62; Britain stands
    alone against Hitler 28, 29; US
    neutrality 28, 38–9, 45; Nazi
    invasion of Soviet Union (June
    1941) 50; early British military
    reverses 62; Pearl Harbor attack
    (7 December 1941) 90, 219;
    'Channel dash' of *Scharnhorst*
    and *Gneisenau* 95, 102; fall of
    Singapore 102; Operation Torch
    154–5, 178–9, 182; Atlantic
    Wall 165, 169; British victory
    at El Alamein 182; Casablanca
    conference 205; Allied landings in
    Sicily 208; Stalingrad and Kursk
    208; German retreat in France
    297–300; German Ardennes
    counter-offensive 309; Innsbruck
    redoubt rumours 310–11, 314–15;
    Red Army arrival in Berlin 314;
    end of in Europe 315–16
Secours Suisse (aid agency) 257
Selborne, Lord 210–11
Service de Santé des Armées 25–6
Sevilla, Jose 130, 131, 136, 137
Simpson, William 64–6, 144, 205,
    348, 353
Singapore, fall of 102
Smyrna (now Izmir), Turkey 15–18
Soviet Union 62, 154; Nazi invasion
    of (June 1941) 50; victories
    at Stalingrad and Kursk 208;
    penetration of US atomic bomb
    programme 329
Spain: officially neutral in WW2,
    29; refugees from France

(summer 1940) 29; VH meets
    Bellows in 30–1; VH's arrival in
    188–9; Civil Guard 189; Abwehr
    in 211; F Section safehouses in
    211, 213, 217; VH's role in (from
    May 1943) 211–15, 217
Special Forces Headquarters
    (SFHQ), London 228
Special Operations Executive (SOE):
    channels of communication
    44, 49, 52–3, 55, 61, 63–4, 93–4
    see also wireless operators;
    most of original papers lost 4;
    creation of (19 July 1940) 31;
    independent French or F Section
    31, 33–4, 36, 41–2, 53–4, 59, 210;
    'ungentlemanly' brand of warfare
    31, 34–5; offices at 64 Baker Street
    33; recruitment methods 35–6;
    repeated failure in early days 36;
    'cooler' in remote part of Scotland
    37; first agents parachuted into
    France 38; old-fashioned attitudes
    towards women 38, 41, 79, 83,
    145; as perforce multinational 39;
    'special' training 39–42; firearms
    training 40–1; lack of up-to-date
    maps 41; flat at 6 Orchard Court
    41–2, 204–5; sickness tablets 42,
    107; Operation *Geologist* 5, 43;
    false papers 51, 56, 72, 73, 78, 131,
    151, 152, 173; air drops of money,
    explosives, weapons 54, 73,
    110, 112–13, 155; orders waiting
    game in early war 55–6; lack
    of guidance/support for agents
    or *résistants* 57; agents' need to
    avoid trivial errors 57–8, 70, 81–2;
    Sûreté arrests of agents (October
    1941) 58–9, 60–1; sabotage of
    food bound for Germany 63; use
    of heroin on German brothel
    clients 68; VH as top agent 78,

79–80, 83; carelessness and irresponsibility of agents 78–9, 82, 83, 111, 113, 114–16, 157–8, 160–1; improved preparation of agents 80–1; survival rates of agents arrested in France 85; Villa des Bois prisoners 85, 93, 105, 106, 111, 125–41, 142; stressful life of agents in field 92–3, 118–19, 122, 149, 159–60, 174–5, 325, 336, 338; *Lucas* and La Chatte catastrophe 94–101; Abwehr breaks codes of 96, 143; sexual liaisons of agents in France 114–15, 157–8; orders VH to return to London 123–4, 131; VH as trailblazer for female agents 146–8; *Prosper* circuit 148, 236; 'maximum disruption' order sent out 191; Top Secret inquiry (April 1943) 202; *Prosper* circuit destroyed 209, 224; accusations of lethal carelessness 209–10; improved agent recruitment procedures 210; H/X (Spanish chief) 211–12; close cooperation with OSS 228; and D-Day 229; agents' training for interrogation 241

SS 183, 190, 195, 286, 320; Waffen-SS divisions 226

Stalin, Joseph 21

State Department 13, 14–15, 21–2, 32, 123; VH resigns from (March 1939) 24; VH resigns again from (1941) 34; delays VH's departure for France 37–8; and Cold War 328–9

Stein, Gertrude 11

St-Etienne 255, 258, 263, 265–6

Stimson, Henry 219

Stonehouse, Brian (*Célestin*) 160–1, 173, 174–5, 176

Sûreté: arrests at Villa des Bois safehouse 58, 60–1, 73, 79, 83–6, 93, 111, 125–41, 142; VH infiltrates 73, 105–7, 152–3; Marshall Vance interrogated by 123; arrest of Rake in Limoges 151–4

Sury-en-Vaux, the Cher 242–6

Sury-ès-Bois, central France 246–7

Suttill, Francis 148, 209

Thame Park, Oxfordshire 218

Thatched Barn, north London 155–6

Thérond, Emile 281, 282

Tillion, Germaine 164, 165, 166, 169

Toulouse 159

Tours 99, 103, 147–8, 233, 239

Trento, Joseph 347

Trotobas, Michael 53, 129, 135, 136, 139

Truman, Harry 316, 317, 326–7, 329

Tuck, Pinkney 179

Turck, Gilbert (*Christophe*) 53, 54, 57, 58

United States of America: Roosevelt's New Deal 21; WW2 neutrality 28, 38–9, 45; recognizes Vichy regime 45; VH sends messages via diplomatic pouch 53, 61, 93–4; Pearl Harbor attack (7 December 1941) 90, 219; enters intelligence war 154, 213; lack of spying tradition 219; McCarthy's 'un-American' activities campaign 334

Valençay, Loire Valley 27

Van der Stricht, Paul 303, 305–6, 309, 310

Vance, Marshall 123

venereal diseases 68

Venice 19–21, 329–31

Vessereau, Colonel 237–8, 241, 242

Vic (Victor Gerson) 53, 107–8, 131, 139, 178

Vichy France: demarcation line 30, 67, 120, 121, 155; denunciation threats in 43, 50, 62; VH arrives in (3 September 1941) 43–4; VH cultivates senior officials 44–5, 46, 73, 102; as brutal police state 45, 47–8, 54–5, 146; USA recognizes 45; Vichy as small town 46–7; fragmented and weak opposition 47–8; propaganda and censorship 50, 52, 62, 63, 91, 102; F Section safehouses 51, 54, 57–8, 60, 66–7, 69, 71, 122, 147, 160, 178; security services 54–5, 58–9; complicit in Nazi plunder of resources 63; abortion punishable by death 69–70; VH's regular returns to Vichy 73, 127; epidemic of scabies 76–7; Nazi slave labour round-ups 86–9, 207–8; mass executions of prisoners 90; belief in Hitler's victory 91; support of Nazi war effort 91; first mass acts of public resistance 102–3; policemen switch to Allied side 103; Operation Torch against 154–5, 178–9, 182; Nazi Germany takes over Free Zone 182–5; mass civil disobedience (from March 1943) 207; Service du Travail Obligatoire (STO) 207–8, 274; Nazis move Pétain and ministers to Germany 295; see also Pétain, Marshal Philippe

Vienna 11–12

Villelonge 269–73, 295–6

Vivarais-Lignon plateau 254–63, 267–87, 289–94, 306–7, 352, 354

Voguë, Count Arnaud de (Colonel Colomb) 249–50, 251, 308

Vomécourt, Jean de (Constantin) 111, 161, 172

Vomécourt, Philippe de (Gauthier, later Antoine) 61, 111–12, 114, 124, 148, 160–1, 175, 249–51, 271, 287

Vomécourt, Pierre de (Lucas/ Sylvain) 38, 53, 61, 94, 95, 96–8, 100–1, 108–9, 111, 161, 164

Wall Street Crash (1929) 13

Wannsee Conference (January 1942) 110

Washington Post 349

Weil, Jacques 150

Weiner, Tim 341

Whittinghill, George 52–3, 64, 70

Wilen, Odette (Sophie) 239, 240, 241–2, 252

Wilkinson, Ernest 151–2, 153–4, 185–6

wireless operators: vital role of 38, 53, 202; lack of 49, 53, 57, 59, 61, 80, 93, 100, 101; Le Harivel arrives in Lyon 54; arrests of 58–9, 108, 151–4, 163, 174–6, 197, 202, 209–10; Lucas and La Chatte catastrophe 94–101; Georges 35's arrival in Lyon 108–9; arrival of Zeff in Lyon 112; workload and stresses 118–19, 122, 159–60, 234–5; attrition rate as high 122–3, 202; Courvoisier arrives in Lyon 131; radio smuggled into Mauzac 131–3; Célestin's arrival in France 160–1; courage of 202; training of 218; VH as radio operator 224, 226–7, 231, 234–5, 245–6, 268–9, 273–4; S-phones 277, 278; see also Bégué, Georges; radio signal detection; Rake, Denis; Zeff, Edward

Wisner, Frank 336, 341–2

women: limited combat role of 3;

alongside men on front line 5; opportunities created by war 6; flappers 9; granted vote in USA (1920) 9; *garçonnes* in Paris 11; Auxiliary Territorial Service 24–5; and international laws on war 38; old-fashioned attitudes in SOE 38, 41, 79, 83, 145; backlash against in Vichy France 44, 49–50, 52, 69–70; Gestapo's brutal treatment of 145–6; VH as trailblazer for female agents 146–8; high death rates of female agents 147; US military attitudes to 224–5; Resistance group attitudes to 259, 271–2; de Gaulle's attitude towards 307; prevailing CIA view of 339, 340, 342; US attitudes in 1950s 339–40; CIA Petticoat Panel 340; progress in CIA since VH's time 351

Worms, Jean 150

Yeager, Chuck 187

Zeff, Edward 112, 113–14, 118–19, 122, 160, 174, 178, 193–4
Zurbach, Dédé 274, 279, 280, 285, 290, 295, 300, 302, 354

Picture Credits

Lorna Catling Collection: 1, 2, 3 (*top right, bottom left, bottom right*), 8 (*middle*)

National Archives and Records Administration: 3 (*top left*), 5 (*top left*)

© Jeffrey Bass: 4 (*top left*)

David Harrison Collection: 4 (*top right, middle*)

Lorna Catling Collection. Held by the Spy Museum, Washington, DC: 4 (*bottom*)

Courtesy of Lorna Catling and John Hall: 5 (*bottom left, bottom right*)

Pierre Fayol, *Le Chambon-sur-Lignon sous l'occupation*: 6 (*top*), 7 (*Fayol*), 8 (*top*)

Courtesy of Lieu de Mémoire au Chambon-sur-Lignon: 6 (*middle, bottom*)

© Collection privée. Courtesy of Lieu de Mémoire au Chambon-sur-Lignon: 7 (*'Bob', Eyraud*), 8 (*bottom*)

The National Archives, UK: 7 (*Buckmaster, Duboudin, Leccia, Stonehouse, Rake*)

Don't let the story stop here

Virago was founded in 1973 as *'the first mass-market publisher for 52 per cent of the population – women. An exciting new imprint for both sexes in a changing world.'*

Today Virago is the outstanding international publisher of books by women. While the cultural, political and economic landscape has changed dramatically, Virago has remained true to its original aims: to put women centre stage; to explore the untold stories of their lives and histories; to break the silence around many women's experiences; to publish breathtaking new fiction and non-fiction alongside a rich list of rediscovered classics; and above all to champion women's talent.

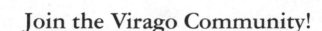

Join the Virago Community!

For our latest news, events, extracts and competitions, visit
www.virago.co.uk

@ViragoBooks   ViragoPress   @ViragoPress

ViragoPress   virago.co.uk/virago-podcast

virago

To order any Virago title by telephone, please contact our mail order supplier on: +44 (0)1235 759 555.